MEMORIES *of*
MAGYARS
PASSED

MEMORIES *of*
MAGYARS
PASSED

ANTHONY E. VIRAG

Mill City Press

Mill City Press, Inc.
2301 Lucien Way #415
Maitland, FL 32751
407.339.4217
www.millcitypress.net

Paperback ISBN-13: 978-1-66283-638-1
Ebook ISBN-13: 978-1-66283-639-8

AUTHOR'S FOREWORD

I chose this title, Memories of Magyars Passed, for its true purpose; to tell the story of the Magyars that lived and died Magyars.

I could have titled it, My Hungarian Heritage, as some thought it more to the point. It is not!

It was the Romans that termed the mounted Huns as Hungari. Those are as stated, Huns; not the Magyars that preceded them into the fertile valley west of the Carpathian Mountains. Indeed, there are stories that state, not many in the surrounding areas of those ancient countries remember witnessing such skilled horsemen as the Huns that fought the Romans; except for those horsemen that settled in those valleys prior to the Hun invasions. Those horsemen were the Magyars.

The history journals and English writings of the years leading up to the 1920s and early 30s, mention the Magyars. During the Great War (WWI), engagements, and even the following peace talks, identify the Magyar country and its inhabitants as Magyars. Their country was, and still is identified as Magyar Orszag (Country of Magyars).

You can see why, as a stubborn Magyar, I insist on adhering to the original traditions. This should absolutely and purposefully identify the Magyar as being different from the Hun. However, because of the Western World people's difficulty in identification, and pronunciation of the name Magyar, convention and convenience advocated these people be called Hungarian. Their country is now identified, and located on English maps of Europe, as Hungary.

It shall forever be a misnomer!

Should Americans ask whence their origin, Immigrants from that country, Hungary, will still insist they are Magyar. Then comes the awkward explanation for convenience of the American language speaker that, this Magyar emigrated from "Hungary". If this does not confuse the American, it does manage to clear up the puzzling name.

The people in my story are Magyars, and they have, since this writing, passed on.

PREFACE

He was firm and immovable, the "Rock of the family", indeed, the very foundation of it. He had been taught and instructed of Prussian discipline at age sixteen, and so he was strict with himself and a strong taskmaster with his family.

His name was Géza. He was my father.

Every time I went to visit the family farm as a young man, he was there, and he was always working. He was healthy, and he was strong; never spent a day in the hospital, (except for that fateful time in 1917). He was never sick. He was not one to complain anyway, and so it was a foregone conclusion that he would always be there when we came home.

Whenever I went home to visit with my wife and two sons, he greeted us with a smile and cheery attitude. He loved us all. He would shake hands, but in the European manner with the free arm we would embrace and I would kiss him on the cheek.

"How are you Dad?"

"Vas I fine. I fine," was his standard reply.

Surely he was an example for us all, in his eighty-second year.

What a happy and contented man he was. He had fulfilled his responsibility to wife and family. He had helped to raise two daughters and two sons. They were men and women now with families of their own. Would that God should grant us all, that we could do as well as he had.

He had seen his grandchildren grow, some of them had married, and so he had seen his first great-grandchildren; how happy, how proud and full of life he was.

He is gone now. The Rock is gone.

They are all gone, that generation of Magyars (Hungarians).

It has been a short two months but how dramatic the change. How we all miss him. Words are not adequate, nor can they be put into sentences that properly define such an abrupt end. We had never known this emptiness! Unless one has experienced the loss of a loved one, one can never realize just what a vacuum is left with their passing. Our relationship with him has ended.

The memories remain.

We could not have expected it.

It was mother who was frequently sick and had undergone surgery many times in her life. Having had two bouts with cancer; she was the one who always gave us cause for concern. She was also four years his senior, whatever significance that has. When two partners in-life are over eighty, we are in awe by their tenacity and bewildered when it is the healthy one that passes away.

No matter how we prepare for what inevitably befalls all creatures of this earth, when it does come, it is a shock. So as I sit here contemplating my sorrow, I truly regret his passing. I am happy that God took him suddenly from us, for he died in dignity. He had retained his faculties and his great strength until the very end.

In my mixed emotions of sorrow, happiness, and thankfulness, I realize that this was the way it had to be. This is what my Father in heaven ordained, and this is what my earthly father wanted. When the two opinions finally drew near they became as one, and so it was done.

He did not want to be sick.

He did not want to be a burden to his family in his old age. He was always so very independent. I remember now, my mother told me he had recently said to her, "come, momma you just shuffle along beside me here, and we will go on together. We will stay together till we reach a hundred."

I am selfish.

I wanted him to be with us a little longer, and then, even then, I confess, a little while longer still. With his passing we mourn our loss; this is why the heart is heavy. Our relationship with this vibrant, strongman has ended. What we have now are the memories he has left to us. We remember, and we do have good experiences to remember also. It is with these thoughts in mind that I write this story.

For now I remember that he told his story to me.

Certainly he also talked with his grandchildren. He remembered his childhood in his stories to them. He told those stories in the broken English that he talked, and he still told them very well.

But he liked best to talk in that language from which the words flowed freely across his tongue, as he excitedly reminisced, and no longer groped haltingly for the proper words. How beautiful to hear him speak the colloquial Hungarian; yes, even when he swore, the words flowed poetically in that language.

He talked with me in Hungarian, the tragedy of it.

Most of his grandchildren did not know what he was saying. I remember, so often now that I reflect back over the years, how the two of us laughed. My wife would elbow me, "What's so funny?" she'd ask.

My children would ask me to retell it, and translate, but at the moment, at that point in time he was talking, how could I stop him? Quite frankly, he was on a roll and I did not want to interrupt him. If he detected the children's anxiety, he would say to me, again in Hungarian:

"You retell it – later."

He was a cornucopia of information from the past, and I enjoyed it.

At those times, if my dear mother was present, she would try her best to fill "them" in, speaking that broken

English, while my father continued his accounting to me in Hungarian.

Why, I remember once, coming back from Wheaton Woods, Maryland, he talked all the way. He insisted on sitting in front with me while I drove, just so he could talk. It was a good eight or nine hour drive at least, and he talked, and he talked.

He started at his childhood, at age six years, then his apprenticeship, then his World War 1 years, and then on and on. Oh, how I wished then, that I would have had a tape recorder on all that distance; but it would have been in Hungarian. My children surely could not appreciate such a wealth of reminiscence if they did not understand a word of it. Try as they might to laugh, to enjoy our laughter when we laughed, was actually laughing at our joy, that of my father and me.

I will translate and set to printed word a record of a man we all enjoyed, this man and his many friends.

In this manner my children will finally know many of the stories I did not retell at the time they were being narrated to me.

I will retell now all that I could remember of what he told me, as well as what my mother has added to those stories. If place names are incomplete; if events in time seem in error, they are my weaknesses and not his, for he had a magnificent memory and a love of history. This made him particularly aware of placing events of his lifetime into proper chronology, tying them to Saint's Days, holidays or birth dates.

I endeavor to tell events as I heard them, knowing that this can never be the same as hearing it from the man that lived it. In many cases my mother verified some stories, my Uncle Pál Valko's life also has reinforced some interesting incidents in those troubling times leading up to WW1, and that which followed.

Finally, I too have done a little bit of investigating, into many of the events that shaped him and brought him to Canada.

It was a long time ago, a very long time ago.

All things seemed so much more beautiful then; the country itself seemed so peaceful. In my imagination I have sometimes walked there with my mother and father as guide. I have never been there but I long to see what they saw; though I cannot feel what they felt, to share their happiness, and to see their lives as they lived it in this faraway land, this land of my heritage.

Could that what they told me, could all this actually have taken place?

It seems so unbelievable, and yet, I associate with their generation so well, with their simple ways, their simple wants and simple lifestyle. I wish to traverse their lifetimes, and yet I realize that life, this life, is lived but once. Each life must be lived by the individual to whom it is given.

I could no more live what they have lived, for the world itself is not what it once was, nor will it ever be again. I could only hope to capture a little of their lives in these memories that I write about as they imparted it to me.

These people are proof of what once was.

They have in their lives' story made a promise; we shall meet again in their world, that world of what is remembered. Things will be as they were then, so beautiful and so peaceful.

They will show me those places that they talked about. We shall walk those trails to pleasant places, paths their memories have worn smooth with these many years of remembering.

Such fairy tale names to villages and hamlets, picturesque and placid scenes; looking back once again, using the imagery of their words, it was another lifetime ago.

The world was younger then, untainted; it seemed as a garden of plenty. In their minds it seems as though it was another place, another world, and yet it was their world.

INDEX

THE WAY IT WAS

He entered the world fists clenched, feet kicking, as if ready to take it on. This pretty much defined his personality for the rest of his life. They named him Géza...he was my father.

He was born in Porpacz, Vasmegye, Hungary, on March 31, 1900.

It was not a cold day, but as days in March are prone to be, it was cool. When the midwife arrived in the house to assist mother Virág's delivery, she took off her heavy outerwear, and while doing so, ordered Mr. Virág to heat lots of water. The midwife rolled up her sleeves and washed her hands in a basin. She then went to assist mother Virág with the delivery.

Very shortly Géza was born.

It was an easy delivery because this was mother's fifth... and he seemed eager to come out into the world.

"János, you are the father of a healthy son. Let's bath him in that water and I'll be on my rounds. There are more in the Village that need my services today."

"But the water hasn't begun to get warm! You just came in a while ago; this old wood stove cannot boil water in such a short time."

The midwife was holding Géza in her outstretched hands. "He's got to be washed", she replied, as she approached the stove with the baby...still wet from the amniotic fluids. "Put your hand in the tub. How warm is it?"

"It's not even tepid!"

"Take it off. Pour it out into the washbasin and let's clean him up. His mother's body will warm his outside, and his mother's milk will warm his inside."

With that said, the washbasin was filled and the baby was cleaned.

"Vas cold water too". Is how Dad would tell in later years.

What an inauspicious birth. The infant that was anxious to come into the world was met with a cold reception.

My mother, Ilona Valko, was born into a Homestead at Szálláshely, Zalamegye, on July 8, 1896. She was the eighth and last child of Pál and Ilona Valko. Szálláshely (literally translated as "Lodging Place") was the name given to the Homestead on this settlement; it had been that name from as far back as people could remember. A name given to it by many people who had received a kindness and a night's lodging there. Even at this time, in the late nineteenth century, people associated the pleasantries about this large Homestead with many generations of benevolent Landlords. It numbered more than a thousand acres and Ilona's father Pál (Paul) Valko was the Foreman (Munkafelügyelö).

This pious man singularly carried out those actions that extended the reputation of Szálláshely. No matter who the people were, just passing through, they had a place where they could eat and rest. It was generally the poorer people, those who could not afford the expenses of regular hostelries. All found that here, was a "lodging place".

My mother's birth was registered in the Town of Csehimindszenti, the largest town nearest this Homestead.

Most villages consisted of several single family dwellings in a close cluster, separated by wagon roads or paths between the homes; perhaps a blacksmith's shop or even a tavern (koscma) on the outskirts, with a church at the village center. Many hamlets had no church at all, and so they would walk or hitch up the farm wagon and go into the nearest village that had a church. Farmers lived in these villages with their animals; the children and animals shared the same backyard; cultivated lands were in the outlying fields surrounding the village.

Poppy Tree (Mák Fa) was a little village on the road between Little Poppy Tree (Kis Mák Fa) and Big Poppy Tree (Nagy Mák Fa). These little hamlets were all within walking distance from one another.

Hiding (Buja) was another little village in close proximity to the others. On any evening it was quite within reason to walk to one, or both from the other little hamlet. It was quite common for boys and girls to walk back and forth between these quaint places. Many kindred experiences existed among the children within these four communities and grew into their maturity.

As young men and young ladies, they would visit to share common festivals. They were married and given in marriage, so that many friendships endured for a lifetime. The four communities' proximity to one another meant that fields surrounded more homes, and also the adjoining fields of each hamlet and village, so the residents learned to live in harmony.

Gravel roads led from one village to another and were trod by peasants who walked those roads with contentment. The roads leading into Hiding (Buja), were bounded on either side by orchards. The trees with fruit filled branches reached upward toward the raised road. Their limbs seemed to extend kindly, offering produce to the happy wayfarers. The travelers, equally kind, took only the fruit which would sustain them on the short walk into Hiding. It seemed so much as though Nature was also in harmony with the people.

There were thick woods between the orchards, and that is how "Hiding" got its name. Because it lay situated between the rolling hills surrounded by these orchards and woods, it appeared to be hiding in wooded seclusion.

The road leading in that direction caused strangers to wonder where the road was going. They were surprised to see the hamlet hiding quaintly, as it came into view. It was a vain attempt at concealment however, for once found, no traveler ever forgot it. Its reputation became international. Far and wide throughout Austria-Hungary, merchants knew that in the orchards that bounded the roads leading into this hamlet were the finest Lasponya—small pear-like fruit with rust colored skin. When ripe it is very fleshy and fibrous. Berkenye trees were also plentiful, bearing a small grainy, pear shaped apple. It is brown or red in color.

In the summer months life was joyful for the barefooted children. As they walked to school little girls challenged little boys to many contests; one challenge was to see who could jump the farthest across the roadside ditches. The girls always outdid the boys; for when the girls anticipated that a particular boy might out-jump the girls best try... they pushed the youngster just as he was almost airborne. Indeed, he was off balance and fell short and into the ditch. The girls jeered and ran away, being chased by the boys, or in turn, the girls chased the boys.

Soon competition was forgotten as one child discovered a bird's nest in the grass. There may be eggs, or small nestlings. Once again, boys and girls, equally curious, equally fascinated with Nature's bounty, would love the poor creatures to death. Children would attempt to feed the nestlings even though the creatures did not want to be fed!

On holidays the children walked the surrounding woods and picked wild flowers, beautiful red and blue Bachelor Buttons (Konkoly) abounded. Wound and braided with flowering Chamomile (Pipitér), they made a colorful bridal wreath for a little make-believe bride.

The make-believe wedding required singing and vigorous dancing in which the little girls allowed no boys. But surely the boys spied upon the girls from the vantage point of thickets among the woods.

Ilona would play with her many friends, but her two best friends were Irén (Irene) and Ziggie. One of the games the three daredevils played in the summer months between the school terms was rather dangerous, but all the more thrilling.

Playing among the sheep, they would taunt the ram as it tried to defend its flock. The ram would run at the nearest girl, and as she ran away the next girl ran nearer to the ram to divert it; it then turned to the nearer girl and chased her. The friends, each from different directions, taunted and tried to divert the ram from the girl being chased. They ran like deer when being pursued, and sometimes they would stumble over their skirts, then they screamed as they rolled and tumbled out of the path of the butting ram's head. Luckily they avoided serious injury.

Finally the youngsters tired, and with skirts in hand jumped the fence, they were safely remote from an equally tired ram that now appeared proud over their sudden flight from his threats.

The girls would walk to the creek for a drink. They 'cupped' their hands and raised the refreshing water to their smiling, rose-cheeked faces flushed from play. Barefoot, they would stand in the cool pebbled brook, savoring the cool water.

Little crayfish, as bold as the girls, would dart among the children's feet, and even settle upon the tiny toes. Squealing in feigned fear, delighted at this almost expected excitement, the girls quickly leaped and bounded to the security of the creek's bank. They had done this so often that summer; the crayfish seemed almost to understand, for they too, never failed to play the game, but did not pinch the tiny toes.

Homeward bound, the children would pick colorful bouquets of wild forget-me-nots for their mothers. Loving mothers remembered from their childhood, when they too picked forget-me-nots for their mothers. Their hearts welled with love from this childish gesture. Soiled clothes and mischief were always forgiven.

As the harvest neared there were community gatherings, work bees, in which shepherds helped one another. They may all be in one village for a week and then move on to another village the following week, or a few days, whatever time it took to complete the butchering.

Whole sheep were barbecued to feed the workers. The three friends sat pensively on the corral fence and watched as the carcasses were hung on meat hooks row on row. They snickered to see the dreaded ram of their summer sport sulking in a remote corral with a few young sheep that were not to be butchered.

It was to no avail that the adults scolded the girls away from one coral and then another. They were curious and wanted to witness all they could in their growing-up years. They understood at nine years of age why their one time playmates, the sheep, had to be slaughtered.

Village children, like farm children of those 'early times', had common sense, and were wise at an early age. Domestic animals are raised to be slaughtered, that is their purpose in life.

The farmers in this cluster of villages ended their harvest in October with a Harvest Festival (Szüreti Bál), which always proved to be a great celebration.

People from the largest cities like Körmond, Vásvar, and Gersë would always attend. This harvest celebration's reputation was well known.

Weather permitting, the fall fruits, pears, apples, and grapes, were hung in clusters on outside arbors and between the trees. At other times, because of the nippy weather, it would be held in a Church basement, or community dance hall.

Then the fruit and grapes were hung loosely from wires strung across and above the dance floor. Everyone danced, drank wine, and enjoyed this Ball more than any other holiday; it was better than the grand parties of the Aristocrats.

Custom required a Harvest Queen and a Harvest King; these were selected before the Ball. During the celebration they would be "married" and reign as King and Queen for the duration of the banquet and dance.

As their position of Royalty dictated, they also had their mock courtiers and guards, gendarmes or police (csendör). These would be given the responsibility to see that none of the fruit hanging on the wires was stolen.

The fruit of course was meant to be 'stolen'. Anyone caught stealing the fruit would be apprehended by the make-believe-police however, and, at a cue from the police, the orchestra would strike up a lively tune as the thief was paraded across the dance floor to be judged. The culprit would be jeered and laughed at good naturedly by all, as he was accused of stealing and required to pay a small fine for his thievery.

If they wanted to attract attention, young men made certain they would be caught. The more cunning however, took the fruit very efficiently like a true thief, without being noticed. He presented the prize to his sweetheart. Once the prize was in the lap of the 'lady', the thief could not be fined. A lucky lady, and there were many in an evening, ended up with a lap full of fruit before the night was ended.

This "stealing" became a fierce competition among the young men seeking a particular lady's favor.

Many children wished to participate, but to no avail for they could not reach the clusters of grape, or grasp an apple. Fathers then put the child on their shoulders in an effort to help the child to steal a 'favor'.

They were caught of course. This brought pleasure to those children and a few more pennies to the purse, as well as keeping the make-believe-police busy.

The three friends, Ilona, Irén and Ziggie, would sneak off following young lovers, wandering to the woods and the creek. Here, the crayfish, frogs or, mushrooms that abounded in the grasses and at the base of trees would distract them. As the youngsters stopped to gather mushrooms the lovers gave them the slip.

The land gave freely of its bounty to the willing workers. Innocent peasants, like children, were content and happy, while the crystal clear creek flowed to water the thirsts of men, beasts and meadows.

Their world was a peaceful place in 1905.

FAMILY
BEGINNINGS

Ferenc Joseph was the German born Monarch of Austria-Hungary residing in the Imperial Palace in Austria when Geza's father, János, had been a guard at the Imperial Palace (circa 1880-1886). It was an honor for any soldier to be selected an Imperial Guard, and one of the greatest compliments to a soldier's military service. The selection was reserved for the most disciplined and physically fit members of all His Majesty's armies.

When János went home on leave, if occasion permitted, he would wear his uniform of the Imperial Guard. This uniform was uniquely different from that of the regular army in the eighteen-eighties. As a result he received much curious and fond attention from the village girls, which he greatly appreciated.

It was then that he met a beautiful girl of wealthy parents. More importantly, she had wealthy grandparents, and so it was that János, when discharged from his military service asked for her hand in marriage. Anna Péntek's parents were pleased to consent to their daughter's future happiness. And that is how Geza's father made the single, most significant choice of his life!

Anna was strikingly attractive, a good homemaker, and the only grand daughter of Mr. and Mrs. Komondi, and she loved János with all her heart. Her grandparents had large land holdings, so it was that grandfather Komondi gave Anna and János a large parcel of land as a wedding present. Not to be outdone, János' father in turn gave them a few acres.

Throughout the first several years of the young couple's marriage they prospered and grew wealthy. The family grew also, as did the families of János' brothers and sisters. To differentiate between the many Virags, villagers referred to János Virag as "Komondi-Virag", as much in need of differentiation from his relatives but also because of their envy!

They knew that Old Komondi was responsible for the young family's prosperity since he saw to it that his "little Anna's family" should not want for anything.

Anna bore János ten children, four boys and six girls. As the children grew, they happily helped father and mother work the land. They were a happy and close family with parents and children talking about a positive future, of high hopes and aspirations.

The Virag family, as with all peasants and families of that time of innocence, toiled on, planning for their future, discussing what this or that child would do. Geza's brother Antal became a skilled carpenter. And a tradesman, in a village eight kilometers distant, approached Antal to apprentice as a Cartwright in the tradesman's shop. So it was that Antal's future was already looking positive. His parents were pleased to consent to his apprenticeship to pursue the trade. He need not explain why Cartwright was a worthwhile endeavor, in those days Cartwrights were important to the wagon makers and commercial shipping industries.

In the early twentieth century every merchant and farmer knew that consumer goods and international trade moved on rails, but between the railheads and towns the goods were trucked by horse drawn wagon. Freight cars received goods to be shipped by the wagon load, and once at the freight destination, wagons again delivered the goods from the railhead to the merchants, farmers and factories. The Country respected the Cartwrights who built these wagons and a good Cartwright could earn a prosperous living.

Antal's parents encouraged him, and he started his apprenticeship after the fall harvest. This left his brother Janos, Gergely, and youngest brother Géza, and six sisters to help the parents farming.

Géza and his sisters were attending school but helped after school and on weekends. This was only because the children in their childish manner insisted on being part of the 'working family'. It was not necessary that they work, there were hired hands that did most of the farm labor. The young did no serious labor, perhaps light chores around the stables, collecting eggs, and of course they brought water to the field hands when the work was in the fields near home. The children's school years were filled with the fun and excitement, with every day being a learning experience.

There were no pressures on the children as they were growing up, and so the Virag children enjoyed their school days. Géza particularly listened to his science teacher's stories of what the future would hold for them. Communications in telegraph stations, and the telephone were marvels to any child of that century. They were impressed when the teacher stated "I may not live to see it, but some of you sitting here will surely live to see that day when people speaking on the telephone will actually see the person to whom they are talking".

This was at a time when there was but one telephone in the entire village. As they walked home Géza and his friends talked about these things of science.

"Gosh, are such miracles possible in the future? Will some of us actually live to see them?"

They marveled as only children could in that peaceful world of 1907.

During the spring, mother and father Virag had arranged for older sister Borcsa (Barbara) to come in from the fields, or stay at home in the afternoons when the field work was near the village. In this manner someone was always there as the younger children came home from school. When Géza reached home, he would run into the house and announce to Borcsa "I'm home". Then like any child of today, dash out again to play with his young friends.

He was playing in the dirt street with his buddies, and as they ran between the homes they spied Aunt Susie (Zsuzsi Néni) the gypsy. This gypsy woman had positioned herself beside a house so that she was not seen from the street front. In turn, the boys were not seen by her from across the yard as they crouched low to watch without being observed. She cast a handful of corn into the backyard of a neighbor to where chickens were scratching and pecking in the dirt. The boys wondered why Zsuzsi Néni would be feeding the neighbor's chickens, while hiding in the shadows.

No gypsy feeds another man's chickens... unless they have an ulterior motive for doing so. The youngsters were puzzled, watching her intently, as she waited patiently with a string in her hand! Just as patiently as a fisherman might, but she did not have to wait quite as long as a fisherman. For as soon as she tossed out the feed corn, it was gobbled up by the chickens.

Among the kernels was one fastened securely to the string (perhaps through a hole in its center). Quickly she reeled in the string hand over hand, as the chicken squawked and flapped its wings, first its left wing and then its right wing haphazardly as it was dragged, but with little resistance since the corn kernel was securely lodged in its gizzerd. Once it was at arm's reach, she twisted its neck to silence it. With swift efficiency, and a strong pull, she jerked the corn from the dead chicken's gizzard. With another quick, continuous motion, the same hand tucked the chicken under her dress and looped its neck under a belt that she had over her many underskirts. The limp chicken now hung beside another that had preceded it!

Had the boys not seen it, they would not have believed it. Her plump body with the many petticoats concealed the chickens. She put the strung kernel of corn into her palm, and adding more loose kernels to it, she cast it into the chicken yard again.

The boys ran to their respective homes to summon grownups, Géza ran to fetch Borcsa. Some mothers came running with the children, but of course they were too late. Before any adult could get to Zsuzsi Néni's position, she was gone (with another chicken it was later deduced by the chicken's owner). No adult saw her; the men were in the fields, and so the mothers were somewhat dubious of the boys' assertions.

Again, the gypsies that did show up on occasion were always friendly, and seemed to have a valid excuse for being in the village. The culprit would have to be caught red handed, and that was almost impossible for the police could not be everywhere.

Géza and Borcsa were the only ones at home; all the family members were in the fields as usual, when the gypsy Aranka (Aurelia), walked boldly into their home. She scanned the walls, cupboards, and shelves with her head rotating from side to side, wide eyes looking for something... anything to steal. She continued to walk and did not stop as she stuffed valuables into her bodice. She was not yet aware that anyone could be in the house when Borcsa ran from the kitchen and confronted her.

"Stop! Put those things back. I saw you."

Aranka did not stop. She moved forward with deliberate strides, and because Borcsa threatened her, she lunged at the young girl snarling. Baring her teeth like a vicious dog, both her arms extended like a clawing animal.

"I'll scratch your eyes out, you brat."

Borcsa turned and ran screaming from the house through the back door, Géza followed immediately behind her. Before the police could be summoned the gypsy was gone. They looked, but could not find her anywhere in the village.

After this instance, the police chief must have influenced the gypsies to break camp and leave. The two women,

Zsuzsi Néni and Aranka, were never seen around the village again. They had broken the confidence of these villagers whom they had falsely befriended, but, so what? They simply moved on to another village and pursued their same actions. It was their livelihood, and they would do so until once more forced to leave, moving again from village to village; that is how gypsy Caravans roamed the entire European continent. Perhaps a generation or two may pass before that same Caravan returned once more to camp outside this same village. By then the old thieves and old victims had passed on, and the villagers were again, albeit cautiously accommodating.

In this same year, no more than twenty kilometers distance to the south, in a Homestead in Szálláshhely, another drama was unfolding.

Ilona's parents, Pál and Ilona Valko (whom their little daughter was named after), were a very happy couple, and raised their eight children; five sons and three daughters, in a Christian manner. Their prominent position at the Homestead meant that all their children received an exemplary education. They went to the same schools as the Land Barron's children, learning German as a second language, and the boys were also instructed in useful agrarian trades.

These children became as God fearing and humble as their parents. They were obedient children, but obedience slips to some degree when children are ten years old and engrossed in play. After the fall threshing was completed, Ilona was playing with Irén and Ziggie in the barnyard. Playing on the fresh straw stack is a lot of fun, but it can be dangerous also, because the straw has not settled. Until it settles, or sets, large sections can freely slide from under a person if one gets too near the edges of the stack.

The girls were warned not to play on the straw and, they remained earthbound for one whole day. The ladder against the stack however, tempted them to climb.

Once they were up on the stack they were not content with enjoying the view from up so high, so they began bouncing in the straw, they then thought it would be more fun to slide down the side of the stack. Very shortly, after having slid down the stack, one was giggling with enjoyment and climbing the ladder again, while another slid down the stack, the third was scurrying away from the foot of the slide to the ladder. It was great fun! The little friends were very enthusiastic, excited, and thrilled with their new found adventure, but in her eagerness to get to the 'groove' now forming in the straw slide, Ilona rolled off the top of the ladder.

She slid down while rolling, plummeting uncontrollably to the ground and landed awkwardly, full weight on her left leg. Her two friends were immediately at her side, eager to help her rise to her feet, but she could not stand up.

She screamed that it hurt...that her leg was broken. The friends looked down to where she was clutching her thigh with both hands; blood was already staining through her petticoats and dress.

Now came the difficult part they dreaded, someone would have to summon the adults. Someone would have to tell the parents that Ilona needed help...quickly!

The adults came hurrying from the field with horses and wagon, with mister Valko running ahead. He was soon at his daughter's side talking soothingly to her, cradling her shoulders with one arm while tenderly removing the little hands that clutched the dress to her bleeding thigh. He then gently lifted her dress and underskirts to inspect the injury. He was alarmed to see the fractured thighbone had pierced through the large muscle in front of her thigh.

He commanded one of the hired hands to fill the wagon with straw. He then made the wagon comfortable for Ilona's ride. Mother brought blankets and pillows to further cushion her, as father consoled their little girl. Then he picked her up gently with mother's helping hand holding the broken leg steady. They lay her in the wagon and took her to town.

The wooden splints applied by the doctor stayed on for a day, but no more than that because Ilona was in pain. Too much pain thought father; she could not sleep at all and continued to cry.

"It doesn't feel right Papa."

At the child's incessant begging, he did help her. Father tenderly prodded fingers between the splints and binding. With more than a layman's knowledge he determined that the doctor had not properly set the bones; furthermore, the bindings were too tight. He completely undid the bindings, removing the splints completely. He then proceeded to set the bone, pulling the leg until the broken ends aligned together.

Ilona resisted only a little; she knew father intended to correct a painful condition. Her older brother held her hips, and father made certain the bones were 'meshed' and now straightened. He then replaced the surface wound bandage. The splints were put back on and bound snugly, but not too tight.

Two weeks later the doctor knew no difference when he removed the bindings. He acknowledged that the bone was healing well, as it was set well. The splints were again put on; the thigh wound had also healed, leaving only a slight scar where the bone had pierced through.

The bones mended extremely well. Had it mended as it was initially set, this one leg may have been shortened, causing a crippling limp in her stride. Throughout her long life Ilona was mindful whenever she saw the scar on her left thigh. It was thanks to a loving and thoughtful father that her leg healed without a serious fault.

Ilona's father was fond of "Natural Medicine", and people from around the Homestead often came to him for herbal remedies, so it was 'natural' for him to help Ilona as he did, and used due care for her proper healing.

The doctor was none the wiser.

ERZSI'S GIFT

I n the winter of 1907, Géza was seven years old, and Erzsi (Elsie), one of his older sisters, was nearly thirteen years old.

Whenever mother Virag made fresh bread for the family, she would send Erzsi with a loaf for Simon Bácsi (Uncle Simon), an old widower who lived in one of the houses at the edge of the village of Porpacz. (The reader should note, adult woman were referred to as 'néni', and adult men as 'bácsi' by the children and younger adults, as a formality indicating respect for their elders. These meant 'aunt' and 'uncle' respectively, although the adult referred to was not actually a blood relative.). In the winter, mother would also send a pot of soup along with the loaf of bread.

The man was always grateful, and since Erzsi was the one to bring these victuals to him he loved her dearly. He could not have loved his own grand daughter more, since he saw Erzsi more frequently than he saw his grand daughter.

His sons and daughters on rare occasions would drop in to see him, but did not stay more than a few days or a weekend at a time. They had their own families, and lived in various cities where they were pursuing a future of their own. The old man was secondary to their personal existence.

Erzsi was on her usual errand to the Old Man's home with the pot of soup and warm bread. She observed that he was not in, but she left the soup and fresh loaf of bread on the table of his small kitchen as she customarily did in his absence, and then she returned home. She told her mother of the situation but neither of them thought anything out of the ordinary, for he had often gone into town for a few groceries.

Returning home he would warm up the soup and eat the bread.

That evening, as the children were preparing for bed, Erzsi was in the kitchen with her mother when an apparition startled her.

"What's the matter child?" asked mother.

"its Simon Bácsi mother" –

"What-- ?"

"There...see him?" She pointed in the direction of a dim lit corner of the kitchen.

"Where?" questioned mother.

"He's dead. He's trying to tell me something!"

Little Géza scurried behind his mother and peered out from behind her skirt to look into *that corner*. His little knuckles were white, as he clutched her clothes and clung to his mother. He had intended to kiss his mother good night, and she in turn, would go with him to tuck him into bed, but he had come into the kitchen just as Erzsi was describing the Old Man's attempt to communicate.

"Child," mother addressed Erzsi, "take care now, and don't get the children excited." Then, she took Géza by the hand and led him into the bedroom; stating calmly over her shoulder, "I'll be right back Erzsi."

When mother returned to the kitchen Erzsi was sitting at the kitchen table sobbing silently.

"What is it Erzsi? What did he want?"

"I don't know. He just faded away."

After all the children were in bed, mother confided the experience to their father.

"What do you make of it János?"

"I don't know what to make of it. Maybe the girl is being too emotional about nothing. Just because Old Simon wasn't home doesn't mean to say she should expect the worst."

Nonetheless, his wife made him uneasy, repeating that Erzsi saw his ghost in the kitchen, and inferred that János should enquire about Old Simon from the police, now.

He put it off until morning.

The next morning he bundled himself up against the cold, and walked down to the Police Station. Much to his surprise, he found that the police were aware that Old Simon was not home. Another neighbor had reported that Old Simon's house had been dark for two nights, and so the neighbor checked on the old man the next morning only to find that Simon was not home. That would make it three cold days ago.

"Oh. My gosh! Erzsi thinks he's dead."

"What?" exclaimed the sergeant, "János, why would she think that? We don't know where he is, but we certainly have no reason to think he's dead. He probably decided on impulse to visit one of his sons or daughters. He just forgot, in his old way, to tell someone that he would be away for a while."

"I hope so. I certainly hope so," murmured Mr. Virag as he stepped out into the cold air, and returned home.

The sergeant meanwhile was running a check through the 'wire' and telephones, with Old Simon Básci's children and other relatives. He may, he realized, be needlessly alarming many people.

"Wait till I see Old Simon, I'll surely give him hell for this."

Erzsi had another restless night, but she got up extra early to go to Church. This morning she would visit the church before she went to school and say a prayer for Simon. She needed peaceful reflection, strength and consolation herself.

Her mother was concerned for her, and much puzzled about Old Simon's disappearance.

"János, I'm troubled about what Erzsi said the other night about Simon's attempt to communicate with her, and the police aren't too sure where he is either," repeated Mrs. Virag

But there was more.

Within the next few days the police had verified that Old Simon was indeed missing. Within those days everyone in the village was also aware that Erzsi had seen his ghost.

"Erzsi, next time he appears, talk to him child," soothed the police sergeant. "Ask what it is he wants and, where we might find him."

The local priest prayed for Erzsi, more than he did for Old Simon. What kind of torment must the child be experiencing?

And then it happened!

Another cold morning some days later, as Erzsi walked to school having been to church and prayed for Old Simon; this was her ritual in the past few days, she went to church before going to school. She was walking alone when suddenly; Old Simon's ghost appeared and walked beside her! They talked as they walked; the conversation was not too long: Erzsi asked what it was that he wanted of her. He, in turn, simply explained to her where his body was, then with a gentle smile the phantom faded away.

Erzsi told her teacher immediately upon entering the school that Old Simon's apparition had walked with her, and talked with her. Since the entire village was aware of the police concern for finding Simon, and also aware of Old Simon's rapport with Erzsi, the teacher addressed one of the older boys to go with Erzsi. They went directly to the Police Station, where Erzsi narrated her experience to the sergeant. She explained carefully, just as the ghost had described it to her, the location of the body, its position, and where it could be found in the woods.

Erzsi stated that the Old Man had sat down on a felled tree trunk next to a larger tree. He leaned against the larger tree for shelter and had died, sitting there with his back against the large tree. He had described that the area was just off the beaten path, and mentioned significant landmarks. The sergeant dispatched police immediately to the location.

They found the Old Man frozen, his back against the tree where he sat in his final moments. The body was exactly where Erzsi said it would be, and in the position she had described.

This experience was phenomenal, but now, the superstitious villagers once partial to Erzsi and her 'gift', were suddenly afraid of her. They accused her of many things, but the worst was to claim her to be a Witch!

The poor, emotionally distraught girl was now kept home from school because school children and adults alike, shied away from her, and made remarks behind her back.

She was bewildered, and confused with this adult reaction. In the first few days of the Old Man's disappearance, all had sympathized with her because she had been visited by Old Simon. The police respected her innocence, and indeed, had relied on her to help locate Old Simon's body.

The priest, God bless him, prayed for the Old Man' soul, and for Erzsi, but now that the apparition had succeeded in communicating with Erzsi, he truly searched the scriptures and his own soul.

On the Sunday following the discovery of Old Simon's body (that is the revelation of where the body would be found) this same priest preached to what was now a "Pagan congregation".

"Don't anyone of you dare to accuse this girl of anything unchristian like or evil. For one so young she is gifted. If the gift is of God it is well for us to bear that in mind."

Whatever else he said was as pertinent, and must have been adequate, for the Villagers left off their gossip to let events take their natural course, and soon things did settle down.

They now realized Erzsi had a gift; the innocent girl was not a witch.

FALCON VIRAG

Austria-Hungry invaded the two Balkan States, Bosnia and Herzegovina in 1908. These states were claimed by ancestral rights dating back to 1089, with King Ladislaus' conquest of Croatia and Slavonica.

While his country launched upon this first adventure, Géza Virag became eight years old. Like any child of that age, his association with the war in a remote corner of Europe was that which he picked up from conversations of his elders. Besides, so the elders stated, Bosnia and Herzegovina were merely being annexed. This, they continued, did not require much of a military action which was of even less interest to young Géza.

In this year however, on March 31, it was Géza's birthday and Antal was expected home. The family waited for their second eldest, but Géza in particular wondered what he could expect to receive as a birthday present from his older brother.

Would Antal remember?

Antal had walked the eight-kilometer distance, down the dirt road from the adjoining village where he was apprenticed as a Cartwright. He was pulling a miniature four-wheeled stage coach, which he had skillfully fashioned to scale, crafted in the trade of Cartwright. He could not carry it, so he had to 'draw' it home. It had a doubletree, wagon tongue, and leather traces for the miniature horses that he had carved from wood. These were in the coach as he pulled it to his parents' home.

His was a most enviable profession, manufacturing horse drawn vehicles of all types, freight wagons, farm wagons, and stage coaches.

As soon as he saw the miniature wagon Géza was enraptured with this superb toy. What a grand older brother he mused, and his eyes sparkled as he hitched up the wooden steeds. No child in the village had anything like this.

As the elders sipped their after-dinner wine, talking politics and discussing the new war, Géza excused himself and went outside to play with his coach and pair. He was, as yet, too young to be concerned about the war and would listen only when the elders talked of bold and heroic escapades. Antal was twenty-one years old and had received verification that he would not be required to enlist. Twenty-one was the compulsory enlistment age, but because he was fulfilling a meaningful service to the country in his profession, he was exempted. His employer had vouched for him also, writing to the recruitment center and stating that Antal was needed for the production and manufacture of wagons for freight, commercial use, and the military. Exemption applied to anyone in a profession or job that aided the war effort. As a Cartwright, Antal was in an enviable trade because heavy freight wagons were needed by the military. He was now exempt from conscription for the next three years, his prime three years. However, if his country experienced a military emergency he would be conscripted and still have to serve three years, regardless of those years for which he had been exempt, no matter how old he may be at the time, up to the age of 42.

In peacetime, a young man of means and position generally "bought his way out" of the three years, gambling that once past twenty-four, he might not be called at all.

As it has been stated, Géza was the youngest of the four boys in the family. Janös, the eldest had not been drafted. He and Gergély along with the six sisters were helping to farm the two large parcels of land...

...Géza liked his toy coach immensely, the only problem was, it had no miniature horses. Antal had carved the two, simple wooden horses, to compliment the child's coach, it's true, but they did not move unless the child moved them. Because he moved them one at a time or one in each hand, it was unrealistic. It left him no freedom to work the doors of the coach! Why would he want to open and close the doors of the coach? He had surreptitiously appropriated his sister's two dolls from among her playthings. They were now the privileged passengers of his new coach. One was her favorite doll, but that didn't matter to Géza. He thought that his sister should be pleased that he graced his lovely coach with their presence. It wouldn't be the same without them as miniature occupants. They were to be his first passengers, and he would see to the horses too.

While the adults and his sisters remained in the house, he hitched up first one cat, and then the other. Both cats were hitched to the miniature double-tree, one on either side of the coach's wagon tongue, just like real, sleek horses. Only the devil knows how that child could entice them, or hold them long enough to secure the traces and the collars. Cats do not like collars! But, sure enough, he had no sooner released the fleeted furry steeds than they took off...literally.

Well, they couldn't go in two directions at once because they were harnessed together, but it took only a split second for those cats to realize their mutual plight as they tumbled and tripped over the traces and wagon tongue. They just could not shake off the rolling wood that followed behind them.

As if with one mind, they bolted up the first tree, dragging the coach with the doll passengers up with them. But they still could not shake free of this rolling wooden contraption. Here it was following them up the tree! The cats must have been mystified, and filled with terror.

Géza ran after them, commanding that they stop, but the cats paid no heed to his childish demands. They fought with one another, thinking perhaps, that one was responsible for the other's predicament. In an attempt to climb higher up the tree, the cats may have thought one was holding the other and preventing it from climbing. They set up a terrible squalling, there in the lower branches. The child got a stick and tried to get at the coach or attempt to break the cats apart. He hoped to at least release his coach...if only the cats would cooperate and come down. But upon being poked at, the cats managed to climb higher still, dragging the coach behind them. One doll fell out of the coach and, for the first time Géza began to realize that he might have a problem.

The cats were by now out of reach of his stick. He would have run away before his sister came out to see what was causing this terrible commotion. If she found her dolls being so grievously abused, she would be put out with him. He was torn between wanting to hide from Anna and retrieving his beautiful coach

On hearing the squalling cats, the adults came out of the house, casually at first, tamping the tobacco within their pipes, the men expecting nothing more than to break up a pair of fighting tomcats. When Antal saw the situation, he sprinted to come to the aid of the treed coach. One cat remarkably broke free, burst out of the tree, and pounced to the ground. In sheer relief, as swift as flash it was gone. Antal climbed the tree to save the remaining trapped cat that hung by the neck from the traces and was dancing in the air as it was being strangled. He could not grasp the cat and help it out of the traces as it fought for life, for surely it would have lacerated his hands and arms with bared claws, so Antal quickly took out his pocket knife and cut the traces. The cat dropped to the ground, shook itself but once, as if to verify its remarkable good fortune to be free, and promptly fled to safety under the nearby shed.

Antal untangled the traces that were cut, and brought the coach to the ground with its single doll passenger still inside. Mother, father, sisters and brothers now confronted Géza. Anna screamed to find her favorite doll lying twisted at the foot of the tree. She clutched it to her breast, grabbed the other from the coach, and ran with them into the house, turning her head to scold Géza for stealing her dolls. But he was already telling the grown ups how sorry he was. He was sincerely sorry now that one set of the traces of his dream coach was cut, and he realized that he was sorry for the hurt he caused his sister too.

Antal pointed out the cut traces that would have to be replaced; father scolded but, truthfully, no one really severely reprimanded the birthday boy for he had learned his lesson.

As the day came to an end, the family learned that Antal had accepted a new position, he would be working in Vienna as a Cartwright, and this meant that he would not be coming home as often, but the family understood. To prosper and progress a young man had to go where the best opportunities lay.

Before Antal moved to Vienna he came home once again and had with him the new traces to replace those that were cut. Geza hugged his older brother thanking him and wishing him well in his new assignment in Vienna. The coach would now bring Geza much enjoyment as he played with it throughout the spring and summer months.

But as the new school year began again in the fall of that same year, 1908, his young mind would be fascinated even more. In the late fall, in the cooling months between fall and winter, Géza went to see his cousin Jószi (Joseph) Virag, who was about 16 going on 17 years old. The neighbors had labeled him Kánya (Falcon) because of his bold experiments at flight.

He had attempted to fly many times before this year, but now young Géza watched with fascination as Jószi first took his wings up onto the straw stack, then came back down for his harness. With that on his body, he climbed the ladder to the top of the stack again. Slender ropes from the wing tips were tied onto the harness belt. Once there, he secured the crude harness to the center position and literally put his wings on.

The wings were covered with a silken cloth stretched over a lath frame. (When I wondered at the strength of these laths, why they didn't break or split, I was told they were 'edgewise' to the fabric, constructed to support the stretched, and shrunken cloth. Consider it; the frame must have been structurally sound because it did support Jószi, as he tried flying, over and over again many times). Jószi now ran the length of the straw stack for his initial speed, and literally ran off the end of the stack.

Once he was in the air, he leaned into the harness and pushed down on the ropes at his waist; the ropes that ran to the wing tips. Apparently he was attempting to flap the wings as he pushed down and eased up, pushed down and eased up, using his body weight.

He did not succeed in flapping the wings and circling the barn as he had hoped, but he did glide, and he did land safely with no broken bones. Géza was duly impressed at this marvelous exhibition! Mocking neighbors did not deter "Falcon" Virag as he continued to improve on his glider for some years, attempting to accomplish his dreams of longer, more successful fights.

I wonder if he could not have gotten to some mountain, or hill top; I wonder also if he had known about convection currents, thermals, and updrafts created by them; just how far would he have gone? .

PÁL'S STALLION RIDE

Gyula (Julius) and Jóska (Joe) Valko, Ilona's older brothers, became restless with life on the Homestead. It may have been the rumors of war, a war they wanted very much to avoid, or perhaps the stories they heard about America from visitors to Europe: whatever their reasons, these young men left to see for themselves the great things that they had heard about the United States of America.

Jóska was just past eighteen years old, going on nineteen, and Gyula was seventeen when they left Szallashély (circa 1908). (We shall find later on that they arrived in America and traveled the country until they settled in Chicago, Illinois, never to return home again.)

This left the three sons Pista (Steve), Pál (Paul), Toni and the three daughters, Theresa, Annüs (Annie) and Ilona to administer the Homestead with their mother and father. The entire family felt that Gyula and Jóska would surely come back home once their wanderlust was satisfied, and the Balkan wars were over.

Mr. Valko had twenty families of agricultural laborers (mezógazdasági cseléd) to concern himself with, so he could not dwell too much upon those two wayward sons. Young Pál would now be responsible to handle the horses. He would allocate the draft-horses for the agricultural tasks of the Homestead, while seeing to the grooming of those horses that draw the Landlord's family sulky and coaches.

He would also be required to break or train the young horses and stallions. The stallions could be very ferocious to the point of being vicious; it took a firm hand and gentle heart to get them to accept discipline. Only Pál could handle the job in the kindly manner that his father wanted it to be handled. Not one man among the twenty families indicated the same confidence, nor had they the qualities that Mr. Valko demanded. Pál had been working with horses since he was adolescent, and he loved it.

Farmers from an eighty-kilometer radius came to have this sixteen year old train their overzealous stallions. He also got to travel from one village to another as he took the Homestead stallions on the yearly rounds for 'stud servicing' the mares in the neighboring counties. Very pleased with his life and his job, he grew tall and stronger each year, as he went about his appointed rounds.

A few years into Pál's responsibility, a Squire from a distant county brought a stubborn stallion to the Homestead. Having heard that Mr. Valko and his sons had succeeded where others had failed, he would test the Valko "reputation", their skill at animal husbandry was one thing, but because of Pál, their success rate with breaking stallions was remarkable.

Father asked Pál if he would like to try to "break" this horse. It was a challenge that the eighteen-year-old accepted immediately. He grabbed the hair on the mane, and swung himself up to straddle the saddle-less horse. The horse was as tall at the shoulder as the boy was tall, and the boy was now approaching a two-meter height (he was almost six-foot tall).

Holding the reins of the bridle while the stewards held the horse, Pál assured the Squire, and his father, that he would not sleep that night until he could lead the horse into the stable stall. He then passed one rein around his trouser belt and tied it to the other rein. In this manner the reins looped through the trouser belt, in effect his body anchored the bridle reins.

This horse had never been led by less than two men, and had never been ridden. It had been transported by wagon to the Szálláshely homestead. It was not a riding horse; more important to the squire was the fact that it was an excellent breed of work horse, much like the big-footed Clydesdales and Belgium breeds. This made it valuable for stud service, if only one man could handle it. It had always been a labor of patience, and determination to get the stallion to "take the bit" (of the bridle), and for this it took two men, sometimes three.

Well, they started out, Pál and the stud on that morning, much to the alarm of the Squire. The stallion bolted forward as though it had been "sprung" loose.

They were not seen in that barnyard until late that night, very late.

People from two counties recited fascinating stories of what they had seen; pieced together, it became a subject of humor, along with respect for the boy. The stories verified that Pál was more stubborn and more determined than that giant of a horse.

The first village that they had raced toward had citizens in wonder at the size of the stallion. The earth shaking stomps of its hooves had alarmed them. Huge hooves they recalled, with large shaggy hair that amplified their size also amplified the speed of the horse. But before the rider and horse had raced through on the main road of that village, peasants working in the fields nearby recalled the giant horse leaping over a hedgerow from off the dirt road and, tumbling like a flowing rag from off its back was this young boy.

The boy fell to the ground, it's true, but he held fast to the reins. The horse could just not get away from him! The mountain of flesh dragged the boy for some distance, and Pál most certainly was thrown more than twice that day. Each time he held fast to the reins, or the reins remained held at his waist by the trouser belt as he was tumbled and dragged viciously; he almost lost his trouser, and it is a wonder they were not ripped off him.

No matter that the horse was powerful; its mouth began to smart from the steel as the bit pinched into its lips while dragging the boy. The halter also dug into the roots of its ears: still the bruised boy comforted the stallion with soothing words. He spoke softly, blowing into its nostrils as he adjusted the halter harness to release the cutting leather from behind the ears, but certainly secured them snug again before mounting. He stroked the mighty muscular neck, and smoothed the horse's nervously shivering muscles as it circled about him marvelously. Somehow, the horse circled less each time, and was reassured more and more by the boy at the center of the side-ling circle.

If Pál had lost the reins as he fell, if the halter had broken, the horse surely would have run away and would not have stopped until it was in its own corral, at its home barn. That is where the horse was headed with Pál, preferably for the horse, without Pál. But Pál maintained control, and worked the reins only to guide the horse as best he could, more than an attempt to slow it. In this manner the horse would associate a rein action with the words of the boy atop his back.

Finally, the horse threw the boy no more.

Its tongue was pinched and bleeding; its lips and gums of its back teeth were chaffed from the steel bit. The horse wanted no more to drag this boy; it was easier to carry him! Then in a distant county, in early afternoon, Pál turned the horse about. They began the return journey. The horse knew now that it was no longer on the way to its home barn.

It walked, for the first time it walked, and cooled its lathered hide.

After a short distance at this easy pace, Pál urged the stallion into a run again, so it would not catch cold or suffer a chill. As the afternoon turned to evening, and the evening air turned cool, Pál would alternately run then walk the horse while still astride it, until at his home village. He and the walking horse approached the village square as a young woman was drawing water from the well. With Pál's approach, she heard the steady clomp of the stallion's heavy stride, and looked up in amazement to see atop this huge horse, a boy whom she knew. Pál greeted her, and asked if she would kindly draw water for the horse. He would still not dismount and relax his control, after the struggle both had gone through that day, he did not want to regret a silly action now.

He remained atop the horse, permitting only two buckets of water to quench its thirst. Several people saw this spectacle of the night, and remembered it for years. The three were silhouetted against the white washed side of a house. There was this big boy astride a huge horse that made him look utterly small, but the girl in front of the horse looked smaller still, almost child-like, yet she was a young woman. And that wonderful horse glistened as it put its nose, which just barely fit into the bucket to drink.

Pál let the horse set the pace while he guided it to the homestead stables. He dismounted for the first time on his own, and led the stallion into an assigned stall. Every muscle in his body hurt, and he wondered about the horse, surely it ached as much as he did. The farm hands full of excitement, circled about him and the horse, offering to help stable the horse.

But it was Pál that rubbed it down and washed the salt lather off its hide, and then he rubbed it dry again, as the stallion munched contentedly on the hay in the manger.

When the horse's needs had been taken care of, Pál went into the house and had a bath. Both the horse and rider slept soundly that night.

VIRAG FAMILY FEUD

Many people in Europe were illiterate during the late nineteenth century and even into the early twentieth century. Very few could read newspapers or write their own name, they merely made their mark on official documents instead of writing a signature. This does not mean that the people were dullards, or stupid, they were simply uneducated and, therefore ignorant of reading and writing — and arithmetic. But the miller knew enough to count bags of grain and skillfully tallied for his livelihood. In turn, the illiterate farmer made "marks", hashes and strokes, that to him meant what a sentence or phrase may mean to one who writes the sentence or phrase.

For civil trade, or transactions, which included the sale of property, legality demanded that the sale be registered at the Town Hall. There was always an educated civil servant for things of that sort. He would read the title, or assist lawyers in communicating with the buyer and seller to the mutual satisfaction of both parties.

The Komondis, Anna Péntek-Virág's grandparents, died of old age. For quite a few years thereafter János and Anna still had things quite comfortable with their large land holdings.

But one day János found that someone had harvested half the grain from that large parcel of land which Komondi had given them as Anna's dowry. When János enquired of the neighbors whose fields adjoined that parcel, they told him that it was his father.

Confused and puzzled, János went immediately to talk to his father. It took a lot of work to scythe the grain, bundle it, and then pitch it onto wagons to haul it away. His father must have had a few people, and a lot of co-operation to do that much work so swiftly. János anxiously wanted to know the reason for such deceit; after all it was his grain!

Confronted by his son who knew not quite how to question him, the father stated flatly that the parcel of land was not János' but his!

"Why that's absurd!" rebutted János. "Everyone in the province knows that Komondi gave it to Anna and me years ago."

"Everyone in the province knows that Komondi gave the land to 'a Virág' over twenty years ago," replied János' father, "and I am a Virág. It could be my land just as you think it is your land".

"But it can't be. I worked it, my family worked it all these years, and now my boys are working it. Everyone knows that it belongs to us", professed János. Then he blurted out, "The next thing you will tell me is that my brothers also have a share in it."

The Old Man was only slightly startled at the last statement. Truthfully, he never would have been so vicious nor so bold, except that János' sisters and brothers had put their father up to it. They were jealous of János' good fortune and the good life that resulted from it for his family. As time went on, it was proven that the brothers in particular had strongly influenced their father into what would be a regrettable action. János had guessed right in his anger of the moment. They would have his father parcel out János' land that each of them could increase their own acreages.

"It had been brought to my attention that the land is not registered at the Town Hall, it is only recorded in the Church," continued the elder Virág. "No title or notice of a transaction, or inheritance has ever been recorded in the

Town Hall for that parcel of land in the past twenty years. So it is as much mine as it is yours."

Then, very guardedly, because he may have realized that his other sons were counting on him to continue with what he normally would not have tried to do, or perhaps because he felt challenged by János' anger, he replied: "Take this for what it is worth, I will continue to say that the land is mine."

Heartbroken and disillusioned he would no longer humble himself to his father. The memory came to him of that glorious day when Anna's grandfather, with smiling face had happily declared that János and Anna could have this land. The thoughts all rushed to this final, cold conclusion—Old Komondi had not transferred title on that day, or at anytime. János could still see that well intentioned old man's smiling face after all these years. The thought was as fresh as if it had been just yesterday.

The conclusion was self evident, and incriminating. In all of those twenty years János himself had not once thought of verifying his ownership. Not once had it entered anyone's mind until his father had...now! He realized that he had no legal argument at present, but he also felt the pain. His brothers and sisters had betrayed him. They turned his father against him.

His trust in his blood relatives terminated.

He must have traversed many memorable years of thoughts on that road through his mind, because as he stood in front of his father he appeared stunned, stone-like, while his mind's eye viewed inner visions. It was as though an eternity passed before him. He came to himself with a start. János suddenly felt his hurt turn to hate. No longer dumbfounded he became the stubborn, determined Magyar.

"We shall see whose land this is. You shall see who will parcel out the land," he replied to his father.

His father felt the bite of these ominous words, paused, only momentarily to shrug his shoulders. The older Virág did not know what was intended by those words; furthermore, it was he who was now bewildered. He did not expect this turn of events. The old man merely shrugged because he had nothing more to say. It was an instinctive reaction meant to terminate the encounter.

From that day forward János was a bitter man. He also became very foolish. He left his father that solemn day, and walked into town, and went into the first tavern. He sat down at a table and ordered a bottle of wine. The Tavern owner knew him; everyone in Porpacz knew János Virág and his wonderful family. The tavern owner also knew that János did not drink at midday.

"A bottle of wine János?" he hesitated and was about to add, "But it is only mid day", but he did not. He quickly presumed that János had a business deal going; perhaps others would join him soon for dinner. The Tavern owner brought him the bottle and a single glass.

"Should I bring more glasses?" He anticipated that János would not drink alone, and if guests were expected to join him shortly it would be better to have the glasses waiting for them.

"No. The bottle and one glass is all I need."

Now the Tavern owner was surprised; a most unusual circumstance here. The owner shrugged. He is rich, his credit is good, and perhaps he wants to think something out. That's it, he's here to think.

János stayed for a second bottle. In the afternoon more townsfolk began to enter the tavern. Many were surprised to see him there as it was not customary for him to be in the tavern that early in the day and with a "glow on" already. They knew something was out of order. Something was not right with János.

Anna was also worried. Her husband had left the house in the morning, it was now well into the afternoon and she had not heard from him. When the boys came in from the remote fields she enquired of them about their father, wasn't he with them? She expressed her concern that he was not home for dinner, and here it was approaching suppertime.

The boys would finish the chores while thinking about this change in their father's normal routine.

One of the neighbors dropped by just as the family was sitting down to supper. He had come from town, and though he did not stop into the tavern himself, had met friends that were in the tavern before supper. They had told him that János was "hanging one on". Because this was not like János, the neighbor felt that Anna and the boys should know.

The boys, János and Gergély, left immediately for the Tavern without eating supper. When they arrived the elder János was no longer sitting alone. There were the town freeloaders, and "ne'er do goods" sharing a bottle, sitting around his table, falsely sharing his remorse. The boys approached, not quite knowing how to handle the situation.

"Father, come on home with us, mother has been fretting over your absence."

He looked at his two sons. "Come boys, sit down. Join your old man in a drink." He then shouted over his shoulder to the tavern owner: "bring us another bottle, my sons are joining me."

"No we're not Dad. We haven't eaten yet. Too much wine on an empty stomach is not good."

He was set back at their refusal to join him, and his incoherent brain took this for an insult. He stood up on his feet, and found much to his surprise, that his legs were shaky. Undaunted, he stepped towards his eldest son János.

"Too damn good for your father?" and he took a swing at him. He lost his balance as he did so; his hip hit the table upsetting it into the lap of his drinking partners. He would surely have fallen but János caught him.

"Gergély, help me. We'll take him home in spite of himself. But it will take the two of us."

The drinking partners settled the chairs about the table once more, making snide comments at the boys as the sons withdrew dragging their sagging father. He did not resist too much: he was weak and tired. He had been struggling with his conscience most of the day and the mental conflict had broken him. Drunkenness was a welcome relief; at least in his drunken stupor he did not have to face up to the reality. He would have to face up to it every day of his life none-the-less, and that was going to be bad.

Tomorrow he would be sober.

The boys got him into bed, mother would undress him, care for him, and he would not be eating tonight. Later on, while the night was still young he vomited. He spewed the wine out and onto his clothes, beside the bed, and into his boots as well.

His loving wife cleaned him up. She took the stench filled clothes out of the room along with the boots. She cleaned the boots; she cleaned the clothes and set them outside into the cool night air, the clothes to dry with the next day's sun, and the boots to just air out.

Early that morning, when she was through cleaning the bedroom up, she lay beside him, with a basin at his head between them. When he vomited again, she held the basin under his spewing mouth, and held his head gently so he would not roll into his vomit.

Relieved once more, still lying on his belly, incoherent as he was, he told her what had happened, dimly contemplating the basin in front of him.

But he was speaking through a foggy mind and with a stubborn tongue. All his wife could make out was that he would show them, he would show everyone, they weren't going to take his land.

Oh! He was shrewd, and he would show everyone, but at what expense to his once happy family? He was never a loving father again.

(During the ensuing months neighbors and people in the entire county, and the surrounding districts sided with János, as they knew the land was intended to be his. Custom had it, since he was known to have farmed it for the better part of twenty years it was his. The Church Record was "good enough" for these honest peasants. János' father, brothers and sisters dared not challenge his ownership now that common knowledge had shamed them outright. Still, János kept selling off parcels of that land; only he knew why.)

He was known to sell an ox, or a steer, leading it to the market in town. He would not come home until he had drunk up the price of the animal in wine or whiskey. Then, when he did come home, home was the place where he would go to when he ran out of money, he knew his home meant security from his shame, but when sober, he would hate himself for what he did to the once happy home.

He would beat his wife or his children, whichever was in reach of his drunken hands. Often he was so drunk that he could not bend over to remove his own boots. He just sat there, mouthing words that meant nothing. His loving wife would pull the boots from his feet. At other times, he ordered one of his sons or daughters to pull the boots from his feet, while he swayed drunkenly on the chair. He would roll in the chair with his right arm reaching for the boots now on the floor. He would pick one up and whack the reluctant helper across the backside. Those whom he could not reach, because they had become wise to his action after time, and now ran clear, he would hurl his boot at, laughing drunkenly.

As he became more of a drunkard, his reputation grew and spread into the adjoining counties. He was unpredictable. When he had no cash to buy liquor, he would eat and drink on credit. When his credit ran out, and he could not get drunk, he was a rational man, and he did love his Anna. But he did not stay rational too long. He continued to sell off parcels of the land that Komondi had given them. He paid his creditors and got drunk again continuously. He was succeeding; he was making his father, brothers, and sisters sorry for antagonizing him. He would be the only one to enjoy the Komondi inheritance – literally, for no other member of the family had any enjoyment, nor did they like this transformed man.

The money could have gone for clothes for his younger children but it did not. Nightly he went to the koscma (tavern), and all night he did drink. Sometimes he walked to town in midday, and stayed in the tavern until it closed. He had no concern. His wife and family farmed and he administrated. Many times in his drunken, foolish pride, he thought what a shrewd administrator he was. There were those false friends who egged him on, and flattered him as long as he bought the drinks.

When he was sober, he hated himself; he must have, because he could not face his wife and children for too long while sober. The children now feared him even when he was sober. Anna of course was constant; his wife still loved him. She seemed to understand his torment and what it was that drove him to drink. Perhaps she felt partly responsible because that land should never have been given to anyone if it was to become a cause for contention. She patiently tolerated János, because she knew he could not stand himself and what he had become in his relentless, defiant purpose.

A good man needs no excuse for being good, because he is inherently good. An inherently bad man may continue to act in a reasonable manner appearing to be good, but only until he finds some excuse to pursue an errant way. Then he pursues that way, and uses the excuse as a crutch... forever.

Old János Virág had found his crutch in a bottle.

LIFETIME CHOICES

It was the summer of 1911, during the hay time of early summer that two young men would make a decision that would affect them for a life time. Though several miles apart and remote from one another, at their young age they were ignorant of how their actions would direct their lives far into the future.

Charles (Károly), Asztalos was his name. He was a boy just eleven years of age, but he was a stubborn Hungarian at that. Because he was the youngest son, he did not work in the fields with his older brothers. It was his task to finish the chores about the barnyard, and then he would lead the cattle to any grazing area along the roadside, or lanes between the farm fields. He would be the cow herder for the day. He was warned not to let the seven cows in his custody wander onto open fields of crops because they would do a lot of damage to the neighbors' possessions. Only gardens, chicken pens and barnyards were fenced. In those early times of the young twentieth century, farm fields near villages in Hungary were not fenced in to show ownership; this requirement came after 1918.

On this particular morning, when he was quite a distance from home, he deliberately led the cows onto Squire Simon's hay field, knowing they would eat well in a short time, and then he would drive them back to the road. They would be led down the road where it crossed the creek, there

41

he would stop. The cows would drink, and he could enjoy the shade for a few hours. The cows would lay contentedly chewing their cud, and make lots of milk, or so he thought.

"And I won't have to chase all over to keep them herded".

At about mid morning, just as he was about to drive the cows out of the hay field he heard a shout. It was young Squire Simon approaching on horseback.

"What on earth are you doing? Get those cows out of the field right now!"

The boy simply turned and looked at the mounted man as he approached. Surprised as he was Károly kept an innocent look on his face, feigning ignorance. He blurted, "Who are you? What are you doing here?"

"You know darn well who I am Károly, and you also know that your cows are grazing in my hay field. Who put you up to this?"

He was now dismounted and standing beside the boy.

"No one put me up to anything, and I didn't know that it was your hay field. The cows just wandered in and I was going to chase them out...now, just as you came." He lied.

The Squire could tell by the trampled hay, and amount of hay tops chewed off the mature hay that the cows had been grazing for quite some time. The Squire whipped the boy's behind with his riding crop.

"Come on now; no more stalling, on with it. Get those cows out of the field and into the lane where they belong".

The boy pouted, but knowing that he was caught red handed, and in the wrong, he ran after the farthest cow. The Squire mounted his horse again and helped to walk the cows out of the hay. They both knew that the well fed cows should not be excited to where they would run in panic.

Károly fell in line behind the cows now as they ambled down the lane to the creek. The Squire dismounted again behind the boy, and would have addressed him a second time, to warn him not to let this happen again, but the boy would have none of it. He was not about to listen, and he left the Squire standing beside his horse in the lane behind him.

He turned around suddenly when he was at a good distance, and interrupted the Squire in mid sentence.

"I won't forget this...ever. I'll get even," he said with a firm set jaw that commanded a firm voice.

The Squire was quite surprised, shook his head but did not puzzle over it. He smiled as he mounted his horse once again and rode away in the opposite direction down the lane.

"He'll get even? Darn, even for what? I should be the one to get even. Ah, but that is it! I humiliated the little man with that rap on his behind". The Squire shook his head and smiled to himself, "the little son-of-a-gun got off easily".

Károly held that childish resolve throughout his early and formative years, well into manhood.

He would get even!

In 1911, when Geza was eleven years old his father bought him a miniature scythe; yes a miniature scythe. The curved blade and twisted handle was proportionate to the size appropriate for a boy, just as the curved blade and twisted handle for a man's scythe was proportional to a man's size. His father paid as much for it as one would pay for a man's scythe, and he intended to get his money's worth; normally meant to be a working toy, it became a working tool. It was not to be toyed with. His father intended it for Geza to work.

Any other father buying such a thing for his son would do so because the boy wanted to copy the working father. In this manner a boy learned from his father to use the scythe before he was required to spend all day in the field; but this father no longer worked.

At age eleven Geza would cut hay or wheat, oats or barley just as skillfully as a man. He was forced to awaken before sun up, harness the horses, and be out in the field by break of day. While the dew was on the hay it was easiest to cut. With tear filled eyes, he struggled to cut enough before the heat of day. It was hard work, as it is hard work for any man. The other farmers would be returning from the fields with their wagons loaded, and they would see this 'sapling of a man' struggling to load the wagon alone. With neighborly kindness and pity too, they often helped Geza make up his load of fresh cut hay. They marveled that one so young, with a scythe that should have been a toy, would be expected to work unceasingly for a father that had, in the last few years grown so unreasonable, and so unkind.

"Why don't you go to school Geza?" or, "insist upon your father to get your older brothers to do this hard work", or "Leave the merciless man my boy, run away".

"Yes, leave the son-of-a-bitch", all sorts of possibilities recommended by these men. "All sorts of impossibilities", pondered Geza. "But why should I stay?" When he wondered why, he thought of his dear mother. It would break her heart, or his, that's why.

If many men know of one man's plight, eventually, someone of the many will carry his petition to a receptive or capable party, and the man will be helped.

So it was with Geza.

At age eleven, a tradesman offered to take him as an apprentice. Indeed there were at least three tradesmen that approached the boy having heard about the hard working youngster, and many good recommendations from neighbors. The neighborhood men urged Geza to accept one of the three offers.

His mother quietly stated her heartfelt hope, and her anxiety for his betterment. She knew that life at home was getting unbearable for her youngest son. His father had become a brutal taskmaster and now robbed the boy of his childhood as she stood silently by. Her son knew her love went with him, and he now faced up to the ultimatum. His father was furious.

"You young pup, I had planned on letting you have everything I owned when I got older. Your mother and I would spend our last days with you. As I grew older you would support me and your mother, here, in our old home. Now you choose to leave? See that threshold?"

He pointed to the floor at the foot of the door. With this gesture, he hoped to raise fear and doubt in the child's mind; more particularly with the following words.

"If you step over that threshold to leave, don't come back. This will no longer be your home. You no longer have a home to come to".

The boy's next words provided the answer. Addressing his mother; "Please pack my two shirts and a trouser, I need a change of clothes".

Red with rage the angry father fell silent. What had he done? He never imagined that this stripling of a man had the courage.

Mother packed his clothes into a small bundle. She stuffed a few slices of her home backed bread into a huge handkerchief, which she also stuffed into that small clothes bundle. With tear filled eye she embraced and kissed him. "God bless you and watch over you. Take care to work well and learn".

Crossing over that menacing threshold her youngest son exited through the door. Her husband's disbelief was obvious; else he would have thrown the young man out without his change of clothes.

The tradesman, a blacksmith, with Geza now in tow, walked down the street and out of Porpacz.

Geza commenced his apprenticeship in a blacksmith's shop outside of Vásvar. This was his reluctant choice and hope for a better future.

All did not go too well for this youngest of the few youth the tradesman had in his establishment. Geza was the "go for". The tradesman was also frugal, so the dinner bowl was passed around in like manner; from the tradesman and his family to the senior youths. Geza got what was left in the bowl and many times there was very little left. It was then, at these times, that he thought of his mother's cooking, and the plentiful food to be had at home.

One night, when all were in bed and his stomach growled from hunger, he resolved to steal home in the dark. He opened the window of his ground floor room and slid out into the night. His young feet carried him swiftly as he thought of mother's cooking. But each time he thought of his father, his feet slowed the pace.

What would Geza do? What could he do? He continued running into the night and after a few hours he was home. He looked desperately into the kitchen window. His mother was alone, so he proceeded to the front door and opened it stealthily, not wanting to wake his father.

His mother turned abruptly, surprised to see her young son suddenly enter. Seeing his tear filled eye, she ran to intercept him in mid kitchen.

"Hush." She whispered, "Your father is sleeping".

"I'm hungry mother." He whimpered.

She led him to the kitchen table and fed him. She warmed up a stew and buttered thick slices of bread. He ravishingly gulped it all down.

"Slow down, you will choke on the bread. There is no hurry. Eat all you can but be slow and easy my son".

"I can't get enough food there mommy. I always get the left overs, and many times there is no left overs."

"Things will improve as you get older, and you will get used to the demands placed on you by your master. He is a good man son, just bide your time. Tell him you would like to go to church on Sundays, and I'm sure he will allow that. You shall do well, just be patient."

She was right of course, and he knew it. He had chosen to be a blacksmith; this will be a good trade and a prosperous future. His mother packed him more homemade bread, and a few pastries. She hugged him, gave him sympathetic words of understanding as he opened the door to return to his master's house.

He did not run so enthusiastically away from home; truth is he couldn't, his belly was too full. But he was contented at having seen his mother, and she encouraged him to return again anytime he felt hungry. He plodded on; when the abundance of food had settled somewhat in his stomach, he began the slow run for it was still dark night. He must return before light of day.

It was still darkness of early morning when he arrived at that open window to his room. He quietly crawled in, tucked his prized package of pastries under his bed, and turned in for a restful but short sleep.

During the course of the next few days he did speak to his master about attending church services on Sunday. The tradesman was more than happy to comply with his young apprentice's request. He even bought Geza a new suit for the occasion. The master was not entirely a terrible task master. He often went to church with his wife and children.

Geza became an altar boy. And his master was doubly pleased to see his apprentice whenever his family attended services.

So it was, we saw that two young boys in that year of 1911, though distances apart, were deliberately determined about the decisions they had made. And their decisions did prevail, affecting them both... for a lifetime.

ANTAL & BOBBIE

While working in Austria, Antal met a beautiful young lady named Bobbie, and was now so much in love that he could think of nothing else but to marry her. (This name, Bobbie, I understand is an endearment, and perhaps a play on the name Borbála, or some Austrian equivalent to Barbara).

Even though he had been exempt from conscription in his first two years of service availability, he still had to get the Government's permission to marry before his twenty-fourth birthday because in a National Crisis he could be activated. Hungary did not care if a man married before age twenty-one, or after age twenty four, but for those years in between, the Country would much rather have single conscripts: a novel idea.

Because of the apparently smooth political overtones in Europe, army regulations permitted him to get married in 1910, at age twenty-two he married his beloved Bobbie. He became a father in 1911. The first child was a boy; their next two children were daughters, born in the succeeding years, one in 1912 and one in 1913.

Such was their passion and love for one another that, before the end of 1914 they had five children. There were no twins, but as circumstances came about, Bobbie gave birth to their second son February of 1914, and their third son was born in December 1914.

It was simply wonderful.

The young couple was pleasantly fascinated by the fact that the entire neighborhood referred amusingly to these two born in the one year as "twins".

With the declaration of war in July 1914, the Virag family had cause for concern. Concern for their many sons, surely they would lose a few to conscription. Gergély would probably be the first to go as he was already finishing basic training.

Now with the large family Antal and Bobbie had, their fears were concentrated more on the possibility that he would also be conscripted and leave his loving family behind.

Mother and Father Virag prayed for Antal's continued exemption.

The three years in which Antal would have served were considered 'peacetime' years, except of course for the second of the Balkan wars which was in 1912-1913, and actually involved Bulgarian troops and their allies.

Bosnia and Herzegovina, though annexed by Hungary in 1908 in a brief military campaign did not affect Antal. Austria-Hungary 'permitted' these states to maintain their elected governing body; it is just that they had no representation in Vienna. Vienna dictated the international policies, and also 'pulled' those Countries purse strings.

Although Antal and Bobbie loved their family of five, their love was greatest for one another. They seemed to be lost without one another when one was out of sight or gone for a long time.

Bobbie waited anxiously for the workday to end, and for Antal to come home that they may be together. She loved her children, providing for them thoroughly as they played around the house and yard. She was thoughtful for their every need, even with the full burden of care for the "twins". But when he came home, Antal was the "center of her attention". She made every effort to make him comfortable, providing him his favorite meals and evening leisure time as he sat in a comfortable chair smoking his pipe and smiling at the many waifs around him. He often held the twins in his lap while he told fairy tales to the girls and adventurous stories to his oldest son as they gathered at his feet.

They were observed holding hands as they watched the children at play, or arm in arm as they walked together in the village behind their playful children. They were always hand in hand, and they always embraced. Antal kissed Bobbie goodbye when he left for work; they embraced and kissed when he returned from work.

It was obvious to the entire village that, here was a happy home and a rare love. These children were most fortunate to have such a "loving" home, but the love their parents had for one another was unparalleled in all the surrounding villages.

In the evening when the children were tucked in bed, Antal and Bobbie returned to the kitchen and sat at the table to talk about their dreams for the future. Thinking of growing old and having grandchildren; the elder boy would surely become a wheelwright just like his father. The other boys would go into the various trades, carpentry, perhaps a journeyman. The girls would all find worthwhile young men to marry.

They held hands across the table, or more often sat side-by-side, as he had a loving arm around her. His arm was always about her or, hers about him. When she got up from the table to warm a pot of water for their evening tea, he would let his arm drop to her waist and squeeze her gently, or he would let his hand fall to the cheeks above her thighs, and he would pat that cheek caressingly. She would turn her head to him as she stepped away, with flashing eyes she would suddenly smile.

Sometimes they did not drink their tea but retired quickly to their bedroom.

Theirs' was the marriage couples read about, and dream for one as complete.

THE HUNGARIAN HUSZAR

C onscription occurred yearly in May and all young men twenty-one years old had to report for registration. Pál Valko was conscripted in 1913. In peacetime the conscripts may be given as little as six week's basic training if they were "city boys" or none at all if they were farm boys. The farm boys were allowed to return home after registration in May because the farming communities needed their young men during the summer and fall.

In October, these country conscripts returned to their regiments for their military training. Throughout the entire winter months they drilled and paraded, only to return to the fields of home again the following May. This continued for three years, until the troops were age twenty-four. If there was no National Crisis the men were honorably discharged.

The new conscripts' commitment did not end here however; up to the age of forty-two they would still be on call in case of a national emergency. After that age, if a national emergency arose, they would still be expected to join the "Home Guard." All males up to the age of fifty-six served in this branch of service in times of crisis.

Pál chose to join the Huszárs (Hussars, Hungarian Cavalry). His love of horses, and his expert horsemanship, made this the natural choice of service for him. Any Huszár Regiment would have been happy to have him. His reputation followed him when officers questioned references.

During his first winter of enlistment Pál was trained to ride, along with many young farmers and villagers who seemed best suited for the cavalry. There were those individuals who took to the horse masterfully, as did Pál. But others, who thought they knew how to ride, soon learned that they were far from what the Hussar standard required.

The men were all given a horse; it became their personal horse to feed, train with, and care for. They were put through a rigorous seven days of bareback riding. In this period they learned to guide their horse around a prescribed course at the gallop, and then at full run. The riders were often thrown, or just simply slipped off their horse because knees no longer could hold the horse viselike. From the daily requirement to flex thigh muscles to stay securely seated, the inexperienced rider's legs often became numb to the amount of pressure he was actually exerting; his knees would often quiver spastically from the long periods of exertion. They would actually throb uncontrollably in and out against the side of the horse; that, along with the fact that his knees and thighs were wet with his perspiration and the horse's sweaty lather... he just slipped off, like off a greased pig. Each time he re-mounted the horse, the inner sides of his knees became worn, and finally, the abrasive action caused these inner sides of his knees to wear raw and bleed.

He would, at the end of each day, first rub down the horse's hide, feed and water it, then "bed down" the horse with straw for the night. Only then, when his horse was taken care of, would he be able to wash up, feed himself, and take care of his personal needs. As he slept that night, a scab would form on the inner sides of his abraded knees, and partial healing would cause the skin to tighten. On awakening in the morning, he would again first feed and water his horse. It was at these times that he experienced the first pain of stretching skin and cracking scabs on the inner sides of his knees. He would rub ointment on the scabs to soften them so they would be more flexible and, hopefully not crack open, only to have the scab wear off completely in its softened state when he again rode the horse! New rawness appeared, now larger in area, causing it to bleed before the day's exercises were through.

At the end of seven days the recruits were given saddles. Now they were taught to jump hurdles, sprint their horses, and stay in the saddle at abrupt stops. They were actually taught some fancy riding, though at times they were in too much pain from saddle sores and healing knees to appreciate their gained effectiveness.

Pál had no such problems, and enjoyed the challenges.

There were those few recruits who took this all in stride and they did not experience the "learning" pains of the semi qualified. These men were soon performing for the ached and healing, and showing off for the Officers. The Officers let them go to the limit of their capabilities; for it was an excellent way of "separating the men from the boys", and evaluating the capable from the incapable.

There was one mounted individual who set his horse to running, then he grasped the saddle horn; took both his feet out of the stirrups, and cart wheeled off one side of the speeding horse while still grasping the saddle horn. As his feet hit the ground he was propelled upward again by the forward speed of the horse. His body was now vertical and rigid, with his head down just at the horses belly and almost at stirrup level, while his booted feet were extended above the saddle. He appeared to be at inverted attention, ankles together and toes pointed skyward when at the midpoint of his cartwheel.

While upside down, he allowed his feet to cross over the saddle by lifting his torso upward; his both feet fell to the ground on the other side of the horse. His head and torso was now upright on that side of the horse. As his feet hit the ground on that side, the speed of the horse again propelled him upward and upside down. He used the saddle horn as a pivot to constantly repeat this maneuver; first to one side of the horse, and then to the other. It was a series of "cross-over cartwheels" atop, and over the speeding horse.

A most fantastic and astounding performance! At the last cartwheel the bold Hussar set himself down astride the saddle. With feet once more in the stirrups he returned to his friends amidst a tumult of cheers and applause.

Immediately, small handfuls of his comrades were off and running to try their skill at this acrobatic riding. They whooped and hollered like a tribe of savages as they cart wheeled. Some fell off their horses, others knew when to quit. The Officers hurriedly put a stop to this carnival. They did however; complement those who successfully completed even one cartwheel. Officers did not exactly discourage the enlisted men from gaining further confidences. It was just that, at this time, it was more discreet to prevent some from killing themselves because of the taunts they may receive if they didn't try what might be beyond their immediate capability.

Before the young Hussars had finished their basic training, they learned to work as a team, men with men, and riders with their horses. The horse so learned that it anticipated the rider's moves. Man and horse drilled as though they were one. The men grew to respect their animal and affectionately groomed them, curried them, and spoiled them with oats and hay; and watered away their thirst.

The Officers instilled upon the recruits to trust and depend upon their horses. They were to be a natural pair, men and mount were attached by a strong tie of trust and affection...one mounted Hussar would be a very effective, courageous, and formidable weapon when the time came.

The Magyar Hussars were the most proud branches of the military. They had carved themselves a distinguished reputation that spanned more than five centuries, in fearlessness, derring-do, and ribaldry as well. Their reputation as hard fighting heroes, and reckless rogues was well known to the enemy whom they met in action. Fun loving on leave and riotous in living was the reputation they left with the women.

The name Huszár comes from the Magyar word husz, which is the number twenty. In the fifteenth century, each village had to supply one mounted soldier for every twenty homes in that village, and so the term 'huszár' originated. These men joined the army as part of a light cavalry, under Mathias Corvinus (circa 1458). This new concept of mounted cavalry was his idea, and he mustered them to fight against the Turks.

The encyclopedia states: "their effectiveness was so dramatic that other European armies decided to institute similar mounted troops."

The Hussar uniforms became very colorful and gaudy, topped off with a flowing cape over the shoulders. A Hussar of the late nineteenth century was outfitted with a sword and a carbine. The uniforms all had some red in them. Red trousers with blue jackets, both trimmed with gold braid. The jacket slung over the left shoulder acted as a twofold purpose now of both cape and jacket. In some uniforms the jacket was red and the trousers of different color, depending on the regiment, but as many regiments as there were, that is as many variations of gaudy uniforms there may be.

Only one regiment wore a totally red uniform, red jacket, red trousers, a red cap with a golden plume on top, black boots, and of course, the ever-present embellishment of ornate gold braid. These were the boldest of all Hussars, a truly fearless unit the 11th Cavalry Regiment called Vörös Ördögök (Red Devils).

When the Vörös Ördögök clashed head on with Russian Cossacks, for that is how it happened with the cavalry, it was as though one immovable wall of men clashed into an equally immovable wall of men, and the devil reigned supreme above the carnage. The Cossacks were as fearless as the 11th Hussars, but as time and frequent engagements took their toll, the Cossacks became exceedingly more respectful of these mad Magyars. Many brave men were killed on both sides, but the 11th Hussars were constantly being replenished from other crack regiments, and the unit appeared to come back in full strength again and again.

There was an oft-repeated story that was put to verse. It goes something like this:

A Cár el ment a Roma Pápá hoz	The Czar went to the Pope of Rome
És be zárkodot a emaszobaba	And shut himself in the confessional
És aszt kért az Ur Istent Magától	And he asked God alone
Hogy van e még a tizen egyes	Whether there could still be any
Huszárbol	Eleventh Hussars

These mounted horse cavalries proved to be a formidable force at the start of the war. They were used much like the British cavalry in the South African Boer War (circa 1899-1901), in an open style of fighting. They would route the enemy once the enemy began a retreat. Cavalries were seriously curtailed however with the evolution of trench warfare, barbed wire, and the increased use of machine guns. The supremacy of aircraft also added to their demise. It soon became apparent that large bodies of mounted troops were not likely to be used in the war after 1916, no matter how brave or bold the men may be.

The Hussar uniforms were changed at that time, from the colorful uniforms, to the drab gray of the Central Powers in 1915. The reds and bright colors were too conspicuous at a distance. The first year of the war, 1914, proved the foolishness of uniforms that were readily noticed from a distance, but in 1914 and into 1915, they still were colorful, and boldly worn.

After 1915, the Hussars were used as the rear guard for the withdrawing troops. Ten good Hussars, strategically placed at a point on the line of withdrawal could harass the oncoming enemy with merciless small arms fire, creating the impression that many men remained.

At the last moment, or at a given signal, the Hussar would leave his place of cover, run to his horse, which was tethered in a concealed place behind him and out of the line of enemy fire. Mounting up, he made a dash to the security of friendly forces.

They were also used singularly as dispatch riders, taking messages to advanced positions. Just before attacking a trench the enemy often "cut the wire" between forward trenches and the trench command post. When this happened, the relief forces in the second line trench were not certain whether or not the wires might have simply been destroyed by a lucky artillery shot. There were those individuals who carried a radio pack on their back, and proved their value for communications because they could, and did, tie into any telegraph wire while standing atop the saddle of the stationary horse, as they sent or received pertinent information.

In any event, when the communications wires were cut and could not be tapped into, and a message was urgently needed, the lone Hussar had to carry a communiqué to and from the silenced salient; no matter how deadly the fire and fury. Not an enviable task, and a most hazardous race, running a horse over cratered country while shells, bullets and mortar are exploding around you. If the enemy did not get you coming, they had a second chance when you were returning.

(Geza's teacher's nephew was a corporal in the Hussars and became a dispatch rider also. Whenever he came home on leave, he would tell stories of close calls, admitting that there were times in which the heat of battle was so intense that he actually "shit his britches" while astride his horse.)

Pál recalled how frightened the peasants were; while scything hay they looked up on hearing the sound of hoof beats, and when they saw him riding into their direction alone, they scattered on seeing the Hussar uniform. What were they afraid of? He had no intention of hurting them. But; perhaps some other Hussar had done injury to civilians before, "riding them down" in cruel defiance. He wondered

The poor peasants had remained on their land in spite of the war raging around them. Some would rather die than leave their homes and land. They did not relish being moved to the "hinterlands" thirty miles from the front, and their homelands. Thirty miles was the estimated safe distance from the artillery in those days.

Quite often a lone Hussar was assigned to a critical position that had no "wire" communications, but relied on carrier pigeons to relay messages. When the pigeons were expended and there was still no relief forthcoming, it was up to the Hussar to run a message through.

Pál reminisced; many times the horse, frightened and confused at the noises of warfare all around, would stand on its hind legs and paw the air nervously with front hooves. "And I was just as frightened as that poor horse, but with shells bursting, and bullets whizzing, it was no time to stand still. One was always on the threshold of death."

As both were exposed to more experiences, the horse became more confident because of the "seeming confidence" of the rider. No longer were they skittish, though still very much afraid, both now veterans, went about their business deliberately.

The fascinating thing about this "one man" situation was that sometimes the enemy watched the rider. You could see the enemy faces! Yet they did not fire a shot! On those occasions they may have been instructed, just as the Austro-Hungarian infantry had been at times instructed, not to fire upon a dispatch rider. At those exceptional times, a critical position may be jeopardized by firing a volley of shots at a rider. Once revealed, artillery could concentrate and obliterate the position that did the shooting.

To allow this decoy to draw your fire would be foolish, and so it was that in these instances the infantry let the dispatch rider through.

HISTORY & THE TREE OF LIFE

S üle Jenö had been conscripted in May, 1913, when he
was twenty years old, because he would be twenty-one
years old before year end. As a farm youth Jenö was permitted to return home after registration for service to help
his parents on the farm until October. He then returned for
the army basic training which continued through the winter
months. In May of 1914, he was again released from his military commitment to help on the family farm.

He was on his way to the train station for return home
from barracks, but near the station was a tavern (koscma).
It was so convenient that he decided to have a 'short one'
for the homeward journey. Inside he met Gergély Virag, a
hometown boy, also returning home. What a pleasant surprise! Jenö now had a drinking companion.

"What are you doing in Vienna Gergély?"

"Jenö"!

What do you think? Where else would they send us for
maneuvers?" Gergély did not expect to see a close friend
here and he rose from his chair to clasp his friend's hand in
a two fisted, hearty handshake. Gergély was with the 18th
Division of the Home Guard, and explained that they had
just finished six weeks of the yearly military exercises.

"If that's the case, there should be a crowd of eager privates on the first train out. What do you say we take the
next one?"

Gergély was agreeable. "I'm not expected into Szombathely until the late afternoon anyway."

The friends had a very lively and entertaining time with one another's barracks stories. They told many amazing anecdotes of barrack life as well as some personal vignettes within their personal lives. After a few drinks, Gergély told Jenö a very humorous story about his father János Virag. He had never told anyone, not a single soul before, but what the heck, he could tell Jenö. The timing was appropriate, and since Jenö knew about János Virag the elder's stint in the Imperial Palace as guard for Old Ference Jozesf, Jenö also knew of the strict discipline these guards were under, with no failure of purpose permitted while on duty.

"As it happened, while on guard duty, dad had a nature call while in that long lonely corridor," continued Gergély, "there was no possible relief in sight."

They both laughed at this double meaning of the word 'relief'.

"No guard to relieve him for a nature break, and no possible place to take a break?" asked Jenö.

"Well," Gergély continued, "he surmised that, if no one had come down that corridor in the last few hours, that late at night, what are the chances anyone would be there within the next twenty minutes? So he walked quietly away from the doors and a short distance down the corridor. Leaning his rifle against the wall in front of a large potted plant; he then got around the other side of the pot, dropped his trousers and relieved himself at the base of the plant."

"He shit right there?"

"Yes, and promptly returned to his guard post. The whole thing didn't take but three minutes."

"Did he tell you that?"

"Of course not, but after he left the service and they were partying, he did tell his Imperial Guard friends. During their drinking get together in later years, one of them retold the story and I overheard the retelling of it. My dad would still deny it today; he might even kill me if he knew that I retold it to you."

"Well, at least he fertilized the 'Imperial Plant'." They then both laughed uproariously, picturing the incident in their mind, and thinking how stupidly bold an action that must have been, considering the consequences if caught.

"A Virag shit in the Old King's Imperial Palace! That took a hell of a lot of nerve." replied Jenö.

(This incident will not be found written in the Magyar History books)

They were enjoying themselves so much that they almost missed their train but, thanks to the bartender's reminder, they made it. They would take the train to Sopron where there was a short stopover. The following stop was Szombathely, this was a somewhat livelier town and they were looking forward to that stop also.

János Virag, Gergély's brother met them in Szombathely, and now the three friends walked toward a tavern. No need to hurry; while the boys are away from home is the time to play, and drink. It is best to run wild when away from home.

--- — — ---

This same May of 1914, there was a wedding in Vásvár. It was the first wedding after the Lenten Holiday. The minds of these townsfolk were planning for peace and perpetuity, and certainly were not in harmony with the minds of the Empire Builders. While politicians planned, and militarists dreamed of conquests, murder, and the manslaughter to be perpetrated on these people, the people dared to dream of expanding families, and living a long life.

How happy they were, and how wise the timing of these lovers; the groom's family would now have an additional helpmate for the summer work. Ilona Valko was almost eighteen years old and she was the Maid of Honor.

On leaving the church, the wedding procession was parading toward the banquet hall to continue the celebration. The bride and groom, the maid of honor and best man, were on a brightly festooned, and gaily decorated cart. The young married couple sat on a bench seat behind the driver and facing forward. With ribboned folk-top-hat on his head, the driver sat alone in the front seat, and happily reined the decorated horses. Behind the bride and groom, on a bench seat facing rearward, sat the maid of honor and the best man. The groomsmen and bridesmaids walked at either side of, or directly behind the cart. Many of the wedding guests also walked, following behind, and on both sides of the cart as it proceeded steadily in this celebratory parade. Ilona held the Tree of Life (Élet Fa), and was guarding it carefully.

The Tree of Life is a large bush about the size of a small Christmas tree (Biota Orientalis). Its limbs were wrapped with cords of pastry, and the entire creation had been baked in a large outdoor oven. After baking, it was ornamented with "holed" cookies that were threaded over the pastry covered branches. Festooned with ribbons, it symbolized a "long happy life." It was the object of attraction during the parade from the church to the banquet hall. The Maid of Honor's task, aided by the bridesmaids and groomsmen, was to keep The Tree of Life safe. She must guard it and protect it from pranksters or lose her place of significance, and her position of honor would be forfeited.

Daring village youths challenged the procession at every opportunity with the intent of breaking a limb off the Tree of Life. With the cookies on the limb, and pastry-wrapped limb itself as a trophy, it became as much an honor to claim a part of it as it was to defend it. Keeping the Tree of Life whole, and safe from harm, assured a happy, prosperous and long married life for the young couple. Remaining intact during the parade, it would be ceremoniously proportioned to the parents, most honored guests and family members, as a special treat after the banquet.

The Tree of Life was an extension of the wedding celebration to the citizens who were not invited guests, so that they too may revel none-the-less, and add to the excitement and joy of the day.

Suddenly, a youth ran boldly up to the cart. As the crowd watched in anticipation, the youth side stepped past the wedding guests that were beside the cart and quickly placed his one foot up on the rolling wheel-hub. Jumping up from there he attempted to break off a piece of the Tree.

Ilona saw the youth when he broke through the crowd and, anticipating his intentions she quickly sprang up to stand tiptoe on the seat. With both hands extended she held the Tree high above her head; quite a daring feat on a moving cart.

The youth missed by slim centimeters, and was bodily pushed away from the cart by the best man. The determined youth could not humiliate the newlyweds. Thwarted, he fell to the ground and tried no more. The crowd in the street cheered him for his effort, and the Maid of Honor for her 'gallantry'. Neither action was expected and, how things turned out merely amplified the celebration of the village wedding. This would be something to talk about for months; for the bride and groom, something to remember in their older years.

The wedding guests and street crowd cheered with glee. But, before any other brash youth would consider a similar action, the wedding guests clustered more closely around the cart.

The bridesmaids and groom's men unloaded the bride and groom, with the Tree of Life, while the cart continued to roll past the banquet hall entrance. A well-executed strategy; the Tree of Life was safe from those who dearly wanted to claim it.

WATER AT
THE STABLES

O ne morning in the final week of basic training, when all recruits had formed strong friendships and gotten to know one another, Pál noticed a laughing group at the water trough as he approached to draw water for his horse. He dipped the wooden bucket into the water trough. This was the customary wooden bucket of those times, with wood side staves, like those on a barrel, and the thick wire inverted "U" shaped handle at the center of which was a wood-roller, the easier to grasp and carry the heavy bucket. As he turned to go back to the stable with the full bucket of water Béla yelled at him.

"Hey Pál, can you do this?"

Pál turned to look back; at first glance he did not believe his eyes. There were four Hussars with Béla, and they laughed at the expression on Pál's face. It was one of shocked disbelief. For a well bred, and a religious young man like Pál it must have been quite a shock.

Béla had a water bucket, the wood handle hooked over his penis! He had a huge erection this morning and was showing it off. The bucket had water in it, and as he roared with laughter at Pál's shocked, open-jawed expression, his penis waved up and down like a vertical pendulum with his belly laugh. The water sloshed onto his knees and feet. Béla quickly took the water bucket from his 'meat hook', and set it on the ground while still laughing with gusto. The bucket was heavy enough without the water in it!

64

Two Hussars were now unbuttoning their own trousers and attempting this remarkable feat. Immediately up went a challenge from the two remaining Hussars.

"Bet you can't carry the bucket all the way to the stables like that."

"How much you want to bet?"

"Two forints!" shouted the one, and dug into his pocket to show the coins. (One forint was about fifty cents in 1914; two would be one dollar; a lot of money in those days).

"You're on," whooped Béla, and he again hooked the bucket over his erection.

The three Hussars began to walk with knees turned outward and bowlegged, so that their knees in their awkward striding would not jostle the bucket. On taking a few steps they began to lean backward also, to give their erect penis a more upright vertical angle and added leverage. This also kept the pail's handle at the pubic hairs, and so a more positive anchor.

Béla caught up to the two who had begun before he had accepted the challenge. It was a very crude, clown-like display, and more of the Hussars came to see this amazing 'parade of pricks'.

"Come fellows; see what is going on here at the water trough. Make your bets, hurry."

There was now quite a gathering between the stables and the water trough, with the laughing numbers of unbelieving men forming a corridor that the "cocky" comrades had to walk through to reach the stables.

One contender straightened up to look at Béla's performance whereupon the wood-handle-grip rolled like a wooden-roller-bushing down the length of his penis. Down fell the bucket, the water spilling at his feet. His penis bounced back up like a rigid springboard; and he immediately tucked in his erection, buttoning up his "fly."

His buddy did not get much farther. He was laughing too severely at the first contender's ridiculous accident. Then, a like action presented itself to him, whereupon the bucket just dropped, staying upright, while his penis quickly wilted.

Béla alone remained, moving boldly forward with his huge penis upright; he relished this exhibition. All eyes were now on him alone and on his proudest attribute. He thrived upon such a display. The barracks barnyard rung with cheers urging him on, the horses in the stables were whinnying and snorting at the outbursts and commotion. Officers behind closed doors now began to take notice also, and proceeded to the stable area.

Béla took bold, deliberate, bowlegged strides to the stable door, while the most virile of Hussars marveled at such an incredible organ. At the door Béla unhooked the bucket just as the Officers pushing through the crowd made their appearance. The men applauded, whistled, and cheered the winner. The Officers were confused, shouting to be heard above the cheering crowd they demanded to know the reason for such a rowdy gathering so early in the day.

The Officers could not see Béla through the crowd. Standing near the stable door he hurriedly tucked his erect penis into the trousers, both hands moved rapidly to enclose it. It remained upright against his belly but was contained, and restrained from bursting forth in all its rigidity by the now overworked buttons.

The entire group related a fabricated story to the Officers, laughing as they repeated that they were merely wagering on a balancing bucket of water.

"See? There is the spot where one contender lost it."

They pointed to the wet circle where the first man had dropped the water bucket. The man with the forints now collected from the losers, and in turn paid the champ, Béla.

Pál, incredulous, and disbelieving what his eyes had just seen, again started toward the stables with the bucket of water still clenched in his hand. It was heavy, and he had stood there dumbfounded all the while watching the comical contest. He believed, and agreed therefore, that what he had just witnessed was indeed a fantastic exhibition.

This erotic exercise's capability was brought on by eight weeks of physical strain in the basic training. The recruits had been out of circulation from women; even so, Pál still thought it was unbelievable; no man could actually do that could they? Had he not seen it with his own eyes he would not have believed it.

To describe Béla, one would say, first of all, because of the preceding exploit, that he was well endowed; he was "hung-arian." He was proud of his penis. This simple man, with simple mind, could not help but admire it, and fondly exhibited it to those less endowed. This was his single and greatest attribute. It seemed natural that he liked to show it off to anyone who had heard about his "magnificence," particularly to the young ladies.

The most experienced, and most adventurous of girls were titillated, they giggled with expectation. In their disbelief they asked permission, "Oh Béla could I feel it?" Perhaps they thought that it was inflated and would collapse at their touch. They desired to feel, to believe with their touch, the impossibility that their eyes were dictating to their mind.

"Where would you like to feel it?" Roared Béla with a most sensuous and stupid leer, then he would reply in a gentle and endearing voice, as they fondled, and caressed it.

Oh, how he loved it. Oh, how they loved it.

If he had as much brain as he had penis, this simple man would have been a genius.

THE EMPIRE BUILDERS

While children played and dreamed pleasant childish dreams; while peasants toiled diligently in similar childish innocence, there were those who dared to dream of Empire.

Prince Otto Eduard Leopold Bismarck of Schoenhausen was an Empire builder. He paved the way for the establishment of the German Empire in 1871. It was Kaiser Wilhelm Hohenzollern II, who was to inherit this Empire, the "World's Greatest Empire". But Bismarck clashed with the Kaiser, and resigned as chancellor in 1890. The World's Greatest Empire was still to be formed; it had however, germinated, poisoning the minds of powerful and ambitious men.

With the Great Empire as its objective, a German organization was created devoted to the development of a 'Great Middle European State'. This State was to include Germany, Austria, and Hungary at its center. It would have Belgium and Holland on the West. Russia, Poland and the Balkan States (Albania, Bulgaria, Bosnia, Croatia, Dalmatia, Greece and Montenegro) on the East, and would extend through Turkey to Asia Minor and into Mesopotamia.

Germany, with the help of Austria-Hungary, and the alliance with Turkey, planned to build a railroad from Constantinople to Baghdad. This railroad would then be connected to the Berlin-Constantinople railroad, and thereby stretch from Berlin to Baghdad. Maps were printed and distributed by this German organization twenty years before 1914. These maps showed the extent of the major expansion to this Empire, with proposed annexations. (In retrospect, it is amazing that the Western World stood passively by as Germany prepared for "Empire." These maps, for twenty years were evidence of Bismarck's ambition to build this Greater German Empire).

Austria-Hungary was the first to initiate positive moves that would begin the annexations with the invasion of two Balkan States, Bosnia and Herzegovina in 1908. Of course any excuse would do, but these States were claimed as ancestral rights dating back to 1089, and to King Ladislau's conquests of Croatia and Slavonica.

When Europe showed 'dismay' at this outright act of aggression, the Kaiser stood by his allies and announced his support of their actions. There was, therefore, no threat or challenge from Europe to back up the 'dismay'.

The fate of these small Nations should have been a warning to the Free World. But it was an alarm that went unheeded. The wicked wind of war wafted the scent of scorched earth upon the breeze like the smell from far distant fires. There were those who sniffed the air but were unconcerned. The dying embers were fanned by the small Nations, and the sparks fell short. Only the subtle breath of rancid smoke fell upon the people of the Western World. Governments and Nations ignored it; their people continued on with their pursuit of humdrum lives, blissfully unaware, while the people of those small Nations of the Balkan States fought futilely the struggle to survive. To them, the scorched earth was in the fields of home.

Croatia, Herzegovina, Montenegro and Serbia were simply place names to those residents of the Western World, but they would soon become familiar to the watchers-of-the-world. These same people would be reluctantly caught up in this, which would become the first World Conflict. Those humdrum lives would soon be filled with excitement; and when concern became the real world, it became horrible.

But they had six more years before the fire, and not the smoke, suddenly engulfed them also.

Germany pursued her advantage relentlessly, while the Allied Nations awoke slowly from their lethargic sleep. No more could any single Nation consider herself free from another Nation's dilemma; what befalls one could befall them all, if they do not maintain vigilance.

The fire, once well established within the small Nations, encouraged Germany to now leap across the European continent. The fiery fingers touched Belgium and France. Russia was about to be seared. Never more would she recover to return to the existence that was once her proud, but arrogant heritage; a heritage in which a population of peasants was blind with religious obedience to the Monarchy. The Monarchy was in turn, blind to remove the yoke from the peasantry, and chose instead to exploit their people into bondage that was tantamount to slavery and Churls to work the Massive Russian Empire.

The grandeur of Imperial Russia was soon to go, lost forever.

Across the Atlantic, an unbelieving Continent watched until it too became a believer. Its people were to be swept up by that same wind of war that they had ignored for so long. Names once unheard of soon would fill newspapers, and would also occupy the minds of men and women. Foreign place names became very significant suddenly, as soldiers wrote letters home to their loved ones from cities and towns with strange sounding names. Loved ones would read, over and over again, the grim facts about how, insignificant towns and villages now became specific battle fields, and Hell.

The war would prove to be so very real.

--- — —---

Historically, as Magyarország (Hungary) had gained provinces from adjoining territories, she exercised a negative repatriation, and a positive re colonization of these frontier provinces. In an attempt to turn these provinces into native lands, she would uproot the total population and transport them into Central Magyar provinces, far from their homeland.

She would, in turn, replace these foreigners with patriotic, volunteer Magyar families, and thus colonized the vacated conquered provinces. In this manner the transplanted foreigners would be, within one generation, assimilated into the Magyar social structure with their children becoming "Magyarized". The transplanted Magyars in turn, remained loyal to their Mother country's cause. They were ready to fight any rebellious neighbors bent on driving them out. In this manner Hungary grew, and stretched out her borders.

She may have started a similar re-colonization of Bosnia and Herzegovina if given more time, but just as German ambitions appeared to be going according to plan, the Balkan wars broke out. Bulgaria, Greece, Montenegro, and Serbia declared war on Turkey in 1912, gaining a great amount of territory when Turkey was defeated.

Then in 1913, a war broke out between these allies who had fought Turkey. An argument about unequal division of the territories conquered from Turkey in the 1912 conflict caused this second war of 1913.

While the greedy allies fought one another over her territories, Turkey took the initiative and exploited their quarrels to her advantage. She re-occupied some of the territories ceded from her by the recent allies. However, Turkey's overall losses robbed Germany of her dream to secure a corridor to Asia Minor.

Bulgaria was now enticed by the "Great Empire," to start another war, in the hopes of regaining some of the territories lost to Serbia. But Serbia, and her past friends, her allies of the 1913 conflict, defeated Bulgaria.

These "games of war" were played for expansionism, as well as to try the determination and strength of the armies of the challenged nations. They continued to be played by greedy politicians and ambitious militarists, while the innocents died fighting for a cause they believed in.

But soon the innocents would be confused and know not what to believe!

It was an embarrassment for the Empire Builders to see their ambitions so rudely halted, and with Serbia enlarged in territory. The events from 1908, up to 1913, had not been as fruitful as they had hoped. The expeditions attempted within the smaller nations had proved disappointing. The internal struggles had cost the "Great Empire" the loss of close proximity to her ally Turkey.

There was only one alternative left, Germany herself prepared for war.

On that fateful Sunday of June 28, 1914, Archduke Franz Ferdinand of Austria-Hungary, and his wife the Duchess of Hohenburg, arrived at Serajevo, Capitol of Bosnia. (This city was founded in 1262 by the Magyar General Cotroman and initially had the Magyar name Bosnavar). As the parade of vehicles passed through a very unenthusiastic crowd of citizens toward the Town hall, a man bolted from the crowd and onto the road. He threw a "hand-bomb" at the royal automobile. The vehicle passed over it, and the bomb rolled to explode harmlessly in the roadway. The would-be assassin was caught while attempting to assimilate himself into the crowd. The young man, Gabrinovics, aged twenty-one, was promptly arrested.

The reception at the Town hall proved to be most embarrassing. The Archduke had not wanted to go to Bosnia in the first place but went at the urging of Ference József, the Old King of Austria-Hungary, who had been initially scheduled to go. Now with this attempt on his life the Archduke was very apprehensive, very excited, and rightfully nervous. He blurted out his anger, humiliating the Serajevo Burgomeister, and insulted the Serbian people because of this scandalous act.

He called it — attempted murder.

The reception was now gone from a cool formality, to one of outright hostility. With such a sham royal welcome, there was no use playing upon the Serbian patience any longer than necessary. The crowd that was unenthusiastic and indifferent earlier now became resentful and ominously quiet.

On the way back from the Town Hall the Archduke's car passed another youth as he stood on the curb; suddenly the youth jumped onto the running board of the car, and fired his revolver, twice. The first shot hit the Duchess in the stomach; the second shot pierced the neck and severed the jugular vein of the Archduke. Both died in the automobile. The youth, Gavrillo Princip, a university student, was immediately apprehended.

The German States now declared that both youths were hired, and that they were trained assassins of Serbia's Radical Party. But circumstances preceding the trial of the youths, and subsequent terms, led many to believe it was the Austrians and Germans who had planned the assassination. Peculiarly enough, both youths received light sentences at a time when death sentences were commonplace for an attack on Royalty.

The assassination however, furnished the excuse that Germany wanted to start the war of her ambitions. Is it a coincidence that the assassination took place just as Germany's preparation for war was completed?

In July of 1914, the entire world knew of the assassination of the Archduke and his Duchess. There were many people in the Western World who were confused, and outraged at this double slaying. Was Serbia foolishly courting fate? It was suicide for this small, subjected nation to ignore an internal political party comprised of assassins. What was happening in the Balkans anyway? Some suspected, but many more were ignorant. The culprits had been caught and sentenced. Was Austria-Hungary justified in waging war because of this insult? At that time in History, who could say that the sister nations were warmongers? They had due cause now, hadn't they?

But not only the people of the Western World were duped, and brought into a false belief; there were many more in

Europe and within Germany, and Austria-Hungary, who were also deluded into thinking that theirs was a righteous wrath. There were many Hungarians and Austrians who were first outraged, then furious. They were now willing to fight because of this brutal attack upon their sovereign.

Were they less willing to fight before?

The peasants had worked willingly, work meant food, clothing and shelter. There was an order and purpose to work. There seemed no purpose in fighting. Perhaps their political leaders anticipated the peasant mind; the peasants needed an incentive to fight, so they were duped into fighting. The Archduke and his wife were meant to be sacrificed. The very religious peasants having the innocence of children, illiterate, and worldly ignorant; these poor people of the Austro-Hungarian Republics would thus be brought to anger. They were provided the incentive to fight. The seeds of war were planted with care; the Empire Builders would now harvest conscripts more willing to fight

--- — — ---

With the declaration of war suddenly upon them in July 1914, the conscripts received orders to return to their regiments immediately. Süle Jenö was now eager for a fight. The killing of the man in premeditated cold blood was a political hazard not unexpected for one in his position, but to kill his wife in such a despicable manner was a most unforgivable atrocity. Jenö's understanding of honor dictated that the culprits would be punished. At the turn of the Century, assassination was an act that had to be avenged.

Hadn't he heard? The culprits had been caught and would be punished.

Jenö did not know the truth, or the circumstances surrounding the assassination. It would be years before the people of Europe would know even partial truths. He was tricked, just as most of the citizens of the Empire were tricked. Theirs became a righteous wrath...as planned.

Militarists and Expansionists saw to it that Nation fought Nation, not caring that the people of those Nations died. The once happy children, and childishly innocent peasants in their pastoral surroundings, did not know why they died.

There was no just cause! The only cause that could be just was that which would prevent these mass killings!

LOVE LUST

The basic training was over and the women-hungry Hussars were now given leave to return home for the summer months, or so it was the Military's intent. But Béla, Pista (Steve), and Lajos (Lloyd), three of the barnyard water bucket carriers, would first go to Buda – Pest and have themselves the time of their lives with the macskas (cats...as in prostitutes), they had heard so much about.

They arrived by train and, immediately stepping off the train onto the station platform they directed their questions to the first csendör (policeman) they met while still in the station.

"Where's the finest hotel in town; what's the girlie situation like?"

They were given an encouraging smile by the policeman, and directions to some of the finest hotels and entertainment centers; needless to say the boys had a few detours along the way. They stopped at the first tavern for a hearty drink and a toast to their good hunting.

After many taverns and much booze, they were sidetracked completely when three prostitutes 'picked them up'. It should have been that the boys picked up the scent of macska, but these ever wary girls-of-the-good-times spotted the boisterous soldiers as they drank and sang, for they sang riotously, and not too concerned about carrying a tune. It was obvious that many people within ear shot could not help but notice the young men.

Jo estét kivánunk	*We wish good evening to you*
Meg jőték a Szabosmegye Huszárok	*The Szabosmegye hussars have arrived*
Jőték, menték győzték	*They came, they went, they conquered*
Sok szép lanyt meg lőtek	*they "shot" many pretty girls*
Jo estét kivánunk...	*We wish good evening to you...*

...and so on it went, to many variations of the same theme, boasting about personal conquests. As the whim of the individual Hussar carried him, he may even insert the name of his recent love interest.

The girls heard the braggarts, and mused among themselves; "seems as though these boys have 'shot' their loads before, and are looking to shoot some unsuspecting girls again tonight. What do you say we accommodate them? Besides it might be fun!"

The boys were handsome, virile, and with their uniforms, the women thought it would be exciting to be seen in the company of these young men, and so the girls made their 'pitch'...got their catch, and took the young men to some decent and comfortable accommodations.

When the girls had seen what Béla had, it was agreed that the three girls would spend equal time with each Hussar... so that neither of the girls or boys would be cheated. The six young people actually got along well, and enjoyed one another's company. They either went out on the town together, or in fours, if one couple wished to have privacy of the mutually shared facilities.

The facilities were a combination of three single, adjoining rooms, on the second floor within an apartment complex that the girls had shared often times before. Each room opened onto the main corridor, so that the rooms had an entry from off the corridor. The rooms also had an interior door opening upon the next room; the couples actually had a large three bedroom apartment.

The young people reveled in one another's company. They often stayed out late at night dining, dancing or carousing. They went to places of entertainment, theaters, concerts and carnivals. Coming home in the early morning hours they behaved wickedly, and lustfully, until exhaustion forced them to pass out into sleep.

The boys soon ran out of money; good thing they bought return train fare. The girls did not mind! They liked the boys, and so the girls spent their own money on the last two days of that one-week 'leave'. The boys enjoyed their entire week with these most co-operative and beguiling vixen.

The girls were proud to be seen in public with these handsome Hussars; and they may have been envied by many a lady when seen in the company of these red uniformed, black booted young men. The red cylindrical, pillbox hat, black visored and gold braided, was topped off with a majestic plume above the visor. The plume towered a few inches above the flat pillbox top. They cut a dashing figure these three in their dress uniforms, with blue jacket-cape slung over their left shoulder.

The last day drew near. It was Saturday night and the boys would be catching the morning train back to their Cavalry depot, from there they would go home to their respective villages.... after aquiring money to do so.

They returned to their bedrooms after supper to enjoy the girls for one last evening... for as long as they could. The doors that fronted onto the corridor were locked, and their adjoining bedroom doors were opened. The boys and girls now moved freely from one bed to another. They enjoyed their partners as often as the desire was with them. They had an ample stock of wine and loaves of bread, so as they imbibed in the wine they also imbibed in the girls.

Couples entwined naked in one another's arms, dozed off as they lay, only to be awakened by another of the girls, cheerfully, with a full glass of wine in her hand and a full desire in her belly. The boys of course were most enthusiastically agreeable and enjoyed these 'fruits of love'. They cut a slice of bread occasionally to reinforce their strength; drank a glass of wine, and loved, napped, and nipped again.

As the night began to wane, the couples eventually migrated into two of the rooms and enjoyed a group session of singing, drinking and petting. Then, ultimately they ended up in only one of the rooms, and this of course, would be where Béla sprawled out flat on his back, legs apart, with one of the girls "oooooohing and aaaahhing" at his admirable equipage.

"Oh Béla, what are we going to do without you and that huge, wonderful muscle? What shall we do when you are gone? I can't bear the thought of it, we have learned to love it...you...all you boys...of course."

"Maybe I could leave it with you. Wouldn't that be nice? Gosh; even I would like that, I could enjoy it."

He laughed heartily as his simple mind imagined the girls in a phallic ritual nightly about his phallus, and by some sort of telepathy he would each night, be the recipient of their most unthinkable passions.

"Oh," chortled the girls at such impossibility. Yet, desiring the impossible they too imagined all sorts of unspeakable things that they could do with this organ...without the man. The thought only made them more longing, and as though with one mind they threw themselves, each upon one of the boys.

The small Island of Delos, in Greece, is stated "to have a huge granite phallus towering about six meters in height at the island center. Young maidens of marriageable age still go there occasionally to throw garlands of flowers at its base. This ritual is said to carry over from two thousand years or more, when all of ancient Hellenic Greece commonly held solemn religious festivals honoring Artemis the goddess of fruitfulness and abundance. Dancers went through graceful ritual performances while wearing a manufactured phallic object upon their persons. The phallic symbols were also related to festivals honoring Dionysius and Aphrodite. The Greeks also had a deity called Priapus; he was portrayed and sculptured with his phallus erect, to accentuate the Greek vitality.

It is certain that Béla and the girls were not aware of this deity, but it is interesting at this time to picture Béla as a twentieth century Priapus, proudly exhibiting his erect member. The girls seemed to worship this member, and certainly entertained themselves with the thought of possessing it as a love object.

The night was soon giving leave, and slowly, as the new day began to dawn there was more drinking and desperate intercourse until all were intoxicated. They were in a blissful and drunken stupor. The boys began to weaken, their sex drives waned; the girls now began to caress the body, the organ; they did anything to have everything. They seemed drugged with their longing, their desire; a craving for all they could get.

The six of them hadn't eaten since seven o'clock the previous night; they had only the bread, slicing it and occasionally partaking of it to "soak" up the wine in their stomach. They had drunk too much wine perhaps? They had too much sex? Finally the boys burned out, just like a fading candle, their organs one by one refusing to cooperate went limp. The groggy girls did not close their eyes, for surely upon opening them the boys would be gone.

The boys simply fell asleep where they lay, Béla again on the bed with legs apart, Pista on the floor, and Lajos on the sofa. The girls dumbly reflected, their minds were numb, and truly they were not thinking clearly that early in the morning. After all they had gone through during the night, who could be sensible?

One girl bent over Béla's penis, she spoke to it softly, caressing it, gently fondling it; it began to quiver, to stir, and awakened like some thick, one-eyed serpent. Oh how magnificent! It was alert! It arose and stood erect...one more time.

It definitely appeared to have a mind of its own, separate from the rest of the body. The groggy girls immediately joined their sister of passion. One girl passed the table that held the wine, the bread with the bread knife. Her heart beating now as she saw the exhibition; the other girls remarked about the inexhaustible member. It was erect. It seemed to be quivering with passion for their bodies.

"It has a mind for us," inhaled the girl.

"It certainly has a head of its own," remarked the other giddily prickling with passion.

"And it shall stay!" whispered the third who held it.

She grasped the bread knife and cut it off, flush at the base, back of the lifted testicles.

The huge mass remained in her hand only momentarily; testicles and all, for it just as suddenly went limp as the blood gushed from it.

An undistinguishable mewing yelp, then a blood-curdling moan, an ever so slight pause of deathly silence, and then like a spring recoiling he sat upright. He realized the pain was real, neither a figment of his stupored mind, nor a phantom of his drunken dream.

Béla screamed!

The scream stirred his two friends, but they were too stupefied. The girl let go the wilted mass which fell between the legs from whence it came, and onto the bed sheet. The other girl no longer sat between the open legs as Béla reached for the origin of the pain. The third girl ran into the adjoining bedroom. Béla immediately felt his loss!

Unbelieving bewilderment made him continue to scream unceasingly.

Like a butchered pig, he squealed, and would not stop squealing. He held one hand over the vacant spot; the other desperately clutched the mattress side. With each beat of his racing heart a stream of blood flowed forth from between his fingers.

He had suddenly sobered from his drunken lust filled state. His mind was totally oblivious to all but the pain. His two naked friends jumped up dazedly at the continued screaming, and strove to quiet him.

What the hell had happened?

They saw!

The girl still held the bread knife.

"He said he would leave it with us".

"Oh my God; Pista stop the bleeding!" cried Lajos.

"How?" Pista was dazed and still incredulous.

He hurriedly gathered up and folded a bed sheet thrusting it on the bloody spot. He had to use force to extricate Béla's hand from the place...immediately the hand was again on the bed sheet over the spot. Momentarily the blood was staunched but the bed was already scarlet. Blood soon continued in torrents again under the hand holding the bed sheet.

The friends hurriedly got into their trousers, alternately applying pressure on Béla's hand, while one, and then the other semi-clothed themselves. This was hectic, for they ran about the three rooms to find their clothes. They had disrobed that night before, and had no recollection now where they had started their individual undressing.

"What are we to do?" was Pista's first concern.

"Girls go find a doctor, hurry. Otherwise he shall bleed to death."

Still naked, the girl dropped the knife to the floor, gasped, threw her head back, sagged to the floor and fainted, folding herself down onto the floor like a wet towel.

Neighbors in the adjoining rooms, and those across the corridor began to be heard outside the bedroom door. They had heard the screams and were questioning and murmuring amongst themselves.

The only girl left in the room with the boys responded. "Do not let them in. There is a doctor on the floor above us, I shall go get him." With that, she exited into the second bedroom to where the first girl had fled.

Béla was beginning to shake; he would have stood up and ran amuck, but his friends held him fast. He had ceased screaming for a while, but now he screamed one more time, and fell back unconscious. With the legs now apart, the blood daubed bed sheet fell, and the friends saw a gaping circle where once had been the manly organs. A constant surging of blood flowed, reinforced by arterial gushes.

Following that last scream, there was a knock at the door, then a continued banging. "Hey, what's going on in there?"

No reply from within.

"Get the police," said a muffled voice from outside the door.

The two friends ran through the bedrooms tearing bed sheets and bed covers off the two other beds. They wrapped Béla's bleeding body into several bed sheets, and then they removed him from that bedroom. Mattress and all, like a mannequin in a hammock they took him into the next room and locked the adjoining door behind them. They left the naked girl still on the floor where she had fallen. They again picked up their unconscious friend, and went into the third room.

The two girls were gone. The boys locked that adjoining bedroom door also, now they were two rooms down the hall from that one in which it happened. The two friends were perspiring heavily as they waited.

Would the girl return with the doctor?

Béla's body was cold; he was shivering, and rapidly turning pale. Should they wait? Time was running out for Béla. What else could they possibly do? They were strangers in this city. They could not haul their friend about to find a hospital; they could not even go upstairs to find the doctor. They didn't know where the nearest hospital was. Truthfully, they were now both afraid.

The sun was lifting over the horizon and now peeking over the rooftops, so they opened the shade to let the sun shine into the room. The bleary eyed friends could see that it was to be a most beautiful Sunday. Their foggy minds were beginning to clear; still they did not know what to do beyond what they had already done to help Béla.

It seemed as though an eternity had passed, the room was silent except for the slow, labored breathing of Béla.

Outside the room, and down the corridor, the excited crowd remained audible. It was curious, as though they were afraid to call the Manager to open the locked door, and to enter the room, that horrible room, now mysteriously quiet, for fear of what they may find there.

How much time did Béla have?

How much time had elapsed? Not more than twenty short minutes; it might as well have been twenty days.

Then, at the door in front of them... a hurried knock:

"Pista, Lajos, open up, quickly"

The girl had returned!

They both ran hurriedly to open the door. She had wrapped a housecoat loosely about her body; it was obvious that she was still naked under it. A pajama-clad man in a house-robe, carrying a black satchel, was with her. The first girl who had run from the 'bloody' room was also with them, loosely clothed as the other.

The girls had brought the doctor!

They quickly entered, to the bewilderment of the crowd two doors down. The door was locked once more behind them.

WAR DECLARED

July 28, 1914, Austria-Hungary declared war on Serbia, and immediately moved her armies to the Serbian border. It cannot be a coincidence that the inventive genius of Germany had built the largest war machine in History and was now ready for war... just at the time of the assassination.

German troops were already on the Save and Danube rivers. On July 29, they began shelling Belgrade from the North side of the Danube. Russia became alarmed at this commotion on her doorstep, and at once began to mobilize in her Southwest provinces.

On July 30, Germany demanded that Russia cease mobilization within twenty-four hours or suffer the consequences! But Russia was desperate. She saw that Germany pressed the war with Serbia, while continuing a full-scale mobilization in all the Prussian States. With the loss of Serbia the Slavic countries would be in jeopardy, and Russia's Southwest provinces would be vulnerable to attack. Serbia surely could not stand up to the Prussian Empire alone; Russia ignored Germany's demands and hurried to assist Serbia.

August 1, Germany declared war on Russia. It was simply a formality, for Germany did not fear Russia, she was so confident that she allocated only six army corps to hold Russia in check. Of the twenty-six army corps that Germany had immediately available, twenty would be sent to the Western Front in France. Russia would be dealt with later, after a quick victory on the Western front, before the

"Big Bear" could muster her total strength and become a real threat. But, the German High Command totally underestimated Russia's ability to mobilize swiftly, anticipating that Russia would be slow in reaching her frontiers in the West.

These same people expected to finish with France in forty days!

On August 3, German troops entered Belgium.

Great Britain, appointed by France and Belgium as an arbitrator for peace, failed in her negotiations with Germany. She could not prevent the German plans of conquest by negotiation.

On August 4, Great Britain declared war on Germany.

August 15, the Germans over-ran Belgium, but before they had completed their push through Belgium, Russia attacked East Prussia! The six German army corps, sparse and now widely spread, suddenly discovered how outnumbered they were. They were ordered into a tactful withdrawal, and to engage the Russians only when absolutely necessary; however, it now became expedient for Germany to relieve this unexpected, strategically threatening situation.

It is most likely that within weeks of the declaration of war, there were about seven million enlisted Russians ready to fight. At least half of these seven million were now on the Eastern Front. The 240,000 troops (six army corps), of the Central Powers were sorely pressed to stop, or even delay, this devastating Russian onslaught threatening to overwhelm them.

German troops were rushed from the Western Front in France, to meet the Russian challenge, and this weakened the drive into France from Belgium. When German troops were needed on the Marne in France on September 15, 1914, they were on the way to East Prussia. They succeeded in stopping the Russian advances, and Russia suffered a horrible defeat. But, France was given a temporary reprieve, paid for with the blood of Russia's fighting men. The 'peasant soldiers' did not disappoint their Czar; they died bravely, though foolishly. Russia, true to the German initial contention, was not prepared, and had actually 'rushed' into war with no strategy other than to depend on her troops of overwhelming odds to defeat the threat on her Southwest Provinces.

Janös Virag was the eighth man of a twelve-man machine gun crew, and it was his task to keep ammunition supplied to the machine gun position. This was accomplished by strapping two boxes of cartridges onto each side of a pack-horse, and getting the four boxes of ammunition as near to the gun emplacement as possible without threatening the loss of ammunition or the horse. If the horse was shot, Janös would have to maintain the supply of ammunition even if he had to personally carry it to the prescribed drop-point! This could prove extremely difficult during an offensive.

From this 'drop-point', two men would take the four boxes and crawl, push, pull, or however possible, get the cartridges to the gunner.

In late 1914, along his front line, during one of the offensives somewhere in Galicia, Janös was having difficulty supplying his gun position. The two men were waiting at the drop-point when he returned with four caissons of bullets. They were very excited, and eagerly took the bullets, bidding him to hurry back as quickly as he could with more. Janös therefore jumped astride the horse and rode it at a run to the supply depot behind the lines; He then led the horse back, as fast as he could lead it to the drop-point. When he arrived it was his turn to wait for the pick up men.

Remembering their explanations of urgency, Janös suddenly became anxious himself when he could not hear the familiar sound of the machine gun firing! The missing two men puzzled Janös, and he was certain that something had gone terribly wrong. He tethered the horse and was about to advance alone on foot toward the gun position to see what was wrong, when suddenly Russian infantry came out of the thickets and surrounded him.

That was it!

The gun position had been encircled and now the crew, if alive, was captured. These Russians had simply permitted Janös to walk into their circle. He and his packhorse were now Russian captives also.

After relieving the horse of the four caissons his captors allowed Janös custody of the horse. All prisoners would be moved to the interior of Russia, and so the German and Hungarian prisoners were herded onto railroad boxcars. These trains took them to their first prison camp where they were interred for a short while.

Some of the prisoners were removed from this prison camp and, Janös believed that they were put to work in Russian factories, and some used as farm laborers. Those prisoners who were not selected at this temporary stop, were again herded, and transported by rail to still another camp deeper inside Russia, where once again, some men were selected while they were interred here at Uralski Vida (Uralski is a city in the West Kazakh Republic on the Ural River in Soviet Central Asia. I hesitate to say for certain that this may be the place, or if it is a play on the Hungarian words *Uralski Vidék,*. This means Uralski Area, the area around Uralski). Janös had been in two different prison camps as the railcars stopped in those two different towns. They were selected by merchants, manufacturers or farmers while detained in camps.

The last town stop was Uralski Vida. Those prisoners that were not selected here were once again boarded, and the railcars continued on to the final Siberian Lumber Camp. During all this time he fed that horse, groomed it, and took care of it, as though it were his own. Janös may not have suspected it, but he later guessed, perhaps that is why his captors let him have custody of the horse. His attention to its care kept him occupied, and the Russians need not worry over the horse's keep. After the initial two prisoner of war camps, and because of the horse, he may have even been designated for that Siberian Lumber Camp. Horses were needed for skidding the logs out of the forests!

SERBIA INCIDENT

Pál was happy to be back out in the country and at home. He would be happier when his enlistment was finally up.

He was not too surprised however, to be called back and into active duty in July. The village, as with the entire World, was aware that the Archduke and his Duchess had been murdered. Many of the young men would not be around to help with the harvest because of this need for immediate mobilization; the country was in a state of at war.

He was back with his regiment before war was officially declared against Serbia, July 28, 1914. The entire regiment by now had also heard from Pista and Lajos about Béla's tragic death.

What a hell of a way to go!

"What a waste," thought Pál, "he was such a virile man. And with his boldness, he could have been an excellent soldier."

Worst of all, his lust had led him to an early grave. How tragic for his parents if they learned the truth. The young Hussars would miss him...but not for long, their minds were occupied by more serious undertakings.

They were now to embark upon life's greatest adventure, from which some of them would never return. The first skirmishes were hardly a challenge to their toughness and training. The infantry were doing a wonderful job of pushing the enemy back, and mopping up. The Hussars were sent in only to pursue the enemy, and keep them running once they retreated. This strategy was meant to prevent the enemy from regrouping in great numbers and, to prevent counter offensives against the infantry's advance.

Those several weeks in Serbia were very exciting for the young Hussars as the Austro-Hungarian army won victory after victory. With their superiority they overwhelmed any temporary resistance that Serbia could offer. The Hussars on horseback marched at the head of the proud army into one occupied city after another. With head erect they marched, and did not much notice that the citizenry lining the streets at their approach were more curious than cheerful. Indeed the citizens were quite dismayed as they watched the long procession of soldiers clad in gray uniforms. There were so many, and the monotonous rhythm of their marching feet; how many could there be? How many divisions of Serbians would be needed to stop them?

They marched on, entering the fields beyond, and fought again and again. They over ran Bosnia with apparent ease, and took Serajevo, that infamous capitol where the cowardly assassination had taken place.

But the Serbians, who had retreated, had regrouped, and reinforced with Montenegrins, rushed to stop the enemy's advance. And now it was the Serbs who pushed on into Bosnia and approached Serajevo. The Austro-Hungarian onslaught faltered, fighting a hesitant withdrawal.

That September, Pál and his buddies experienced just what it meant to stand and fight when the odds were reversed and against them. In spite of the superb retaliation of Serbia and her Allies, the Austro-Hungarians held. The Hussars advanced many times onto an area from which the enemy had been pushed, and went so far that they had to fight their way back because contingents of the enemy had closed the gap behind them. There were engagements in which Hussars had to leave their horses behind. Because they were so much attached to them from the days of basic training, and had learned to rely on these horses like on a friend it was a course of last resort.

It was difficult to think of leaving a friend behind, but, in the last measure of survival, one had to remember that a horse was, after all an animal. The enemy did not deliberately shoot to kill the animal without his rider. Indeed the animal was more likely spared if found behind enemy lines; a better fate than that of a soldier who was found behind enemy lines.

It was a Hussar's duty to escape and return. He would be mustered another horse.

Individually they fought their way back, sometimes waiting for darkness, With the night as their cover, they stealthily crawled back to friendly lines three or four kilometers distant.

With the first three months in their favor, and the engagements with the enemy now mainly an infantry duel, the Hussars had more respite from action than the infantry. They had more freedom also to imbibe in the wines and whiskeys of the occupied territories. They were emboldened to "imbibe" with the women folk also. If officers went with the detachments, then the Hussars remained orderly, and duty bound. But there were those assignments in which only one, or perhaps two, Hungarian Hussars were sent to carry a message from one company commander to another. In safety behind friendly lines these may be uneventful but proved to be a welcomed break from the tedium.

It would have been an ideal situation for two friends to accompany one another when an assignment called for two men, but the officers did not exercise that viewpoint. Officers alternated the men within the two man teams instead of keeping the same combinations of two men as a team. In this manner all the men learned to depend equally upon one another, and not just upon friends. The officers thought the men were more reliable and responsible this way; two men working for too long together may develop bad habits.

Pál had the uncomfortable misfortune to be assigned to go with Lajos of the water bucket episode, on a message delivery (and so he thought at the outset he was in for trouble). He could not bring himself to be companionable with Lajos; they were of two different schools of thought, and so Pál remained quiet during this ride.

He was, therefore, in the awkward position of having to listen to Lajos talk and expound about himself for the entire distance to that village rearward of the active lines.

Pál was relieved when they finally reached the village, but Lajos immediately took the advantage, telling Pál he would meet him in the canteen, and Pál should drop in to "fetch" him for the return trip. Lajos apparently had been to this town before, so he described the location of the canteen. Pál continued alone to deliver the message to the infantry Company Commander. It took him but a few minutes of waiting for a reply and Pál was mounted once again. The officer returned Pál's salute and, gave him casual warning to avoid the canteen in the village. A dozen or so of his men were spending their twenty-four hour pass. The soldiers had already been drinking for a few hours and may be brewing for a brawl. Most infantry envied the Hussars because they were always seen riding, mounted on a horse that carried the man and his gear. Hussars were also quick to run with the speed of the horse while the infantry had to carry their back packs and equipment themselves "on the double".

With that warning, Pál was dismissed and nudged his horse forward. When the officer was again behind the closed door, Pál spurred his horse anxiously to speed. Within seconds he made it to the canteen where he saw Lajos' horse tied to a support post. Pál reined in, jumped off the horse before it stopped, he could already hear the commotion coming from inside. He bounded in through the door almost tearing it off the hinges.

The sight that greeted his eyes disgusted his disciplined mind. Lajos was doing his damndest to ward off the blows, and to return a few, but he was no match for the crowd of men that encircled him. They were pummeling him mercilessly with their fists. At least three Serbian civilians, canteen help, were aiding the Hungarian infantry to beat up on their countryman. Lajos caught a fleeting glimpse of Pál.

"Pál! Attack! Help!"

But Pál was already in the mêlée, tearing into the circle of men, he threw men with his left arm to the left, and with his right arm he threw them to the right. He threw them like sagging sacks of grain, to the left and to the right. Pál could not allow this mob of soldiers to beat up on a regimental comrade no matter that it was Lajos.

As the soldiers became recipients of Pál's blows, they immediately gave ground to him, opening a path for him to the weakened Lajos. A few soldiers were reluctant to stop fighting; the two Hussars should not be allowed to disgrace them. Pál appeared to be immune to their blows. Finally he grabbed two of the civilians in his vice like grip, one in each hand, he literally tore the shirts from their chests as he lifted them to bash one against the other. With the force of their rebounding bodies he flung them upon the soldiers, battered and bleeding, one to the left, one to the right. His six-foot three was quite a spectacle to behold as broad shoulders and brawny arms hammered the mob down to a smaller number. The soldiers threatened, cursed, and in angered expressions vowed to kill the two.

Some of them ran out of the building bleeding, however, one well-pitched beer mug got Lajos broadside his head, and he sprawled out unconscious on the floor. Pál advanced and bodily lifted the kicking soldiers off his fallen companion, fighting off the few who dared to come within arms reach of him. Then the action just as abruptly stopped.

Not one of the soldiers dared to accept the challenge of this lone Hussar! The few, who had encircled him, slowly broke up as he stood his ground, feet firmly planted, with the unconscious man safely protected at his feet.

"Where the hell did you come from? We didn't see you come in".

They marveled at this mountain of a man. His uniform wasn't even disheveled; why he still had his hat on! And, as they looked about their thinned out numbers, they conceded the fight to him.

"Let us go as we came, in peace," he said quietly, but determinedly.

The soldiers began to slowly set tables upright, and to place chairs around the tables. No longer was Pál ringed by opponents, the soldiers were embarrassed.

"You should be ashamed of yourselves," began Pál, "is this the brave Hungarian infantry? You fight well only amongst yourselves, or when you outnumber a foe. Do you not get enough action from the enemy to burn up your energy?"

"We...were bored...I guess".

"Think of what you are doing" and as he gazed at the two blooded Serbs, "Don't give our enemies cause to rejoice over our differences".

With that, he stepped from above Lajos and bent over to pick him up. He carried Lajos in his arms across the floor to the door, like a man carries a child. No one stood in his path, one soldier on looking about, saw Lajos' hat on the floor, picked it up, and walked toward the door after Pál. Another soldier opened the door and Pál was quickly outside with the unconscious Lajos cradled in his arms. The soldier caught up to Pál outside and placed Lajos' hat upon the limp Hussars' stomach.

"There's a water trough around this side of the building... there", he pointed, "Take your friend and revive him".

Pál walked to the trough, it was not quite full of water but as he lowered Lajos into it and let go of him, the water over ran the sides. With one hand he removed the floating hat from above the stomach. Lajos awoke in the trough, startled and sputtering. With both hands he wiped the water from his face and eyes, and stood upright in the trough. He looked at Pál with astonishment.

"Come Lajos, it's time to go back," said Pál, as he handed the drenched Hussar his dry hat.

Lajos stepped out of the water trough to the great amusement of the soldiers who had followed Pál. He caught up to his comrade, and fell into step beside him, putting his hat on and adjusting it to a cocky angle. He felt proud and tough; the two of them had beaten ten...maybe twenty soldiers. He will exaggerate when retelling of this experience to the Hussar back at the camp.

Pál noticed the jaunty angle of the hat and said, "Seems to me Lajos," in a dry voice with no attempt at humor, "you are at your cockiest around a water trough".

Lajos observed the pun, smiled, and thanked Pál for saving his neck in that canteen brawl. After Lajos emptied his boots of water, both men mounted their horses and set off at a gallop. No point sticking around longer than necessary, some of those drunken bastards may actually take a shot at them. They fell into a good speed and followed the road back to their regiment.

VARGA JÁNOS
& FERKÓ

The drummer went through the village, as other drummers had done through every village that year, escorting the 'Conscription Officer'. The Conscription Officer announced that any soldier home on leave and any veteran up to the age of forty-two as well, must report to his registration center or to the regimental headquarters from where they had been discharged.

Varga János was a forty-two year old siege artilleryman (vár tuzer), conscripted in 1893, and saw action in the war of 1896; he also volunteered in 1908, for the Balkan wars. Now that his country was in crisis again, this veteran was among the first to again volunteer.

As Geza reminisced about his childhood, he remembered that Varga János had a lot of fruit trees at one time; apples, pears; every type imaginable that can be grown in Hungary. And as a child, Geza's father also had many fruit trees, but it was more fun to sneak into Varga János's orchard to snitch a few fruit, since it was handily nearby. It was exciting and challenging to see if one could get away without being caught. But many were the times, while Geza and his little friends were up among the branches of the fruit trees that János approached very quietly, and unsuspectingly, under the trees.

"Just come down from there, right now", he would say casually.

Oh boy!

The children began to cry before they started to climb down to the ground. They knew that a good spanking awaited them once they were earthbound.

János casually reached into his tobacco pouch and packed his pipe as the children slowly, and very reluctantly, made it to the ground. This was a very fancy tobacco pouch, shaped like a cat. The tie was at the neck, and its legs were fancifully worked leather thongs tied in a knot at four places. Janös kept his bag of tobacco in that cat shaped pouch and on his person at all times as he worked, because he did like his "pipe". He now waited patiently, and deliberately, which made the fear and anticipation of the spanking waiting for them more terrible for the children.

Once they were all on the ground, he systematically went about the task of spanking every single one of them!

"Now you can get out of here, hurry before I kick your ass".

He then he lit up his freshly packed pipe, and continued to go about his work, as though the incident with the children was forgotten.

The children whom he had spanked at one time or another were several years older now, and many were at the railroad station with their parents to see a brother or cousin off. When they saw Varga János and Ferkó (Frankie), Janos's younger brother, they could but wonder:

"Does he still have that fancy cat-shaped tobacco pouch? I'll bet he's taking it with him".

Even now, at age forty-two, János was a stubborn man, strong willed, and equally strong physically. His brother Ferkó was also strong, but more of a troublemaker, always getting into scrapes. Ferkó was also more uncontrollable; when drunk he became totally berserk. If he had his heart set on a girl and he desired her, he went to call at her home, should the girl's parents not open the door to him, and indeed, some parents did not open their door. Ferkó then broke the door down. He became so enraged he wanted to beat up the entire family.

Ferkó had learned a lesson many years before this; he was only seventeen years old when he had an altercation with another youth in a koscma (tavern). He had beaten the youth up so badly that the young man's older brother took it upon himself to revenge the beating. A chance encounter, not planned, presented itself as Ferkó was walking through a field on his way home. This youth's older brother was scything hay in the adjoining field, ran and attacked Ferkó using the scythe as a sword, attempting to cut Ferkó's head off. Instinctively Ferkó caught the swinging scythe blade with both hands. The man drew the scythe through the clenched hands; cutting off one finger and causing such severe lacerations on both palms that Ferkó was now crippled. Though he was twenty-one years old, these crippling scars exempted him from military service in 1914.

The man who attacked him did not get punished! There was no crime, the authorities knew Ferkó, and therefore presumed, if they thought about it at all, that Ferkó finally got more than he had bargained for. He could only wonder at what price his life was spared.

Ferkó maintained that if he would have had a knife that day, things may have been different, and so it was that he always carried a knife. Even now, as he escorted his older brother János to the railroad station, perhaps envying his brother and those who were going to war, Ferkó was itching for a fight.

Because Szombathely was the embarkation point, there were many hundreds of people from the outlying districts at the railroad station that day. Many of these hundreds were there to bid loved ones, or friends, farewell. There were fifty or sixty rail cars of all types, maybe even a hundred. There were so many men being shipped out on the initial induction that box cars and coal cars were put to equal use. The poor recruits; young men in coal cars could not see out because of the steep sides of the coal cars. If anything, only the tops of their tall bowler folk-hats showed periodically above the steep sides as they jumped up in an attempt to see over the sides to view their loved ones on the platform before the train pulled out.

There were many who got drunk. Wine flowed freely at the station bar and nearby Taverns, and so there were fights also. It was inevitable that Varga János and Ferkó would become involved in a brawl. Three men, so their story goes, were beating up on an acquaintance of theirs, and so the brothers went to his aid. Ferkó cut up the three men very badly while extricating the friend. One of the three died, the other two were hospitalized. Because he was a 'cripple', Ferkó received only one to two years imprisonment for his actions. In reviewing the stories told about Ferkó, it can be concluded that he was a mentally unstable young man!

The authorities had seen to it that all the able bodied veterans were on the train out of Szombathely and so, János wasn't even implicated in the knife fight. He was already in uniform and on his way to the Eastern Front when Ferkó was sentenced.

Later on, as the war proved costly to Hungary, and so many men had not returned, the two men whom Ferkó hospitalized were now recovered, and were very thankful for the incident. They were never inducted as a result of their wounds, and were strongly convinced that the incident had spared their lives. Most of the men shipped out of Szombathely on that day only received a two-week refresher-training course and were swiftly distributed to the various front lines.

Before the fall of 1914, Geza's older brother János was also in a war zone on the Eastern Front. János Virag (I had mentioned his capture previously) was followed into active duty by his cousin Jószi (Falcon) Virag. Jószi had registered for military service in 1912 at age twenty-one. When the war broke out he had already two years credited service, and so he was activated immediately. Another cousin was on the

Western Front; if any more troops were required Gergély would surely be activated out of the Home Guard.

Antal was fortunate, so far; because of his job classification he had still not been drafted at twenty-seven years of age. He was working very hard for the war effort, and Bobbie was expecting their fifth child. Mother Virag was quite concerned about Antal's young family.

"God be with them. Keep their father home dear Lord", she begged in her daily prayers in front of that wall on which all her saints' pictures were hung.

While mothers, wives, and sweethearts prayed; fathers, husbands, and young men in the Home Guard gathered up their old swords, and daggers, bringing them to the Blacksmith Shop, to get them honed and sharpened. The fourteen-year-old apprentice from Vásvar was kept very busy now that most of the young men were gone. Geza learned a lot about human nature that year, he also learned how to sharpen swords, daggers and axes; but best of all, he had finished his apprenticeship, and on receiving his certificate of accomplishment, got a job at the Magyar Alomi (Magyar Government) factory at Szombathely, the provincial capitol. This government factory had many skilled trades that the apprentice could experience and choose, from mechanics, millwright, workshop sciences, forge workshop, etc.

HUSZAR
INCIDENT

Those once idled and bored infantrymen who had fought Pál and Lajos in that Serbian tavern, were soon very active, and fought desperately for their lives while retreating. That Austro-Hungarian army which had advanced like a prairie fire, and penetrated deeply into the Balkan provinces soon found itself routed by the Serbians, Montenegrins, and Bulgarians. They were forced across the Drina River and back into home territory. The Allied successes continued until September 1914.

It was in September that the Austro-Hungarian troops were reinforced, and again took the initiative in October. They re-crossed the Drina River, and advanced until they had reached the "Oriental Railroad" which ran from Belgrade all the way to Constantinople (present day Istanbul) by way of Nish, in Serbia, and to Sofia in Bulgaria. Belgrade was outflanked, and the Allied troops garrisoned there had to evacuate and retreat. The Central Powers forces reached as far as Valievo in Bulgaria and swiftly conquered the small nations of Dalmatia, Montenegro, and Serbia. With this deep penetration of Bulgaria, the corridor to Turkey appeared once more to be opening; Turkey was allied to the Central Powers and so the road to Mesopotamia looked encouragingly clear by this ambitious advance.

It was in these campaigns that Pál saw the trenches of past wars. Those positions, dug for the Balkan wars in 1908, which Varga János may have fought in, still existed. The earthen work on the forward side was overgrown with grass and shrubbery that now effectively concealed the trenches. Small trees grew, as though the slopes were natural to the area topography, but the insides of the trenches had been maintained and kept clear for future troop activity. It seemed ironic, that these same trenches were used again in this war, and were still to be used in the engagements of 1915 and 1918 also. Counting the 1912 wars, a total of five campaigns found use for these same trenches.

There was a Company of about fifty Hussars who were given the task of routing the retreating allied armies. The fifty men came from Pál's Regiment. Although I do not believe my uncle Pál was part of this Company. But it was an interesting story when I heard it... a few times in my 'growing up' years, and I thought it would be interesting enough to submit here. After all, they were bold Hungarian Hussars that executed this marvelous action, with or without my uncle Pál.

They had penetrated too deeply into enemy territory however, and they were now forced to cautiously work their way back to friendly lines before the enemy could entrap them. When he found a tenable site, in a shrub shrouded ravine, the Captain ordered the men to dismount. All but ten men were positioned on both crests of the ravine to command a view of the surrounding area. The ten men cut grass and saw to the needs of the horses; forty Hussars kept vigil with carbines in a tight circle about their saddled horses, saddled for a quick get away, and not a man slept that night. They lay awake as sentinels for their mutual safety. No campfire was permitted, and the men ate cold rations, even the horses felt the tension and did not stir. Fifty horses rested quietly while fifty men kept watch for danger.

At first light of day, the Captain ordered the men to retrieve and lead their horses as they moved forward toward friendly positions. Not a Serb was spotted; not a single enemy engaged. The Captain appointed a man to ride quietly forward to scout the terrain that seemed devoid of men. With this as encouragement, the Captain permitted the men to mount up at mid day but still did not permit a stop for rest, nor did he care if they ate, so the men ate as they rode in the saddle.

Perhaps mounting up was a mistake? Fifty men walking, leading their horses, cast a lower profile in the fields than fifty mounted men with their red trousers elevated above the grass. Serbians forming a group of reinforcement for their Allies on the fighting lines facing the Austro-Hungarian trenches must have spotted part of the column of red from quite a distance. The Serbians now came forward to meet that lead Hussar who was scouting one kilometer ahead of the column. The Serbians concealed themselves and permitted him to go forward; remaining concealed as he returned on the run. Again they let him pass, knowing that the main body which they had glimpsed, was following in his direction and were even now approaching and coming closer to them.

They observed the scout enter, and disappear into a dense grassy spot in the thick forest. The Serbians now moved toward that position, not knowing for certain the total number of the Hussar Company. They had seen a number of mounted men, but before they could ascertain their number, the column disappeared from view at that spot where the scout was also now lost to their sight. Apparently they had seen only the tail of the column. The Serbian group had not received reports perhaps, nor had they knowledge of enemy troop movements behind their lines, so they probably anticipated it was a small patrol scouting for weak positions within the Serbian lines.

The scout now reported to his Captain that he had seen the Serbian lines, some trenches, and he deduced that opposite these lines were friendly troops. He admitted that he had not seen evidence of friendly forces (he had not seen the concealed Serbians either). The Captain decided to move in a direction parallel to the trench line, until his scout could verify the presence of friendly forces at any position along that front.

He ordered his men to dismount again, and lead their horses, in this manner they unknowingly moved away from the Serbian troops that were attempting to surprise them, and by walking, their red trousers were again obscured by the tall grasses and thickets.

Two hours later, the Captain ordered five men to tend all the horses, as the men moved to a place of concealment surrounded by trees and shrub. Several of the men removed their jackets for freedom of movement to cut the grass, leaving only their loose white shirts on; others gathered the grass by the armful to bring it to the horses. He again designated another Hussar to scout the enemy lines. This man was now off again in the direction of the trench positions. The Captain would alternate the men in his command so that no one man or one horse tired. In this manner each man also shared the dangers and risks of being a scout or point man. The Captain then ordered two sentinels forward of the trees, to guard and watch the one side facing the trenches.

The Serbian infantry had run on the double to keep up with the Hussars, they somehow hoped to gain an advantage on their unsuspecting quarry. Now as the scout Hussar rode out from the concealed location, he rode at a right angle away from the Serbs that were also concealed from him. The Serbs now knew where the scout had come from! They quickly moved into that direction, and soon they spotted the Hussars, and tried to count their number. The two Hussar guards did not see them because the guards were vigilant in the direction of the trenches, the direction in which the scout had gone. The Serbs probably could not see the five men each holding the reins of nine or ten horses, nor did they see the men who had returned to the horses with their arms full of grass. The Serbs did not see the entire Company, bending and gathering the cut grass. They saw only too clearly the white shirted Hussars that were cutting the grass.

The infantry were only about twenty in number themselves! The advantage must be theirs before they dare attack. While they waited for more of their soldiers to catch up to them, they wasted no time; they began to encircle the secluded area with their fewer numbers. They wished to get the Hussars in a cross fire, where they stood. They would deal with the horses and attendant Hussars after wiping out those that mowed the grass.

But time favored the Hussars!

With time, more of the men swathing grass returned with armfuls to feed the horses, and they loitered about in small groups now, quietly joking, some groomed their saddled horses. Some even sat down by their horses, eating cold snacks while the horses ate the fresh cut grass.

Only a few remained in full view of the Serbs.

So intent were the Serbs to encircle and surprise them, and so eager were they to maneuver and get beyond the trees, anxious to catch the Hussars off guard, so anxious that they were caught by surprise themselves as the scout Hussar returned hurriedly running his horse. The Serbs were now about thirty in number as more of their troops had caught up to the first few. The scout clearly saw the intended ambush, as crouching bodies presented their backs to him.

Not breaking the horses running stride, he unsheathed his saber and veered left to run along that flank of the crouching line of ambush. The infantry did not hear him, and now he spurred his horse because there were fewer riflemen to the left. As his saber hacked the first man's unsuspecting head, the rifle discharged in the dead man's hand.

A warning shot!

The scout need not trouble to cry out to warn the others. The shot caused a few rifle men to turn towards the commotion that was directly behind them. Where they stood;

they too were slashed, hacked or decapitated by this one wickedly whirling blade.

The majority of the Hussars that had gone back to the horses and were lounging casually; instantly reacted at the gunshot; they sprang astride their horses. No orders were needed as instinctively the mounted men parted their numbers, they would not be caught grouped together. Then, in this random scattered manner some of them rode into the direction of the shooting. The two Hussar guards stood their ground and returned fire with their carbines at the shooting Serbs.

The Captain swiftly directed a three point charge with those few Hussars who were already mounted and orderly; one upon the grassy clearing to aid their compatriots so openly exposed and helpless there; two to circle the grassy clearing, one from the left and one from the right.

The Serbian riflemen shot those defenseless Hussars as they were cutting grass. Other Hussars still on foot grasped their comrades' waist as the mounted troopers rode toward the shooting Serbs, and they swung themselves up behind the saber wielder. For those Hussars caught on foot with no where to go, the scene was chaos, and they sought to ride double mounted as one or two of them had done, in order to get out of the cross fire. Others shrewdly hit the ground, and lay prone as their fellow mounted troops bounded over them; they would not trample their white shirted comrades.

Now those hurriedly shooting Serbs flattened to the ground also, they had best lay prone, or those Hussars already mounted up and joining the fray would carve them.

Seven Hussars were shot, never again to mount up; a few were shot from their horses. Had the Serbian infantry not been forced into shooting randomly, and hurriedly, the situation could have been far worse. But forty some odd Hussars, was a greater number than the Serbs had expected! These maddened Magyars rode fearlessly head on at the riflemen because of this despicable act, this attempt at ambush. They would not now stop until all resistance was silenced. They rode back and forth across that half circle, turning and returning, to trample under hooves those Serbs who cowered, and lay on the ground, fearful to stand else they too would be sliced by saber strokes.

Those who did rise and attempt to run were ruthlessly run through, decapitated, or shot by carbine wielding Hussars; no Serb could get to the cover of woods or rock.

The worst thing; the most feared thing for the Hussar, was to be caught like this, without his horse, and in an untenable situation. So it was that all evidence of such a possibility must be wiped out, that others would not dare to try. The Hussars must kill to a man, all those who were perpetrators of such a strategy, and thereby put the fear of certain death into the hearts of all their enemies.

Kill they did; every last man of those who shot their help-less comrades. There were at least thirty Serbian infantry that died around that grassy spot that day.

The Serbians approaching to aid their faster comrades, who had started the fight, were now aware of a heated engagement. The fight had started without them and they wanted to share in the blood spilling. What a remark-able turn of circumstances they thought, as they eagerly approached. Surely there would be little fight left in the Hussars now. As they converged onto the position only a few commanding voices could be heard.

Was the fight over already? There sure had been a lot of screaming, and shooting for a short while. The late arriving Serbians felt cheated of this piece of action, and lowered their guard as several more came eagerly near, and now into view of the Hussars.

The scout Hussar remarkably had survived, he now related to the Captain that he sighted a number of riflemen approaching from the left; he had seen them crouching attempting the ambush.

The situation at the trenches?

Again, there was no activity noticed in trenches in that sector; the Serbians encountered in the skirmish must have been from that position of trenches sighted by the previous scout, two hours ago. With a bold charge they could rush across this sector and break through to friendly forces. But first they had to engage those Serbian soldiers approaching their position. They had to discourage them from following the Hussars in their escape attempt.

The Captain left one able-bodied man to tend to the wounded; the Serbians they had engaged were dead, or had run. In a fight such as this, the Hussars would show no quarter. The one man, and the wounded men began immediately to drape the dead comrades over their horses' saddles, they secured hands to ankles as the lifeless bodies hung from the mournful steeds.

"We shall be back to get you, and together we will return these dead friends to their homeland", replied the Captain. He hurriedly ordered the remaining thirty-nine men into a single row for an attack on the approaching infantrymen.

"Sabers...tip-to-tip, space between horses," he ordered.

With this order, the men formed a straight line and extended sabers towards the man next to him, on either side of each trooper. His saber extended at arms length would touch the extended saber tip of the next man. First on his right, with his right arm, then on his left with his left arm; in this manner no Hussar, nor horse would suffer wounding from another Hussar as he slashed from left to right on his charging horse. Thirty-eight mounted men then became a line of about 90 – 100 meters long, and at its center, ahead of this line; the Captain led his men into the charge.

With sweeping sabers they charged; the first dozen Serbs nearest this point of charge did not fire a single shot, as horrified and wide-eyed they died. The single long row had the effect the Captain wanted; the approaching soldiers thought there were many more Hussars than there actually were, and instinctively the soldiers turned to run. A fatal mistake; the Serbians who dared to approach were met by their panicked, and running comrades who were yelling and screaming. They also saw behind this line of charging Hussars, more mounted Hussars and more horses (the wounded and dead on horse back followed).

"Good Lord, they have penetrated our defenses; they are too many. Run for your lives! There is no hope", and much more cries of doubt were shouted.

That company of soldiers were turned and routed, leaving many dead upon the ground and in the fields. Those who survived the forward charge, and then the return charge of the withdrawing Hussars, must have quickly spread the word of this impending doom from behind their lines.

Of course they exaggerated. Those would-be perpetrators of the ambush were dead and the true number of the Hussars was not accurately determined. The line of thirty-nine became a hundred. The mounted Hussars and horses seen behind the charging line were seen as reserves of at least the same number. No enemy came near enough to see three wounded Hussars, now mounted. Nor could they see that the remaining horses were draped with dead men. There was but one able bodied Hussar with these, but they would suffice for the hundreds of reserves the Serbian survivors would report.

The Captain returned with the thirty-eight blooded, but now bolder men. The situation was one of mixed emotions; elation at their success against the greater number was restrained because of their sorrow for the seven dead comrades. The number of enemy soldiers trying to ambush them, and killed, indicated no other alternative but that the Hussars also had to loose a few of their own. A situation that could have been grievously worse was turned into a satisfactory victory, thanks to the timely return of the scout Hussar; that point man.

The young Hussars, now emboldened by their success, were all for immediately charging the rear of the enemy lines, and crossing to the security of friendly forces. Smarting with victory they wished to bloody their sabers. The understanding Captain smiled knowingly, and congratulated them on their fearlessness, but experience cautioned him to wait. They again walked, and led their horses, to conceal-ment about one kilometer from that day's last engagement, and then once again the troopers encircled their horses, and with carbines, guarded against possible attack.

In late afternoon, a few hours before nightfall, they moved into the position which the scout had indicated, still leading their horses so that they were a lower profile than mounted men, (and the red trousers were nearer the ground and not easily seen). The dead, draped over the horses were at the center of the column.

They were about one hundred meters from the enemy lines. They could not see any activity, and so assumed that the Serbians and their allies were keeping low and within the security of the trenches. By now, that mid-day engage-ment would have been communicated, and carried along this entire sector. Caution was to be expected on the ene-my's part. The Captain ordered half the men to mount up and then he led a charge on the rear of the suspected enemy trench. The last half would wait until the enemy were in disorder, then charge, in this manner the Captain hoped to again create the effect of two separate Companies, if the ruse did not work, he was gambling that some would get through. The seven horses with their dead comrades were to follow. He could not risk more lives by staying behind enemy lines another night. It would be too risky.

But there were no enemy forces, no resisting infantry!

The first half of the company leaped over empty trenches and rode hurriedly for another fifty meters before con-fronting their own forces. Luckily there was still light of day for the Austro-Hungarian forces would have surely opened fire on them, but the bewildered infantry heard the shouting "huzzas" of the Magyar challenge, and hap-pily exposed themselves, to return the same elated, gutsy defiance. The surprised Hussars cheerfully dismounted on the run, and now, filled with the giddiness of adrenalin pumped into expectant bodies, they hugged and "bussed" their countrymen.

The Captain had not dismounted; he sheathed his sword, and turned about when he saw what had transpired. He rode, now faster still, to meet the second half of his valiant band. He guided them, and urged them on quickly, before the enemy had time to converge upon them. He did not rest until all his troopers were among the friendly infantry and out of harms way. The Hungarian infantry Commander in that trench line was about to hear a remarkable accounting of the Hussar escapades as reported by this Captain. His men were already hearing many versions, and different accountings of the day's events from the young Hussars. Many of course would be exaggerations, but none-the-less; the fact that they had survived these few days behind enemy lines was, in itself, remarkable.

What had transpired?

The Serbians and their allies must have quickly withdrawn, and cautiously enough, that those Austro-Hungarian forces facing them in the opposing trenches, were not even aware of their evacuation! When news of two hundred Hussars at their rear was reported, the Serbians may have suspected an outflanking attempt. Unwittingly they opened a gap that allowed the entrapped Hussars to get out. The Hussar Captain's decision to wait until evening before attempting the dash across enemy lines was an excellent decision. His eager troops wished to confront the enemy when their companions were killed in ambush, might have proved suicidal. They would have, no doubt, met with the hurriedly withdrawing enemy forces. As it was, their concealment one kilometer distant from the enemy trenches, and waiting, had spared more Hussar lives.

The unwitting Austro-Hungarian infantry had faced empty trenches for half the day. Now it was up to the Hungarian Infantry Commander, on hearing the Hussar Captain's report and faced with evacuated enemy trenches in front of him, to press his advantage.

The Hussars were very pleased with their marvelous response; they were proud of their personal contact with the enemy. The enemy had been met on his own ground, and had been beaten at this vicious game of war. This was quite different from routing him as he retreated. The young men were most happy to have the experience of serving under such a fantastic Captain; all the men in the company felt the same, about this great leader.

There was a short lull in battles for these Hussars. Now as they joined the full contingent they sat down in the field to write a letter home to their families and loved ones. Pál would dedicate some space for Mom and Dad. He would have much to tell his sisters also. He would mention this Serbian engagement only casually, and not tell about seven of their company who had died. In particular, he wished to tell them about the wonderful group of men he was serving with. Most particularly, to tell his sisters of that grand Captain who had brought Pál's friends through an exciting experience.

"Hey Pál: do you have any more writing paper?"

Three of his companions approached.

"No, as a matter of fact, I'm down to my last sheet now. I'm writing small, and hurriedly to get it into an envelope for today's mail pick-up. I'll have to buy some more next time we get into town."

"Never mind Pál," Then the speaker turned to his companions, "we will simply resort to that most versatile of ancient paper suppliers. Come on boys, follow me."

They went into the woods. Over his shoulder he yelled, "we'll be right back Pál: I want you to give me your address," said the man.

"What the heck is this 'ancient' suppler of paper?" queried one puzzled companion.

"You'll soon see," he stopped at one of the many birch trees in the woods and pulled out his pocketknife. He commenced to strip a reasonable, rectangular piece of the bark from the tree. Showing his companions how to peel off the outer loose-flaked layer, he retained the tanned center layer that is nearest to the stiff cellulose trunk. As they worked meticulously, each at a different birch tree, the worldly-wise man proceeded to educate his friends.

"Do you know that this fine tree provides man with many useful things? All the parts of this tree are usable. The farmer or peasants around here, are smart enough to utilize every part of the tree simply because they are poor and cannot buy, for example, woodenware dishes. These people use the tough wood to make spoons, buckets, shoe-heels, and even oxen-yokes."

"Well I'll be damned. Do you know; I can actually realize what you say? My father buys birch tree boards and makes his own slats for our well bucket. That must be because we don't have birch trees on our farm. I wonder if Dad knows what else is possible from birch wood." With that he shrugged his shoulders, and proudly displayed his paper *shingle,* a piece of passable parchment twenty-five centimeters on a side.

They now walked back to where Pál was seated, and the 'scholar' continued to educate his two friends.

"The birch tree can provide strips of bark for wicker work, and peasants thatch brooms with it. With the stringy bark and roots, they can weave a passable rope. The leaves produce a dye – tannin – that is practical for tanning hides. The sap from the tree leaves also contain sugar, so if one makes a mash of leaves, you get a reasonable 'birch-wine'."

"Hey, what do you know?" exclaimed another companion, "how long would it take to ferment if we start now?"

The three friends laughed as they sat down around Pál.

"Now I shall show you the how to utilize this birch tree bark that you observe here," he turned his piece over and over to show his companions, "it shall be our paper".

"What side do you use?" asked the eager companion.

"This tanned side – here; Pál if you're through with your pencil can I have it next?"

"Pál, what's your sister's name?" asked one.

"Yeah, give us the names of all your sisters," said the man who had asked for Pál's address.

The fighting men of the Eastern Front had written many letters on birch bark paper to their friends, families, and sweethearts back home. All they needed was a pencil or pen, and they could write whenever the mood hit them. Postage was free for the men in active sectors. Surprisingly enough, the military mail couriers were reliable; their civilian counterparts were also conscientious, and eager to help the moral of the fighting men. With such a civic minded and patriotic combination, it is no wonder that most of the birch bark messages arrived at their destination even when the paper and envelope kind may be tardy!

It provided excitement and humor, not only to the recipient, but also to the entire village or to the community whenever a birch bark letter arrived. The mailman, as he did his rounds read it of course, and so did everyone who saw it before the person for whom it was intended got the letter. It was a wonderful and exciting way to start a pen pal, or correspondence with an unknown potential 'sweetheart'. The girls were very nice about it, and felt duty bound in most instances, to reply to these birch bark letters from soldiers. Indeed, a hasty reply was more likely for these types of letters than for the regular paper and envelope type. Pál's sister Ilona received her share of "parchment" letters, and dutifully answered every one.

PÁL A PRISONER.

The conquering Austro-Hungarian forces suffered an unprecedented set back in December. They had pushed the Allies back relentlessly and became confident with their superiority, but with confidence there should still be caution! They had intruded so deeply into Bulgaria they felt that in no time at all, they would meet up with their Turkish allies.

On December 9, 1914, at age seventy, riding upon horseback, King Peter of Serbia led his troops and civilians into the battlefield. This gray haired monarch instilled a new morale, and such courage, into his demoralized armies that they stopped the conquering foe, and hurled them back from Valievo. They routed those proud forces of the Empire all the way back to Belgrade and across the Drina River, the Save River and the Danube.

The Magyar Hussars were now pressed into service to rear guard the infantry's withdrawal. More and more they began to work in smaller numbers of ten, and sometimes five: most often they were engaged as couriers, message runners. Many now acted as riflemen for the infantry, serving with the infantry; they were also issued new uniforms that complimented those of the infantry. No more were they to wear the colorful uniforms of the past. All Hussar units wore the gray or beige to coincide with 'earth colors'. Some Hussar regiments also had the infantry 'officer' type jacket with shoulder epaulets, which replaced the dapper jacket-cape of the past, and they had riding pants that matched the gray jacket, but they kept their black boots. I understand that all cavalry units in Europe made similar changes for the common sense safety of the mounted regiments. Eventually all mounted cavalry were disbanded; the mounted horse cavalry's time in History had come and gone.

Pál was re-assigned and now became a very dependable dispatch rider. The infantry battalion Commander that he was attached to recalled how Pál had often got through to summon help in the form of artillery support to cover their withdrawal, or had led reinforcements to their position in a timely manner. They would have surely been lost without this dependability.

Many were the times when Pál would see a line stretched between telegraph poles that had been broken, ripped apart. This of course caused a communications break down. He would then stand up on the saddle, and tap into the working end of the wire announcing the problem. Repair crews were dispatched when Pál could not repair the severed wire himself.

Pál was behind the friendly lines when headquarters lost contact with his forward infantry detachment. Headquarters immediately summoned Pál, and his Captain ordered him to investigate, because reinforcements from the second line of defense were already moving forward to relieve the front line...Pál's detachment. His horse was willing, and ran over the shell-cratered fields. They were now ahead of the second line relief forces, as these men marched at a deliberate pace, expecting no enemy confrontation, thinking that their front line troops were still between them and the enemy.

With his horse running a good pace Pál reached the front lines and saw enemy uniforms! He looked at the line of entrenchment where Hungarians should have been. The trench had been over run! The captured men were already being led towards enemy lines! Bulgarians, Serbians and Allied soldiers were in the trenches; many others at both ends of the entrenchment appeared to be preparing to advance toward the oncoming Austro-Hungarian reinforcements approaching the position.

This was not the first time an attempt was tried to capture the second line of defense as it advanced to relieve the front line troops; both sides had executed this strategy successfully at one time or other. The front line was enveloped when their communication wires were cut, unable to inform headquarters, reinforcements advancing to relieve them were encircled also, captured without firing a shot!

Pál spurred his horse; he had no choice but to attempt to turn about. He must warn the reinforcements of the trap awaiting them. He successfully executed a speedy turn, but while he was parallel to the trenches, the Allies suddenly became aware of this lone rider... he was among them! A shout went up, and then many others; as the enemy infantry were now eager to stop him. They must prevent him from returning to report what he had seen!

His fleeting horse charged the shortest distance, straight as a lance, to make warning. The Allied infantry shot at horse and rider. Pál knew he should have zigged and zagged, and done some fancy riding to avoid a direct concentration of fire, but there was just no time. Both the enemy in the trenches, and the intended Austro-Hungarian reinforcements, were too close. He could see the relief forces from where he sat atop his horse. In a few short minutes the enemy would have them!

The first shots were in haste, made amidst confused shouts of "surrender, stop or die!" Duty bound he paid no heed to threats of death and whistling bullets. Rifles opened up on man and mount from the two flanks on either side of him, and from the trench behind him, but not a bullet found their mark! The shooting just as suddenly stopped now that many infantrymen barred his path. Running in front of Pál and his horse, they managed to grab the horse's bridle and turn it swiftly.

As the horse abruptly turned about and was stopped, Pál continued forward, catapulting out of the saddle and tumbling to the ground. Pál rose momentarily onto both elbows, and looked forward eagerly to see that the reinforcements had been warned by those shots fired in the ensuing confusion to stop him.

The reinforcements were already falling to the ground, and in the prone position were returning shots with the outflanking Serbians. He lifted his right hand to wave them off, and would have raised his voice to warn them still of what to expect at the trenches, but he saw nothing more than darkness. His words were silenced as he faded into unconsciousness. When he tumbled from his horse, he had hit the ground hard, tumbling head over heels.

As he awoke from unconsciousness, he found that his hands were bound behind his back. He was a prisoner of the Serbs, and had been laid to rest among the wounded as they were being prepared to march toward the interior of the country. He was not wounded, badly bruised, but hail and hearty. This good fortune cost him a ride. He was made to walk in a column that followed the carts and wagons. The wounded had been loaded onto farm hay-wagons, two wheeled carts, and whatever conveyance was available.

With rifle shouldered, armed guards walked on either side of the column at intervals of perhaps five meters. At evening, the prisoners were halted for supper, but the column of wagons and carts continued, as urgency dictated need for aid and comfort to the wounded. The nearest village as their objective could be reached in a few hours of marching; the wagons could make it sooner and within the light of day. The able prisoners were to walk that distance in the morning.

The higher ranking officers continued with the wounded. They desired the creature comforts of the village, perhaps a bed to sleep on that night, and wine with a home cooked meal. The lesser officers and subalterns were left with the guards and the prisoners. The guards could become resentful and disorderly towards the prisoners without officers to keep them orderly and disciplined!

They had stopped at a bridge, a small fieldstone structure that crossed a flowing creek. The prisoners were permitted to drink, and could wash up also, but Pál and the few others with hands bound behind their backs remained bound. Pál resented this and asked an enemy subaltern.

"Why? A few of us are bound like cattle and the rest are free handed?"

"Orders," said the Serb. He shrugged his shoulders and walked away from the haughty Hussar.

The prisoners who were not bound assisted those who were bound at eating their portion of the hurriedly cooked meal. If the bound prisoners managed to get their hands forward from behind their back in an attempt to feed themselves, the guards reprimanded them, untied their hands and rebound them again behind their backs; this second binding was tighter and hands became numb.

The ground was well chosen, it was a clear field nestled into a corner made by the road that intersected the creek, and continued over the bridge. The guards were positioned on the road, which was about one meter or more above the field. Guards were also positioned along the creek bank and the remaining two sides of the field. A plowed field was beyond the clear field as the third side of the field.

A sparsely wooded pasture, one side bounded by the creek was its fourth side. A cow had been heard beyond this pasture, no doubt within a stable somewhere. Two guards climbed over the fence to investigate, one would suppose, anticipating a drink of fresh milk with their portion of supper. As the evening began to wane, the bound men, like creatures with something in common, began to form a group by themselves apart from the other prisoners. They questioned one another, attempting to puzzle out the reason for this harsh treatment of them, as opposed to the other prisoners. They could find no sensible answer, and as the men milled about, they sat down finally to rest on the slope of the road's shoulder and near the flowing creek.

A struggle from the crowd of prisoners sitting within the open field suddenly created a rush of excitement among the prisoners and their Serbian guards. Campfires now burned in the approaching darkness...just what was transpiring in that struggle? The bound prisoners could not see from where they were. They did not even stir to stand up, but continued to sit at rest on the sloping shoulder of the road.

One of the guards at the creek bank rushed forward, more from curiosity than to investigate. The remaining guards along the creek surveyed the agitated prisoners, and glanced at these bound prisoners who appeared unconcerned. The struggle across the field became more intense, and now a few prisoners were running toward a tree that stood at the opposite end of the field.

Pál observed the guards on the road, they too were intent upon the tree and the struggling prisoners, and so were those that guarded the creek and bridge.

Backwards, like a crayfish, he moved so that not even those prisoners who were with him noticed that he was moving out of their group and nearer to the shoulder of the bridge and below the roadbed. The guards on the road were out of his view in this position, so in turn they could not see him.

Someone, a Hungarian from within the field shouted a barely heard cry, it sounded like a challenge that came unintelligibly to Pál's ear. The words stated something that sounded as though, "a prisoner...hands bound...was tied to a tree...the Serbians...were attempting to emasculate him".

The guards at the creek now stared in fear at the defenseless but angrily milling Hungarians. Someone shouted, "...defense!..." Another strange voice retorted, "...lie". But the guards were few in number and very nervous as they closed in upon the quickly rising crowd of prisoners.

Pál quietly slipped into the water. It was ankle deep, and he strove to stay next to the stone shoulder of the arch of the bridge. He had to stoop low as he walked slowly along, silently feeling his way by rubbing his left shoulder against the stone structure, using it occasionally for support. His hands remained bound behind his back and he did not want to slip on the uneven bed of the creek bottom. The water remained below the level of his riding boots in the flowing creek as he struggled to stay against the field-stone wall of the bridge.

He crossed under the bridge and thereby under the road, and stepped up onto the creek bank. On the opposite slope of the road he sat down and quietly but quickly moved his bound wrists under his buttocks and thighs. He then lifted his two feet through the loop described by his bound arms. In a stooping position, with his wrists still tied, but now in front of him, he looked over the top of the road. The guards on the road were still intent upon what was happening in front of them to consider a backward glance.

Pál saw, by the light of the campfire, that there was indeed a prisoner tied to a tree. Other prisoners were releasing him with the assistance of one of the Serbian subalterns. Pál thought instantly of his own fate... if he were recaptured? He quickly turned and crawled noiselessly on hands and knees away from the road and into the descending darkness.

He followed the meanderings of the creek, away from the guarded field; then continued in a stooped over fashion, until he was a safe distance from the bridge. It was a dark, shadow-less night, and he now felt secure enough to stand erect to walk along that winding path which the creek had led him. It had already taken him through many fields beyond the road and his wrists were still tied. Pál resolved that with the next opportunity, in some secluded area he would struggle free from his bonds. The Allied soldiers had taken anything that may be used as a weapon therefore; he looked for sharp rocks, boulders, any natural assist that would spare his teeth the task of unknotting the rope about his wrists. He found what he needed as he entered another wooded area.

While he struggled to wear away the rope against the jagged edge of a granite boulder, he had time to think about the long walk back to the battle lines. He did not have a plan, and didn't try to form a plan, he would simply walk back. He was bold enough to attempt any reasonable risk, but he

122 ~ *Anthony E. Virag*

resolved not to do anything foolish. With luck he had come this far and he would accept the fortunes, or misfortunes of fate, taking opportunities as they were presented.

With his wrists now free, he walked on in the darkness. He turned westward; this was the direction of withdrawal for the Austro-Hungarian forces. Since he had made up his mind to walk the distance, he also resolved to do it in the safety and dark of night. That's it! He would rest in the security of forests or wood lots during the daylight, and walk only at night. He would eat off the land, village gardens, whatever he could find in the countryside of that December, or eat nothing at all.

Pál calculated that, as prisoners they had walked about five hours. It should not take him, at the most five to ten hours, walking in the dark and across the fields to get back to the front trench line where they had begun... given that the Allied troops had not advanced too far, too rapidly on that front. He walked briskly for some time, and thought he heard the occasional sound of artillery in the distance. As he walked up and over the slope of a stubble hay field, he came upon a road that ran along that hay field and turned sharply westward. He placed himself upon that road and now walked on more eagerly, for he had suddenly entered upon the audible range of guns. He had kept deliberately to fields, and avoided roads, but now he would stay on this road convinced it would take him to the front lines. He walked with a smile on his face and very little fear in his heart; because he knew that he would make better time on the hard surfaced road with its straight westward course.

He had walked for a few hours on that road, and, given that he had initially walked the fields always going westward, he calculated that his westward progress had been maintained for about six hours (he had no watch, so he approximated these times). Within two or three hours the sun would be rising. He began to hear movement in the darkened woods on both sides of the road. Were the noises he heard in the woods the noise of the enemy troops regrouping? The occasional small arms fire he heard in the distance had died down; as had the artillery he heard at some distance ahead of him earlier in the evening. As a precaution he stepped off the road, and walked in the ditch beside it still walking briskly.

With the first light of dawn beginning to break behind him, Pál became anxious; he was not near any distinguishable line, or entrenchment. He soon would have to hide for the day. But within a few minutes, with the sun casting long shadows in the morning's first light Pál was at the Serbian lines. He saw a stone culvert that crossed from the ditch, and under the road.

Pál could see the dark shadow of a dry gully beyond him on the left that snaked towards the culvert and meandered through the culvert into the fields to the right of the road. Pál looked over the roadbed, the fields, some of which were wooded, ran off at gradually dropping elevations that appeared as a continuous gentle slope.

He may not have to hide for the day!

His heart began to rapidly palpitate as he weighed the options; he gambled on the gully's direction beyond the culvert, and to the right of the road. It may mark the front line course! But if it moved forward from the culvert and curved back toward the road ahead, he would be exposed to the line of fire parallel to the road. The gully seemed to continue to the right, and directly across the road into those low slopping fields. He gambled that the road was the high ground elevated above the fields, and that the gully cut straight across to pass under it at a right angle to the road.

He proceeded cautiously, hurriedly to crawl through that culvert and onto open woodlands. He was soon within front lines of the Central Powers troops. He had made it!

When it was over, all who had witnessed it simply shook their head in disbelief. Admirably they granted the man a true respect, he had earned it, whoever he was...he had gotten away with it.

The soldiers in that area were bewildered by his sudden appearance; all of them exercised disbelief at his action, and were amazed now when they considered how easy it was. All but Pál, as frightened as he was, and doubtful of the outcome, he knew what he did was what he had to do. He took a calculated risk, and so it was that in true Hungarian fashion he now shrugged off the compliments of courage and bravado. He had gambled and won!

Aki mer – nyer! [He who dares – wins!]

This has been the motto of many generations of Hungarians.

The gully did drop away slightly as it left the culvert, and luckily, at right angles to the road. Pál's escape was a good example of lots of luck. He presented himself to the infantry Major and enquired about the nearest Hungarian detachment. Given instructions, and permission to join them, Pál set out for the Austro-Hungarian lines.

It appears that his amazing "rush through enemy lines", and stories of a dramatic escape had preceded him. Mounted Hussars rode to greet him as he came to their encampment, there were some familiar faces among them, and for this Pál was happy. But better still, his Captain, that bold, cool, calculating man, walked out of the command post to meet him. He returned Pál's salute and shook his hands exuberantly.

"Corporal Valko sir, begging forgiveness for this delay," smiling, "but reporting for reassignment, and a return to active duty," Pál clicked his heels together.

"Congratulations sergeant, you are a corporal no more. It was good thinking and determination to escape in the manner you did. What you have succeeded in has instilled your fighting friends with high moral. I am happy for you and proud to have you in my command." He again received a hearty handshake from the Captain.

With Pál returned, it was just not enough; the Central Powers still could not prevail over the Allied efforts. The Serbian King Peter's inspiring example fired his troops to wipe out the invaders. Finally, with the Germans, Austrians and Magyars back beyond the Danube, Serbia was free again, for a while. Thanks to this remarkable king, who thought it better to die at the head of his loyal troops than to live subjected to foreign tyrants. He continued to command his armies in the field until the end of the war.

(He lived long enough to become the first King of the new country of Yugoslavia, in 1918. He died at seventy-seven years of age in 1921. May his soul rest in peace.)

But Serbian freedom was short lived, General Mackensen, fresh from his victories in Russia, where he was with Hindenburg in East Prussia, and had commanded troops in the area of Angerburg and the Masurian Lakes, now reinforced the Austro-Hungarian troops that had retreated in December 1914, with fresh German troops. In October of 1915, he began a new drive on the Slavic countries and into Serbia again. The Serbians fought bravely but were no match for the replenished, determined forces and this wily General.

Furthermore, the Bulgars who were Serbia's ally in the 1914 campaign, now became allied with the Central Powers, and attacked Serbia on her eastern flank. The little nation reeled at this unexpected overpowering and encircling threat. Greece would not offer assistance to Serbia from the south, and dared not get involved in a war that would threaten her suzerainty. King Constantine of Greece had made a farce of his treaty with Serbia, and was further reluctant to permit the landing of Allied troops on Greek soil, troops intending to cross Greece in an attempt to aid Serbia.

Bulgarians were fearless, and conniving, deadly fighters. If they were outnumbered or out of ammunition, but determined to fight another day, they did not always retreat. An entire battery of men resolved to give themselves up; with arms held high they suddenly exposed themselves to their foe, and walked forward feigning surrender. Arms still held high in mock surrender they were soon rounded up by their anxious foe. What the unsuspecting captors did not know, until it was too late, was that each man held their hands high to hide a shiv, or bayonet concealed in his sleeve. When the group was herded behind enemy lines by a few guards, never the number equivalent of the troops they had faced; the Bulgars attacked their guards. Taking the guns from the dead men, they fought their way back to friendly forces.

Just as often when the fighting stopped, while still at the fighting positions, or trenches, and with arms held high in mock surrender, they observed that the enemy were fewer than expected, they attacked openly, then and there, with nothing more than their concealed blades, now that they were within arms length of their foe. They were bold and determined soldiers!

By October 10, 1915, Belgrade was again in German hands. The Bulgarian troops, and combined German forces had now completed a meeting of their forward forces in Northeast Serbia. The Bulgarian forces took the city of Nish on November 7, and their armies also continued to sweep westward. They reached Monaster (present day Bitola), on November 19.

In December the Anglo-French forces that had landed in Greece with the hope of saving Serbia, now fell back to Slavonika, because of King Constantine's cowardly refusal to permit them to cross Greece overland. There was no point in jeopardizing these troops as well; they were too late to reinforce their Serbian allies.

The German High Command had ordered him to take the Balkans, and he had won the Balkans, Von Mackensen had successfully completed his mission.

THE IRON CROSS

S üle Jenö's regiment was on its way to the Russian Front. Rumors circulated that Von Hindenburg was seen at the railroad station. It occurred to them that Von Hindenburg himself might command this regiment, and would be joining the many reinforcements rushing to the aid of the German Armies in East Prussia. Other rumors had the General in that very same procession of troop trains now speeding across Austria. General Paul Von Beneckendorf Von Hindenburg would be commanding them. This would be a great experience!

The General was sixty-seven years old, but he had come out of retirement volunteering his services to aid his country. Because of his reputation, these troops were very proud to have the opportunity to serve under this most famous Old Man.

He had offered to serve his country earlier, and the Empire Builders had ignored his offer. But the Russian threat had surprised the German High Command; they now accepted his offer. Could he succeed with reinforcements against the onrushing, confident Russian Armies? Their Generals in the field in East Prussia, doing their best with the few troops they had, were no match for the force of two Russian armies, and they now had to give ground.

After his retirement in 1911, Hindenburg continued to study the Masurian Lakes region in East Prussia where he was born. He foresaw that this would be a major battleground in any future war with Russia...and now the war was here just as he had predicted! No General in all of

Germany was better prepared for fighting in this area. He had devised strategies, and alternative actions on updated maps; he was as familiar with the terrain, the rivers, and forests, as any native.

The German High Command reconsidered his voluntary offer to serve when the seaport of Danzig was threatened. They would now watch him apply what he had learned in his study of East Prussia. So it was that the old warhorse was once again in harness, speeding toward the Vistula River.

Von Hindenburg immediately took over command of all troops in East Prussia with General Erich Von Ludendorff as his assistant staff. Even with these reinforcements the German, Austro-Hungarian combined forces were greatly outnumbered by the two Russian armies of the Grand Duke Nickolas Nickolaeivich. Hindenburg however, very masterfully dealt with both armies by engaging them separately. He kept them confused, and because of the poor communications between the two Russian armies, he prevailed. The Germans freely intercepted the Russian messages between the two armies, then in the crucial last days; cut the communications wires between them! He defeated one of the Grand Duke's armies by September first, and went on to deal a crushing blow at Angerberg, pushing them to still another defeat around the Masurian Lakes. His 'homework' proved to be well studied! The results are History.

The Russians fell back eighty miles to a new line of reinforcements, onto the Nieman River. Here they stayed, never venturing into East Prussia again.

Jenö's troop train had made a few stops along the way, and in these stops the troops read the Village Station names. It was then that they became aware they were not going toward East Prussia but were going due east, through the Carpathian Mountains and more likely toward Galicia; they were disappointed. The rumors therefore proved only partially true, Hindenburg did come out of retirement to fight again for his country, but would not lead Jenö's detachment into Galician While two Russian armies engaged the

Germans in East Prussia, with Russian manpower superiority of two to one, Russia pushed another four armies against the Austro-Hungarians in Galicia. The manpower superiority was obviously in Russia's favor here also, and a reasonable estimate would put it greater than four to one on this Front.

The initial plans of the German High Command required the Austro-Hungarian army to engage, and hold the main Russian forces in Central and Eastern Galicia until the German Army had won the war in France. Then Germany would transfer a greater number of men and weaponry to the Eastern Front. This left two alternatives open to the Austrians and Hungarians: they could await attack and attempt to hold the Russians at a stand still, or they could take the offensive and attack the Russians who were superior in numbers. If they chose to wait, the best line of defense was on the San River between the Carpathian Mountains and the Vistula River.

But, in the European 'handbook of Martial Tactics' of that time, if one fought against Russian troops, theory dictated, "when in doubt, attack is the best defense". This would resolve all doubt as to what should have been the best strategy! The Austro-Hungarian forces therefore pressed an offensive, and with their inferior numbers smartly pursued to take advantage of such a bold venture.

With hindsight to our advantage now, to wait would have been the best choice, and they could have, by an active defense, successfully held up the Russian advance for a reasonable time. They could also have won small successes with skirmishing counter attacks.

However; after that initial Austro-Hungarian offensive was halted, the Russians countered with an offensive and were more successful than the Austro-Hungarians had been. Jenö's regiment arrived at this crucial time as reinforcements for the badly pressed Austro-Hungarians. He had finished one winter of basic training, and did well as a machine gunner placing the bullets where the officer directed. He received a medal of merit for gunnery, but had not yet seen action; this first engagement was his baptism of fire. He was pleased afterwards when the infantrymen congratulated him. They appreciated his cover fire as enemy troops threatened their withdrawal

Time after time, Jenö's withering machine gunfire turned a helpless situation into a decisive standoff, as the Russians turned back. Those first few days were exciting for Jenö as his infantry forces held off the overwhelming numbers. It was August when the Russians again pressed upon the Austro-Hungarian positions which now fell back from the onslaught, fighting a hesitant and tactical withdrawal. The Austro-Hungarians counter offensives were no longer intended for regaining lost ground but were more opportunistic; executed to inflict as many casualties upon the enemy as possible in an attempt to throw the enemy off balance from their steadily forward progress. They would hold their position for as long as possible in doing so.

There were many stories after each engagement of how combatants individually, or in groups... sometimes just a handful of men against a superior number behaved superbly, and turned back the surprised and bewildered larger force. The Hungarians exposed themselves at the last moment, leaping from cover to toss grenades into the advancing forces, and with small arms fire attempt to open a gap in the enemy ranks. They fell upon the onrushing troops suddenly, in a screaming counter charge, cutting and cursing. The Russians in front were literally butchered with bayonet, or bludgeoned to death with rifle butts. If they stopped momentarily, or hesitated due to the upstarts confronting them, the troops behind pushed them into the merciless Hungarians. Such engagements continued to thin the ranks of the defenders however, while the attackers still outnumbered them.

Jenö was proud to be a part of all this as he and his gun crew were called upon to hold delaying rear guard actions while their infantry redeployed. There were many hand-to-hand engagements which shattered the nerves of some of the best of men, but not the true fighters like Jenö. He surprised himself by his seeming lack of concern and disregard for his own life. He did what he felt had to be done, convinced that the job his crew were performing was critically important to the infantry. The infantry relied upon his crew, and he had no intention of letting them down.

He was really too cool, calm, and many times foolhardy in being just about too late to retreat. The Russians more than once almost closed the gap on him and his crew, as they encircled his gun emplacement to get at it from behind. Some of the infantry that had already fallen back would then be forced to stop in their flight, turn about, and shoot at the few Russians approaching Jenö from the left and right behind his position. There were times when the Russians actually came between the redeployed Austro-Hungarian positions and Jenö's gun.

Too often there were only Jenö and one or two of his crew left! In such a case, the gun was left behind and they fought a running battle in retreating, or crawled on their bellies back to friendly positions where they were patted on the back, bear hugged, and greeted with cheers. Cheers which must surely have been disconcerting to the Russians. His friends had seen it all, how he had slowly, methodically scanned the total perimeter of his range with chattering bullets, until he had described almost a complete half circle with the steaming gun barrel pivoting purposefully on its tripod. He would continue to hold his position as long as the gun continued to fire, and that meant as long as the cooling water-jacket was not damaged, and there were bullets left to dispense. He was a fighting fool, and soon earned the reputation as one who could be relied upon in a tight situation.

Still the Russians came!

The Austro-Hungarian troops continued to fall back!

There was no help coming to relieve them, it was they who were the reinforcements! They had come to assist the badly pressed troops that, without a doubt, would have been overwhelmed by now. Each time they fell back to a new position there were fewer of them to continue the fight; then from out of nowhere, a troop of men would charge the Russians, running out from behind Jenö's gun emplacement. Jenö would stop shooting as these men moved forward, if they held the position they would beckon him forward. His men would set up the machine gun in this advanced position, and with those few troops hold it until the Russian counter attack. At that time they again would fall back to their old position while inflicting large casualties on the enemy.

The fight would seesaw back and forth over the same terrain until there was very little cover left. The machine gun bullets, mortar and grenades, and the charging of men back and forth had leveled the underbrush, and turned up the soil. Only the dead and dying remained as stark, fixed symbols of the frustration of this kind of battle.

A few days after his baptism of fire, Jenö and his crew set up the machine gun in a stunted-cut-shrub area, skirting what was left of the woods. Behind a hurriedly prepared dirt work cover, the crew hid the position with a few shrub branches and clumps of tall grasses. The position commanded a clearing that the enemy would have to cross if they were to get to him. The water cooler was replenished, and his sergeant allocated the men for his crew. Eight men constituted a machine gun crew when the gun emplacements were far apart. In these cases more men were needed to keep the gun supplied for covering a wider area. In this grave situation however, eight men would have more than they could handle. At these times the crew also had rifles and "covered" with small arms fire when not being dispatched after boxes of ammunition, or containers of water for the cooling jacket.

His munitions carriers had just delivered the last caissons of ribboned cartridges when the Russians began their attack; his crew waited. All along the perimeter of what was left of the woods, artillery concentrated upon the attacking enemy. Mortar and machine guns ruthlessly cut spaces in the Russian ranks, and still they came. Small arms fire began to concentrate on specific groups of Russians that were pinned down. The force of the fusillade caused the attackers to disperse into many directions, but the concentrated direction was always forward. Some onrushing troops faltered and were pinned down in spots, others progressed forward, the movement of men was forced to feint and skirt the defended woods. This skirting, feint action directed them into the clearing, and into the range of Jenö's gun position.

Still the crew waited.

They saw the booted men in baggy pants for uniforms; the number of rows deep, and the line that extended far to the left and were now charging at them. All those men had gleaming bayonets fixed on long rifle barrels before them.

"There are so damned many of them... so few of us", thought Jenö.

"Fire!" The sergeant gave the command.

Jenö did; and would not stop until told to do so. The fighting was without parallel! The gun crew had never seen at any time, what was now unfolding before their eyes. Generally a ribbon of bullets cut a swath through the enemy and left a gap. Men appeared to the left and right of the gap... to be cut down, and so it should go, until all around there were but sparse troops left standing. But now, men kept coming onward, some crawling on their bellies, some ran upright pell-mell into hell... and oblivion...but they kept right on coming through the gaps!

There was no stopping them!

The rifle regiments spaced within the advancing bayonet-fixed Russian infantry, dropped momentarily onto one knee calmly shooting as they came, picking off the defenders. Where there was a gap made by machine gun bullets, men again quickly appeared; there were too many to notice any slowing of the forward surge.

His sergeant was hit and fell over backwards. Jenö was hit in the left arm, so that his left hand slipped from the left-hand-grip of the gun. He continued to fire one hand-edly while attempting to place his left hand back on the handgrip. Dirt and dust was kicking up all about him as the Russian mortar cover-fire sought to stop this line of resistance. His gun steamed a tremendous cloud now, and Jenö shot through the steam. Before the mortar debris had settled, he was shooting through it; he tried hard; they all tried hard, but the best shooting would not stop this advance. The ribbon of men in front of him came closer as his ribbon of bullets got shorter! He resolved that he would stay until his last bullet was gone, and then get his ass the hell out of there...*but he would not waste the bullets*, he would make every one count.

Two more of his crew were gone.

They had either run for it, or had been hit by shrapnel and crawled away from the gun emplacement so they would not hamper the rapid movements of the crew who were left. Speed was imperative in this very close situation. As soon as a ribbon of cartridges reached its ending, another was slapped into the chamber, and the instant that the top lock was released – lock slapped down; the murderous steel missiles of death were chopping into the flesh in front within split seconds, no longer wonderment, but desperate necessity.

As he struggled awkwardly, with one good hand, Jenö was again hit. Wounded in the side, he refused to quit. He was too intent on what was threatening in front of him, to the left and right of him. Only one man remained of his eight-man crew, and this faithful man kept diligently feeding the ribbon into the chamber while Jenö sighted and kept shooting. His shooting now was sporadic but accurate. He was not shooting randomly; he just did not have much ammunition left to be foolish with it. The sporadic bursts were deliberate and aimed at the greatest clusters of charging men.

They did not hear the shot; there were too many shots, but Jenö saw his ribbon feed man roll over. Now alone, and bleeding badly at his arm and left side, he was stubbornly oblivious to the danger facing him.

"Damn it! When will they stop?" he cursed.

The Russian artillery and mortar cover fire had stopped, the charging troops were too close, and already they were over running the Austro-Hungarian positions.

They had closed the gap!

Jenö now fired continuously at point blank range.

He had his pistol... there were at least two rifles within reach of his gun position, death was facing him yet he dared prepare to fight the troops advancing in front of him. But until then... expend the machine gun bullets, shoot... keep shooting!

The Russian was alone, with bayoneted rifle poised; he rapidly approached Jenö from behind. He had succeeded in circling the gun emplacement, and now observed the blood stained back of the gray uniform; he also saw the left limp arm; bloodied, that arm hung from the left shoulder, and though the Russian saw it move at the elbow, it definitely appeared to impede the man that tried to use it.

This Russian must have been a reluctant soldier; he more likely was a peasant conscripted into the Czars army. Being a peasant, he was probably from a strongly religious family. Perhaps killing was against his moral conscience, maybe, plain and simple, he just did not want to fight and kill, or be killed. Maybe he felt sorry for this wounded human, just as he would feel sorry for an injured animal.

Why did he hesitate?

An experienced soldier would have dispatched his enemy without hesitation. Many of his comrades were killed during the previous days of fighting. He may have thought at that time, what many of the peasant soldiers think... the dead are lucky; they are in heaven, free from the bonds of earth and free from the strife of men.

Why did he hesitate?

Could it be he admired the courage of this wounded man? This man who stood alone against the advancing horde that was about to engulf him? Did he feel a sudden kinship with this pathetic figure? The two of them appeared to be so much out of place... this man who wanted no more to be in this position than he did. How bold! The man must have seemed unreal...in this nightmare. The Russian was behind Jenö, and so, he was also in front of the charging Russian infantry that came like an enormous wave about to engulf him. Jenö was between him and his maddened countrymen. In that instant, the Russian took in that awesome sight; in that instant, he could have imagined that it was he who was alone, and the charging horde was about to engulf him!

The sight would paralyze with fear a less disciplined man.

Was he horrified? Surely he did not relish the thought of being on the receiving end of that charging, murderous mob.

Just how is it that this... this wounded man could stand so defiantly, and not flinch at the onslaught? Surely the man knew he would be killed; yet he stood his ground where no other man would dare to stand. Death was imminent, but still the man dealt out death... death to my countrymen.

Suddenly! A sharp hit delivered to the side of his head!

"Another bullet?" thought Jenö as he lapsed into unconsciousness... and he had almost reached his last bullet in the ribbon.

The Russian had used his rifle butt and now stood over him. The fighting had stopped for Jenö.

He was the last of the gun crew and the position was now overrun. Only a few of the marauding troops gave a sideward glance at the limp, lifeless forms in gray uniforms around the machine gun.

That solitary Russian could have run the bayonet through the unprotected back, but he did not. Why not? Only that one Russian would know why he didn't. And his reason? Being otherworldly was probably not even clear to him.

Why does a soldier in the heat of battle have mercy, and spare his enemy?

Jenö was extremely lucky.

He remembers only a few events, those between intervals of unconsciousness. He would awaken, and then black out again; he recalls only vaguely the image of a uniformed Russian with bayoneted rifle in his hands, standing over him as he fell away from his machine gun. The man's face was passive and peaceful... oddly not grim faced, as one may expect of a killer. His countenance was much like the childish innocent peasants back home thought Jenö. The image comes through a hazy, undulating fog on the edge of the real and unreal as he passed out. Did the Russian kill him? What was that sharp pain felt suddenly against his head?

"Did he shoot me?" then Jenö slept...

"What was this?"

Through the darkness of a dreamless sleep he heard voices.

Was he still sleeping? He could not be dreaming the pain was too real. He actually heard voices in his native Hungarian! Quickly he opened his eyes; they were Hungarian! But how could this be, how did they get here?

They were discussing his fate when they saw his eyes open, and his apprehensive face; they smiled.

"How did you get bandaged buddy? Our medics haven't caught up with us yet".

"I don't know...I passed out. I just remember the shots to my arm and side, fighting...a sharp blow to my head... here." As his good right hand touched his head at the spot, he winced.

His head was wrapped; his left arm was bandaged as was his left side, after Jenö noted this, he asked, "Will you guys get me out of here?"

He was still lying pretty well near where he had fallen, at his machine gun position. The two soldiers remarked about what Jenö already knew, the others of his crew were dead.

"We counter attacked. Thanks to you, the Russians in this area were cut down in numbers so that they couldn't hold the position for long. We're still not sure how the battle will go, but we're trying to push this little advantage".

They looked across the battlefield, in the area in front of the machine gun there were many dead Russians, only a few wounded lying among the dead were bandaged, but they too were left where they fell in the open field!

"Apparently we didn't give them enough time to carry their wounded out," mused one Hungarian.

"Why would they bandage me, and leave their own men in the field? They should have left me, and removed their own men to safer positions," thought Jenö. He tried to raise himself to see across the field, but he could not.

"Come, good fellow; you've done your fighting for the day. We'll get you to some place that is safer than this open space."

Bullets were again kicking up sprays of dirt around them. The soldiers quickly hung their rifles over their shoulders, they then sat Jenö up; he damn near died from the pain, but he knew the need and their urgency. They swiftly formed a "seat" with their interlocking hands on one another's wrists, and then squatted nearer Jenö. They ordered him to raise his butt onto the "seat". With his right hand and arm he pulled himself onto their wrists by embracing the shoulders of the soldier on his right, and he held himself there. This action was hurriedly done, as the pained Jenö could only allow so much.

Jenö knew that he would surely die in the field where he lay if he didn't co-operate and so he suffered the extreme pain to help himself. He held his arm around the neck of one soldier as they ran, trying to prevent his left, wounded side, from hitting the soldier on the left by rolling towards the man on the right. It hardly mattered! He was tossed from left to right anyway as the soldiers ran. Just as the pain was about to overtake him again, they reached an earthen dugout; a bunker not far behind the position he had held.

"That's odd," thought Jenö, "I didn't think we had dug in this well. On the other hand, it could have been the Russians who dug this".

"As soon as we have secured this sector again we will return for you."

They lay him outstretched, and into as comfortable a position as they could, near the farthest wall of the dugout directly opposite the entrance. Their words were meant to encourage of course, their counter attack after all could fail, but with a few cheerful, parting words, they left him alone lying on the dirt floor and they exited the bunker.

He felt secure – somewhat – in this large earthen dugout. It could contain about six, maybe eight men with not too much crowding...men would have to stoop to enter. Once inside a man could stand, and the floor sloped downward slightly to flatten out at the main enlargement where he now lay. He did not think too much, he was tired, and it pained him to be alert, as apprehensive as he was, he finally acknowledged his helplessness. He knew he could not defend himself, and acknowledged he was at the mercy of the circumstances around him.

He had lost a lot of blood, and had exerted himself to help the soldiers that carried him. He is not sure but it is obvious he must have passed out again. It is possible that he passed out often; even when the soldiers carried him he wasn't sure what was going on. He does know that he was constantly extremely tired. He felt an exceedingly great pain, was in and out of consciousness as the conflict raged about him and above him.

He awoke: he did not start up suddenly; he approached consciousness as though struggling through a veil of fog. The fog made the darkness of the bunker even heavier. It felt as though he had to cast off this cloak of darkness physically, but he could not. When he finally woke up he was still in darkness.

"Where am I?"

It took a while before he became aware that the darkness was the natural dark interior of this bunker. What had aroused him to consciousness was the sound of many feet running on the ground around and above him. He remembers the sound above was much like that of a stampede. There was a lot of shooting, small arms fire and screams of men; others cursing and shouting...now plainly heard in his bunker hideaway. What was happening out there? Which way would the tide of battle go?

"God, I want out of here!"

He was not actually in fear, but doubtful of his personal capabilities, and in his weakened state he did not like that helpless feeling.

Very shortly he heard voices, Russian voices!

He could turn his head to the right, and plainly he saw their silhouetted forms against the light of day outside the bunker entrance. There were two men, one on each side of the entrance. In their foreign language he thought they threw a challenge into the darkness. They both extended their rifles into the bunker, and upon no reply to their challenge, both men shot into the darkness.

They listened.

Jenö was afraid to breath, fortunately the bullets had passed harmlessly into the darkness. He had not answered their challenge, and he was most fearfully reluctant now to let his presence be known. They could very well shoot again, and at the direction of his voice. He thought that he had better be quiet: perhaps they would go away.

Satisfied with the silence, the two entered the bunker!

Cautiously, they slowly stepped forward, with rifle barrels extended in front of them to feel their way into the darkness. One stumbled against Jenö's prone body, and fell to strike the dirt wall. The Russian cursed the darkness and felt about the body. *He then sat down on it.* He laughingly remarked to his crouched companion...something. His companion also sat on the body and felt about it. They were satisfied to feel the wetness of the bandages and surmised;

no doubt they had killed this man. It sure beats sitting on the damp, dirt floor. Perhaps they were laughing because they were pleased with themselves at having shot into the bunker before entering. Had they thrown a grenade the bunker may have collapsed, they would then have to continue fighting...outside.

They talked with subdued voices for quite a while, as they sat backs to the wall, and facing the bunker entrance. They planned on sitting out this fight and they were heavy! Jenö could not breath, he was afraid to move a muscle. He couldn't move a muscle! He was in agony, and began to perspire; their combined weight had opened up his wounded side. He began to bleed. He could feel the bandages getting warmer and wetter. Maybe the men would soon realize that he was not dead. He could not continue like this much longer. Mercifully he blacked out again.

Finally, some commotion, or lack of commotion outside, caused the soldiers to get off of Jenö. They crawled to the bunker entrance, weighed the situation, and listened a moment, then left in silence.

When he awoke from unconsciousness Jenö was happy to find that he was alone. He breathed deeply with the weight off his body...how good it felt. The two vagrant Russians were no longer in the bunker, thank God!

He passed out again, the loss of blood and pain of his wounds were taking a toll on him.

He was on a softly floating, gentle wave...rising. He felt as though he was being lifted up, and was now gliding effortlessly above the ground, there was a peacefully pleasant humming about him. He anxiously opened his eyes to see the sun shining above the dreamy landscape of broken treetops; leafless they swayed in the cool September breeze.

"This must be the way to Paradise", he thought, "Everything is so quiet and peaceful". For just a moment he felt no pain and, then it descended upon him! Reality overpowered him pitilessly: he was in severe pain!

When he regained consciousness he was outside, he had been carried on a stretcher, and his comrades–in-arms were with him again, laughing and joking now with the surge of adrenalin. Happy to have survived the countless attacks and counterattacks, they enjoyed a respite from battle. A medical corpsman came over and began to change Jenö's side bandage, his arm bandage had already been changed. Proper dressing and cleaning would wait until they could get Jenö to a hospital behind the lines.

Some of the troops of his decimated regiment were here and recognized Jenö. They came to talk with him, and con-gratulate him. They had seen his stand and how he had fought; they had feared for his safety but they were help-less to do anything in that situation of yesterday to help him. (So he had been out for one entire night?) The Austro-Hungarian troops were busy at that time, each soldier trying to save his own neck; regrettably it became every man for himself.

They marveled even more as they talked, and he told them all that had happened to him during the Russian attack. His experience in the bunker with the two vagrant Russians gave them a particularly hearty laugh...at Jenö's expense, but he didn't mind. He was actually happy that he was alive and once more could make his friends laugh.

Apparently the seesaw offensives and counteroffensives he had experienced were the decisive battles of yesterday, though he felt as though each offensive had lasted one day in itself. He was too tired, he was sick and in pain. There were many injured and wounded Austrians, Hungarians, and Russians. In turn all of them received medical attention in the field from the German doctors behind the fighting front. They were all then loaded into motorized ambulance vehicles, or horse drawn wagons. As they lifted Jenö, many eager hands suddenly extended to help carry him. He was loaded into an ambulance amidst compliments, words of good cheer, blessings, and handclasps from his comrades.

"Why do they treat me so?" he wondered, "Other soldiers, and good men had died. The dead had given all they had for their Motherland."

Soon he was transferred from the ambulance into a hospital train. The train would carry him away from this man made hell. In a few hours he would be back among civilized people. Oh how good it will be to be home again, in the fields free from strife and the conflicts of men. It never occurred to him that he would be hospitalized for a while.

The troops had treated Jenö with respect because they were grateful to him. They had carried the day against a superior force in his area, mainly because he had held his position. Each minute that he had stood his ground he had considerably thinned out the Russian ranks. Every one that fought there that day knew it. He had made it possible for the mortar crews to turn their weapons and concentrate on the large groups of Russians. With his sacrifice for their time...he had delayed the Russian charge and the mortars would have been too late to do any good.

He was being unloaded with the wounded at a hospital in Vienna when the ill-fated news was announced: that very same day, in which he and the wounded were evacuated, the Russians counter attacked and carried the offensive.

Final victory was to the Russians!

Jenö was heart broken and disgusted. He reflected on that peaceful Russian peasant's face. He had not killed when he could have killed me...he was an exception. What purpose was there to all this sacrifice of young men? Austrians, Hungarians, Germans, Russians and their Allies, they were all alike...like so much "meat to be ground up by the war machine".

In such games as these, soldiers always lose.

There will be many tears from many families of the dead, and in time, even they will have forgotten. There will be new threats, new tears, and new wounds for new people, which will make those of old forgotten, as though they had not existed.

The Old would not be remembered because the importance of the New would be dwelt upon and emphasized. There will be need for more wounds, more "human meat to grind", and more tears in the future.

Hindenburg had won a great victory on September 1, 1914, and drove the Russians back eighty miles to the River Nieman.

The Russians had succeeded in repulsing the Austro-Hungarian forces and had won a great victory at Lemburg, the Capital of Galicia on September 2, 1914. From this victory they advanced twenty-seven miles westward to threaten Hungary and thereby the road to Berlin.

Point and Counterpoint: Who then really won?
The battlefield dead on both sides were no longer symbols of Glory. They represented the callousness and stupidity of Man.

Jenö received the Iron Cross for this engagement in Galicia.

SIEGE AND RELIEF

R ussia continued to press her advantage after this Victory in Galicia. Her armies actually went over the Carpathian Mountains, pushing the Austro-Hungarian forces from Ravaruska, and they besieged Przemyl (Premeez-lee). Steamrolling on to occupy Jaroslav, they made gains in their advance along the Donajec River.

By September 23, 1914, their artillery began shelling Cracow, (which was then a possession of Austro-Hungary, but after the partitioning of 1918, it became a possession of Poland), and the Russians were now spread out over the entire Carpathian Mountain Range.

Varga János, the old, siege artilleryman, was in Przemyl as the Austro-Hungarian artillery dueled the Russians at every engagement of the siege. He remembers how reluctantly the Hungarians gave up the Carpathian Mountain passes that led to their Homeland, and how Przemyl continued to hold out under the Russian siege even though it was a most trying time for the inhabitants and defenders.

"If only we had some reinforcements we could push them back. It is difficult to stand what they are dishing out; we should give them a taste of their own medicine."

János got his wish!

With the beginning of October the Austro-Hungarian armies were reinforced and began a counter-offensive to push back this threat to their Homeland. It seems that Von

Hindenburg had convinced the German High Command with his victories in destroying the two Russian armies in the Prussian Campaign. They were now confident that the Old General knew how to cope with Russians. So, fresh from his victory in East Prussia, he arrived on the scene and was given command of this offensive. The Empire Builders knew now they could rely on him

The Russians were quickly driven from the Uzok Pass in the Carpathians and forced to abandon their hold on the besieged Przemyl. The embattled Hungarian defenders had, remarkably, held out against the Russians in spite of the extremely greater numbers.

Kerekes Lajci (Lajci is a 'pet' name for Lajos –English, Larry), a young siege artilleryman, was among those troops sent to relieve the besieged city, and he was now assigned to the same artillery unit as Varga János. Since both came from the same "home town" of Porpacz, the young man received a hearty welcome from the Old Veteran. With all the news from home, and the many mutual friends they had at home, they simply felt fortunate to be brought together. The twenty-one year difference in their ages did not trouble the soldiers, and they became very close.

When either of them wrote home to their respective families, they would be sure to mention the other in their correspondence. In this manner each family was kept informed as to the welfare of their man.

The Austro-Hungarian forces recaptured Jaroslav, forcing the Russians to fall back to a position beyond the San River, in Eastern Galicia.

But in mid October, with fresh reinforcements the Russians again counter attacked. With Campaign and counter Campaign; the battle once again seesawed like some massive tug of war. Slowly, painfully slowly, the Russians gradually gained and re-entered Jaroslav. The Russian reinforcements attacked the left flank of Hindenburg's armies, and he was forced to withdraw all along that line.

Von Hindenburg's troops executed a perfectly ordered withdrawal as he moved his troops swiftly and tactfully, so they were too fast for the Russians. He had outwitted them, saving his manpower. They had withdrawn successfully and lived to fight another day.

But by mid November 1914, the Russians had again besieged Przemyl, and also again surrounded Cracow. Kerekes Lajci was genuinely scared, and Janös had an awful time attempting to keep the young soldier's spirits buoyed.

"This is entirely different", cried Lajci, "We are surrounded, and there is no way out!"

"Look son, while there is food left in this city we can hold out. While there are shells left for our artillery those Russians will keep their distance. It is as simple as that. They push: we push back. We stood them off before, and you were among those who helped relieve us... remember?"

"But, what happens if we are not relieved?"

"We will be!"

"How can you be so sure?"

"Look damn it, that is how it has always been. We don't like it; but we have to put up with it. When you've been at this war business for as long as I have you'll know. Either we fight and hold; both fight and die or, we are taken prisoner when we have nothing more to fight with," determined János, "and that is the worst of it in a nut shell. Lajci it's not an easy life, this soldiering. We have it better than most soldiers though, we artillery men, you see we do keep the enemy at a distance. How would you like to be in a trench out there, somewhere, on the receiving end of our shells?"

The Old veteran went on like this, resolving to harden the 'boy'. He and Lajci were constant companions for every day of that siege. They stood their duty at the gun together; they ate together and even slept together. They became more like brothers and remained so to the end.

Hungary was raided again from the mountain passes of Carpathia, and her forces once again driven from Bukovina.

Home on leave after release from the hospital, Jenö had been exercising to bring back his strength. The army physician told him to return in a month for a physical check up when released from the Hospital. His left arm muscles were still stiff and weak but he kept exercising it to bring it back to normal strength. His left side had healed dramatically well, but internally? The doctor would have to decide.

He had been reading newspaper accounts of the war, and weighing the eyewitness accounts of his returned buddies against the propaganda of the newspapers. He was not too anxious to get well; some of his recuperating friends had already been called back, as they were needed for active service again.

"Things must be bad," thought Jenö, as he took the train from Porpacz, Hungary, to Vienna Austria. He spent some time in a koscma with his friends before reporting to the doctor. His left arm was still in a 'sling' but he had a girl on his good right arm as he stood at the bar. Not wishing to remove his hold on the 'warm body', he would remove his left arm from out of the sling, and drink his glass with his injured arm. The girl was flattered; his companions laughed at his mockery of the wound.

"Exercise," remarked Jenö. "I'm following the doctor's orders. He told me to exercise my wounded arm." Then he joined in the hearty laughter.

With much reluctance, and some apprehension, he prepared to report to the doctor, that same Colonel who had released him from the hospital. He stopped off at the Company Barracks and dressed into his uniform with the Corporal stripes. He centered the Iron Cross onto his tunic, with its ribbon hanging from around his neck. He was deliberately trying to dress in a manner to 'psych' out the doctor. He took a last glance into the mirror; he looked great! Damn it, he looked too good. He tried to change his countenance by putting on a long face.

"There, that looks better," he remarked to his reflection. "Well, that's the worst that I can look."

He entered the Colonel's office.

"Well, well, well, you look like a model soldier corporal; those broad shoulders, you stand straight like a rail, and with a very military countenance." The happy doctor seemed pleased to see Jenö.

"Oh boy, now how do I get him to give me more time," thought Jenö. "My long face was complimentary? A military countenance?"

"We need more fine soldiers like you, you know, there are not too many men who earn the Iron Cross as you did, and live to enjoy it", continued the Old Colonel. "We are anxious to get you back into action."

"Oh shit! That was it, the Old Colonel has said it openly," fretted Jenö, "They are anxious to reactivate me".

"You know, the Russians are still being stubborn, and trying to give us a difficult time," went on the Colonel. "It is up to men like you to get back and teach them a lesson again, huh?" With this last remark he laughed good-naturedly.

"Doctor, with all due respect, sir, my arm is still weak. I doubt if I could lift a caisson of bullets with it. You know, if I were alone at a gun position and again pressed by oncoming infantry...it would be awkward for me to wrestle a box of bullets." Then as an afterthought he added, "This handicap could prove fatal." Pressing his luck further, "You really don't want that on your conscience do you?"

Jenö had not raised his voice at all, he stated these points in a soft, methodical, but deliberate manner, matter of factly, and all the while he looked directly into the Old Doctor's eyes. The remarks were truthful; the facts could stand-alone, and he hoped to 'play' the doctor to gain more time off.

The doctor reflected but a moment. In that moment he looked respectfully at the Iron Cross located strategically and purposefully in the center of the tunic. The Old doctor hesitated.

"Let's see your arm lift a few weights son. We shall both try to be reasonable today."

Jenö nodded in agreement.

"Remove your medal; take off your tunic and shirt."

Jenö did as he was told while the doctor checked his heart with a stethoscope, and then prepared a stack of weights, all the while tallying on a clipboard, checking his heart again. The doctor tested that arm for quite some time. He bent and pulled the arm, felt and probed his wounded side also, finally:

"I'm satisfied with the results. Do you know how well your arm is healing, or do you want to know?"

Jenö winced at, 'satisfied with the results' but puzzled over 'arm is healing'. "Of course it is, and healing well," under his breath.

The doctor continued, "You have now actually been away from active duty, let's see." He went to his desk and consulted Jenö's record again. "Yes. In mid October you were released from here, and you've been home for a month." He mused, "Yes, yes, of course. How much does a box of ammunition weigh, machine gun bullets, how much?"

"Huh? I guess," Jenö stammered "about twenty five, maybe forty kilo. I never gave it much thought" He hesitated and added – "recently."

"W-e-l-l," the doctor dwelt on the word, and said with a smile, "You can just about lift one case then, can't you?" He added quickly, before Jenö could reply, "If your right arm carries the heavy end!" He chuckled to himself at this joke.

"Corporal, tell you what I'm going to do. Take another month! Take all of December."

Jenö's eyes bugged out wide. This good fortune was totally unexpected!

"And the New Year holiday at home! Then come back here. It should be a good trip on the train from Porpacz to Vienna just after the New Year. It will be a few days "after the night before", and you can recuperate from your hangover while resting on the train; report to me on Monday, January 3, 1915."

"Yes sir!" exclaimed Jenö. He snapped to attention and clicked his heals snappily together as he did so. His bare chest thrust out above his flat, sucked-in belly.

Boy!

He looked like a strapping, model soldier now.

"Put your clothes on Corporal, and get your ass out of here," snapped the doctor as he sat down and made out the necessary papers. Still seated, he gave the credentials to the now clothed Jenö, and smiled again at the Corporal. Looking at the Iron Cross he saw that it was not carefully centered, as it had been when the soldier came in; he had redressed in a hurry.

Jenö smiled, saluted; his joy was hard to hide.

Still seated, the Colonel raised his right hand in an attitude of indifference, and returned the salute with a wilted and casual hand. He threw the salute at Jenö, and then his hand landed to again hang freely from the desktop.

The happy Corporal exited the Colonel's office.

Jenö Returns To Fight

Time flies quickly when you are having a good time thought Jenö.

It is odd how, mathematically and scientifically, physics will prove that time is the same no matter where you are, and whatever you are doing. The seconds pass by, ticking away methodically, and with precise regularity whether you are happy and enjoying yourself or whether you are waiting desperately and tensely for an uncomfortable experience to end. Yet, in those desperate and tense moments, the seconds seem to last longer. He pondered these things on the train that was taking him back to his military commitment.

How interminable the time appeared to pass now.

"How interminable it was when I lay wounded in that bunker, with the Russian soldiers sitting on my body", he reflected. "The mind's biological clock must not obey the rules of physics, that's all there is to it."

The last six weeks had gone too quickly.

During December of 1914, and January of 1915, with a series of campaigns and battles in the Mountains, in the winter snows, the Russians fought desperately to gain control of the mountain passes.

Jenö was again with the Austro-Hungarian forces that were sent to check the Russian advance. The fighting seemed more pathetic than any that he had previously experienced because of the bitter, sub zero cold. Among the many men who stood guard at night at a machine gun post of some lonely salient commanding a critical pass, there were those few who were found the next morning to be frozen stiff. In death they were still 'standing guard', in that squatted, seating position of last warmth, with no defense against the merciless, bitter cold winter wind; that deadly wind that numbed the senses and made the already ruthless cold more unbearable.

The snow made the mountain fighting the more treacherous, and the Central Powers were again grossly outnumbered. They had no choice but to fight a holding battle, and slow withdrawal. Both sides suffered dearly; every foot of ground was paid for with the bodies of soldiers. The second attempt to relieve the besieged Przemyl would have to wait.

The defenders of this encircled city now resorted to eating the dogs and cats. There just was not enough food to feed soldiers, women and children, so the artillery draught horses were also butchered, and eaten.

"Boy! What a stew we made of them," said János, implying that cat stew or dog stew is tolerably good. Perhaps it is, when one is starving.

Przemyl had changed hands three times. It was occupied first by Russians, taken by the Austro-Hungarian army, and then recaptured by Russians during the last siege. The Central Powers and their Hungarian Ally held on for three months. Imagine the stubborn individuals among the populace that endured all three sieges as well, in a manner that indicated nothing more than a bold tenacity to hang onto their homes and possessions. It is amazing!

Kerekes Lajos would not eat!

He could not eat dog, cat or horse.

"Damn your dainty gut," cursed János. "Won't it tolerate the last food that's left? You will surely die Lajci; you've got to eat."

"I can't – I won't" and he didn't!

Despite all the persuasion, and all the threats of death, Lajci ceased to eat. The old veteran did not know what to make of his young countryman, but he did continue to nurse him. Occasionally he gave the young, delirious artilleryman some horsemeat broth. But when Lajci regained consciousness, he could only think of the 'foul food', and vomited it back up again.

Lajci finally died.

"Damn it," thought János. "He could have prevented that, but only he could help himself, and he wouldn't."

Now the old artilleryman had to take care of himself. So he went about it the more diligently. He always had chunks of raw horsemeat in his food pouch to cook or prepare in any manner, and he did sustain himself. When the Central Powers were finally forced to surrender the city, János still had a chunk of raw horsemeat in his pouch. This is how he got the nickname 'Nyers János' (Raw John)

There were many who starved in Przemyl, and many who did not have to starve, but they too, were just too damn squeamish about what they ate.

"Bele Istenét," cursed János (God curse his guts).

On March 22, 1915, the Russians finally captured Przemyl, though they had besieged it twice since September of 1914, they had always been driven back. Encouraged by this success they again swept towards Hungary. The Hungarians rallied their forces, but again they were greatly outnumbered. Still they held tenaciously and stubbornly; they were fighting for their homeland; the battlefield was in their backyard, this made the defenders more fiercely determined, and unrelenting.

Varga János suffered as a result of those three offensives on Przemyl. He was a nervous individual for many years thereafter. As stated before, he was a very strong man physically, but he was also a strong willed free spirit. To be imprisoned after that three-time siege ordeal at Przemyl, and then confined in the still smaller types of holding structures, made him paranoid and unstable. His Russian captors often locked him in a loft, since there were no prisons, nor any place to hold a prisoner, short of keeping him confined in an attic or in a chicken coop, which they did, he was constantly surly and made trouble for his captors.

The Russian captors allowed the prisoners to drink vodka, apparently the strategy was, drunken men are easier to corral and hold, but of course, given the vodka, János drank to excess, and when drunk he caused even more trouble for his captors by getting into a fight with his guards. They in turn beat him senseless many times, as he was drunkenly helpless. When he awoke, he cursed his guards, accusing them of taking advantage of a drunkard that was unable to defend himself.

--- — —---

Perhaps Russia was allowed to encroach upon Hungary at the expense of the Hungarians troops? There appeared to be a plan formulating among the German High Command, and it needed time before its execution.

It would be difficult to convince the troops in the field that there was a plan however. They were told to fight a holding battle, but did so more out of frustration for their homes, their families, and their own will to survive.

Finally, in November of 1915, the strategy began to materialize; Von Hindenburg struck at the Russians again! He was hitting them on both flanks, and once again threatened the Russian armies with a pincers movement. One of his armies came down from the North, along the Vistula River from east of Thorn. The other advanced northeast from Czstochowa. The Russians were in danger of encirclement and acted hurriedly upon realizing their plight. They pulled back their total manpower to Lodz, they would have been further set upon and forced to withdraw farther still except that, as they waited at Lodz, their reinforcements arrived from Warsaw, and immediately attacked Hindenburg's army as it came down the Vistula.

That Northern pincer of the encircling Austro-Hungarian army was now hard pressed to continue! In this manner the battle for Lodz began. But when the Austro-Hungarian forces also received their German reinforcements the Russians were pushed back from Lodz to the Bzura River, twenty miles west of Warsaw. With the Central Powers so strengthened, and the Russians newly strengthened, both armies dug in.

A long trench siege began. The front lines paralleled the Vistula River in the north and continued to the Galician border in the South. For months this position of stalemate existed all along the entrenched front, with neither side making any gains. All was not quiet however; bitter fighting ensued in campaign after campaign and each time it was the Russians who became weaker in the north, but stronger in the south.

It has been stated already, that at the outset of the war in August 1, 1914, about seven million Russians were actually ready to fight in a matter of a few weeks. Half of their troops were immediately sent to support this Eastern Front; we did not cover the fact however, that an estimated manpower of twenty-eight million men between the ages of twenty and forty-three could be conscripted into military service in August 1914. It is easily concluded then, that as the duration of the war continued, in time, more Russians were added to the standing army and the balance of manpower was obviously always in favor of Russia. There is no reason that we can think of, why the Russians did not simply overwhelm the Austro-Hungarian forces that, for the whole duration of the four year war, numbered no more than seven million.

It is possible that Russia could not provide arms for that great a number of soldiers, nor was Russia capable of re-supplying them with the necessary food and ammunition.

It was here, in the Carpathian Mountains that the Hungarians stubbornly resisted the Great Bear. Jenő's regiment had fallen back each time that the Russians advanced. He was more often in the rearguard of the tactical withdrawal. (The reader will have noticed that the Russians were making all their gains in the South, on this Eastern Front. They were most often soundly beaten in the North.

We can only assume that, the Russians starting with four armies in the South generally had more men in that theater and that they hoped to succeed in beating the Austro-Hungarian forces by sheer numbers). Once they penetrated Hungary they would have a clear road to Berlin.

Jenö was all too familiar with the current situation. The Hungarian infantry to the left and right of him had very little chance to dig in thoroughly. They were on open ground to meet a Russian attack. The soldiers dug a small hole; a mere few spades full of dirt thrown up from the hole were tossed directly in front, to form a small earthen mound. The soldier would thus lie; chest in the hole, and the slight pile of dirt in front was his shield. He aimed and pointed his rifle from around this small mound of dirt. The ground was simply too solid, unmercifully uncompromising because of the frozen surface. If the unfortunate soldier did not strike a soft spot of dirt in which he could hurriedly dig this crude little shelter, he was invariably shot down.

There were many grain fields, and hay fields that were not harvested. Because of the war the peasants had left the fields and evacuated their families to areas remote from the threat of bombs and bullets. These un-harvested fields of grain were a particular threat to the infantry when, invariably, machine gunfire emanated from somewhere in the field as they were crossing it. The soldier had nothing to hide behind for protection in these fields; there was no refuge except that which they could provide themselves. This was again, that little hole which they scratched with their entrenching tool. But to get good leverage to dig, they had to extend their arms, or try to chop into the ground while lying flat against it. In many of the grain fields, the parched hardpan soil itself would have been very hard to dig into; the frozen fields amplified the problem. If a soldier used his body in a position somewhat higher than the prone position in order to achieve leverage on his trenching tool, many a good man died where he struggled, cut down by the withering bullets coming through the standing stalks of golden grain, from a source he did not even see.

Jenö's crew had no more opportunity than the infantry; they no sooner had checked out the gun and loaded it, than the Russian counter offensive began.

"Damn, look at all those Russians! Where the hell do they get so many men?"

The infantry to either side of Jenö did not open fire, the sergeant ordered all soldiers to wait for his command. Then, when the entire field was crowded with charging Russians all hell broke loose! The sergeant ordered to fire, and Jenö did! True to the sergeant's command, the infantry, as few as they were, put up a deadly fusillade, and the Russians went down, rolled over and fell on their faces never to get up again.

The sergeant was gone from the gun position just as suddenly as he had given the order to fire. There was no senior officer among them, so the sergeant rallied the infantry, and commanded the small group of fighters to their greatest advantage. He called them back from behind the line of fire of Jenö's machine gun for cover. Jenö was too busily occupied, but he did notice that the sergeant ordered these brave men to fix bayonets and follow him!

They obeyed!

They followed the sergeant in a flanking effort at a distance to the left of Jenö. The sergeant had no more than a pistol, but as soon as he emptied it into the oncoming infantry, he picked up a Russian rifle and continued to lead the few, what few remained of the Hungarian infantry...into that grain field.

Jenö never saw him again.

His crew stayed to the end in a desperate effort to stop the tide of charging men. The machine gun spit out as directed and men died. The crew used their rifles as support fire when the ribbon of bullets was in-loading from the machine gun... but to no avail. The Russians were so great in number that they just could not be stopped.

Two Russians had encircled Jenö's gun emplacement, and now as they approached from behind, only two men remained with Jenö. One fed the bullets to the machine gun; the other lay prone and kept firing his rifle until he was shot. The two Russians ran at the remaining Hungarians, one of them stopped, knelt and took aim, and shot the ribbon feed man while his partner continued to run at Jenö's back. The sharpshooter took aim again, and just as he would have squeezed the trigger to finish off Jenö, his comrade was at Jenö's back and in the line of fire. Both men were intent on stopping Jenö quickly, the sharpshooter was certainly smarter. He would not waste time. He could have done it easier and more neatly from a distance. But his comrade's impulses were dictating to the individual. He was intent on reaching the gun and whipping it out of that damned hand that held the trigger.

That is exactly what he did, clubbing Jenö's both arms with one blow and sweeping him off the gun.

Jenö continued to turn around completely where he was, in that squatting position sitting in front of the now silenced machine gun. He had a surprised look on his face; indeed he was surprised, and only now did he realize the gravity of the situation. As he faced the bayonet wielding Russian, he also saw the second man approaching with angry eyes and bayoneted rifle. Jenö's first impulse was to draw his revolver and shoot them both from where he sat, but both his arms were still numb, and the first Russian was already menacing the bayonet in his face. The second man arrived to stand beside his comrade, both now exclaimed, in a furious tirade, and indicated their intent with sweeping gesture of their bayonets upward.

Jenö immediately understood this universal language, though he did not understand their Russian. He thrust both hands upward, straight up, so eagerly and so swiftly, that, in standing upright at the same time, it appeared that the thrust of both arms upward had lifted his body into the standing position.

Still they motioned menacingly with their bayonets, to his left side. Oh yes, of course, my revolver! He lowered his right hand and reached across to his left side where his holster was. He would unclasp the holster flap and lift out his gun. He immediately received a rifle butt to his right forearm for this effort. It smashed his arm painfully against his chest.

"You filthy son-of-a-bitch," he cried. "What the hell do you want me to do? How else can I disarm myself?"

Jenö furiously attempted to reach for his gun again, but just as rapidly as his right arm crossed his chest, he withdrew it, raised it into the air again.

"Damn it!"

Many bayonet-wielding rifles now surrounded him; the charging troops had passed on, but for these few who surrounded him. He could tell that half of them were waiting to see what would become of him.

"Damn it; isn't there one of you that understands Hungarian? Tell me what it is you want me to do." And as they pressed forward upon him from all sides, he clenched his teeth in anger.

"Anxious to make a pin cushion of me is that it? You bastards! There certainly is strength and courage in your numbers. Do you feel braver now that I am helpless?"

The sharpshooter had consistently leveled his bayonet at Jenö's belt, now he jabbed the point into the gun belt buckle, and picked at it as though to open it. The gun belt was wrapped loosely around Jenö's greatcoat. In his anger and fear, Jenö had not been thinking clearly. When the bayonet proved inadequate, Jenö barked at the man, and extended his right hand palm toward the man.

"Stop!" He cried. "Let me try one more time, please."

With that, he very slowly lowered his right hand to the buckle. He continued to hold his left hand above his head as he deftly undid the belt and held it in his hand. The buckle end fell to the left of him from the weight of the holstered gun. It swung like a pendulum suspended from his right hand.

Jenö dropped it.

The many Russians surrounding him broke into ready smiles. (They really seemed not to want to kill him). Jenö gave a sigh of relief and muttered to himself.

"You dumb peasants! Believe me; I was more than anxious to stay alive. I would have done what you wanted, I just didn't know how, or what it was you wanted." Then cursing himself he continued, "You dumb ass."

He almost got himself killed.

He looked about him. His crew members were dead, or missing. He had not realized that he was alone when those two came at him from behind.

They prodded him on to the rear of the lines, one of them picked up the holstered gun from where it lay; several infantry men stayed with him, as he walked arms extended Heaven ward the entire distance. He arrived at an encampment, still accompanied by at least twelve bayoneted rifles and their infantrymen. A group of Russian officers, through an interpreter recorded his name and rank. They knew by his uniform markings what regiment he belonged to and who was commanding it.

His escort went into an excited description of how they captured this corporal. They must have mentioned that he stayed at his machine gun until the very end. The Officers, now grim faced nonetheless congratulated him, and made record of this fact along side the record of his name, rank and serial number.

"You have served your Fatherland well. Pity, but you are out of the fighting now for the duration of the war", Remarked the interpreter. With this remark the several Officers smiled, relieved that there was now, one less true 'Prussian' that would no longer decimate the Russian ranks.

It is a fact that some officers on both sides of this war admired and respected courage, even if it was revealed to be of the enemy.

Jenö was already contemplating escape!

Still, it was late in the year, and the winter was severe; "Maybe I had better stay for the winter," he mused to himself. Then to the other Hungarian prisoners, "We shall see what the room and board is like boys."

The captured Hungarians laughed good-naturedly, still nervous and giddy from their capture. The events which unfolded in the heat of battle, their hopelessness, and fear for their life was now behind them: they were alive! For now, that was the most important thing. Jenö was just as lightheaded and giddy, so exhilarated was he at being alive and whole.

He had come through this one unscratched. Bruised arms, but he fared extremely well, better than many of his comrades. He enquired about that brave sergeant, who led the charge against the Russian flank, had anybody seen him, or his men? No one could answer positively. (Süle Jenö would remember that one man and his bravery for many years.)

Russians, Austrians and Hungarians had many wounded there, behind the lines. The able bodied prisoners helped the wounded of both sides. They lifted the injured onto two-wheeled horse drawn carts. They noticed the scarcity of medical assistance, and the lack of motorized ambulance vehicles. These prisoners were, in an odd way, gratified to know that on their side of the front it was a totally different world.

The armed forces of the Central Powers were well cared for when wounded. Expediencies were exercised to cleanse and bandage wounds quickly, and then the wounded were hurriedly shipped to hospitals in motorized ambulances where they received prompt, life saving surgery.

On the Russian side of the front, in most areas, first aid was administered to the wounded once they were distant from the battle. There were those medics however, depending on the commanding officer of that salient, that risked their lives to aid and comfort the wounded on the battlefield between heavy active engagements.

The serious cases were placed on hospital trains that took them to City Hospitals inside Russia; here is where they received surgery. It just took longer on the Russian side to treat wounded soldiers.

Time cost lives.

Jenö was marched overland under armed escort, along with the few Austro-Hungarian prisoners. It was cold, and as they walked through the snow-covered paths, their great-coats gave them welcomed comfort from the chilling wind. They were finally far from the fighting, somewhere inside Southeast Galicia.

"With the onset of spring we shall see," mused Jenö. "Yes we shall see."

The thoughts of escape in the winter months of 1915-1916 were not too inviting. He would have to cross the Carpathian Mountains, and those passes are treacherously cold. He did not relish the thought, and shuddered to shrug it off.

"Let us keep our wits: meanwhile stay alive and keep warm."

TWO VIRAGS CONSCRIPTED

U nfortunately for Antal, that blessed double-barreled event, the birth of his two boys in 1914, was followed by a heartbreaking injustice. In May of 1915 he was called to active duty. At age twenty-eight, with six dependents now, he had wished that this war would somehow pass him by as the war of 1912 had. He was duly concerned for Bobbie, and hoped that he could have stayed home to help her raise their children. He would like to watch his 'twins' grow up, and wanted so much to see these boys attain manhood. Forced into an escalating war created horrifying doubts for him, and more so, for Bobbie in particular. She would be lost without him being at home and she would worry incessantly.

His brother Gergély was also conscripted in that May of 1915. With basic training completed, both brothers were granted leave before being shipped out to the front lines.

Antal was overjoyed to be home once again in Vienna with Bobbie and the children. On many of those days his 'twins' were, one on each of his knees as he told them childish stories and fairy tales. The two boys were entranced by his thick handle bar moustache; how it danced as the upper lip moved with the formation of words. Antal would deliberately flex and unflex his upper lip so that the moustache wriggled, and the older child would snatch at it playfully. What a happy time it was!

It had been too short and he was off again.

Gergély visited Mom and Dad Virag in Porpacz. Geza visited from Szombathély as well, to see Gergély once more before he was shipped out. When the women, sisters and mother, were not present they discussed their brother János. They hadn't heard from him, nor knew anything about his fate. They also expressed anxieties for Antal's future, what would Bobbie do while he was gone? She had already asked her mother to stay with her until Antal's return. The young wife was delirious because of her love for her husband, and her fear of losing him. She would surely go insane if the war kept Antal away for too long for she loved more than most women. She did not easily accept separation from her loved one. She would not be able to cope: thank goodness that her dear old mother would be with her for the first while.

Gergély also visited the various places that he had worked during the winter months, when for him, farming came to a stand still. He downed a few 'glasses' with his old friends and companions, and practiced talking 'Slavic' with his Slavic speaking friends and the more agreeable prisoners of war whom he had met in the Szombathély stockade.

"You never can tell," he laughed. "Knowledge of another language may save my life out there. If someone is creeping around in the dark with the intention of killing me, I may be able to say something in his native tongue to persuade him to spare me."

They all laughed at the thought.

Finally, Gergély too, was shipped out with a contingent of infantry, and immediately reinforced a hard pressed regiment in Galicia.

All too quickly the new recruits received their baptism of fire. Gergély was in the front line trench, somewhere east of the Carpathian Mountains in western Galicia.

Directly behind the front trenches at a distance of about 100 meters (300 yards), was a second line, or reserve trench. This reserve trench was a secondary line of battle, a point to which the front line may fall back if the enemy pressed an attack. And in the event that their own artillery found it necessary to shell the front line closely, as when attempting to stop an advancing enemy. With prior warning the front line troops would withdraw so that stray, shortfall shells would not incur harm upon them.

Of course the secondary trench was also the reinforcement trench; should assistance be needed, men from this trench rushed in through intermediary connector trenches to help the front line soldiers.

The Russians launched a surprise attack without artillery cover on Gergély's front line, and within minutes the trench was overrun! Russians were in front of them, behind them, and even in the trenches. The struggle in these dugouts was too close; the Hungarians had to get out of the trenches to fight effectively. They had no better choice, they could be killed in the trench as the Russians above the trenches bayoneted and clubbed those struggling with their Russian comrades within the trenches. And it was as deadly above because logically, the second line of Hungarian troops opened fire from their positions to clear the surface terrain of Russians in an attempt to protect their comrades struggling above the front line trenches.

The second line troops were ordered to hold their position within their trench line. They were not to get up and out to assist the front line. They nonetheless shot at any Russian uniform in the mêlée between the trenches hoping that the bullets intended for the enemy would not strike a friend. The second line held; and when a cease-fire was called, these Hungarians could see only a few of their friends walking beyond the front line and with hands upraised in front of the retreating Russians; too few. The rest were dead, or too severely wounded for the Russians to be concerned about.

The Russians marched their prisoners, with Gergély among them, to internment camps in the interior. Here it was possible for some skilled tradesmen prisoners to find a job for the duration of the war. As a prisoner of the Russians he could still get paid for his work. But most of the neighborhood Russians coming to 'pick out' prisoners, wanted only farm laborers. Of course, for this purpose, they picked the men that looked the strongest.

Gergély had acceptable expertise in the Russian language, having exercised his understanding of the Slavic language. It now proved to be helpful when he spoke to his Russian captors, and the farmers who came to the holding camp. As a result he had many choices because all farmers wanted him, a prisoner to whom they could communicate their orders and have them understood. He reinforced his position by letting them know that his father too, had many acres of land in Hungary.

A kindly faced Old Kulak – wealthy, large farm owner – laughing and arguing with his Russian neighbors, turned to Gergély and spoke in Russian, "I don't only want you; I need at least six more hired hands that don't mind doing a good day's work for good food and lodging. Pick six of your friends there, and come with me".

That is how Gergély met the man whom he would grow to like, and whom he would refer to affectionately for many years afterwards as "The Old Kulak".

Gergély called to his fellow prisoners in Hungarian, and asked which six would want to work with him at the Old Kulak's ranch here, in the area of Uralski Vida. (It is exciting to presume that he was in the same town where his brother Janös was temporarily interred, and that their paths may have crossed. But Janös passed thru Uralski Vida in 1914 on his way to Siberia; Gergély was there a year later in 1915).

Prisoners who had preceded them in the early months of the war, and who were now working with tradesmen in the close proximity of Uralski Vida, felt obliged, and when possible, made it their duty to meet the prison trains that stopped on their northeast journey from the battlefields, they quickly advised their newly arriving countrymen to –

"Accept any job offer in this place. Lie if you must about skills, but try, try to avoid going on to the next internment camps. There aren't many stops between here and Siberia".

The seven Hungarian soldiers went happily with the Old Kulak; their spirits were high, for they had avoided being shipped to Siberia.

A soldier who was in the second line trench, and had been wounded in that same engagement at the front when Gergély was taken prisoner, returned to Porpacz shortly after his release from the hospital. The Virágs heard about him and in turn, invited him to visit. Mother and Father were eager for news from that front because they had not received any letters from Gergély, and were now anxious to get information that might be helpful in their search, which they could pass on to the International Red Cross.

The Virágs had searched for proof of their sons existence but received nothing more than a cold confirmation that he "was missing in action".

The soldier now told the story to them in the best manner that he could, uneducated as he was, and as excited as any soldier home on leave from the front where he had been with death and survived it. He was not eloquent, nor did he think of moderating the dangers of front line fighting for the sake of these concerned parents. He was not tactful, and was not about to 'soften the story', after all, he had survived it, and to him, that experience was worth the retelling.

"My detachment was in the second line of trenches. We could see everything clearly, for we did defend our position, sticking our heads up to shoot at the Russians. They were all over the first line trench where Gergély was. We saw our boys leaping out of the trench to fight the Russians who had encircled them. Believe me, there were so many Russians in that attack they seemed to cover the trench like maggots on a rotting carcass. We were certain that they would overrun our trench position also, so we kept shooting."

"Our boys in the front trench had an awful time; they were so greatly outnumbered. We were sure that no one could have survived, yet when the shooting stopped, we saw the Russians move back to their trenches. And a few of our boys were being led ahead of them. We could not tell just how many, nor could we recognize them from our position. It seems a miracle that anyone of them lived to walk away."

Fearing the worst, mother sobbed, "It is possible that God took him."

But the sisters and Geza kept up a continuous search through the International Red Cross, until the Red Cross replied simply, "When we hear of him, we will immediately notify you."

And that was it for Gergély as far as friends or family could know of him, and after that attack, the military did not identify any of the dead bodies as being his.

Jószi (Falcon) Virag was captured and taken prisoner by the Russians in 1916. These captives were put on railroad boxcars and moved to the interior of Russia, and yes, one of the towns they stopped at for transitional internment was Uralski Vida. (Jószi was captured in the year following Gergély. Things surely would have worked out differently for Jószi if their paths had crossed at Uralski Vida. Perhaps Jószi could have worked for Gergély, it would have been a more pleasant experience to be on the Old Kulak's farm where his cousin became foreman, than to spend wretched winters in Siberia; but it was not to be.

The Fates ordained otherwise!

Again the Russian farmers selected the prisoners for farm labor, but could not accept all of them, and the rest were sent on to Siberia. There were thousands of prisoners of all nationalities in this Siberian prison camp. Those Hungarians who had been in prison for a while were eager to greet the new Hungarian prisoners, anxious to have them in the same barrack to hear news from home. Each barrack contained about one hundred prisoners, with so many men in a confined area, and with each nationality attempting to stay in barracks with men of their common language, the cousins, having the same name, were thus brought quickly together. Jószi shared news of relatives and mutual friends with János; (János had been taken prisoner in 1914). Happily, they bunked together, and began caring for one another in that cold winter of 1916-1917.

They stated that it was so cold; a man's eyelids would freeze shut as he ran the short distance between the barracks squinting his eyes against the sharp, smarting wind. Smarting from razor sharp cold blasts their eyes watered, and the tear filled ayes simply froze. The harsh cold, along with the prison camp environment, made the survival rate extremely low. Prisoners were shamefully underfed and severely overworked.

Many men collapsed from malnutrition; others developed scurvy, or being weak, had no more resistance to colds, and a fever ultimately took them. Many died from what the prisoners called consumption,(pneumonia?), or just simply from the bitter cold life. The prisoners slept on wood cot-like shelves covered with rags, or they improvised the shelves into troughs and filled the troughs with straw. These straw filled troughs actually kept a man warm. A man could imagine he was warm when he bundled up in rags, but the straw filled troughs were more apt to keep a body warm, much like a dog in a manger.

Occasionally the prisoners from some of the barracks were taken out in groups under armed escort to scavenge for wood or to cut down trees. They were then forced to cut and split the wood for the barracks stoves; each group would have to cut enough wood fuel for their barracks and for the Russian guard shacks as well.

ANTAL'S EXPERIENCES

As the Hindenburg offensive of November 1915 pushed back the Russians toward their own frontiers, and cleared them from Hungarian soil, Antal was with the Hungarian troops. He was dug in with the infantry along the line of trenches that extended from the Galician border to the Vistula River. This long trench siege was a new kind of warfare to the old veterans of both sides. With these new tactics came new experiences also!

It happened rather surprisingly, and without plan, sometime during those winter months of 1915-1916, that some Russians and Hungarians exchanged comments across that cold, quiet, expanse of no-man's land. Perhaps it began with those Slavic conscripts. Antal was not quite sure how it came about, but there he was; there they were, Austrian, Russian, Hungarians and Slavs, in that undefined, snow covered void between trenches. They swapped wine for vodka, German pipe tobacco for Russian pipe tobacco, and they walked, and they talked together. Those familiar with the Slavic languages had no difficulty, they were all genuinely pleasant towards one another and behaved as civilized people.

One would have thought that these were not bloodied warriors but "friendly" troops. In this action of neutrality they seemed to be rebelling against the ungodliness of war. In this white landscape they learned that there really was not much difference between them. They were similar people, regardless of their nationality or racial origins, all had likes and dislikes characteristic of all humankind the world over.

All mankind are the same. They all have their fears, and they all have their confidences as they also have doubts. Above all, they truly want to live and let live.

Nervous officers on both sides of the trenches, with revolvers drawn, menacingly threatened their own men. After the first two days of bewildered indecision, they ordered the men back into their trenches. The Russian soldiers were chastised bitterly by their officers. The AustroHungarian troops now in their trenches, could hear the ravings coming from the Russian trenches across no-man's land, just as, no doubt, the Russian soldiers heard the shots and shouts from within the Austro-Hungarian trenches.

Soldiers were being shot; others shot back at those furious officers. It was obvious that a rebellion was eminent.

Headquarters Command in that immediate sector acted quickly, recalling most of the superior officers familiar to the men, and replacing them with new officers of equal rank. The new officers were intent on doing what was expected of them; what was expected to be done in any war; cause the soldiers under their command to fight...or else!

Headquarters ordered artillery bombardment onto the Russian trenches, in like manner, the Russians, having replaced their officers, ordered retaliatory bombardment. Thus a mutual bombardment of horror began, lasting several hours without ceasing. The newfound friends, the foot soldiers on both sides were punished for their show of humanity, punished with volleys of unfeeling steel and cordite. The officers totally disregarded the suffering; the hell-on-earth-without-mercy being inflicted upon their own troops, even when some shells fell short and onto the friendly' positions.

Before it was over, the men hated their officers; some officers hated the circumstances that created the need to abuse good men. When the bombardments ended, all men in that theater of fighting were filled with hate for one or the other cause. It mattered not what the cause; the once civilized combatants, those whom had participated in that gesture of peace, now became the devil's madmen.

All hell broke loose upon them as the men were ordered to fix bayonets and go over the top.

They were murderous!

Filled with an unexplained rage, and with heads still throbbing from the concussions of the ceaseless bombardments, those whom a few days ago were extending the brotherly hand of friendship, were cutting off that hand that begged for mercy, and bayoneting the would-be-brothers.

--- — —---

The opposing armies had encamped in the frozen woodland. They were facing one another but not engaged in any action, intended to feel the strength of one another's forces. They only knew that the other was there, somewhere near and in front. The Austro-Hungarians were on the alert, but not dug in for the night; still portable, and flexible to make change of position before nightfall and final encampment if necessary.

The river ran at a proximity inviting to both of the military camps, but both the enemy, and friendly forces could not determine if the river would be an advantage to have on one flank. Perhaps the enemy was already on both sides of it? How would the army be best deployed? They arrived at a new position and were in the process of setting out their bivouac for the night.

On both sides of the river mounted Hungarian scouts were dispatched for a quick reconnoiter into the area. The Officers first favored occupying both banks of the river as a precaution, and thought it may provide a strategic advantage, until the mounted scouts gained more information about the Russian camp.

This could be done before darkness set in.

These troops were the forward detachment for the main body of the army coming to join them. They were only one corps in strength, and the river now separated this corps; a contingent of men being on both sides. It was intended that when the main body of the army would join them tomorrow, and they were in full strength, they would engage the Russian camp.

The scouts found that the Russians had encamped on only one side of the river. Now both halves of the Austro-Hungarian forces prepared their camps for defense, a contingent on each side of the river. Several soldiers gave their canteens to one infantryman to go to the river and fill all the canteens. With true abandon, canteens hanging loosely from both hands, the infantryman approached the river. He walked casually along the riverbank looking for a clear spot from which to draw water. His canteens clanked and clacked as he walked looking for a rock or sandbar, some promontory to put him out into the mainstream a little distance from the shore and encrusted ice of the riverbank.

After filling his canteens he walked to the riverbank's wooded edge and sat down on a felled tree trunk to relax and enjoy the peace and quite of the scenery, listening to the babbling brook as it gurgled on its way downstream. Laying the excess canteens on the ground beside him, he relaxed and sipped the fresh cool water from his own canteen; as he did so, he looked through the leafless bushes and saw another soldier.

It was a Russian!

The Hungarian soldier froze where he sat.

The Russian, canteens in both hands that clanked noisily, was casually walking toward him, but looking out into the river, just as the Hungarian had done a while ago, looking for a place to dip his canteens.

There was a fresh, clean, smell in the frosted woodland. Their winter greatcoats comforted both men and so they found it easy to tolerate the crisp evening air.

The Hungarian continued to sit.

He thought, and hoped; perhaps he will pass me by. Maybe he will simply fill his canteens as I did and he will leave. I will not challenge him. The poor fellow and his friends want water just as my friends and I do.

As the Russian drew nearer, he turned his head away from the river and looking onto the ground saw the Hungarian soldier's foot prints. He then looked through the leafless bushes to where the footprints led.

He saw the lone soldier.

The choice was his!

The Hungarian continued to sit remaining motionless because he sincerely did not want to fight. It was too peaceful, on the edge of the woods with the river babbling nearby.

The Russian seemed momentarily paralyzed at what he saw: then he dropped his canteens and immediately sprung to the attack.

The Hungarian was abruptly up on his feet to meet the burly fellow.

My God! I wished to let him go by peacefully; what a fool I am.

Was it destiny? Does a soldier believe in destiny, fate perhaps?

They met in peace. Could they not leave in peace? Here in this quiet, peacefully inviting place, could they not fulfill that purpose, to fill their canteens. Who would be the wiser? Why could they not be peaceful?

The devil wishes peace for no one!

The Russian was upon him.

As they grappled one another, try as he might the Hungarian could not free his hand to reach the bayonet on his belt. If only he had not been so foolish; the encounter had been so unpredictably sudden. He was hoping for a peaceful encounter but, what the hell, it wasn't his idea and damned if he will suffer an insult to this rude man.

They struggled, standing upright the entire time. The Hungarian, at the best of his exertions, could only keep one hand on the chest, then with that same hand to clutch the throat of the big man. The Russian now held the Hungarian's other hand above their heads.

The Hungarian soon realized that he was no match for the man who, now suddenly left the Hungarian's hand in the air above their heads, and quickly applied a crushing bear hug with both his strong arms. They turned about as they struggled. Frantically, the Hungarian tried to reach the bayonet in its scabbard. Once he even had his fingers on its hilt, but to no avail. He was now gasping for air in that deadly bear hug.

He became frantic.

What more could he do? He felt certain that his back would be broken and his ribs would be crushed in that awful squeezing embrace.

Suddenly, the pressure on his back and aching ribs ceased. He could breathe again! The Russian had released him, and now stood before him with a look of disbelief on his face. With arms opened, but still in an attitude of clutching, the Russian bear fell onto his knees. He would have fallen into the Hungarian's arms, one of which now held the desperately sought for bayonet, except that the Hungarian stepped back gingerly and to one side. The Russian fell flat onto the pebbled riverbank. With his face on the snow covered ground, his two hands clutched the pebbles beneath the snow, and then he relaxed.

The Russian had been shot in the back as they struggled!

Run! No stopping, run!

Back along the way you came! Leave the canteens where they are, and run. And run he did. The bullet could have been meant for him. A Russian may have shot at his back... just as they had turned about!

Returning amongst his friends he was greeted with laughter and much jesting. He did not have to explain his terror, or why he came back empty handed. His friends explained it to him; a Hungarian from across the river had noticed the struggle and shot at the big man in enemy uniform. His friends had heard the single shot and ran to see if "he had bought it". They saw the body behind the running man, and looking to the other side of the river they also saw the Hungarian who did the shooting. With rifle extended high in one hand, the other hand waving his hat at them, happy that he had saved a countryman.

As he thought about his unknown savior he heard such comments as, "you were lucky friend".

The more he thought about it, the more he wondered, and agreed with them. As they struggled, and as they turned about, suppose it was his back suddenly shot by his own countryman? He also reflected on how often he had seen a bullet rip through a man's body and continue in flight. This bullet, remarkably enough did not, but it could have penetrated both men.

Yes, he agreed that he was truly lucky.

He suddenly felt a chill, and so he went to the campfire to warm himself. The shaking was more from fear, but he let his friends interpret it as due to the crisp evening. He met Antal who was also seeking the warmth of the campfire, and recited the events of his recent experience. Antal could not disagree, his friend of the campfire was indeed, miraculously fortunate

Antal continued the conversation for he saw that this man would be troubled for a while, besides, Antal needed someone to talk to. His own mind was heavy with the thoughts of home. He told the man that his brother Gergély was somewhere on this Russian Front also, only his younger brother Geza was left of all the boys. The family had not heard from the older brother János since he left for the front in 1914. And, Antal told his new companion that he had wished to be passed over for enlistment because of the concern he had for his young family. He also explained, with halting words, how reluctantly he had bid farewell to his beloved Bobbie.

The May 1915 conscripts had been sent to the south of the Eastern Front because the Russians were encroaching upon Hungary. They had swept over the Carpathian Mountains in March of 1915 and pushed on into Hungarian territory, threatening Buda-Pest. Throughout the summer the Hungarians had stubbornly fought a restraining fight to check the Russian progress.

Antal dreaded the many bayonet attacks and counter attacks against the Russians who so greatly outnumbered the Austro-Hungarian troops. Waging death and awaiting death, are horrible enough, he reflected, if we were all Austrians and Hungarians; then you could depend on one another. The next man fought with equal fury as you did against the Russians.

But many of the recent reinforcements were conscripts from occupied Slavic-States, and these men simply refused to fight. They had no reason to be patriotic, and had no desire to fight in defense of the Central Powers. When outnumbered in combat engagements they were the first to give up. They were ready to surrender when the attack was against their Slavic brothers the Russians. The AustroHungarian had observed on many occasions that, the Slavs ran slowly in charging, slower than the deliberate pace of the determined AustroHungarian fighters. One could imagine the terrible plight, if a situation presented itself, where the Russians greatly outnumbered you in the front, and suddenly from among your own ranks the troops of Slavic origins turned their bayonets on your back.

The Officers had difficulty in allocating lieutenants and sergeants in a manner that, these subalterns would follow the Slavs into battle and threaten the reluctant fighters from behind. But still, at first opportunity when the going got tough, they threw down their guns and threw up their hands surrendering to the charging Russians. When it was their infantry that charged the Russian positions, these Slavs ran slower, hoping that the bayoneting and butchery would be over before they got to the entrenchments. When he was being watched, the Slav would run the bayonet into an already bayoneted and helpless Russian.

The deceptive action was intended to imply that he had fought and killed the man. This was more disgusting to the Austro-Hungarians than their obvious unwillingness to fight.

FRUSTRATION
AND FUTILITY

I n May of 1916, Italy was in dire straits and requested help from Russia. Field Marshal Conrad Von Hötzendorff's AustroHungarian armies were advancing virtually unobstructed in the Trentino area of Italy, and there were no major forces left with which Italy could challenge Hötzendorff. Russia yielded to the cry for help and attempted to relieve the pressure on this ally. Russian General Alexi Brusilov began a massive offensive on a 115-kilometer (70 miles) long front in Galicia. At first he was successful, and advanced a full 96 kilometers (58 miles) against the outnumbered Austro-Hungarian troops. But, as though to herald in the last spring of Czarist Russia, Von Mackensen rushed with German reinforcements to meet this new challenge and, assumed command of all Central Powers troops in the Galician area.

He met Brussilov's forces and defeated them!

There were more than one million Russian casualties; Russia never did recover from this defeat. She had, however, succeeded in relieving the pressure from the Trentino, since it was from the Trentino that the Central Powers troop reinforcements were drawn, and rushed with Mackensen to Galicia.

If my reader will pause for a moment's reflection: in 1914 the Central Powers never expected that Russia was capable of mobilizing quickly enough to become an effective threat to Germany's ambitions. Yet, Russia sent massive numbers of troops to attack East Prussia; and in so doing, caught the German High Command totally by surprise. Russia was, truthfully, obliging her ally France; but she should not have jumped into the war so hastily and so ill prepared. Germany's military strategists guessed correctly, Russia could not be effective if she jumped into the fight suddenly and without proper preparation. Russian military leaders also gravely erred in many of their decisions. They lost thousands of troops at Tannenburg, Annenburg, and in the Masurian Lakes region. Two whole armies of her own were shattered and broken...but she did relieve the pressure on France.

The German troops that defeated Russia in East Prussia were the troops chosen originally, in the allocation of manpower, to fight on the Marne. On September 5, 1914, when the Battle of The Marne was being fought, the French were fortunate, and should thank Mother Russia that they did not have to contend with those additional German forces.

In like manner, the Italians were most fortunate that they were spared in this May 1916 attack on the Trentino...at such a terrible expense, again, to Mother Russia. I wonder if the Western Allies realize just how much more Russia actually bled for them. Was it necessary? Would the Allies have done the same for Russia?

The politicians quickly answer in defense, and exclaim; but she had the troops! She had millions to draw from, whereas we did not. If you don't have them you can't use them! Obviously then, Russia's Allies could not help her when she most needed help.

Von Mackensen was a most merciless opponent. His strategy was to break the resistance of the opposing army; it mattered not how he did this. When the opposition broke ranks and retreated, he pursued them and continued the pursuit to piecemeal every pocket of resistance. If there was only a slight breach in the enemy's defenses, he poured his troops through that little breach, and kept pouring them in until all resistance on either side of the breach weakened and collapsed. With the enemy forces in retreat, he kept pushing them, and they rolled over, unable to stop the thrust. He kept up the advance behind the broken line of resistance, until all possible chance of stragglers regrouping was wiped out. He pressed every advantage and left none for his opponent.

The picture I have of this man, (and from what was told by those who served under him) was that of a very stern face, with firm set jaws under a thick bushy handle bar moustache. His eyes were piercing, bright, hard and very cold; one would say the icy eyes pierced the personality of those who were viewed by them. In turn, the expressionless face was a shield for the thoughts that went on behind those eyes. An observer could not fathom the General's thoughts by looking at him. His silver hair was crowned with a huge fur hat; this fur hat was massive, and appeared to be huge in proportion to the head that carried it.

The aggressive General shattered the Russian forces, and pushed them back. He continued to push and did not stop until they had crossed the San River. The Russians abandoned Przemyl for the last time, and on June 22, lost Lemberg also, that expensive gem in the eyes of the Czarist armies. Lemberg was the greatest victory that the Russians had in the war and, it came at a time when they needed a victory, after their terrible defeat at Angerberg against Hindenburg on that fateful day of September 2, 1914.

Von Mackensen mercilessly pushed his attack into northern Galicia, while Hindenburg pressed the Russians in the region of Estonia and Petrograd. By mid July a great struggle existed along a front almost 1600 kilometers in length (about 960 miles). The German forces set Warsaw and Ivangorod as their objectives, and reached these objectives August 5-6. By mid August, Hindenburg's armies reached Brest Litovsk.

In August of 1916, Roumania entered the war thinking to aid the Allies. On the 27th of August she had the audacity to invade Transylvania. Her armies actually crossed the

Carpathian Mountains behind the major Austro-Hungarian forces that had pushed so far eastward in chasing the Russians. This brashness on her part was most commendable, and intended to relieve some of the pressure on the Russian forces retreating in that region. But she came upon the scene too late. Russia could not recover, and could not join forces with the Roumanians to cut off the Austro-Hungarian troops in the southern sector of that long eastern front.

Von Hindenburg continued his drive against the Russians and drove them to East of the Dvina River by mid September.

Von Mackensen pushed on also to Pinsk in Russia, on the edge of the Pripet Marshes.

--- — — ---

A lot of lives had been expended in these last few months thought Antal, as he extended his hands toward the heat radiating from the campfire. His friend of the 'water canteens' had finished the story of his frightening experience at the river. Antal reflected again upon the circumstances about him, and sighed. The Russian was dead; no doubt his body at this moment, drained of its warming lifeblood was beginning to freeze where it fell. Antal's companion was still at the fire, warming his hands to ward of the winter chill and the inner fears that caused him to shiver. What a paradox, one body is cold in death another is cold in life. The dampness of the marshes thoroughly chilled Antal.

The Pripet marshes border the sides of the Pripet River. They are predominantly on the southern bank, but still surround both sides of the river. The city of Pinsk is on the northern side of the river and to the west of this area of the Pripet Marshes. The marshes south of Pinsk go by the name of Pinsk Marshes.

The infantry would be pressing on tomorrow against the Russians. It was mid September and Mackensen was anxious to take Pinsk before the year ended. They had come a long way on this offensive, and gained a lot of territory since their first encounter with the Russians, and now had completely pushed them from Galicia.

Perhaps we shall be home soon. Antal turned to thoughts of home and to the memories of his one leave from active service in July of that year, 1916, and here it was September already. The flames of the fire were windows through which he could see another life, another existence. In his minds eye he was home again, at home with his lovely Bobbie and the children. His twins were again, each on one of his knees, as they sat by the fire; the fires of home are the warmest. He told the oft repeated childish stories, the fairy tales that the children enjoyed so much. The one born in February of 1914 was just about two and a half years old and the one born in December of 1914 was nearing two years. Their father bowed his head over them as they sat on his knees, and the twins were entranced as always by that thick handle bar moustache. How it danced as the upper lip moved, and daddy deliberately wrinkled the lip to make it move.

The two boys looked at the bushy caterpillar, then at one another, they wrinkled their faces and giggled as they hunched their shoulders and drew in their short necks: this childish motion that no adult could duplicate. As the father talked, the boys began to reach for the moustache. First they touched it cautiously, and then withdrew their hand quickly when father deliberately wriggled it. Then they began to pet it. It jumped as though alive, and they squealed with childish delight until finally bold enough, they grabbed it. One on each side, they pulled and tugged on it, and father made all sorts of snorting sounds, and deliberately formed curled lips to cause a tugging on the two ends.

Bobbie smiled, and took in the peaceful scene.

"Apu (Papa), enough of that, you shall get them so excited that they will not be able to sleep to-night". Then to the boys, "come now, wash up and into bed with you."

It had all ended too quickly. Antal now wished Bobbie would have let him enjoy his sons at play a little longer;

how he longed for his loved ones, he wished they were here. (Here in this God forsaken cold frontier?) He wanted to hold his boys on his knees just one more time, to hug them and hold them close to his breast. It was painfully unreal. To be dreaming like this, to long for Bobbie; why torture yourself?

You are here and they are not; forget, or go insane.

He returned to his buddies and lay down for the night. Their great coats and one rough woolen blanket were all that comforted them, unless they dug into Mother Earth for warmth beneath the crusting surface. They slept close to one another, side by side on the ground, some of them around the campfire.

The winter of 1916-1917 was one of the coldest and bitterest of winters. It started early in September, as some winters did in Europe one hundred years ago, but lasted well into February of the next year, with the harshness that reaches to chill even the marrow of men's bones. In Galicia, and the Carpathian Mountains, and in the mountain passes in particular, the wind swept in sub-zero temperatures that season. The men's thoughts turned to home, warmth, thoughts of loved ones and friendships. But many would stay here frozen to death. Those of the Russians infantry who did not die that winter, readily deserted in the spring of 1917.

On the morrow morning they arose at first light of dawn, and gratefully ate a hearty breakfast. Immediately after breakfast the troops moved about the wooded landscape and through the sparse clearings in the marshes. They redeployed at a distance paralleling the river and waited for the contingent on the north side of the river to cross back over and join them.

During the night scouts had gone as far as the Russian camp's perimeter on the north side of the river. They reported that the Russians were superior in number, as usual, and also had artillery that was already set up parallel to the river and ready to fire onto the contingent of Austro-Hungarians that were on the Russian side of the river.

The one corps of Austro-Hungarian troops could not hope to engage these superior forces while one half was on the same side of the river as the Russians, so they rejoined, and their small number moved westward. It was the intent of this small number of troops not to engage the Russians at all, and let the Russian artillery bombard an emptied camp. They did leave a small detachment behind as a rear guard, hoping to lead the Russians to believe their camp was still on the north side.

The Russians were a little later breakfasting, and the Austro-Hungarians had redeployed when the Russian artillery barrage commenced, intended to wipe the Austro-Hungarians from that side of the river, and then to offer cover to the river crossing Russian infantry. The small rear guard detachment stayed and fought, incurring casualties upon the river crossing Russians, but also receiving a great number of casualties themselves. Throughout the morning the Russians pushed the rear guard southward, but could not find the rest of the Hungarian forces. By the afternoon, Russian scouts had found where the main body of the Austro-Hungarian Corps had dug in. The river bent northward, so that the Corps was now on the west bank. The Russian troops continued their sweep onto this position but suffered heavily without their artillery cover. They had been strategically turned onto this marshy spot. The main body of Mackensen's forces would be coming shortly, and they would now be capable of outflanking the Russian infantry. The position was a good one.

If only the Corps could hold!

The Russian artillery was redirected, and turned almost eighty degrees to bear more effectively on the entrapped Corps. Once repositioned, the shelling was not too effective because of the soft swamp ground of the marshes.

The distance between the Russian infantry and the Corps was too close! But with each hour they did whittle away at the size and reduced their numbers. Desperately the small force hung on knowing that reinforcements were already moving towards them. The Russians would be outflanked, and the pressure would be off them. (But Mackensen was to have joined up with them yesterday! Where was he?) A runner had been dispatched as soon as the Corps had dug in, that was in late morning; the scout should be intercepting the advancing army, surely to urge them forward at a faster speed.

Each time the Russians charged, the Austro-Hungarians saw that they were shoulder to shoulder, there were so many of them.

My God! Whenever we stand to counter charge we are six meters apart! The best disciplined soldier would have been paralyzed by such a sight, but these Hungarians had been taught of Prussian discipline.

They expected no mercy and gave no mercy.

Without being too particular in the calculation, a quick guess would put the odds at more than ten to one.

The Austro-Hungarian officers ordered a counter charge only as a necessary expedient; otherwise the troops so exposed were cut to pieces. They could only do this as long as they had some troops left, and if the officer chose to take the risk of bewildering a wave of Russian infantry with their small group opposing it. The Russians were still not certain of their opponents' strength or numbers. It was, therefore, necessary for the Austro-Hungarians to keep throwing the Russians off balance.

It was a pathetic sight to see these brave men charge; they look across that six-meter space to the next man, and then turn to face that onrushing greater force. Oblivious to the dictates of conscience, they charged with a furious yell of outrage and cursing, this Prussian discipline made the enemy's blood curdle! The pride in adhering to the call of duty was awesome, and most frightening to behold.

As the day was drawing to a close, the Austro-Hungarian troops were running out of ammunition, and still the

Russians continued to push relentlessly. They had fought all afternoon without let-up, confident that they would be relieved, but there was no sign of Mackensen's approaching army; and now this small number of men was forced to fall back and give up their cover time and time again. Each time they fell back now, their lesser numbers began to show.

Resistance was weaker and the enemy pressed all the more furiously upon them.

Many of the troops simply escaped. When they fell back, they fell back completely and out of sight. There seemed no point in dying. They had fought well; if they could intercept and join Mackensen, ah, then, they would live to fight another day the more fiercely.

There were many dead and many wounded now among them in that position of last resort. The remaining officer shouted an order to fall back from the carnage of bodies and await the Russians. They didn't have to fix bayonets; bayonets were on their rifles continuously that afternoon. They would stand on the clear ground of that marshen edge of the woods covered with tall grasses and farthest from the river, while the Russians stumbled toward them over this last line of battle. The Austro-Hungarian troops appeared rooted to their standing positions. Defiantly they waited, fixed in that attitude of a final challenge.

The Slavic troops among them who had surprisingly fought bravely, and had survived the day hoping against all hope that help would ultimately arrive, now saw the finality; this was to be a last stand! To them it was an exercise in futility. Even though many of their people had escaped, the whole day had been boldly spent. This last act was unfathomable.

Why?

It was not necessary to die!

Just throw down your weapons; throw up your arms, and surrender. It's simple! They had seen it often enough that day.

The thinned out Corps were standing with bayoneted rifles along that line of attack. There was not a moment of hesitation; it just seemed that with this sudden change of events time stopped; *stopped as the occupied-territory Slavic troops threw down their guns and approached to meet the advancing Russians — - to give up without executing the final challenge.*

To the left and to the right of Antal the men raised their arms and stepped forward.

He was alone.

These brave Slavic bastards had survived the day unscathed, only for this; to surrender now? He would have shot them, if he had any bullets. He would have shot them in the back as they walked with upraised arms and showed their backs to him.

Desperately, he looked to the right, and to the left...and behind! Not one Austrian or Hungarian could he see! Even the officer, that last officer was gone. Was he killed? Was Antal the lone survivor of this once proud corps? What happened to the remainder of the troops?

(Obviously many had fled into the thickets and disappeared from the fight. They saw what the Slavic troops had done, or anticipated it, and very wisely escaped while escape was still possible).

He turned completely around, his eyes searched desperately for help, for some encouragement, for hope.

But there was none!

There were heavy brush and thickets to the left and right of this clearing, and marshes with their shallow ponds in between at other clearings. He ran instinctively to the right, attempting to make it to the thickets before he was engulfed by the oncoming tide of men.

He yelled as he ran.

"Are there no Magyars left? Is there no ally to stand and fight beside me?"

He still had time; the Russians were only temporarily slowed in coming through the swamps as they gathered up the occupied-territory Slavs into a group. The surrendering Slavs momentarily stopped the advance, as the Russians eagerly corralled and encircled them, happy to lead their blood brothers away from the fighting, and so to, to save their own necks by leaving with their prisoners.

But the surrendering Slavs told their captors that only a few troops remained, that this was to be the last stand. The Russians, now assured of victory, anxiously came through the tall grasses and every clearing; they welled out of the thickets behind Antal. These woods; that just moments ago were to the left of him when he decided to run to the thickets on his right, were exuding Russian infantry. He continued to run; yelling while running...for just one man to stand with him against the foe. With God's help, perhaps he too could escape.

If he could circle these marsh ponds, and make it into the woods beyond he may be able to cross the river!

Antal did not entertain any thought of surrender.

The Slavic soldiers had almost panicked him with their sudden surrender. Even if he expected it after all these months when it finally happened it was unexpected. Antal thought their surrender was a cowardly act. Now however, as he looked back upon it, it was not his courage, nor his patriotism, nor his sense of soldierly duty that made him stubbornly pursue the fight. It was one thought, and one thought only, that of his family...he too could escape...he could still survive!

Worse still was the second thought, that with just one more Magyar, they could beat a path through the Russians, and make it to the security of the woods. Surrender was out of the question. To him it meant internment in a foreign country, and he could not stand being away from his beloved Bobbie for the duration of the war. Why, he might even die in that country. He would take his chances on a fight to escape.

There was no one to decide for him what action or what choice was best. He had no guarantee that surrender in itself would not mean death. Soldiers on every front had heard stories of prisoners taken, and then executed while helpless to do anything about their fate. Antal would take no stock with capture, and he doubted a Magyar's safety as prisoner among the vengeful Russians, since this day the Magyars had killed so many of them.

Antal did what he had to do.

Each man thinks in terms that he feels is best for him and his family and so every man thinks differently from other men. In spite of what others would advise or suggest, not one of those giving the advice knows the total circumstances that shaped the man to think as he does, nor does any man mentally weigh conditions equal to another, and so each man's predicament is truly unique, and the predicament is his very own.

Now the Russians were coming out of the woods in front of him as he approached the expected escape route through those same woods. One, faster than the others, had already intercepted him as Antal turned to now attempt to skirt the woods and cross the marsh. Antal let out a bellow, and without stopping, parried the Russian's bayonet thrust with the broadside of his rifle, deflecting it with the rifle butt and turning his body into the Russian, he knocked the man to the ground. Immediately he swung the bayonet-end forward into, and through the prone Russian. He paid no heed to the Russian's plaintiff cry!

What the hell? He was alone! Outnumbered and marked for death; if he hesitated for mercy's sake it is he that will die. His was such an angry fury that the rifle barrel almost entered the wound. Retracting of the rifle was also equally furious and powerful, as the finger guard of the bayonet pulled out entrails.

He was a savage, a wild man, now desperately fighting for survival. He lashed out with superhuman strength and purpose. He thought only to survive! He must survive!

The instinct of self-preservation is marvelous. Unless one has experienced this, or seen it, it cannot be fully understood, nor can words explain in a comprehending manner what motivates a living creature to continue to struggle in the face of impending disaster...when all hope is gone. Antal's breathing became measured and deliberate; his mind was nimble and alert. All his senses were suddenly keener.

He had, at the moment of committing murder, heard a loud cry:

"Over here!"

He looked while he ran toward the cry. It was a soldier in the familiar gray uniform and great coat of the Central Powers. This figure ran towards him so that very quickly the two running men closed the gap between them. They faced one another, they were the last; they did not recognize one another. They only knew that both were Magyar and warmly received the other's presence.

They met, no words were exchanged; their glances were a grim acknowledgement of their purpose as they quickly turned back to back.

They would defend one another's back!

It was warmly encouraging to have a countryman to back you up. *You knew that you could depend on him.*

The bayoneted rifle, extended in front of the body, was their only shield, and none too soon.

Countless Russians quickly encircled them. They too with bayoneted rifles, like a mob they pushed and jostled one another to get a jab at these two ridiculously defiant Magyars.

And they lost a few.

The two could not actually, in all safety; thrust and bayonet at will, for this would leave their sides and underarms exposed and open. They had their hands full and wits at end to simply deflect the thrusts, and ward off the blows of rifle butts and jabbing bayonets. The few Russians that did go down in that deadly circle, were probably pinioned or clubbed by their own anxious comrades as they bayoneted and battered blindly in the direction of the two men. The two men may have, with lucky blows, killed one or two.

Foolish Russian rabble!

Behold, the two lowly creatures' courage. How awe-full they stand, to strike, slap, and thrust but will not cower from your numbers. For indeed, there could be at least forty Russians encircling the two at any one time...but only six, or less could actually strike at once at either man.

So, what matter the size of the mob? The madmen dared, and defied death.

How long they fought? They knew not.

The Russians did thin out. They left these two to a goodly number more intent upon the outcome. Their greater numbers went on to scour the swamps and marshes for more of the enemy.

The two did tire.

The rifles themselves were heavy, let alone to wield and batter with. The final encounter that broke up the circle of death was like all the encounters before it...except that now, now the arms were tired and numb.

Three Russians attacked Antal at once using their guns as clubs, grasping the barrel and using the heavy butt-end. In this manner they succeeded in staying a rifle length distant from Antal's bayonet. They had learned from their wounded comrades to stay at a distance. As the rifles swung above their heads, many Russians were forced to back off, for fear of being hit by their own men. Three battered and battered at Antal, until he warded off the impending blow to the head, and received two to the arms. His arms, numbed from the blows and the fatigue of fighting, now became useless.

His bayoneted rifle fell forward out of his hands, as he crumpled to the ground onto his knees in anguish.

God! Are both arms broken?

But the most horrible thought!

He did not like the feeling that he left the vacant back of his countryman exposed as he fell to the ground. He did not like it at all, but he was now helpless!

As his knees hit the ground, he threw himself forward to avert another blow directed at his head, and received it on his back. His numb, unfeeling hands hit the ground; as his hands touched the ground he was in a crawling position. He felt the crisp frozen ground, trampled underfoot by so many men. He looked forward from his half-meter height above the ground at his aggressors' legs... and saw a tunnel of escape there before him, with legs astride for its roof. Without thought of consequences, more from desperation, he entered, and crawled, bowling over a few startled men as he went, he crawled through to the open, stood up, and ran as fast as he could, great coat flying at his knees. It seemed to carry him above the marsh grasses, and he ran pell-mell through the tall grass and dry bullrushes.

Not once did he look back!

He looked only forward to the other side of the pond in front of him, where it was now free from men. Perhaps there, on the other side, he could penetrate the thicket and escape. His heart heaved with hope. He ran through the swamp grass, the thin ice-crusted surface; into the water, and through the mud he ran... until he was brought down!

It must have been a powerful son-of-a-bitch that dealt him the blow. It was delivered to the small of his back and the force continued to propel him forward, faster than his legs could keep up with. He plummeted to the ground on the other side of that shallow pond, and lay there. Up to his breast in the water he lay face down, with his shoulders and hatless head on the frozen mud of shore.

He rolled over to look up.

Where the hell is that Russian? He would have had to been in the water to hit me like that. I saw no man in the pond.

Antal did not realize it then; he had been shot in the back.

His adversaries could not tolerate the thought of letting him make good his escape after defying them so boldly.

They had shouted at him to stop, but of course he had not heard, did not understand or would not yield.

His mind was like the mind of a fleeing animal, oblivious to the shouting and loud cries of man. He had only the thought of open space and freedom ahead of him.

Since he continued to run, and escape seemed imminent, many Russians had cast a hurried shot after his fleeing back. One lucky shot had found its unfortunate target.

The poor creature was felled!

Antal felt at peace with the world; he had tried. He had fought all day. He was tired, and now, as he lay partly on the ground and partly in the pond, he heaved a great sigh, and rested. He just could not move. He had spent his energy, and no matter how uncomfortably cold his body felt as he lay immersed in the marshen mud, he could not move.

He looked up at the sky. It was gathering dusk; soon the night would be upon him with its warm comforter of darkness.

Maybe...just maybe, he thought, as he looked at the graying clouds moving like phantoms overhead in the quickly darkening sky, all is not lost yet.

The Russians had now reached the spot where they saw him fall. Antal saw a semicircle of emotionless faces around him silhouetted against the gray, still sky. What a horrible nightmare. He did not yet know how badly he was wounded. The cold water mercifully deadened the pain.

Even now that I am down, they won't leave me alone.

They were jabbering above him as the blood stained water encircled in an enlarging circle about his waist. They noted that he slowly closed his eyes, and in a final relaxing of muscles his head rolled to the right, and he lay very still.

Nonsense what they jabber about, were Antal's last thoughts.

He didn't feel the broadside of the boot that kicked him in the back of the head. Thus, with no response from the body, they left him.

ANTAL'S ORDEAL

The cold, September night was filled with stars that occasionally peeked out from behind the slowly moving cloud formations. The night was very still, with the hush of a Cathedral-like silence, as though in reverence for those who died that day. Not one warm blooded woodland animal stirred. None had dared to stay, for they had seen the carnage and slaughter wrought by those warm blooded two legged animals during the "ritual of the bloodletting".

The woodland creatures had escaped this sector with all the shelling, shooting, chaos and violence. It would be several days before animals would again have the courage to come back. And if the frosts of winter were not kind, they might be forced to leave again, the stench would be unbearable...except to the wolves and carnivores of similar appetites. These lowly creatures would eat the flesh of the two-legged dead who could not be found by their two-legged kind, to be spared from such a fate.

It was so very quiet. By mid-time of the darkness hours, even the wounded had stopped their moaning; the frosts of that final darkness had stilled their breath for all time.

Antal awoke, shivering.

He could not stop from shaking, his teeth almost chattered out of his head. He looked about him trying to determine why he was so cold. Foremost in his mind was to get warmth, warmth of a fire for heat. He remembered the warmth of two nights before, its flaming warmth upon his outstretched hands, and the warm thoughts that it also provided. In his mind's eye, he again enjoyed the sight of his two boys tugging at his handle bar moustache, as they sat each astride one of his knees.

That moustache was now crusted with frozen mud; his right cheek was caked with mud. He looked up at the dark night sky, and wondered if he would ever see his loved ones again. But, he had tried before, and he had come so close; hadn't he?

He must try again! While there is life there is hope.

While there is the slightest ray of hope,
he struggles.
His mind stays troubled, as it tries to cope
and he suffers dreams, misty eyed.
With hope, he struggles: again he tried!
For the dreams torment, thoughts please,
and encourage mercilessly – again he tries!
His body, wracked with pain, fights against the lies –
but can find no cease.
Logic screams: "Remove all hope!"
That the man, no longer troubled by hope –
Can rest in peace.

His mind wracked with anxiety, struggled confusedly to combat the cold. His body was getting numb from the cold, but he was now also aware of his wound and loss of blood; warm blood that he needed so much to keep him from freezing.

Thoughts very slowly took the form of action. Very tediously, the dictates of his brain reached his freezing muscles.

Like some ponderous, otherworldly creature, he slowly flexed muscles to move, to slither his body up onto the cold shore and out of the ice forming on the pond. He would not roll onto his belly. He knew that he should surely die if he exposed his wet back to the freezing night air. And so, slowly, ponderously, painfully, he extricated his body from out of the muddy bottom. His two arms were very willing. Even his feet pushed heels into the bottom mud, and strongly urged muscles into obeying, but the best that he could do was to inch his way up onto the shore.

Inch by inch, on his back he struggled. Occasionally he saw a star as it peeked at him from behind the gray clouds moving slowly through the night sky. The thought that kept him actively striving, trying, was the thought of home.

But he had one more thought, *one that may defeat him!*

He felt ashamed. A horrible guilt descended upon him as he thought of his last companion; that Magyar that had been his ally, back to back they were two against the mob.

Is he dead? Surely he was killed.

There is no other possibility except that, with his back exposed, his countryman had lost the fight...and died. Perhaps he lies there, somewhere on the other side of this pond. Antal wanted so much to go to him now, to apologize, and to talk with him about that good fight.

For they had fought the good fight; and like many good men before, they too had lost.

Talk?

"Why we had not spoken a word to one another; I don't even know his name," thought Antal. Tears came to his eyes as he thought of the fate of that Magyar. "Our eyes met, we acknowledged our commitment to one another knowing our fate, *and I let him down.* Because of me he died. I should have stayed upright and suffered the blows...that he could have lived."

But of course the outcome would have been only slightly different.

None-the-less he wished he could talk to the man, to ask forgiveness or, just to talk and know the sound of his voice.

Then again, maybe he had not been killed. But, was he? Was he also out there on the cold freezing ground? Antal had many doubts. But to go on thinking unknowingly was futility and torture.

He cried in shame. Tears filled his eyes, only to freeze on his face.

His efforts were not to go unseen; those stars, and the moon itself, bore witness to his struggle. It was as though the heavens urged him, prodded him, and softly, slowly, coerced him not to give up, not to stop, but try. That body, wracked with cold moved, and exposed more of the blood weakened torso to the heavens above. His great coat, soaked with water, was an unbearable weight to lift. Yet he dared not unbutton it that he may crawl out of it. His arms were both still full length in the water, as when he had fallen.

He moved them more frantically now, and pushed against the bottom mud to raise his body. His legs moved underneath the water, to push against the mud and help raise the body higher, but from the waist down he was almost paralyzed by the wound and the cold water.

How long he struggled; in wretched misery, quietly, in agony? He had, after an eternity, raised himself to where his body was now in the pond from the buttocks down. His wound was just about out of the water. The small of his back became difficult to move and painful to bear. He relaxed his taught muscles, sunk down on his back into the mud again, and with teeth chattering, not so much now, moved both hands out of the water for the first time. Out of the water and onto his chest, he pushed each hand between the buttons of the great coat, and next to his body underneath the coat. Here they stayed. They would not suffer frozen fingers, he thought.

And then mercifully, he again blacked out, with that determined, stubborn head facing up to heaven, with the tears that he had shed for his last companion frozen on his cheeks.

--- — — ---

The youthful soldier looked across the short stretch of water and ice. That entire perimeter of the marshen pond was ice encircled, with a three meter encrusted width paralleling the shoreline. It left the entire center of the water open, glass-like. Not a ripple moved on the surface. He had turned to see that there was no escape from that clearing if the enemy came through the woods except across the marshen pond, there in front of him.

There in front of him, across the pond, in the morning still-air, a wisp of vapor. Was it smoke? No. It slowly rose like a plume of warm air, it rose mysteriously, mist like, challenging the mind as to its very existence, but with tedious regularity. It was such a thin, almost transparent white wisp.

"Bog gas?"

What was it on the other side? What was the origin of that rising column of bog gas?

He was young, and he was curious.

With quick strides he followed the shoreline around to the other side. His rifle balanced in his gloved right hand, his left hand in his greatcoat pocket, he circled the marshen pool and kept his eyes constantly on that almost invisible column, only glancing occasionally to the ground at his feet to pick his steps through the frozen mud puddles. The bulrushes and the grasses had been trampled around this shoreline. Hoar frost lay in the hollows, as heat of the sun struck the low lying ground so shaded by the 'rushes'. The hoar frost melted.

The mist may have been a trick of the sun, he thought, as he walked, the more curious now to see how this phenomenon came about. He was almost two meters from the source, and saw the plume like, wafted mist, through a space between the perimeter bulrushes. It looked to him that this narrow spot had been trampled by many feet, exactly around that odd looking hulk, *from which the mist was being exhausted.*

He almost jumped to the form. Were his eyes playing tricks within the shadows of the morning sunlight?

Oh, my God! That form, the very thin vapor exuded from the death mask of a face with a head of matted hair.

The breath of life!

The water had frozen around his waist, and his legs were still submerged under the ice-encrusted surface. His great coat was frozen thinly crisp and hoar frost covered. His arms were over his chest, the hands were under the now whitened great coat.

The youthful soldier bent over to touch the icen cheek from which frozen tears fell at his touch. He sprung up, surprised and frightened.

He bellowed; "Over here quick, somebody; anybody, help me!"

A few soldiers skirting about the woods heard him but apparently did not move fast enough for him. He pointed the rifle skyward and fired a shot, and then another. This brought an excited response, and more than enough soldiers to help him.

They freed Antal's body from the ice and mud. They carried him quickly into the woods to their campfire. The medical men were already heating water and awaiting any possibility from the last day's battle. There may be a few fortunates who survived yesterday.

The tear choked youth was blubbering an explanation to those about the camp fire about Antal; he never would have found the spot but for what he thought was bog gas. He narrowly missed seeing it as he stood in the clearing between the wooded thickets to survey the battlefield of yesterday from across this pond.

That 'bog gas' turned out to be the faint, weak breath of life.

He was among his own again, and alive! God had answered his prayers of that long, lonely night.

How grateful he was.

The medical corpsmen removed all his wet and frozen clothing. They drained and bandaged his wound, and now he lay wrapped in layers of warm blankets. His ear-tips and cheeks were frost bitten, but his fingers were not. Was he all right? He was very weak, very tired, and very hungry and, he was very happy.

They gave him plenty of warm fluids that morning to warm his body and replenish his loss of body fluids. Then they carried him far from the scenes of fighting. They intercepted the railroad tracks that led to Pinsk. Other trains were moving eastward, these carried troops and ammunition. Troops to feed more fodder to the cannons and to those damned war machines with their insatiable appetites for the meat of men. The choicest of a Nation's manpower, the cream of the country; no longer could they live a happy, uneventful life among loved ones, their bodies were needed for sheathing bayonets and blocking the path of bullets... their meeting with destiny was to be very eventful.

The trains would soon unload their war material in the east, and hastily return to the west for more.

But they did not travel empty on the return trip, they brought home the wounded, the maimed and the dead.

Von Mackensen won the battle for Pinsk, and he stopped, just as Hindenburg had stopped after driving the Russians across the Dvina River. The armies held their positions only because Germany was content with these fantastic gains. The Grand Empire had extended its eastern frontiers just as the founders of the Great Middle European State had laid it out twenty years earlier. Von Mackensen was needed now to stop Roumania's incursions behind this solid front.

Antal was bound for home at last, to Bobbie, his five children and his twins. Bound for the best hospitals in Vienna, how wonderful! They would heal his ailing body. True, they could heal his body from the effects of the cold water immersion, but could they cure his raw and inflamed wound?

My God how raw it felt. Just what damage did that bullet do?

What matter; if he was to live but three weeks it would all be worth his suffering? He would be happy to die after he had said his good-byes. It was worth that one, lonely, horribly cold night of struggling, to gain this time, to hold, to hug and tell each member of his family how much he loved them. This was better than to have died alone; so alone in that frozen marsh.

In Vienna the specialists did all that the latest medical knowledge could do in 1916, but his insides continued to stay inflamed, and *infection did set in.* His suffering from the effects of severe cold was rapidly over, and they did 'patch' him up, leaving a tube in his stitched wound that would drain off the infection. In three weeks they released him, and he went home to his parents in Porpacz in October.

There was nothing else they could do for him.

The doctors informed him about the seriousness of his wound and the condition it created. He was a good soldier, so he took the bad news like a good soldier. *His kidneys and his liver had suffered drastic exposure to the frigid water, his bladder was also inflamed.*

The bullet had opened him up, and as he lay in that pond all night, *the frigid water had entered his abdominal cavity.* Statistically he should have died! It was only his stubborn will, the desire to live to see his loved ones that had kept him alive!

If the infection miraculously cleared up he would indeed be most fortunate. The Vienna specialists did not intend to give him false hope, telling him the truth, and let him know that he was living on borrowed time. They gave him no more than two months to live, if the infection and inflammation did not subside.

But he was home! This is all that mattered to Antal.

He could embrace his wife; he could kiss her, pat her fanny caressingly, and feel her warm, sensuous body next to his again.

She was real, no more a wisp of fantasy conjured up to the mind in the flames of a campfire on a desolate and lonely battlefield.

He bounced his boys on his knees again! The war, with all its injustice and suffering no longer existed.

It is just that he was very sick... That's all.

He had received more than many dying soldiers could hope for, a reprieve from death. He considered himself most fortunate, and he thanked God every day, for God had given him the short stay of death that he had asked for;

the stars and the moon of that night in the frozen marshes were witness.

His older brothers reported missing in action somewhere on the Russian front were still not heard from. The family was very concerned and many a tear was shed. Only his younger brother Geza, sixteen years old and too young for conscription, remained of the four boys in the family.

Yes, Antal considered himself very fortunate to have a short stay among his own. He often romped on the floor with his children as the "twins" sat on his chest and tugged at his moustache. He laughed so hard at their childish glee, surely this vigorous play would loosen the infection, and miraculously it would drain out of that tube.

Bobbie took the children off Antal's chest whenever she saw them there. She knew it must be painful even though Antal said nothing.

She cared; she worried.

He reported to the specialists in Vienna once each month, other than that, the doctor in town would be available to look at the drain tube and his healing wound. There was nothing to be done in this impossible situation.

It did not last long.

He died in December of 1916 at the age of twenty-nine.

They placed his coffin in the living room as was the custom of those times. They lay him out in his uniform for his friends to view, as they gave their farewells. It seemed as though the entire town came to their little white washed cottage.

They shared in this tragic loss and offered their sincerest condolences.

Bobbie was grief stricken!

The last two months had been most trying for her. She had been on the verge of hysteria many times, and almost gone berserk. In her frenzy for his life she neglected the children. She could no longer hold a conversation with people; her mind was always on Antal. At times she was incoherent, and the thought process of conversation simply trailed off to nothingness.

But with Antal...she was his everything, as he was everything to her.

Such star-crossed lovers cannot exist, one without the other.

The tragedy here, her tragedy, ignored the five children. They were now without father, without mother, for she could not care for them. Her family and her in-laws resolved that some one must be with her constantly, at least until she gets over the initial loss of her husband-lover.

How wrong they were in their thinking.

She would never get over the loss of Antal.

He was dressed in his uniform, minus hat; his 'twins' thought it simply grand. They loved to see their father in uniform with his black curly hair and bushy moustache. But since Daddy had been put in that box, they hadn't seen much of him. Because of the height at which the coffin was, normal for adult viewing, they could not, as short toddlers, see their Daddy.

What is more, to their childish disappointment; they wondered why Daddy did not sit up to let them see him.

These two boys did not see their father except whenever an adult lifted them up to show sympathetic endearment to them. No matter whom the adult was, neighbor or relative, the children immediately turned to look at their father laid out in the coffin. While in the adult arms, they paid no heed to endearments of their person. They were more intent upon observing their father.

Why was he so still? Why did he just lay there?

He wouldn't even wave back when they waved to catch his eye. Why did he keep his eyelids closed?

One boy was almost three years, the other was just two years old, but both were frustrated because they could not look over the side of that box. They had tried to climb up onto a chair on occasion to see if Daddy was still in there, but adults always shooed them away, or turned them back from their childish efforts to climb the sides of the coffin.

Now, as evening grew late, the friends and neighbors had all gone home. Mother, grandmother and grandfather, and uncle Geza, were all in the kitchen sadly reminiscing, while the older children also sat and listened to these adults quietly recalling Antal's life.

The 'twins' pushed a chair next to the object of their curiosity of these two days, and climbed up onto the chair. Helping one another, these little men clambered into the open coffin and onto Daddy.

They had often played like this when Daddy lay on the floor; and they were both now sitting on Antal's chest, again pulling on that moustache. They snickered, giggled, and laughed as they used to laugh at his wriggling caterpillar of a moustache.

Only now it was still. So very still, and it just did not move. It was not much fun to play with Daddy when he made no sound, made no response, and he felt so very cold to their touch.

He would never again bounce them on his knees.

This was the scene that confronted the adults when they emerged from the kitchen; two playful boys enjoying their father for the final time had mussed his hair and disheveled his uniform.

Bobbie screamed and fainted.

Grandmother reached to lift one of the boys from off the dead man's chest. Grandfather caught up the second boy hurriedly, and the superstitious women through tear filled eyes, scolded the two.

The boys now also began to cry. They were confused in their childish innocence. They did not think that they had done anything wrong, and could not imagine why they were being scolded.

Grandfather uttered an audible curse up to God for this last gruesome playtime.

Geza will remember how, compassion pulled upon his heartstrings, and tears filled his eyes.

They buried the father of five in mid December.

The man of the house was terribly missed that Christmas.

For the children's sake the adults made as though Daddy was gone back to the war, and that he was not gone forever. The children somehow managed to grasp that explanation, for he had been away to the war and he had come back.

They had seen that he had returned.

Bobbie was at her wits end. She was totally helpless and incapable of caring for the children. The neighbors and grandparents had to step in for the family's stability.

The children reveled in their Christmas celebration, their stuffed stocking gifts, and ate a lot of delicious Hungarian pastries. They were, in their childish innocence, amazingly, very happy.

MISKA THE P.O.W.

Pista Valko was seventeen years old in 1916, and not yet shaving. He was, as most young men at that age, getting a 'fuzzy' face. But that didn't matter; his country needed him, desperately. And his country took many fuzzy faced young men to secure the cause of victory that year, and the next. The Central Powers were experiencing set backs in France; the long Russian front also required more soldiers; and the Italian campaign needed new recruits to relieve their thinning ranks.

He was, in short order, assigned to the Forty-Third regiment, and that regiment was immediately sent to the Russian front. The 43rd always took the ablest men; out of every Company of 'regular' infantry perhaps only two or three men were selected. When those selected numbered a hundred, (száz; a group of one hundred is a század and the officer of this group was called a Százados, in the English military a Captain), they were assigned to an 'elite company' to receive special training for their role as Storm Troopers, (rohamosztág).

Storm troopers comprised the qualities of grenadiers and riflemen. Not all enlisted men had the 'mettle' to qualify, for these were not only the most physically capable but also the most disciplined, and with a blind obedience to orders. Yet, most of their ranks were made up of young men, in their prime of youth whom life had not yet toughened up like some of the older men may have been. Through intensive training however, they learned to be unrelenting. These men were the first in battle, the first to charge the enemy.

Can you imagine Pista, this mild mannered, and gentle, Catholic youth in the ranks of the foremost killers?

How cruel it was to subject these Christian, God-fearing boys to fix bayonets, and run headlong at their fellow man, defying the older men that tried to stop them. If they were afraid, and they certainly were, their boldness was the more bewildering, the more 'wonder' full, the more 'awe' full that they did it! They obeyed orders dutifully and blotted out the will of God. That man can be so dehumanized and so brutal, is incomprehensible.

Only the devil could know how it was done.

Only the devil could imagine why it had to be done.

Only the devil could define it!

These storm troopers were drilled, and taught that they would be the first into the field of battle. It was they who executed the charge when necessary, and punched a hole through enemy lines for the infantry to follow. The Central Powers fire power in that sector was concentrated at the point of penetration; machine guns cut a swath on either side of their path, while the artillery and mortar rolled over their heads continually forward and just ahead of them, in a synchronous bombardment intended to keep the enemy heads down until the storm troopers were upon them and breaking through.

The grenadiers charged, tossing grenades at pockets of men that were dug in and might try to resist, and the riflemen troopers knelt shooting at specific targets of fleeing enemy. It was a deadly sight to see: more deadly to be a part of it.

Pista always wrote letters home to keep the family informed of his welfare. After the 1917 revolution broke out in Russia, he was sent to the Italian front, and again, he continued a steady stream of reassuring correspondence, when suddenly the letters stopped.

At all fronts, on both sides of the lines, friend and foe alike, generally listed the names of prisoners. The Red Cross of the captors in turn, registered these listed names, and exchanged them between the National Red Cross Services. In this manner the Red Cross was a godsend, and relieved the worst fears of loved ones who, without the Red Cross lists, would presume the worst when letters no longer came from their soldier sons, and husbands.

When the letters from Pista suddenly stopped, the Valko girls wrote to the Red Cross enquiring about Pista's whereabouts. The Red Cross unfortunately could not account for him, and needless to say, the worst was feared. The Red Cross did state that they would notify the family as soon as any news of Pista could be verified. This correspondence terminated with the Red Cross in late 1917. The family heard no more about Pista until the Red Cross again notified them in 1918.

--- — —---

Near Szombathely, in Vasmegye (Iron County), there was a 500-600 acre Prisoner of War camp. It had a surrounding fence, about two and a half meters in height, topped with curls of barbed wire. At the top of this fence was the typical overhang, angled upwards and over the prisoners. At strategic points, and the intersections of perimeter fences there were guard towers. The towers were about six meters high; atop these towers was a fabricated wooden shack where three or four guards maintained a continuous vigil. The occasional tower may have had a searchlight, but not every one of them had a searchlight because electrical service and wiring in Szombathely was sparse. The perimeter wires were not electrified either, and so, cutting through them was no problem, but only a few determined prisoners did escape.

Most prisoners were content, and seemed happy to sit out the duration of the war behind the wire compound. Still, others willingly worked in town. They received special privileges and volunteered for work which utilized and sometimes improved their special skills.

Some prisoners helped pick the fruit in the various orchards; with the start of cherries, then peaches, plums, pears, and ending with the fall apple picking. Others worked for the neighboring farmers helping in the grain harvest, or whatever crops the farmers needed assistance with. In short, these prisoners continued the work that normally was done by the young Hungarian farm boys who were now off fighting the war.

Prisoners with the related skills helped in the dairy industry, butchering, barrel making (coopers), wagon meisters, and blacksmiths.

Mihail was a thirty-seven year old, husky Bosnian, having served in the Serbian military, and was now a POW. Along with other Serbs, Montenegrins, and Russians, he was depoted here at Szombathely. It took very little attention to keep the prisoners in check because very few would leave even if the opportunity presented itself. The Russian prisoners in particular expressed the fact many times, that their 'welfare' as a prisoner of the 'Hungari' was much better than their lot at home. Many expressed their willingness to stay in Hungary when the war ended.

They felt no qualms, no regrets for their families in Russia. They expressed only their good fortune at being captured by the Hungarian military. It was a blessing to be here in a beautiful land of plenty, until military hostilities ceased.

Miska, as the citizens called Mihail, was none-the-less somewhat too proud of his personal war exploits against the Hungarians. He took too much liberty explaining in detail how he was captured, only because he was one of the last survivors of the Serbian rear guard. This Corporal was too damned arrogant in his comfortable position, and never failed an opportunity to expound about his exploits.

Truthfully, he narrowly succeeded escape from capture except that his Hungarian Hussar horse was shot away from under him...

...He had remained at his machine gun until all the rounds were expended and the rest of his gun crew were dead; then, looking around him at the carnage that both Serbs and Hungarian's had wrought, he thought it the best part of valor to get his ass out of there!

He proceeded to belly crawl as rapidly as he could rearward of the gun emplacement, hoping to reach the bridge and to cross the river into friendly lines. In this manner he kept his head down, and even the slightest clump of grass aided to hide him.

But Hussars were enveloping the Serbian infantry survivors on Miska's side of the river. They were either cutting them down with sabers or encircling those from whom the fight had fled. As a result they kept coming closer to the crawling Miska who, remained shrewdly low, glancing only occasionally back over his shoulder. It would be most embarrassing he thought, to be trampled by an angry Hussar's horse while in this lowly position. After fighting so successfully he could not bear the thought of it.

At one of those glances over his shoulder it happened!

He spotted a Hussar that had seen him, and was already charging furiously at the prone soldier, saber pointing menacingly forward and horizontal with the horses back. Miska was not about to extend his arms upward in surrender; hell, he was having difficulty getting to his feet to meet his executioner. He looked desperately for a weapon, a bayonet ...are there guns lying about, a rock, perhaps a stick?

Anything!

If he were fortunate, he could hit the Hussar, or just distract the horse's onward flight before the blade split his skull. Furiously he scanned the ground at his feet for any object. But how, pray tell, could anyone take his eyes off his executioner, particularly when the executioner approaches on a speeding horse?

And then, suddenly it was over!

The Hussar's chest burst into a massive red and his eyes rolled upward clearly showing their full white orbs as he

212 ~ *Anthony E. Virag*

hurtled backward over the onrushing steed. Just as he had extended his body in the stirrups in preparation for the decapitating slash a bullet had hit its mark.

Well aimed by a distant Serb?

Miska would never know, nor did he at that moment care!

Here comes the ride to safety.

The now rider-less horse was almost in front of him; just as the rider had led it. Miska braced himself; the horse passed him, so very close. He grabbed the saddle horn, and swung both legs into the air while pivoting his body to land astride the speeding horse. The forward momentum of the horse placed him neatly in the saddle. He gathered up the reins, and urged the horse onward, toward the wooden bridge.

The other Hussars immediately observed the enemy uniform upon the horse speeding toward the bridge.

They were furious!

The only horses in the area were theirs. This could only mean that the current rider had dismounted one of their numbers! Those nearer in position promptly attempted to intercept the rider, spurring their horses to give chase. Shouts continued from one Hussar to another as they hastily raced after the runaway.

Miska had no way of knowing that the Hungarian infantry had already crossed the river at several places, and were busily engaged in mopping up remnants of the Serbians that had held the bridge. Miska only knew that he was successfully eluding those horrible Hussars. As he narrowed the distance to the bridge he thought he would soon meet with help. Help that would shoot at his pursuers and chase them off, turn them about.

He did not know that he was rushing headlong into the hurriedly set up Hungarian bridge-guard.

As he sped over the bridge his happy heart surged with hope. He turned once to see the Hussars rapidly approaching the bridge and immediately behind him. He turned hastily forward again, eagerly he looked ahead; what he saw froze him in the saddle!

The gray uniforms; Hungarians were to the front of him, Hussars to the rear of him. Already the clomping of the hooves told him that the Hussars were on the bridge with him. The small arms fire in front of him was hesitantly directed his way and awkwardly aimed at stopping him in his flight, because of the possibility of hitting the pursuing Hussars.

Miska may have frozen in the saddle but his mind was hot. It was alert, ever trying, hopeful for any possibility.

His instinct for survival prevailed.

Just as his horse cleared the bridge, Miska forced it to jump down the embankment and then onto the dry shoulder of the river bank. He left the dust of pursuing horses on the bridge, and the smoke of battles still lingering was behind him. The Hungarian bridge guard was now to the right of him. Alas! That was a horrible misreckoning; they were all around him! As he spurred forward, ever widening the gap between him and the relentlessly pursuing Hussars, the Hungarian infantry on the side of the river that he had left when he first mounted the horse, opened up with all they had.

Firing from across the river there was no fear of hitting Hussars.

This was like shooting at the last duck in a flying flock; if you miss you're not going to hit anything. Small arms fire and machine guns hurled bullets like hail at this fantastically situated Bosnian. His Hussar horse was more than willing at his anxious prodding, over pebbled watercourses, logs, trunks of fallen trees, and boulders. But there was too clear and an unobstructed view from across the river; he could not do better than run parallel to that course now. He was committed to pursue that direction to which his decision had taken him.

He was a sitting duck in that shooting gallery.

Finally, a machine gun from across the river scanned the ground ahead of him and, rippled up the side of the saving steed and Miska. The horse went down, forelegs buckled, the proud horse slapped down to the ground with the hair of the mane like flames leaping in fiery defiance, unfurled, still in an attitude of speed. The speed that was just not enough to beat the bullets.

Miska was catapulted from the saddle to land head over heels, somersaulting, but still striving to gain ground from his adversaries. Before his body stopped rolling he was crawling on his belly, crawling into the overhanging underbrush, awkwardly dragging his left arm and left leg. It was more like a side-ways crab crawl but he did move.

He would still desire escape after stopping seven bullets, all on his left side, leg, thigh, and arm. He was bleeding profusely and in much pain. He finally stopped crawling when his right hand struck a booted foot.

He was thankful.

It was an infantryman in front of him. Miska's soiled face uplifted, looked into the grim face holding the bayoneted rifle, and could not help but smile wanly.

The Hussars had not got him!

Their horses were being reined to a stop amidst shouts of slaughter. The Hussars demanded the prisoner. The infantrymen exchanged assurances but would not give up their prisoner, and gusty laughter rang in Miska's ears. The Hussars admitted that he had given them a damned good run for their experience. They now turned about, and retraced their path to a friendly encampment shaking their heads with laughter, and in disbelief.

How the hell had this Serbian soldier outwitted them?

He certainly rode skillfully, and appeared to have been a master in the saddle. Yet his uniform was that of the Serbian Infantry.

He was not cavalry!

"Damn good thing there are not too many like him. We would be chasing Serbs all over the countryside like hounds after rabbits," replied the light-hearted...

...So it was that Miska was recuperating from his wounds in the Vasmegye detention camp. He proudly showed his bullet scars to those of the villagers who listened to his story and may have doubted the truth of it.

This exploit was remarkable, and the villagers conceded to his heroism.

But in the name of all that is right, sensible, and sane, you just do not brag about how many of the enemy you have killed — *to the enemy!*

After all, they had bandaged him; had nursed him, now they gave him food, shelter and drink. He was even privileged to work in the Government Factory at Szombathely, to further strengthen his mending muscles.

He had been a blacksmith at home in his native Bosnia, and now enjoyed his work here, in Szombathely. In one of his moments of self-praise, he may have deliberately exaggerated, and then again, he may have been entirely truthful, but he was spitefully so whatever the case. He knew in particular that Geza Virag could not, with his youthful sixteen years, and quick Hungarian temper, tolerate his tirade as well as the elders could.

So it was that Miska purposely picked a time when Geza was working with him, to goad the boy. Geza was to be his unwilling sounding board.

They worked together, this youth and the war prisoner. As they worked at the forge, Miska talked intermittently. This is precisely how it was with Miska while he was healing; it was that he chose to work...intermittently.

"My wounds," he would say, "need time to rest occasionally."

He expounded on another exploit in which he gloated too much, while the now licensed apprentice, and Graduate, Geza turned a deaf ear.

"My commanding Officer had asked for volunteers," boasted Miska.

The story went on this way...

...Miska willingly stepped forward, as he had often done. The purpose was to scout out the enemy, get behind the enemy lines and either harass them, or report unusually massive troop movements. Corporal Mihail took an eight man machine gun crew and skirted the Austro- Hungarian lines. They succeeded in penetrating, and then moving rearward of the lines for a considerable distance without being detected. They kept low by traversing river washes, ravines, and low lying terrain when not in wooded or shrub land. They were, for some time now, walking in a shallow gully, more like a ravine, and so they stopped to rest as one of them climbed to the top edge to observe signs of the enemy.

The man quickly slid back down into the ravine. What did he see that excited him so?

"Hussars!"

"Oh hell, let's get out of here, fast!"

"But they were not on their horses!"

"What?"

"They are cutting grass."

A smile formed on Miska's lips; a somewhat satirical smile. "Ah, feed for their horses."

With that, all eight men climbed to the top edge of the ravine that was no more than two meters high to observe. They appeared as eight heads in a row on top of the grassy edge of the ravine. Sure enough there must have been about ten Hussars, uniform jackets and hats off, using their sabers as scythes. They were mowing the tall grass; some cut, others swathed the grass into armfuls.

"Our chances looked exceedingly good— —-" Narrated Miska to Geza.

"Stop right now. I don't want to hear any more," replied Geza.

But Miska continued his narrative because up to this point he had gained a small group of interested listeners. His audience gathered around the forge.

He ignored Geza, and now went on for their benefit.

"We quickly passed the machine gun up, ammunition and tripod, leaving the supplies we carried in the ravine. On our bellies we then crawled as close as we dared to the unsuspecting Hungarians who were still a short distance from our position. Quietly; but where are the horses? No sign of them. How many Hussars may be attending the horses? Are they mounted?"

With these expressions, Miska articulated, and made body motions of stealthily sneaking up above the ravine and crawling towards the unsuspecting quarry.

"You had better stop Miska." The sixteen-year-old Geza dreaded to hear the outcome.

"If there are mounted Hussars what are our chances?" Miska continued to ignore Geza's plea. "Many thoughts entered our minds, but never that one thought which told us to stop, retreat, and consider a more timid objective. No objective could be as helpless as this one before us. It was most inviting and tempting. Their white shirts were stark targets against the green of the grass."

"Miska shut up! For your own good shut up!", implored Geza.

Miska only glanced at the agitated youth. He wasn't even upset to see that a few men had left, there were still some who appeared intent on listening.

"When we were as close as we could get," continued Miska, oblivious of Geza, "so that our hurried assembly of the gun to tripod would not be heard, we put the cartridge ribbon into the firing chamber. With rifles ready, my crew took positions about me in a line facing the Hussars. If we had missed our guess and there were more, we would have to fight it out as they charged us."

[They did what they had to do; what any good soldier must do.]

Miska slapped down the chamber top and, before the Hussars turned toward the audible "click", the trigger was depressed. Bullets spewed forth instantly! The crew with rifles also concentrated on any who remained erect.

They were, every single one of them mercilessly mowed down. The Hussars were butchered, with less consideration for their lives than that which they had for the green grass they mowed down to supply feed for the horses.

"Damned you!" cried Geza. He swung the sledge-hammer in a swift arc horizontal to the ground determined not to miss.

The small group of listeners scattered to get out of the way as the hammer struck Miska's side!

"You bastard! I told you to stop! Don't you know when to stop? Then I'll stop you." He screamed as he approached Miska who had fallen into the quench barrel butt first, and was now desperately struggling to stand and face this mad Magyar youth.

Geza would surely have crushed Miska's skull with the next blow. With deliberate premeditation he was raising the sledgehammer as he approached; the hammer was over the bent-in-the-barrel Bosnian. But fellow workers restrained Geza as prison guards appeared on the scene.

In the confusion, this hesitation was sufficient time for the broken ribbed Miska to extricate himself out of the wooden half barrel with the help of fellow prisoners. Once on his feet he ignored his agonizing and painful ribs. After all he had endured, and successfully come through in the many battles of war, this sixteen year old was now to be his executioner; with a sledgehammer?

Never!

He gritted his teeth; let out a blood-curdling roar from deep within his throat, and stormed headlong at Geza. He tore the boy from those hands that restrained the youth. Both went down, with Miska on top and grappling at Geza's throat. He would have surely throttled the young Magyar, but the same crowd rendered him immobile too, and help-less above Geza. He tried to kick the downed youth as the crowd lifted him off, but even his legs were being held. And, those restraining hands severely abused his broken ribs. He stopped struggling, now primarily intent about his pain.

Geza was now on his feet, still defiant as he searched eagerly for the sledgehammer. Who had taken it from him when it was poised above Miska's head?

"Let me have one more crack at his skull." He spit out the hateful words.

The guards restored order. The civilians were sent back to work. The prisoners were rounded up and taken back to the detention center. Miska was carried on a stretcher for treatment with the doctor at the prison compound.

Virag was sent back to the forge to continue working.

The next day it was reported to the Colonel that one Serbian Infantry prisoner, named Mihail, had received two broken ribs due to a 'fall' into the blacksmith's quench barrel; this Commandant, Colonel Carpatti, immediately questioned if the man was drunk. A person, no matter how they slip, cannot fall into a quench barrel with that severity, to break ribs.

Well; it was said that a sledgehammer struck him.

"Indeed? And how could that happen; like his slipping into the quench barrel?" Queried the Colonel..."He slipped against the sledgehammer?"

Finally, in a statement given by a sergeant Svetkovich, the truth was told. It was mentioned that the fall was due to a sledgehammer blow directed at the prisoner by the recent apprentice graduate tradesman, Geza Virag.

"Reason?"

"The prisoner provoked Virag."

"How?"

"He boasted about his exploits in killing Hungarian Hussars sir."

"Bring this young upstart Virag to me... at once!"

In short order, Geza was found at his work station and escorted by sergeant Svetkovich and two guards, one on either side of him, out of the forge area and blacksmithing compound, and down the road past the remaining working P.O.W.s, and the villagers. A sort of dirt path 'sidewalk' led to a white frame house at the center of one side of the Compound, and at a short distance outside the encircling fence.

He felt some apprehension. "Boy am I going to get it." He thought.

And so thought all that saw him escorted up to the Head Quarters building. He must have looked pale and nervous, because even the guards outside the Colonel's Office smiled nervously back at him; they anticipated what Geza dreaded. The Colonel would severely chastise him; he would be most fortunate if he did not receive a jail sentence for attacking a P.O.W. They entered the Colonel's Office and the two outside guards, one on each door, closed the double doors behind them. The four men stopped in front of the Colonel's desk, sergeant Svetkovich in front and to the left of Geza, the two guards behind, one on either side of the sergeant and Geza.

The Colonel looked up from his desk as the sergeant announced that they had delivered Geza Virag, licensed tradesman, as ordered. The sergeant stepped aside so that Geza now confronted the Colonel face to face.

"This is the man" – Exclaimed the Colonel, as he sprang from his chair – "who strikes at prisoners? Get out all of you! Leave this young upstart to me. You are Geza Virag?" The Colonel asked in a stern voice.

"Yes sir," meekly replied.

But looking at Geza, he was very surprised at how young Geza looked. The Colonel must not have been informed that Geza was just sixteen years old. For one so young to do such a bold thing, he had to have been seriously provoked, and have the 'guts' to go up against a man. If the Colonel had the facts correctly, Miska the prisoner was a thirty-seven year old, hardened veteran. What could the Serbian soldier have done to cause such a youth to behave in a most murderous and bold manner? It took some courage for a boy to go up against a big man like that.

"Do you know what you have done?" bellowed the Colonel. "I cannot stand for such behavior from any

Hungarian toward a prisoner in my custody." His face was livid, and the windows rattled as his voice boomed. He commenced to walk around his desk to approach this humbled Hungarian.

The sergeant and his guards now exiting the room glanced back quickly to see the Colonel's angry countenance. They closed the doors to leave the boy at the Colonel's mercy.

"What could a defenseless prisoner do? How could he have justified such an attack? With a...a sledgehammer! Why you could have killed him. What could he have possibly said to cause such a hostile behavior? Do you hear me? Young man you are going to answer for your actions!"

A crowd had assembled outside and around the perimeter of the Head Quarters, but stayed a safe distance from the building. These people acted non-chalant, not to be seen as obviously interested in the proceedings. They all suddenly found some work they had to do in the vicinity, work that kept them within earshot. Prisoners, villagers, and the ever-present guards avoided actual crowd gathering, but there were many more people to be seen about the building than there were to be seen under every day circumstances.

But, curious they all were; and a sufficient number did hear the venomous voice, now cursing, now chastising. All whom had heard were convinced that the boy was getting his come-uppance, they conceded that the boy was in a most uncomfortable and grievous position.

However, they did not see how the boy stood his ground.

He may have realized within his Christian, 'altar boy' conscience, that to attack a defenseless man with a sledgehammer is most unbecoming of manhood. To attack a prisoner protected by a prisoner's confidence in the rules of war captives, was most severely unforgivable to his civilized mind. Yet, his instinct told him he was justified in doing so and he prepared himself to expect the worst from the Colonel. He would take the punishment.

"Do you understand young man? We treat our prisoners with respect!" The rafters rang with the emphasis on "respect", and the Colonel was in front of his desk, facing the boy now but one meter from him.

"Sir, you asked me to answer as to what provoked my anger." A controlled, only slightly quavering voice dared to speak, and only momentarily silenced the Colonel's stormy words.

All the people outside noted the silence but did not see the boy hold his ground with the Commandant.

"This man was boasting of his murderous actions" – Geza spoke but was unheard by the crowd.

"I have been informed of that," interrupted the Colonel with a loud voice. "Tell me something I should know."

The people milling around outside again heard the bellow; prisoners smiled approvingly.

"Well sir," gulped Geza, "I have two older brothers missing in action somewhere on the Russian front. We haven't heard from them at all. One has been missing since 1914; I have several cousins still fighting on the Western front. We just recently buried my older brother Antal who left a loving wife, now a young and bereaving widow with five children to care for, and each time she sees the two youngest boys happily playing she burst into tears, thinking of her lost husband who loved them so particularly. He was wounded on the Russian front in Galicia; they brought him home to die at twenty-nine years of age."

Geza thought of poor Antal's frozen body and the agony he must have endured to see his family for a final time. But, he did not stop; he continued to tell the Colonel.

"I could not help thinking of my own family, my flesh and blood butchered by someone as arrogant and unfeeling as Miska. He was stupid to boast about such things to me. I begged him to stop, several times, but he carried on. The Colonel may judge me wrong," and he blurted out his last protestation, "but, damn it. I will not stand that kind of talk from a captured son-of-a-bitch...whom we bandaged, whom we nursed back to health. He should be grateful that he is alive and cared for, by the countrymen of those whom he boasts of butchering.

With that last outburst he stood firmly erect. He had said his piece. He could now take the Colonel's wrath.

"You won't stand for it, won't tolerate it?" bellowed the Colonel.

The prisoners outside were happy to hear from him again after that short silence, but they could not see the dubious expression on his face as he observed Geza. The vehemence coming from this boy belied the gentle nature of an altar boy; the Commandant would have been the more surprised had he been aware of Geza as an altar boy. The Commandant approached, he placed a gentle hand upon the boy's shoulder. He grasped the right hand in a most heartwarming and firm handshake to indicate his understanding.

He turned his back and walked a few paces away from the youth, to continue storming and cursing, for all to hear.

"Under all that's holy, we cannot allow your action to go unpunished!" He turned to face the boy, and placed his pointer finger on his lips to indicate silence; nodding his head, he motioned with his right hand that he was aware of the outside attention. Again he approached the boy with another blast.

"Do you realize, if word of this gets out to the enemy, how they may treat our countrymen who are their prisoners?"

Approaching the boy again, he put his arms around the boy's shoulders; in a squeeze of admiration. This scenario continued, with the lead actor the Colonel, expounding loudly enough for all to hear. Anyone who did hear was satisfied, and the crowd was unanimous in approving the Colonel's expressions of responsibility.

The loud cussing out may have begun seriously, intended for the serious chastisement of Geza, but now the loudness was deliberate, and for the benefit of those who were listening.

In this manner Szombathely and in all of Vasmegye there were no further problems from the prisoners, or from their

224 ~ *Anthony E. Virag*

own citizens in actions or confrontations within the Prison Compound. But no one saw the Colonel's acceptance, and acknowledgement of the act, nor did they suspect that he could have whispered, "Not a word of this to anyone Virag, do you hear? For if the prisoners become aware, they will think that I condone such action. They may seek revenge on you or me, or which is worse, on the villagers. Go in peace and try to curb that damn temper boy. I sincerely wish that you shall not see the war." These last words were an afterthought expressed with a sincere concern for the boy's future.

"Guards, enter. Take this man back to work. Get him out of my sight before I whip him with my swagger stick."

The guards burst in before he finished with his threatening. Quickly they ushered Virag out of the office, and out of the Head Quarters Building, but not before the Colonel had swiftly winked at Virag. Only Geza saw the friendly gesture.

Apparently Miska also got a severe talking to by the Colonel, and was thoroughly word chastised. But the Colonel also let him in on some personal insights of Geza's hurt; and the concern the boy had for his brothers missing in action, particularly the heart ache about Antal's death. Miska must have understood, and showed a sincere compassion because a new friendship grew between the old veteran and this young Hungarian.

Thereafter, very little animosity existed between the prisoners and the citizens of the County of Vas. A pleasant understanding and acceptance of this unfortunate situation that they were cast into because of the war, created a mutually tolerable harmony.

Miska never forgot the sixteen-year-old boy who broke two of his ribs, with the intent to kill him.

And what of the boy?

Geza would always, and forever remember that thirty seven year old Bosnian. This was the first, uncontrollable emotion Geza had experienced. It remained in his memory all his life. This was the first time Geza had experienced a will to kill.

Miska restrained himself from boasting of his dramatic exploits for the total duration of his internment as prisoner of war. He did make more friends with this new personality change and with one other Hungarian in particular, Tegla Karól (Carl). The three, Miska, Geza and Karól spent quite a few good times together so that Miska even promised to send a barrel of plum whiskey to his friends when he got back home to Bosnia after the war. The plums would be from his father's orchard; he would tell his father of these Hungarian friends and how well they treated him. He took down Karól's address, and memorized it also, in case he should lose the written address.

The Magyar friends made it as simple as possible for this foreigner to recite. The address they constructed was in four short lines but with sufficient accuracy to remain legible to receive mail delivery, and in particular that barrel of whiskey.

Tegla Karól (name of recipient)
Nemes Böd (location of residence)
Posta Vép (City Postal Station)
Szombathely (Post Master's City)

This friendship continued until the end of the war. The time with Geza lasted until Geza was conscripted into military service in 1917, at age sixteen, just before his seventeenth birthday. Tegla Karól was the most likely to stay at one address since he was not drafted. Who knows where Geza would be?

So the plum whiskey would be delivered to Karól when Miska got home. Geza could certainly partake of the barrel if he survived the war.

GEZA
CONSCRIPTED

Von Mackensen returned to Germany in triumph with the victory in Galicia. He did not rest too long from his successes in the Balkans however.

Italy had declared war on Austria-Hungary on May 1, 1915. Just when the German troops were severely occupied with fighting on the Western Front in France; the Austro-Hungarian forces were engaged in Galicia and the Balkans. There were German and Austro-Hungarian forces active at various places all along the Eastern front against the Russians, when the Italians set upon the unsuspecting Austro-Hungarians in this Southern Front.

The World thought that Italy would stay neutral, or ally with the Central Powers. France however, was convinced that Italy would join the Central Powers and, fearing an outflanking maneuver kept several divisions of troops in those southern provinces. But early in the war, Italy began to court favors of France and England. Secretly conveying a message that France could get her troops out of the southern provinces in France; and with further assurance that Italy would not attack. In this manner, France's general Joffre pulled the two army corps out of the southern provinces and reassigned them against the Germans on the Western Front.

Italy particularly desired return of the Trentino territory that was, at that time an Austrian possession. If she became actively involved against the Central Powers she may have it. Now meeting with promises from the Allies,

Italy pressed successfully the unsuspected in this disputed territory, against her former ally Austria. Initially she was quite successful, but the Austro-Hungarians forces held fast in Northern Italy despite the Italian treachery.

Central Power Troops were diverted from the Eastern Front in Russia to meet further assaults on this New Southern Front, and Italy's campaign began to weaken. The Italians reached the west bank of the Isonzo River on Austrian soil, and a small advance was made into the Trentino territory, but that too, was soon halted.

If one were to look at the territories gained on this Southern Front in 1915, the battles favored Italian gains in territory. However, when Von Mackensen was reassigned to active duty here, with German reinforcements, the Austro-Hungarians were exceedingly more successful in 1916. With help from these reinforcements, the Central Powers made huge gains on expeditions into Italian occupied territories, recovering all that the Italian surprise assaults had taken from Austria...and more. One year from the anniversary of Italy's declaration of war, on May of 1916, found Italy no better off than when she had started.

It was in May of 1916, that Von Mackensen began an offensive to destroy the Italian armies, cutting rail Communications, and he stopped on June 3. But in this short offensive his troops captured the Arsiero territory, and reached into the Italian plains.

Italians had tried a counter offensive, and succeeded, only because General Brussilov of Russia started a drive into Bukovina and Galicia. (Remember? Von Mackensen was sent from Italy to Galicia with his Austro-Hungarian troops to stop the Russian threat. These troops were withdrawn from the Trentino front; please refer to Chapter 24. Von Mackensen met Brussilov's forces and defeated them, incurring more than one million Russian casualties.)

With General Hötzendorff's Austro-Hungarian army again halved, the one half going with Von Mackensen to the Brussilov challenge in Bukovina and Galicia where Antal met his fate, Italy launched a drive against Sabatino, San Michele, and the bridge across the Isonzo on August 6, 1916. On August 8, they reached Goritz and routed the Austro-Hungarians from the Carso Plateau. In September the story was the same, with Italy making more gains beyond the Carso Plateau.

In October-November of 1916, the fighting shifted to the Trentino area, and now the Italians felt securely placed for further operations against the thinned forces of Austria-Hungary. (The greatest concentrations of German troops were fighting on the Western Front. Austrian and Hungarian troops would continue to be preoccupied on the Eastern Front until March 1917). Those few army corps serving in Italy would have to cope until reinforcements arrived, or new conscripts were sent.

--- — — ---

Rum-a-tum tum, rum-a-tum tum, it was a most ominous sound when first they heard it. It was heard faintly across the village and became louder as it approached the blacksmith's forge and compound. Just like a pied piper, it gathered a following of laughing children and barking dogs. Dogs that had never before heard a drum, barked furiously. However, there were some children, and their mothers, who slunk back into their cottage doorways. Mothers grasped up and held infant children to rapidly beating breasts. The drumbeat sounded dreadful to those who instinctively feared the worst.

The excitement of children, and some of the elders, soon drowned out the steady staccato of the drumbeat. Finally the drummer and his civilian entourage reached its destination, the village square. They were two mounted men; one had a drum, which hung sidesaddle as he drummed upon it.

A final and very loud drum roll quieted the noisy chatter of the women folk, the lilting laughter and squeals of the children. He was the army conscription Officer's drummer. The Officer immediately took advantage of this momentary silence, experience had taught him, and in a booming voice he read the proclamation to the villagers.

"Good people! My countrymen and countrywomen, I am called upon, by order of his Excellency Emperor Charles the first, nephew to our late Archduke Franz Joseph, beloved father of the Hungarian people, to make this declaration."

He eloquently tried to impress upon the crowd with emphasis on "beloved father of the Hungarian people." He continued:

"With victory eminent, and within our grasp, the glorious troops in the fields of the western battlefields, and those in the battlefields of the east, and those in the south of our homeland, are in need of a few men to assist them in the final push against our enemies. It is with this noble, and most honorable undertaking, that the Prussian, and all our allies, the Germans, Austrians and Bulgars are asking that we share with them, in this their finest hour."

"We call upon all able bodied men, married or single, between the ages of sixteen and forty-two to assemble within the next three days, to register with his Imperial Majesty's Officer herein represented."

"For those of you who are veterans and have served, and are therefore experienced soldiers, we ask that you return to that city, to the military depot from which you were discharged. Register with the conscripting officers present for those regiments."

And so it went, in somewhat this manner; many a father who thought he was through with war because of his past service, now reluctantly kissed his wife, and hugged his children goodbye as he held them to his heart.

The young men and older bachelors, some of whom looked upon this as a grand adventure, quit their jobs instantly!

Geza was furious!

Frustrated and confused, he threw his blacksmith's hammer onto the floor. It skidded for a considerable distance before it struck an anvil across the room abruptly stopping. He too quit his job instantly.

"They" finally got to the last of János Virag's sons. Now all the sons of one family were forced to face their fate! "Damn it!" He declared, "I shall not work another day if three days of liberty is all I have left."

Another young man of eligible age, who also worked in the same shop in the Government Factory, followed Geza's example.

Here was the excuse that some men needed to get good and drunk. Every koscma and hotel was dispensing wine, beer, and whiskey without let up, day and night.

For the next three days, while the conscriptions and registration continued, the good people celebrated as though it was Festival Time. Many a young lover got lucky with his sweetheart, where it was an unheard of possibility before marriage. Of course many married on impulse and on the spur of the moment.

None seemed to regret their actions.

Men and women gave of themselves freely to one another. It was as though every one either suddenly became bold, or they became very desperate. Lovers longed for one another. Their joining was an urge, a primitive instinct; that desire to be as one flesh, so that they would never have to part. For in parting, wife knew that husband might not return. Sweethearts knew there would be lonely nights; for some, an eternity.

The realists remained cool, and showed no desire for revelry. They talked of their possible fate. Perhaps desertion would be the better thing. Stories circulated how a family had hidden their kinsman, and he was yet undetected by the police. Other stories told how deserters were caught, tried, and shot. In many instances they were shot where they were apprehended without the benefit of a trial. The military police were judge, jury, and executioner.

There were as many thoughts in Szombathely as there were people. Geza had misgivings and fears too. Returning to Porpacz, he shook his father's hand and kissed his mother good-bye, his beloved, God fearing, religious mother. She promised to remember him in her prayers every day. Geza knew she would. He could picture her as she knelt before the crucifix hung upon the white washed wall of her living room.

The crucifix was surrounded on either side by religious pictures of Saint Joseph, Jesus as an adult, the Immaculate Mother Mary of The Bleeding Heart, the Christ as child piously extending two fingers of his right hand heavenward; the Blessed Mary again with the Blessed Child in her embrace. The adult Jesus was at the center position above the crucifix and the others were balanced in a manner on either side.

He had often seen her kneel there, before her *Holy Wall*. Yes, she would pray for his protection there, he could be sure of that. At mass on Sunday she may light a candle for him, and sincerely toll her beads; those same prayer beads that she fingered daily in her home. She would be content and secure with her confidence in God her Heavenly Father.

The religious pictures of the prime saints were mounted in simple wooden frames. In the corners of these picture frames she had inserted smaller pictures, photographs of her sons and daughters. She now had also inserted pictures of grand sons and grand daughters, and daughters-in-law. The saintly pictures had quite a gallery of earthly beings to support.

On a chest of drawers directly below the wall hangings, she had still more photographs of her loved ones, and saints displayed. So that whenever she viewed the saints, she saw her children also, and suffered a short prayer to thank the saints for her blessings. In turn, if she wished to see the photographs of any child or grandchild, she saw the saints; again, she prayed to offer a short, respectable "thank you".

Yet, thought Geza, all these prayers, her daily rituals were exercised for János, and Gergély, the two brothers unheard off for so long now. And Antal, for him prayers were of no avail. His young wife cries herself to sleep these months mourning for her husband-lover; and more and more depressed, more and more she pays less and less attention to her fatherless children.

Geza had much heartache.

He shook hands apprehensively with his friends, Miska, Tegla Karöl, and many others, and wondered: "what will become of us?"

Miska was particularly concerned about this Hungarian boy-soldier, he had taken a liking to him after their initial "murderous tussle". As bold as the boy may be, battle was meant for men. Miska grasped the young boy's hand in both of his, and sincerely wished him luck.

Geza reluctantly joined the new recruits as they marched through the village streets on their way to the railroad station. The many youthful conscripts converged there, on that cool February day of 1917. The singing and riotousness may have abated somewhat over the past few days, but now it increased in volume, and would not let up until the train pulled out of the station with all these young men, some very drunk and totally unaware. The train would take them to Vienna (Bécs), Austria. There were those dreamers among the multitude of recruits, who sang idiotic bachelor songs, some were cheerful songs, others senseless, and some were patriotic. There was one song in particular that went something like this:

Peter, a Serb Szar	*Peter, the Serb Czar*
Fel maszot a fára,	*Climbed up on a tree,*
Hogy ö onan a Magyar bakát	*So that he, from there the Magyar foot soldier*
Orbu le puskaszja	*Nose-on could gun down*
De piszkad le, piszkad le	*But poke him down, poke him down*
Aszt a Magyar bakának mondták	*Is what was told the Magyar foot soldier*
Vagy vegy suron hejdejre	*Or take him on your bayonet's tip.*

Baka aszt mondta:	*The foot soldier replied:*
Nem piszkalom, edje meg a fene	*I'll not poke at him, damn him*
Gojot a fejebe!	*A bullet to his head!*

Another song of that period went like this:

Meg áll, meg áll, kutya Serbia	*Watch out, watch out, dog Serbia*
Nem lesz tejed Herzegovina!	*Herzegovina will not be yours!*
Mert a Magyar nem enged	*Because the Magyar will not yield*
Meg a scöpp vere meleg	*While a drop of his blood is warm*
Akar menjit szenved.	*No matter how much he suffers*

Geza did not join in the singing of these songs. Those who sang such songs had no idea what a fighting Serb would be like. Among the sixteen year old recruits of his village and the surrounding areas, not too many had a better conception of what to expect than what Geza had; he had tangled with a Serb soldier. He reflected upon Miska, that was one hell-of-a-Serbian recruit. If the tenderfoot recruits tangled with the likes of him they would be singing a different tune. To dream of heroics how one would dodge bullets, and to dream of slaughtering the enemy easily, was a fantasy unbecoming of any sane man that had not yet experienced the battlefield.

The enemy is human as we are, as all men are supposed to be human. He has fears of death, just as all men in battle have fear of dying. Some men are simply luckier than others. That is the only difference,. Luck! The enemy too, have loved ones for whom they must fight and persevere. Survival is just as important to an Englishman, Frenchman, Italian, Russian or Serb, as it is to the Austrian, Bulgar, German or Magyar if he is to return to his home and loved ones.

The recruits boarded the train amidst cheers, and of course tears; as the train slowly eased its strained engine.

The serpentine length of the many railroad cars was painfully withdrawn from the cheerful and happy scenes at the station platform. Many young men with their heads out of open windows, extended arms and waived a brave farewell to friends and family. Young lovers smiled encouragingly, and with words of cheer comforted the young girls as they walked. Some recruits on board were still holding hands extended from open windows to those girlfriends on the platform. Hands ultimately parted, and still the girls ran slowly to the end of the station platform, and then, heartbroken they turned their backs on the receding troop carrier. The station became dramatically quieter. Only those people on the platform who remained in view of the men still leaning out of the windows of the train, continued to wave as though in a last gesture of confidence and to lift their own spirits and their recruit's moral.

Aboard the train the silence was not as sudden. Excited farm boys who were on their first train ride, continued to exchange remarks about the scenes outside that were beginning to rapidly flash past the windows as the engine picked up speed and overcame the inertia of the many heavily laden coaches and freight cars. The windows began to close one by one, as the train continued in an effort to reach its travel speed. Now, only pockets of revelers continued their boisterous thoughts in songs and bold words. Those who had drunk too much, now either passed out or slept, others recoiled into a corner and remained quiet.

Inevitably, with the passage of miles, the daylight did not interfere, but still permitted the quietening crowd to dream dreams, and thoughts of home were plentiful. The home that many of them were leaving for the first time; some would never return to. Yet there were those fools among them who commented how nice it was for the Government to give them this free train ride. There were those perhaps, who had no spectacular thoughts and simply went along with the mood of the men around them. But there were the silent ones, who had many thoughts; the older married men who had families and were reactivated again, were very apprehensive. They worried, and were most frustrated in this grievous position. It was not only the young home-sick recruit who turned his tear filled eyes away from his companions.

Geza wondered many thoughts too, when soldiers meet in a battlefield and are equally furious as they oppose one another, unrelenting, unflinching and merciless, what happens? Antal had recited several such examples to him.

Many die!

When Antal told the stories to Geza on his return from the Vienna Hospital, he invariably ended with a heavy sigh of "Ah Galicia, Galicia", as though it was a horrible nightmare too painful to recall, and yet, he felt he had to let his youngest brother know the futility and the hell of war. Survival is no longer to the fittest, nor to the best of men; survival is but to those most fortunate.

In days gone by when men fought men, personal prowess accounted for a lot. Even a boy could kill an older man because wit and, keen mind could help the less physically capable to prevail over the most powerful of men. Today however, what good is physical strength against bombs and artillery? All the intelligence and alertness of one mind is no match for the impossible.

The impossible was an artillery shell shot from 120 kilometers away that could strike anyone, and send them into oblivion while contemplating the fact that, they didn't even hear the shot that killed!

There was a gun located in St. Gobin woods that fired a mammoth shell to bombard Paris; a distance of 120-125 kilometers, about 75 miles.

The aircraft overhead, spraying the troops in the fields with lethal machine gun fire, or dropping a bomb, while in both instances the infantryman is struggling to stop the advance of his enemy, was another missive that could not be ignored. Intent upon coping with the death that is facing them, they are struck down from above or behind. The devil has the last laugh as friends and foe alike go to hell.

Modern warfare they called it!

A man is taught and trained to prepare for the unexpected; yet, it is the unexpected that strikes him down. Does he know what is in the barbed wire ahead? If he knows there is something in the field he must cross, then where will he find it? That is the unexpected! And as he shrewdly, and nimbly, sets about to ferret out the trap, machine gun bullets kill him while he is hung up over the barbed wire.

The earthly paradox: wars were not meant for man!

No one can justify warfare!

Feeling, emotional man, conceived of warm flesh and blood was never meant to be pitted against emotionless and unrelenting steel. Flesh was never a match for bullets, shrapnel, poison gas and flame throwers.

All the courage and shrewdness that could possibly be possessed by any one man will not make him indestructible!

If he is not lucky he will not survive.

BASIC TRAINING
THEN FURLOUGH

February 17, 1917, Geza was conscripted into the 83rd division of the AustroHungarian army at their Head Quarters in Vienna, Austria. The Armory for the Hungarian contingent of the 83rd was actually at Szombathely, Hungary, but the basic training for this batch of conscripts was done in Vienna to expedite them into active service.

The soldiers were housed in wooden barracks at their drill camp. The barracks were long, and contained two rows of bunk beds, (with head to wall and feet to center aisle), one row against either of the long walls, extending almost the length of the building. The soldiers slept billeted on these bunk beds, one above the other. In the evening, after a hard day of maneuvers, and after supper, there would be little time left for cards or idle talk. The general behavior in the first days was; the recruits being exhausted simply retired to sleep. They needed the rest; early rising meant early retiring.

The older men observed the younger recruits drop to their knees to pray at the side of the bed, just as they had been taught to do at home. While the young recruits recited their evening prayers, the older men hooted, and simply mocked and made fun of the 'foolish children'.

"Say a prayer for us while you're down there;" or "what are you praying for; sweet dreams?" And, "Do you want the sergeant major to tuck you in and kiss you good night?"

Geza was about to join the youths on their knees that first night, as one would expect from a former altar boy, but when he saw how unmanly the older men thought it was, he held back. He felt embarrassed for the youths being ridiculed, but said nothing.

"God save us from these faithful wretches," pleaded an older man. "Can you imagine? Our lives, our fate is in their hands, and at the slightest hint of trouble, when the enemy is charging us, these foolish kids will throw down their guns and plop to their knees. Instead of throttling throats, they will have their hands clasped in prayer!"

"Oh hell," said another; "What chance will we have when man must depend on man...and we have only these children to depend on."

As the religious recruits sheepishly got to their feet one by one, Geza climbed into his upper bunk. Some, more stubborn in their faith, finished their prayers quietly. Others, red faced, hurriedly jumped into bed, saying nothing, and covered themselves completely. They felt embarrassed and sought to hide their humiliation under the covers. Even though they covered their heads, they could still hear the severe word abuse handed out by the unbelievers.

In a short while the lights were turned off as were the abusive remarks. The barracks became quiet as each man gave himself over to sleep. Geza turned to face the wall, and with the blanket drawn over his head, he executed the Sign-Of –The-Cross, like a good Catholic. He placed the palms of both hands together in front of his face and said his prayers.

There were good sergeants, and there were bad sergeants. One of the latter was named Talös, and he was a bastard! In civilian life he was a roof tiler. He knew the art of working "burnt clay tiles", the tiles one sees on wealthy European homes. He had been on the Russian front, captured and taken prisoner. But with the Russian troops demoralized and deserting in the winter of 1916-1917, the prisoners were let loose. He returned home and was re-inducted keeping his rank.

He was a rotten leader, well remembered by the men he attempted to "lead". Geza was assigned to his regiment in February 1917.

One cold blustery March day of basic training, sergeant Talös, walked down the line of men to review them before the officers appeared, his ever present swagger stick under his arm. If a soldier was a bit too thrust forward out of line, and some with beer bellies invariably were, this bastard hauled off and whacked the fellow across the stomach with the swagger stick. This son-of-a-bitch expected every man to be in a straight line, as though each soldier was in profile, an image of the man beside him.

At another time, Geza's friend Forgács Jószi was hit so hard in the stomach that he simply folded up and fell forward.

This blustery day Talös wiped Geza's runny nose with a swift swipe of his swagger stick. Through a thick and swollen upper lip Geza "thanked" the sergeant for wiping his nose.

The men warned him; they told Talös, "god damn you, when we get to the front, the first bullet we fire is yours." The men stood together against him. They had nothing to lose once they were in an active salient and facing the enemy. On hearing these threats, Talös went, literally crying, to his superiors. He begged to be transferred to another regiment, because he now feared for his life. And those bastards in charge did transfer the cowardly sergeant. He could dish it out, but when it came payback time, he couldn't take it.

When the Officers asked the men why they threatened Talös, they replied truthfully. But the Officers couldn't care less about the many privates' personal resentments. They leaned heavily on sergeants to whip the men into discipline, in spite of the sergeant's personal unmanliness. Ranking Officers generally protected those sergeants in most circumstances. Many Captains and Generals resented the officer who could be a buddy to his men; a man who understood and sympathized with rank and file, even though it was later proven that these officers got more out of their men.

The Generals belonged to the old school, they believed that fear and discipline was all that was required.

With the transfer of Talös completed (he was sent to France), the Captain later admitted that Talös must have been unnecessarily harsh a disciplinarian. "But you should have reported him, instead of waiting until we got our front line assignment".

"Bullshit!" was the unanimous reply. "Not one officer in this man's army was about to listen, until we threatened to shoot him".

No matter what the men could have said it would have done them no good, but now, when they could not be punished there would be no courts martial. The officers were obliged to pay lip service to both sides of the argument. They realized that these soldiers meant business, and by saving the sergeants life, another regiment gained a veteran officer.

--- — — ---

The German drill instructor, a Captain Rozenfeldt, had been very pleased to get these new recruits. He taught them the basic commands in German while he trained them, but spoke primarily in their mother tongue, for he liked the Hungarians. He claimed that he preferred to have Hungarians with him in battle than his native Germans. This old veteran had commanded Hungarians in action, and truly took a fatherly interest in the new recruits. It is incredible, to look back on it, now that we have the luxury of distance and time, but all the officers were German in the Central Powers International regiments, and orders were given in German. The Hungarians had to understand their German officers commands if they were to survive.

These men who comprised the 83rd were the Közös Összegy (Common Troops i.e. Central Powers' replacement troops) and they could be expected to reinforce any of the German, Austrian, or Hungarian forces no matter where the Central Powers needed troops. Among them could be found troops of many Nations and languages that made up the Austro-Hungarian Empire, but regardless of their origins, these troops learned the German commands. Instructors taught the pertinence of the German commands during basic training.

The National troops of course made up the National Army, and officers spoke their nationality. Magyar troops reinforced the Magyar armies, and so, drilled with Magyar officers. Troops of the Közös Összegy had to be somewhat bilingually versatile as to commands and orders since most depleted armies were headed by German Generals who received these "Common Troops"

Geza and these Hungarians in Vienna received an intense and concentrated basic training, shortened because of the need of reinforcements for the Italian Campaign.

Captain Rozenfeldt remained a hard taskmaster, and firm instructor it is true, but as the recruits came along in their training he let them know how proud he was of their accomplishments. He shook his head sadly and remarked, "That's good, good, but if you forget too quickly, you are dead. Remember all that I have taught you my boys, for every bit is important. My training experiences can only contribute to the skills you will need to survive, the rest is up to you to remember, and use those skills."

There were farm boys among them who knew the names of all the grains and grasses but they did not *know their left foot from their right foot.* For these poor farmers, the Captain tied clumps of straw to their left leg and clumps of hay to their right leg. Thus he paraded them at extra drills apart from the rest of the recruits, and shouted szalma – szena, szalma – szena, (straw – hay, straw–hay), for the customary left – right, left – right.

He was a good instructor, and best of all, the men admired him; he would not expect the men to do anything that he could not do!

One day he was emphasizing the importance the "belly crawl", crawling on one's belly under fire; this one skill alone could get many through blazing gunfire.

"You keep your head down and bullets pass harmlessly over you while you continue to move forward...and move rapidly. Grenades and mortar fall behind you if you move faster than the enemy expects. If the grenades do fall among you, they strike fewer of you because you are low and moving, always moving forward."

In the training fields the entire division lay down with rifles nestled into the crotched elbows of both arms. Standing behind them, Rozenfeldt gave the order, dropped to the ground himself, and they all crawled one hundred meters only to find him standing at the end of the course already upright, erect and waiting; he cursed them in Hungarian.

"Faster you block heads! I told you speed was important. You must not lie down and dilly dally as though you were on Sally...there is a war to be won!"

He actually crawled the distance in one-third the time that it took most recruits. With an example like this, the recruits soon learned to 'burn the buttons off their tunics'. They doubled their time, crawling uphill, downhill, even over rocky terrain.

He was remarkable.

During combat training, the 'grenade toss' was executed on a field much like a current football field, but white lines marked every two meters distance from the center of an upright barrier which looked much like the two-pole and crosspiece of football goal posts, except that the barrier poles were very high in the inverted "U" shape. The crosspiece on top of the U could be raised to ten meters, twenty meters, or even twenty-five meters. The soldiers were to toss the "dummy" grenade from a measured distance forward of the "post". The object was to teach the effectiveness of a high toss, with a high toss the grenade would 'plop' down after its high arc. Bounces were fewer, and rolling was minimized.

To simply throw a grenade like one would throw a rock was not effective because it skittered across the ground. Such a throw may cause a grenade to skip over a trench and explode ineffectively. A high toss would, theoretically, plop it down into the trenches.

Basic training was now completed and the Captain issued passes to his trained men. He shook each individual's hand; he was seen to have a tear in his eye as he told them in their native Hungarian, how much he wished them well. After their furlough he would not see them again because they would be shipped out while he stayed behind to train more recruits.

As a wounded and much decorated German veteran, his experience was most needed in the training of more replacements for the thinned out fighting forces. He would not be going to the front with the 83rd division.

Geza's birthday was coming up, March 31; he had passed three weeks of basic training before his seventeenth birthday and Germany was anxious to get these troops to Italy; General Hötzendorff needed reinforcements for his army: he was at a standstill and handicapped because of Von Mackensen's recall to face the Russian front.

Geza had written only one letter home in which he stated that the recruits expected a furlough after completing three weeks of basic training; if that proved to be true, he would be home for a short while. Sure enough, sometime after March 10, 1917, basic training ended and he had a one-week furlough.

His mother was very happy and now anxiously awaited him. She pondered that her son had become a soldier, and a man, before his seventeenth birthday. She had informed Father Sekés that his one-time altar boy would be home for a final visit before leaving for the war.

Geza brought many fine staples home to his family, food stuffs not readily available to the public but sold only to those in the military; fine German tobacco for his father's pipe, (father had long forgiven the brashness of the child now turned soldier), whole cuts of meat, links of sausages, and butter for cooking the Hungarian pastries that mother would make. He carried all that he was allowed, and all that he could handle alone, including wine for the family, candies and souvenirs for all his sisters.

Everyone greeted him joyfully. They were all happy to see him looking so well, so much like a man. He was a fine figure with black curly hair and natty uniform, and as he lay down his many bags of gifts; "Ah!" sighed heartbroken mother Virag, as she held her arms open wide to embrace him.

"How grand you look."

They celebrated his birthday early, as they knew he would be gone within a week, who knows where he would be on March 31. The entire family ate a lot heartier that week, of good spicy foods and delicious, fattening pastries. It was a continuous party as friends dropped by every day to wish Geza well. He spent a good part of every day in uniform because everybody insisted on seeing how this boy-turned-man looked, now that he was a soldier. Many of the older and wiser citizens just could not believe that the 'Empire' was so badly in need of these boys, and seeing Geza now in uniform, was but a bitter reminder that the end of the war may be nearer than most citizens thought, though they dare not express that opinion openly to anyone. But Geza heard it often enough.

The family reminisced about the past with the many good times. Mother reminded them about the time when Antal carved and created that unique two horse coach as a toy for Geza's eighth birthday. The grown-up Geza now laughed along with his sisters, as mother related the story. Anna reminded him however, that at the time it was heartbreaking to think that she almost lost her favorite doll.

"Suppose those Tom cats had decided to take off together instead of in different directions...instead of climbing the tree, what would have been the fate of my doll? They could have ended up in the next county."

On the last day of Geza's furlough his father and Father Sekés the priest, sat back after dinner and filled their pipes with the German tobacco that Geza had brought. They each enjoyed their 'pipe' for the rest of the afternoon and talked neighborly while sipping wine. Idle but happy talk for a happy family; Father Sekés amused the family with a story of Geza as an altar boy. How mischievous those boys had been, these young novitiates. When Father Sekés was in front of the altar imploring the blessings of the Holy Host for the communion sacrament, he lifted the chalice up to God, and repeated a prayer. Then he would turn to the altar boy who was supposed to pour the wine into the chalice, but the altar boys had a conspiracy going between them; they would tilt the decanter only slightly, and quickly, (no matter what altar boy officiated over the wine). Their intent was to pour only a small amount into the chalice and save the rest, to be shared amongst them. Father Sekés was often, suddenly red faced in front of the congregation, to think what these boys intended was blasphemy.

He became wise to them, and when the boy balked from pouring an ample amount, he was forced to hold the chalice with one hand and with the forefinger of the other hand held the decanter's neck down to get more wine into the chalice. He then prayed that additional prayer, that none of the congregation had seen his two handed deftness.

Mother was shocked at this new revelation. She had not known about it before, because Father Sekés had never told the parents. Now he and Geza asked her forgiveness at this deception. Jokingly they chided, but it had been a long time ago, too long to be of consequence now. Geza smiled sheepishly as he stated that he did not always cheat on the wine, it was the older boys that had put him up to it. It was the older boys that always enjoyed the wine...he did not admit that he got his share none-the-less.

It was all over, and much too soon. The one-week was too short. Geza could only leave regrets and regards behind as he embraced his sisters, sister in-law, and kissed his mother brushing a tear from her eye. When she released him from her embrace, she muttered mournfully, choked with holding back tears.

"You are the last one my son."

Over her shoulder the seventeen year old, taller than his mother, caught a last glimpse of the religious saints' pictures hanging on The Holy Wall in the living room. Within their borders framing them, were inserted many older photos but there was a new one now, showing him in uniform. His sisters' photos were there; his brothers were there, the grandchildren too. That wall held her all; her holy family and her earthly family; one place of veneration to all those above for all these below.

Antal was dead. János and Gergély were not heard from, and yet she will persist in praying for Geza. His mind's eye could see her now, kneeling before the saints and that crucifix, praying for his safekeeping. He was becoming too much of a man to accept her unshaken faith. He had suffered silently the heartaches of those prayerful recruits in the barracks, as the older and wiser men lashed at their childish faith with stinging words. But he would not show his wavering faith to her. He truly loved her, and, who knows? Her faith may keep him whole.

They all wished him goodbye, good luck, prayers go with you, "but be careful."

Only Antal's widow appeared downcast at times during his visit, to the discomfort of the others. Her children were very happy however, all the members of the extended family were spoiling them, and they enjoyed it. The children were sorry whenever it was time for them to leave, for their mother had begun to act oddly at times when they were alone as a family in their own home. She would fall into moods of depression. Wrapped up in a world of her own thoughts, she seemed to cease thinking of her children. And, each day the children were left more and more to their own keeping. The mother – children relationship was deteriorating to the point where grandparents were concerned. Good neighbors had begun to assist when they could, but they to, were too busy. Everyone in the village began to notice Bobbie's neglect of her children. She was seen to wander alone at dusk as though she were hunting for someone. At times she walked with deliberate steps as though she were going somewhere... as though she had a meeting, or someplace positive as a destination, only to be seen much later, walking slowly alone and sadly to her home. The neighbors advised the grandparents of their common concern for her. Soon, some action on the part of the children would have to be taken.

Bobbie smiled sweetly, and embraced him affectionately. She stepped back holding him at arms length and marveled at just how much he looked like Antal. Antal must have looked like this when he was a young seventeen, black curly hair, tall trim body; Geza's youthful face lacked only the handlebar moustache. She remarked to Geza how much like a man he looked in his soldier's uniform. She attempted to be cheerful at their farewell, but remembrances of Antal only made her slip into depression. She was beginning to retreat into her own world of memories.

Geza's heart ached for Bobbie... for Antal.

One last look at his family, his village, and he stepped onto the train for Vienna once more. Not much packed this return trip, just his memories. The army would care for his clothes now, and his necessities, as they saw fit.

His hand went to the chain around his neck.

His mother's farewell gift was a small, long box, much like a locket, with latches on the front cover. Within this box was a small likeness, a metal statue of Saint Christopher the Protector.

She had paid Father Sekés to bless it, and with the Holy Water Father Sekés had imposed a prayer and blessing that was meant to safely see Geza through the war.

SÜLE JENŐ
RETURNS

As Von Mackensen pressed relentlessly forward in early 1917, the beaten armies of Russian General Brussilov scattered ahead of him. The Central Powers' soldiers taken prisoner by the Russian forces in the 1915 winter campaign, and in Brussilov's offensive of May 1916, were left to fend for themselves. There were several hundred internment camps beyond the Donajec River, but many of these prisoners managed to escape, or were released by the now threatened Russian troops guarding them. Some compounds nearest the advancing German army were left without guards, as many Russian troops deserted and went home.

The Central Powers armies were all the more deliberate and methodical along the entire Eastern Front. They encroached further into Russian Territory, and in so doing liberated many prisoners of the past campaigns. Cheerful Germans, Austrians and Hungarian prisoners greeted their liberators with a hearty welcome, as they happily thought of the return home.

Among the many Hungarians walking anxiously westward towards the advancing armies of General Mackensen, was one very confident and resolute corporal... Süle Jenő.

The advancing armies met with their comrades amidst cheers and jubilation. The erstwhile general however, required that every man be registered by rank and regiment; and provide information as to where the soldier was taken prisoner etc? The German High Command needed such information, as well as the returning prisoners. They must be reactivated and added to the depleted army.

When the corporal finally returned to Vienna with the other repatriated prisoners, his regimental major and captain remembered him. Many veterans also had verified his capture under trying circumstances in action against the Russians during the Carpathian Mountains Campaign. His reputation and valor preceded his arrival; he was given much praise and consideration.

Within the next few days the Army was 'arranging' things for this old fighter, but that was yet to come.

One of the first things Jenö did was to go to the Quartermaster's Stores; he had literally "walked out" of his shoes; they had holes in the soles and were badly worn, so he asked for a new pair.

"I would like a new pair of shoes?" He stated.

The quartermaster sergeant approached the corporal attempting to intimidate with his superior rank. "Are you demanding a pair of shoes or are you asking for a pair... with please?" He stated boldly.

"I want a pair!" exclaimed the corporal, now nose-to-nose with the sergeant. "Don't you have any?"

"I have shoes but," now pointing at the shoes on Jenö's feet, shortly and curtly replied, "those are still good enough for you."

Jenö immediately punched the sergeant in the face; "Are you going to give me a pair or aren't you?"

When the dazed sergeant picked himself up off the floor, Jenö ordered him, stating his size. "Bring me a pair of shoes."

The quartermaster sergeant reluctantly brought him a pair. Jenö took off his worn ones and put on the new pair; they fit well, and they looked good. He then picked up the old worn out pair, thrusting them into the sergeant's hands; deliberately pushing the sergeant's fingers through the worn soles.

"Hold these, see how well they feel----- -"

"You're not scaring me;" Replied the stupid man.

"No?" smiled Jenö; "well don't think you are going to worry me by reporting me to the Captain." He laughed. "Go ahead; while I'm sitting in the guard house I'm not in the battlefield." He shook his finger at the sergeant. "Know this *son*... know this! I walked up and down the Russian front with those boots. Not on one side, but on both sides of that damned front, up and down its length. I was wounded and then sent back, and you were here at home fingering your balls, sitting in a supply depot."

The sergeant made a move as though to lay down the filthy shoes and get them out of his hands.

"Don't you dare; you better keep hold on those shoes!" yelled Jenö.

The sergeant made no further effort to lay them down, but it was obvious that he didn't want to hold the dirty things either.

"Hold onto them you son-of-a-bitch." Jenö again pressed the sergeant's hands against the shoes, and then into the man's belly, forcibly crossing the man's hands over the shoes making certain that the fingers protruded through the soles. Then he grabbed the sergeant by the scruff of the neck and shoved him forward.

"March! You want to see the Captain? Let's go."

Jenö led the man ahead of him to the regimental head-quarters offices. Jenö opened the door with one hand and thrust the sergeant forward, still holding him by the scruff of the neck. The sergeant still embraced the worn shoes at his belly.

All those in the office stood up at this sudden intrusion and those already standing turned to face the scuffling at the door. Everyone in the room now faced that door through which these two men had burst upon them. Those who recognized Jenö, and knew the hotheaded corporal, wondered what that poor unfortunate fool sergeant had done to "piss him off".

They stood in expectation now.

A first lieutenant familiar with Jenö's behavior broke the silence. "What's the trouble corporal?" He knew enough that whatever it was, Jenö was at the root of this issue with the sergeant. No point addressing the sergeant.

"I went in to ask for a new pair of shoes from this snot of a man...there, he is carrying my worn pair in his arms. I told him that they had walked far enough and he was to give me a new pair. He replies, 'If you please? Or do I demand a pair?' Then he said that those shoes," Jenö pointed at the ones in the quartermaster's arms, fingers were still appropriately protruding through the worn soles "are still good enough for me...and he would not give me another pair."

Jenö stopped momentarily. He had an idea.

"Lieutenant Sir, let's make him put those shoes on! Let him walk in them. After six years of service don't you think I'm entitled to another pair of shoes?"

"All right, all right," replied the lieutenant, patting Jenö's shoulder to settle him, "Of course you are entitled to a new pair," and turning to the sergeant, "Not another word of this incident."

Observing all this, the Captain smiled knowingly, but did not interfere. The lieutenant appeared to be handling the situation very well, and needed no help.

The sergeant and first lieutenant were younger than Jenö, whether that meant anything in the lieutenant's behavior is hardly likely, except that the lieutenant exercised good sense and knew when to appease the old soldier.

Stubborn as he was, Jenö respected veterans; but he could not abide soldiers whom he knew were not veterans and 'played at soldiering'. The young lieutenant was not about to tangle with Jenö; the Quarter Master sergeant was a good example why not to. Jenö didn't give a damn. He had clashed with a first lieutenant (örhagdnagy), when he reported back from Russia the first time.

"Because they were snotty corporals (önkintesék), when I left for the front, and now they are lieutenants not having been at the front; how the hell did you guys get your promotions? By pumping your pricks on the home front while I was pumping bullets on the man's front?"

Jenö could not stomach the inequity he saw...because many officers hadn't earned their rank. These bastards were young soldiers, became young officers, and never fired a shot in anger. Yes, Jenö just didn't give a shit for them. He showed absolutely no respect for these pampered peacocks. He was older; he was a veteran. He didn't worry about a clean uniform, clean tunic, or cape. If he wore it...he slept in it...even if it looked like he had slept in it.

He was now toughened and indifferent.

He had proven himself. He was mean, and he looked mean if angered. The young peacocks did not dare challenge him.

The army had finished with the 'arranging.' They would now see to Jenö's appearance also. The Military made a hero out of him. They manufactured a hero's welcome for Süle Jenö. They publicized his accomplishments in the newspapers. They spoke highly of him on radio.

He was a fighter, and his awards were because of his courage to stand and fight. Every Staff Officer found reason to publicize his accomplishments. They awarded him the Ezüst (similar to the U.S.A. Silver Star) to go along with his Iron Cross. For quite a few weeks he went on tour throughout the Prussian Empire, Germany and Austria-Hungary. He was encouraged to tell of his experiences, exaggerate if need be, but promote pride in service.

The German High Command needed recruits to fill the growing needs of what was now becoming a two front war; many more men were required to bolster the ranks against the growing ranks of the Allied armies.

Jenö the hero would promote conscription.

He was not patriotically moved after two years of active service; but he was no fool and would play their game willingly. The room and board was considerably better than what he received as a Russian prisoner; it also meant a good life away from the front lines. What the hell, it did not bother him in the least to get others to do the fighting.

In 1914 he was eager, and anxious for a fight to settle the dastardly deed of assassination of the Archduke's wife Sophia. Now, having seen the injustice of war, he had become quite indifferent.

For a period of time he toured the cities, then the training camps, occasionally he would also engage in the instruction and training of new recruits. He certainly lived well, and he enjoyed it. He got home to Porpacz more often. Yes, Jenö conceded that things were going just fine, and he played the role of returned hero quite naturally, but he also toured the military canteens at night.

In Vienna he was frequently seen with the choicest, most attractive and most grateful young women. That was the standard for his evening life.

While he made his tour of the drinking establishments one day, now dressed in a tailored uniform, and displaying the Iron Cross and the Silver Medal, along with his service ribbons; he was ordered to always display his honors to impress the men in uniform. He never forgot to wear them however, because he found that they also impressed the women.

He stepped up to the bar in one of the canteens of his intended evening tour, and met with friendly conversation from two veterans at the bar. He downed his first shot of whisky among the good company, and soon the entire room full of soldiers bantered back and forth their war stories, and just good, manly conversation grew into a mutually satisfying evening of companionship.

Jenö enjoyed these veterans; the feeling was mutual, they enjoyed him. He surely would have stayed longer because of this good companionship except that two young German Officers stepped into the canteen. They appeared to be fresh from military school, they had tailored uniforms also, and to the veterans it was plain to see the boys were 'green'. Yet both had *Iron Cross, Silver Medal and a board of service ribbons* as ornaments on their tunics! Their attire and bearing smacked of Aristocratic snobs.

Their attitude? Pomp and arrogance!

The canteen suddenly fell silent. The silence was too obvious, timed with their entrance. Still they moved to a table that was centrally located and would have sat down but for Jenö.

Too disgusted at what he saw, he stopped them in their tracks. He was instantly angered, and now as he moved from his position at the bar, thoughts rapidly raced through his mind. He had fought for his honors, many men around him, and in front of his gun had died bravely, men more becoming of military recognition than these...these pampered brats.

He confronted them.

"Who the hell are you?" Jenö white with rage stood before them.

The two young officers feigned unconcern, and did not initially appear to be set back by this upstart... until they saw Jenö's medals.

"I beg your pardon, soldier?" replied one, showing no respect at all for the man and his medals.

"Soldier?" shouted Jenö; "You're damned right, I am a soldier, you young peacocks." He emphasized. "Where in the hell did you buy your decorations?" He slurred the word 'buy' as though it were a profanity, and had particular emphasis for 'decorations'.

Now all eyes were on Jenö. Every combat veteran in the canteen heard from Jenö's mouth what all would have wished to say. But the veterans did not defy the Officers' rank. It seemed to them that Jenö was doing fine, for he totally ignored their superior ranks.

The veterans waited for those young Officers, still wet behind the ears, to make a foolish move. If Jenö could not handle them; if they insulted Jenö-- — the veterans would forget rank also!

They needn't fear. The display was gratifying, and bold, as the veterans watched and listened.

"How do you have the gall to wear those medals?" He demanded, and exploded with, "When you haven't earned them!"

"We...also represent the German army...Corporal ...just as you do. We must have no differences here." Replied one bold peacock, now somewhat taken aback by the belligerent and defiant corporal.

"No differences? Why you dumb son-of-a-bitch, there is a world of differences ...between *us*" He emphasized 'us', and swept his right arm to include the veterans in the room, "...and you." Jabbing the young Officer's chest

Jenö pointed at the Officer's chest, and kept jabbing the chest with his finger. "I represent the fighting men of the Hungarian Army, and the combined armies. Some of these men, again his arm swept around to indicate all the men in the canteen, had been fighting when you were still sucking tit. They defended your privileged right to be pampered. Now, in your pompous, asinine behavior, you insult these men, and the things for which those medals truly were intended."

"Damn you both. What you represent is arrogance and inconsideration!" He was hot, now red faced, as he shouted the insults into their faces. "The least that you could do as a sign of intelligent Officers is to respect what the fighting man knows; don't try to make fools out of proud men." He slurred the word 'officers' again, as though it were a dirty word. "Don't buy your medals because they appear as pretty jewelry on your tunic!"

He clutched at his own medals with his right hand, and ripped them from his neck. "These you can have, you young asses. You don't even have to pay for them. I earned them with my blood, but I would not be caught wearing them in the company of such ignorant asses as the two of you. Be the privileged, and most honorable, if you think bought medals make you more of a man."

In one final gesture of contempt and disgust, Jenö vehemently threw his medals onto the table, that table which they were about to sit.

One medal amazingly stayed on the table; the other bounced off and rolled, bounced and rolled again across the floor to strike the booted foot of an older soldier. There it stopped.

Jenö turned his back on the peacocks and stormed out of the canteen. He could stand no more. Had he stayed he could not restrain himself from striking the two spoiled brats.

The old soldier slowly reached down and picked up the 'Silver' from the floor at his feet. In all the years of active duty he had not earned a medal, but he respected the bravery and courage they exemplified. He was there; in battles where many men feared and yet, others dared. He admired the dedication to duty and to fellow man which the medal represented. Now as he sat in the chair with the Silver in his palm, he fingered it, and was, momentarily, alone with his thoughts. He wondered about that bold man who had earned it.

The canteen was silent. The two Officers had not yet sat down. The old soldier interrupted his contemplation and turned to face the young Captains. Both were looking at him. Everyone was looking at him. What would his actions be? How would he respond?

He got up, and with deliberate steps paced the distance to their table ignoring them, and looked beyond them to the Iron Cross lying on the table.

One of the young Captains, clearing his throat asked, "What is that Corporal's name? Soldier, do you know that man who just stormed out of here?"

The old soldier reached beyond the two fools, deaf to their words he picked up the Iron Cross, holding both medals in his hand he must have suddenly felt as one with Jenö, which emboldened him too, to make a fist with the hand that contained them. When the lump finally left his throat, he replied quietly but clearly.

"Sir, I do not know that bold corporal's name. I never saw him before this night, but again...I never saw you before either, and I don't know your name, or the name of your friend here. But I don't give one damn for the both of you"

Stating that last phrase coolly, he added, "but I shall find the corporal and return these to him." He held the clenched fist up to the officer's face, holding the medals. "After all he earned these medals."

Putting the medals in his tunic pocket, he again raised his finger, and not quite pushing it into the young man's face added, shaking that finger, "Good sirs, sit. Take a drink, if a drink is what you came for, but drink it and be gone quickly, that is my advice to you, until you mend your minds, for these veterans do not take kindly to arrogance and fools."

With this last statement, he turned and exited through the door, anxious to find Jenö.

The two Officers looked about. The canteen was too quiet. The faces of the remaining occupants were too grim and unfriendly. They felt as though they were alone, so the two thoughtless fools left. They were not quite that foolish... to stay where they were so obviously not welcome.

Jenö had gone to another canteen, and now decided to get drunk.

Before the evening was over, and he was not quite drunk yet, two military police came in. They knew this much-celebrated hero, and wished him no ill but they had a duty to perform, and so they talked him into leaving peaceably. They did not choose to fight him, and they did not wish to carry him out...perhaps the other veterans would intercede on Jenö's behalf if a fight started. Should such a challenge happen, their duty would be impossible to obey.

Feeling disgusted and moody Jenö decided not to make a scene, and was quickly ushered outside. There, one policeman each, grasping under each arm, led him to a waiting vehicle and all three sat in the back seat. He was promptly thrown into the stockade when they got him back to Head Quarters.

Early the next morning he was ushered into the Colonel's Office.

"Jenö! What the hell have you been up to? I have a complaint lodged against you from two Captains."

So! They had got to the Colonel before he could. How did they find out who he was? Oh yes, the newspapers had many articles about him. They now planned to put him on the spot; how could he hope to explain to the Colonel? They had cunningly put him on the defensive.

"You behaved with conduct unbecoming a soldier." Continued the Colonel. "You ripped your military honors from your person...and threw them...*threw them onto the floor in a canteen.* Those medals are the highest honors that your Nation can bestow upon its heroes, and you insulted them with your lack of respect for what they represent. What kind of foolishness was that?"

I guess those Officers were not so dumb after all; to cover their ass they had out maneuvered him. He was the villain in the eyes of the Colonel. The only defense remaining for Jenö was to tell it like it was and he would tell the truth, whatever a corporal's word was worth against two captains.

"Foolishness? Damn it Colonel, sir, that was not foolishness that was a display of genuine disgust."

"What? Then it is true, you did insult your fellow officers and your country?" queried the Colonel.

"Officers? Shit! They're not officers that I would be proud of. They're not fellows of mine! Further more, I did not insult my country! It is they who are an insult to officers and country. Damn their hides."

"What are you saying? Be careful, you could be court marshaled for what you say in the next few minutes," threatened the Colonel.

"Sir, did I not earn those medals on the field of battle?"

"Yes. Yes of course you did."

"Then I refuse to wear them if any pompous peacock could buy them!

To buy them is shame enough...but to be *permitted to wear the purchased honors is disgusting and disgraceful.* They *should be locked up for impersonating a soldier."*

"Peacocks? Wear the highest medals of honor?" The Colonel was taken aback by this statement and confused. "Jenö are you still drunk from last night? Didn't you cool off in the brig? They... the Officers weren't wearing any medals when they wrote out a complaint against you."

The Colonel quietly puzzled the pieces out, while Jenö ranted.

"They probably removed them from their tunics for the benefit of lodging the complaint. What was their complaint?" He raised his voice. "To be present when those two bastards paraded into the canteen was too much of an insult. Just ask the veterans who were there."

"Now calm down my boy; let's hear your side of this charade."

Jenö proceeded to narrate the incident truthfully from the beginning, just as it had happened. He highlighted with his exact words spoken to the young Captains. When he was through, the Colonel understood only too well what an insult the Officers had tortuously endured. But he agreed, they deserved it, flaunting such disregard for medals of bravery, in front of veterans. They were lucky that they came away unscathed. They had been shown disrespect for their position.

In lodging the complaint however, they were shrewd enough to forego the truth. Instead they emphasized a fabricated story of the disgraceful action of a true hero. It was their intent to belittle the man who had belittled them. They would have succeeded except that they under estimated the man.

Jenö defied the Colonel, and would have the truth of the matter known just for what it was, an insult to the fighting men of the combined armies of the Central Powers.

"Well, you are after all, a noble son of the Motherland. I am not going to stand in judgment over you, nor am I about to say that the young German Officers represented themselves falsely. They are, after all, your superiors in rank. Whatever insult you presented them was not befitting of their rank. You must respect rank, and you will respect rank! Understand?"

His words were an officer's words, menacingly demanding discipline for the sake of discipline.

Damn it! Of course he had given them respect, along with a piece of his mind; else he would have flattened their noses and tore their medals off. Didn't the Colonel understand that?

"You have had too much leisure, corporal. I think you are bored with inaction. You are spoiling for a fight and I am prepared to accommodate you. You will be sent to the Italian Front."

"What? But sir – "

"Don't interrupt me. I am promoting you to sergeant that you can give the benefit of your experience to a larger group of men."

"Sergeant? Influence a larger group? But sir, I can influence more young recruits here at home."

"Like you impressed those young Captains, eh?" Smiled the devious Colonel. "My boy, along with your medals, use your rank proudly. You should have had this promotion at the time you received the Silver Medal. Perhaps now I could have promoted you to Captain," kidded the Colonel.

"Then what would you have done to the young Captains? You would have been more defiant I'm sure."

The truth is, and the Colonel may have known it at the time, Jenö had been a sergeant twice before, only to be stripped of his stripes. He had, throughout his war years been promoted, and as often been threatened with court martial for insubordinate behavior.

They gave Jenö a platoon to drill while he was waiting to be shipped out. He would take the men away from the others on the drill field and out of sight whenever he could. There they would lounge about and tell war stories, a group of men just enjoying the day, and learning from this veteran's experiences. Yes, he told how it was on the Russian Front, the good and the bad of it. He minced no words. If any of the drill instructors looked in his direction, not hearing the conversation, but noticing that Jenö had the whole platoon's attention; they surmised that he must have been giving serious instructions.

When the bugler sounded the evening recall for the men on the drill fields, his men picked themselves up and marched in behind the rest of them. After supper he would address the men and enquire:

"Who wants to get away this evening?"

If anyone expressed a wish to go home, Jenö would issue a pass, and then scratch the lucky individuals name from the attendance sub-list. If challenged by an Officer about any man that was absent Jenö would say that the man was on an errand, or give some other acceptable excuse. He just didn't give a damn. He had twice ripped off his sergeant's stripes and twice he was threatened with court martial because of the insult designated by anyone who had earned the rank. He certainly was not concerned about these new sergeant's stripes.

He was quite a soldiers man, a straight shooter and honest. He knew what was proper even if the military didn't think it was proper. He lived by his own code and thus earned the respect of his men.

On his way to Italy in the summer of 1917, Jenö had reason to reflect upon what he had done to deserve this. Looks like that Hungarian temper had done it again. If only he could curb his tongue, but that would mean restricting his feelings also, and no hot blooded Hungarian could do that.

The first official act he performed as örmester (sergeant), when he got to the Front was to issue a three-day pass to eight of the thirty-two men in his command.

"Okay boys, which one of you have not had any time off? Who has been in the Service the longest?

His men liked him, admired him; best of all they respected him for being a soldier's soldier.

THE TROOP TRAIN

The 44th and the 83rd infantry divisions (regiments?) boarded the long troop carrier of boxcars and freight. There were a few coaches in the long line of cars, but these were for the officers of high rank, Colonel, Major etc., and for those few among the wealthy civilian population that were also traveling south from Vienna. Each boxcar accommodated thirty-two men and their sergeant, field equipment, backpacks, ammunition and rifles; three freight cars held the equivalent of one Company (100) of men.

The freight car arrangement of the two divisions of men were alternated by threes; that is, after the line of coaches, there were three boxcars of the 44th infantry, then three boxcars of the 83rd infantry, followed by three boxcars of the 44th, and so on, alternating to the final and last cars carrying soldiers. From that last car extended the remaining boxcars carrying freight and commercial goods; these commercial products were dropped off at cities enroute south.

In the last three cars, before the cars containing the freight, were a Company of the 83rd infantry. Geza was in the third car from the freight carriers, and immediately next to that car carrying members of the 44th. Military theory was that, in the event of aerial attack and bombing, should several carloads of troops be destroyed, this dispersal of troops was best Not all men of one division were strung-in together, and both divisions would share in the casualties, thus, not all casualties would be incurred by one division alone, making it ineffective as a fighting force.

The locomotive pulled out of the station and went directly south from Vienna. All trains carrying commercial goods, and locomotives carrying civilian passengers and other freight would yield the right of way to this military transport as it rumbled through many stations non-stop. It did stop at designated depots that had been cleared of civilian traffic, and the troops would disembark to partake of a prearranged dinner, supper or breakfast.

The men could have no respite, and were forced to relieve themselves within the boxcars or out the open door. Not too many were brave enough to relieve themselves through the open door while the train was speeding. They had use of a 'honey pot' shared by all men in one boxcar as the train sped heedlessly on. (Soldiers named the common commode used for this purpose the honey pot). Should a soldier get bored or tired along the way, there were straw piles to recline on, though these proved to be not too soft a bed in the rolling and swaying boxcar.

At their first stop the men eagerly disembarked, hurriedly and in disarray, hastily unbuttoning their trousers and turning to urinate at the iron wheels of the boxcar. The sergeant barked orders to the men, that they should form up in ranks and stand at attention, though he was hard pressed himself and sympathized with their need for a nature call. Finally all the troops were at attention in front of their respective boxcars, one long line, as long as the troop carrier, awaited the Major's command.

They would march in line to meet each succeeding contingent, up to the third contingent. Then in columns of three, the troops marched in companies of one hundred to an improvised military kitchen. Those companies nearest the kitchen were seated and eating before the company in the center boxcars had arrived, and the first company was through eating before the last company was seated. It took about two hours but at separate sittings all the men had eaten. The first company left the dining area and was returning to the boxcars and boarded before the last company returned to their boxcar.

They formed ranks of three after eating and marched back to the freight boxcar from which they had disembarked. One man had remained as guard at the boxcar to watch over the rifles, knapsacks and materials. These single soldier guards all ate after the entire number of troops had finished eating. It so happened that some men, those of the 83rd, began to take notice of the boxcars behind their own. Curious about the kinds of freight traveling with them, they wandered to the side of the car immediately behind the last troop carrier. They were surprised to find that the manifest tacked to the board on the side of the car clearly indicated that it had a *full cargo of barreled beer.*

A pleasant thought entered the minds of the men simultaneously. They were unanimous; an after dinner drink of beer would go very well. The sergeant happily agreed! He helped formulate a hurried but adequate plan before the order to 'board' again was given.

Being situated where they were, the last in the procession of troop cars, they were at some distance from the station platform and the officers. While the majority of one hundred men from three cars milled about and talked in an unassuming and casual manner, six men darted between the freight cars. Once behind the beer carrier, they were concealed from the station side and the rest of the troops. They broke into the freight car and took three barrels, one for each of the three cars that carried troops of the 83rd division. The privates guarding those three troop cars discreetly opened the doors on the opposite side from the station, and accepted the barrels.

When all the troops had boarded, and the train was rolling, the men in those boxcars unplugged the barrels and drank cheerful draughts of the German beer. Of course, the barrels were emptied before the next stop when they again disembarked, this time for supper. From their outward appearance the beer drinkers were not detected as behaving differently from the other troops who did not have beer in their boxcars. Some of those who were drinking had relieved themselves out the door as the train rolled on; with the drunken mind came the bravery to attempt it. So they did not seem any more anxious to relieve themselves once the train stopped.

As they finished their supper, the friendly camaraderie had revealed to those of the 44th, immediately in the car up from the third boxcar carrying the 83rd that they too could have a draught of beer to wash down their supper, and if the troops of the 44th could share, then certainly the troops of the 83rd immediately up from the cars carrying the 44th would also appreciate their buddies' consideration also. Quickly a lone soldier was quickly dispatched to inform the guards aboard the three original boxcars about the need for *more barrels of beer*.

This man found that his guards had already returned the empties, and exchanged them for full barrels; barrels that were already hidden within the three separate cars.

The four men now hurriedly returned for six more barrels.

There was a barrel of beer hidden in each of the nine trailing boxcars when the troops returned. The train pulled out from the station with three hundred happy troopers. With the approaching darkness the train would travel all night making no stops until the next morning. Occasionally, as the troops in the next cars tried to sleep, they thought they heard the hearty singing of happy Hungarians. Drinking and singing in an enjoyable manner, the beer drinkers thought they could not be heard above the roar of the wind speeding across the boxcars roof, and above rumbling, clacking iron wheels.

At their breakfast stop, the soldiers disembarked most hurriedly. Three hundred troops seemed more eager than the rest; they wanted food on their stomach. Again the guard privates made their barrel switch while the troops ate. Nine empties returned and nine full barrels stashed one in each of nine boxcars. While eating breakfast however, those troops of the 44th who rode the boxcar immediately next to the ninth one containing the beer drinking troops of the 83rd, curiously questioned their comrades about their nighttime singing.

Now, hurriedly the guards willingly accommodated the new group of 44th would-be beer drinkers, which of course would also include *the next three cars of the* 83rd. Those of the 83rd who had discovered the beer first just did not want to forget the others of their company. If the beer was to be shared, it was only fair that more of the 83rd should share also. There were now fifteen freight cars of troops *drinking beer after breakfast* ; four hundred and fifty plus, happy howlers.

At the next dinner stop it became somewhat noticeable that there were too many men that appeared happier than the rest! They were backslapping one another, and very boisterous as the Major stepped off the coach. He glanced back at this company of men. The sergeants had ordered the single line formations in front of each boxcar; good. But some men were weaving slowly. Their feet were in line but their bodies slowly weaved back and forth!

What the hell is going on out there?

The Major commanded the troops to 'stand to'. He wished to look them over before their march to dinner, and before they formed into columns of threes. He was beyond the twelfth car from the freight and nearer the ninth car when he detected a familiar odor emanating from these men at the tail-end of the troop carrier.

Those who had drank the most these past twenty-four hours and, after a weak breakfast, were having difficulty standing still. The Major ordered the responsible sergeants to walk along beside him as he viewed their men. He was not quite sure what was happening, and could not yet puzzle it out, but one man cleared up the Major's mystery in a hurry. For just as the private swayed back and forth, weak on his feet and weaker still in his stomach, fighting to restrain himself from bringing up his breakfast.

Perhaps he could shut his eyes and the Major would pass, then, he could puke his guts out.

There is no man that could succeed in fighting back that force.

As the Major approached, up belched the private; vertical as he was he almost splashed his beer soaked breakfast onto the Major. That beer-odored vomit cleared up the mystery.

The Major now knew what had happened, but he questioned the man's sergeant anyway, while walking quickly away from the now bowed over private who was thoroughly emptying his stomach. The men were ordered to march to their dinner, while the Major and a few subordinates followed the trail of boxcars for possible beer possession.

The guards of those fifteen boxcars meanwhile had not stood idle.

When the troops had disembarked from in front of the boxcars, these men had jumped to the ground behind the boxcars. They were returning the empties and bringing full barrels back to the troop carriers. Even now, while the Major and his men approached the beer carrying freight car from the station front side, there was quite an active rushing about behind the beer car. As one might guess, those guards were already taking more barrels for more boxcars. When the troops returned from dinner there would be one barrel of beer in each car that carried the men of the 83rd infantry.

The Major was not surprised to find the front of the freight car locked. He knew that his men were smart enough to keep the front, station side of the boxcar as it was. But he was not prepared for what he saw when he ordered the door to be opened. It was just like pulling the curtain open upon a stage. The open door revealed the actors on stage; one man handling the returned empty barrels, while two men lowered a full barrel to two men standing on the ground, others waited with arms ready at the freight car door opposite the Major.

Surprised, the men stopped in their tracks when the door suddenly opened as the Major looked directly across the freight car floor at the wide-eyed privates on the other side of the car.

The men were so intent upon their task that they had not even been aware of the activity out front. They had been neatly stacking the empties to one end as they were returned by the guards, and removing full barrels from the other end of the boxcar.

Quite an orderly process for the disordered privates.

They were caught red faced and red handed.

The Major had done them in. They were ordered now to return all full barrels from the troop carrying boxcars. When the task was completed, a subordinate counted the empty barrels. Since the 83rd division soldiers had been the instigators, they would be the ones *to pay for the beer consumed!* The Major threatened that a small amount of their monthly pay would be withheld.

The freight car doors were now wired closed until the train reached the first large city with a rail yard. Here the commercial goods and the beer cars were side tracked from the rest of the train. The railroad yard crew shunted the boxcars back, and into a siding. This caused a short delay in which the soldiers ate their assigned meal and rested.

The train now truly became a troop carrier and within the next day they approached their destination in Italy.

The beer was had free gratis, as not one soldier had any money with held from his pay at any time throughout the Italian Campaign.

That major was after all, a fine man.

SERVICES BEHIND THE LINES

The train lumbered on, and when it stopped, somewhere in northern Italy at a troop marshalling depot, half the contingent of soldiers disembarked; all of the 44th. The other half, which was the 83rd, continued on the train headed for Caporetto Vittorio. It knew no geographical boundaries as it simply, and swiftly, pursued the serpentine trail of tracks.

Caporetto is situated in the Julian Alps. It is just about at the foothills of the mountains that terminate, and come down from the Bainsizza Plateau. The Isonzo River flows nearby, through a pass in the mountains. The train finally stopped at a German troop-marshalling depot about twenty kilometers from Caporetto, which was still held and occupied by the Italians. The troops were separated again and split into half at this second marshalling depot. The train was not permitted to approach much nearer, staying back for safety while it unloaded half of the 83rd troops.

The Allied aircraft had a penchant for striking troop trains, and destroying the tracks as well.

Geza was with the troop contingent that headed south toward Vittorio. These men were sent in Companies as replacements, and reinforcements, for several divisions already engaged and fighting opposite the Italians. Designated Companies went off on a regular road to march to their assigned fighting area.

The Captain leading Geza's Company had decided to approach their designated area overland and cross-country, electing to stay off the traveled roads. He was on horse-back while his troops walked, and from where he sat in the saddle he pointed out to his troops that their comrades would suffer the consequences of their decision to march with the comfort of the open road. (He was proven to be right...in this instance).

They descended a slight slope and then began their ascent from the valley floor to circle the left of a mountain. Shortly after departing the road they heard the sound of air-craft motors coming from around the mountain side, near the road from where they had begun this cross-country slogging. These aircraft, (it was found out later), carried on a bombing and strafing of the road, incurring casualties upon those Companies of the 83rd that had marched down that road.

Geza's Company was not attacked; they were spared because of the Captain's decision to stay among the woods on the mountainside. He had a map in a cylindrical leather case that hung about his neck and was slung behind his back. He was observed viewing it, supposedly, mentally plotting the path to their destination. It would be an all day march to camp and supper, if they wished to eat that day. The Captain rolled up the map and put it back into its cylin-drical case, swinging the case behind him again.

"Let's hurry boys, and we shall get there soon".

The Captain's horse led the way and so the troops fol-lowed the horse's ass leading them.

They marched vigorously for five hours, and were led around that mountain; they were back to where they had started, near the same road that the second half of the Companies had embarked on. The least intelligent of the infantry could tell this was the same spot where they descended the slope and had ascended from the valley floor. A few men in the Company openly grumbled at the Captain's ignorance, remarking that they had truly followed a horse's ass.

Needless to say, the Captain was a bit embarrassed, but he was not ashamed. Even though he had lost his way, he had not lost any men. It was certain that the second half of the Company had lost some men before they had even engaged the enemy. What a hell of a baptism of fire those green troops must have had when the allied aircraft attacked them.

The Captain's tired troops were allowed to rest here, while the Captain further studied that damned map. Some soldiers were so tired that they just fell back against their knapsacks and slept. They were dog-tired! Others ate half their rations, beef and bread from their knapsacks, and they too, rested. They rested all night.

In the morning they were off again without breakfast!

They marched, again for five hours without rest. When the Captain observed that they had indeed progressed and had not again circled the mountain (it took five hours to circle the mountain yesterday), he let the troops rest for ten minutes. Their knapsack shoulder straps were lathered with their perspiration.

This knapsack was unofficially referred to as "Borjú" by the infantry. Borjú, in the Hungarian language is calf; in this instance with the 'lathering' straps it was called a 'sucking' calf, implying that just as a sucking calf lathers at the mouth while sucking the cow's teats so was this weighted bag lathering the straps with soldiers' sweat.

At about this time a unit of mounted Hungarian soldiers overtook the resting infantry. The mounted men noticed that the foot weary soldiers were perspiring from the long hike and their shoulder straps were lathered white with their perspiration; they taunted the miserable infantry.

"Hey! Szopik a borjú?" (Hey! Is the calf sucking?)

"Don't let that stop you from sucking my ass!" retorted a private.

The horse soldiers laughed all the harder at the wretched infantry, and openly discussed their lather potential.

"Ask your unfortunate horse about his sweat"...and "How would you know about sweat, your horse carries the weight", etc.

Had the mounted horsemen not continued moving on it is possible some hot headed foot soldier would have taken a pot shot at them. They were angry enough with their Captain. It was because of his map reading error that they were taking unnecessary punishment, and now these horse-riding bastards mocked them. It was easy for them; the horse had the labor of carrying their sorry asses.

"We carry ourselves and knapsacks too".

They continued their march, the Captain probably following the horse hoof prints of the mounted troops to make certain he did not get lost again. At dusk they finally reached the assignation.

The cook's kitchen had expected them twenty-four hours earlier so they now received that day's breakfast and coffee, yesterday's dinner and supper – all at one sitting. Many men ate it all, every bit that was rationed out to them. Many did not eat at all, because the cabbage soup was found to contain the cabbageworms as well. It was a fine way to greet the queasy stomach of fresh recruits. Later on that year, during the fight to break the Italian hold on the plateaus, they would have rotten pumpkins thrown in with the cabbages. The entire contents of whatever vegetables could be found were thrown in to make one batch of vegetable soup.

The now queasy troops were led to a marshalling area directly behind the front line trenches where they saw the troops that they would be relieving. The veteran troops passed through an elongated, open slit trench to the side of the main trench. It was a dugout area in the ground where they were sprayed with a white powder to fumigate their lice ridden bodies. The nozzle of the sprayer wand was inserted under their shirts, their tunic, and also down their trouser front.

"What on earth is that for?" The young troops mused; until they saw an old veteran put his field cap on the utensil table. The cap actually moved as the head lice carried it!

"Oh my God! How long have these guys been in the trenches?"

In their advance up and onto Caporetto, the fighting was getting gradually easier as more and more reinforcements added to their numbers. The prime concern was the aircraft harassment and the brutal artillery fire. The Italian artillery gunners on the plateau and surrounding mountains, kept a constant concentration of fire upon the Austro-Hungarians advancing upward and toward the mountain entrenchments, endeavoring to keep the pressure off the Italian foot soldiers engaging the enemy.

The Italians tried in vain to strengthen their numbers and descend the slopes to reinforce their armies in and around Monte Grappa. Try as they might they were left with the major concentration up and on the plateau, above the Venetian plains. The artillery from the Central Powers now began to duel those guns above the mountains, and succeeded in keeping the major Italian forces west of the Piave River.

The Central Powers also kept pressure on the Italians around Caporetto, and pushed an aggressive front at and beyond Vittorio, hoping to make a successful advance to, and across the Piave River a short distance to the west. At night, both sides would venture forth among the barbed wire entanglements; the Italians to reinforce the strands laid out in front of their positions; the Austro-Hungarians to cut through them in an attempt to affect an opening through which a daylight attack could be made.

When sent as replacement troops (közös ozség) for a decimated front line, many of these troops were 'tried out' on night patrols first. If they 'understood orders' well in German, the officers used them with confidence as the need arose.

Italian and Austrian, on these night patrols sometimes met in the dark. They saw one another face to face, but would not fire upon one another. They knew that their rifle fire would be returned, past experience had taught both sides that these few men would be killed needlessly should searchlights scan to find the fight and answer rifle fire with artillery fire. Then the entire front line would suffer for this slight infraction and on both sides soldiers would die.

Knowing this, both patrols would quickly melt away into the darkness without firing a shot.

Such are the rules of 'contact combat'. The Generals did not know that their men ignored the rules of war for the greater good of all the men in that sector.

As the troops of the Central Powers made forward progress, the barbed wire laid out at strategic positions was now rolled back, ends opened up on a fixed center. This made open-ended sections with wide gaps between the still strategically placed wires through which the advancing troops could pass. In case of a hurried withdrawal, these same barbed wire entanglements could be drawn, and the gaps closed behind the retreating troops, thus slowing the enemy should a counterattack follow.

In May of 1917, the Italian General Cadorna began an offensive that swept over the Bainsizza Plateau northeast of Goritz. He also succeeded in taking practically the whole Carso Plateau. The General had thought to encompass the Julian Alps, and take Trieste. He was pushing his troops eastward and too much northward. He may have even thought that he could encircle the Austro-Hungarian forces.

It has since been concluded that his successes here were permitted by the Central Powers, as they deliberately pulled back and allowed this deep incursion in order to draw him and the greater number of his troops into a trap. The Central Power's armies would attempt to cut him off and prevent his chances of a safe retreat.

The Austro-Hungarian forces attempting to get up onto the Bainsizza Plateau left off this futility and concentrated on Caporetto. Their initial attempt was to silence the Italian guns concentrating down upon them from the mountains. Their artillery dueled the Italian artillery and the troops by-passed the Plateau cutting off the Italians as they attempted to withdraw westward into central Italy. The Austro-Hungarians intercepted the Italian withdrawal by breaking through at Caporetto, and with a deep penetration westward to the railhead at Udine. At Vittorio they also succeeded and advanced to cross the Piave River, then proceeded forward to the Brenta River, but were met with a stubborn Italian resistance from atop Monte Grappa. They would have to take this mountain fortress in order to move on to the west and the Brenta.

Geza remembers that the Cannoneers (artillery men), who were very tired, tied their belts to the cannon and allowed themselves to be bodily tugged along by the horse drawn cannon. Poor souls; they practically slept...a form of sleep walk, until they were jerked abruptly as the cannon was jostled crossing a ditch or other road hazard. Their eyes suddenly popped wide open as they struggled not to fall... not to be dragged through the ditches.

During a lull in the fighting, several of Geza's friends decided to attend Sunday Mass, and Geza, like any curious ex-altar-boy, went to see how these services were conducted in the field. Just what was a religious service like behind the battlefield?

Geza had often seen the Company priest among the troops as he visited giving the soldiers moral encouragement, and had heard him talk with the troops in and out of the trenches. He seemed to be the soldiers' friend, usually riding upon a very small horse behind the trenches, but looking somewhat ridiculous because his legs were so long that they extended lower than the small horse's belly.

Now as Geza and his friends walked to the field far from the reach of artillery, and from the scenes of action. He noticed the improvised wooden, folding-altar in the open field. Some soldiers were already there, reclining in the green clearing between two hedgerows of trees, a few of the trees had shell torn tops and limbs missing. This was all that marred the otherwise peaceful scene, and reminded them that the war was not too far distant after all.

The priest actually blessed the soldiers' rifles! This seemed sacrilegious to the young seventeen year old because he did not feel that God could condone the blessing of man killing machines. After blessing the rifles of those who presented them to the priest, the priest then read from a large opened bible on that make shift pulpit. Throughout this service the good priest constantly prayed blessings upon the troops sitting on the ground before him. He talked of God as waiting with open arms to receive the honored dead; those who had died in action. He glorified death in battle with words such as:

"God will give you glory in the after life if you prevail over the enemy...if you fail, the devil will take you!"

To stand your ground, and to die a true Christian was the only way to go.

Softly, but in ever increasing crescendo, a motor was heard overhead. The trained troops heard it before the priest had, but hesitated to turn to see what its markings were, since the priest was so fired up with his spiritual Glory for death-in-battle. It wasn't that they thought it would be disrespectful to run for cover, they just wanted to see what his reaction would be.

But the priest saw the aircraft markings first, since it approached from behind his congregation. It was an allied plane, lazily it leveled off in its course, and the undulating wings straightened out as it approached the open field between the trees behind his congregation. The troops turned to look at the approaching fighter, and then turned with their backs to the aircraft's approach, intent upon observing what the priest would do.

He did not disappoint them!

He slapped the open bible closed, tucked it under his arm and ran for cover, gown and surplice flying in careless disarray. He abandoned all his religiosity for the preservation of life!

The troops burst out in laughter and, mocking him, swore after his receding and frightened figure.

"Hey father, don't you want to go to heaven?"

Others, bolder, stood their ground even with the airplanes' approach, beckoned openly and yelled after him.

"Stay with us! Let us glorify God with our death in the battlefield."

Some spitefully mocked, as they too, ran for shelter.

"Hey, father, wait for us. We don't want that glory either."

Then just as suddenly, all the men cleared the field, like running rabbits, but some were amazingly still laughing heartily as they ran, leaving only that small improvised altar to stand alone as a deterrent to the aircraft.

Geza remembered it too well.

It was several days before the priest dared to venture among the troops again. He was obviously ashamed. However, he had a duty to perform and so he swallowed his shame, and went about his business as usual. But now he carried a canteen full of his best wine. When that was gone, fine brandy, and sometimes whiskey, that he offered freely to small groups of men as he went about his duty *behind the front lines.*

"Perhaps, if I share some favors with them, in time they may forgive me." he thought. But he would have to live down his cowardly act somehow.

JENÖ MEETS GEZA

Sergeant Süle Jenö heard that the 83rd infantry had sent up reinforcements, and since their Home Quarters were in Vasmegye that would indicate that someone from home may be among them. So one morning he paid a visit to the camp that got the reinforcements.

"Is there anyone in this outfit from Szombathely or Porpacz?"

"Yes there is, but he's out on patrol now."

"Well what's his name?"

"Virag."

"Virag? Well I'll be damned! I'll wait for him if it takes all day." Jenö of course presumed that this Virag must be Gergély his old friend.

He had a good visit with Geza's Company; they enjoyed his humor and appreciated his stories. He told them of his many campaigns on the Eastern Front, and of course there were those among the recent recruits who had heard about this much decorated hero or read about him in the newspaper. Jenö also narrated what it was that caused him to be sent to Italy; it was his insubordination with those two Captains in Vienna.

"A fine thank you for your Services," He laughed.

Geza showed up in the late afternoon as his patrol returned for supper; he was then led to where a group of his detachment was gathered around Jenö.

"Well damn it! Is it you Geza? My God! Things must be getting bad when they start taking kids." With a slightly more thoughtfulness he continued. "I fully expected to see

Gergély...any one of the Virag boys but you! The furthest thought from my mind was that I should see you. Why you were only an unshaven brat when last I saw you!"

He placed a hand on each of Geza's shoulders. "Have you heard from your brothers?"

"János and Gergély are missing in action. Antal is dead."

"I had heard that János was missing, but with the war on the Eastern Front soon coming to an end, I hoped that he would surely be repatriated by now. I'm truly sorry about Antal, he was a good man, and he leaves a fine family behind." He shook his head sadly taking his hands off Geza's shoulders. "Don't worry about Gergély, he'll be alright, and you? Damn it son, if you are required to fight like a man, we will treat you like a man. Let's go into town, I'll buy you a drink, a few drinks, as we reminisce about the good times. Your brothers and I...Geza...we had a lot of fun together...you and I now, we will carry on the good times."

There was plenty of wine in Italy, and it was sold quite freely to these troops, for a good price. As a matter of fact, many hungry and thirsty troops drank wine instead of water on their marches between engagements with the enemy because their officers had warned them that the water wells might be poisoned. In the towns however, it was safe to drink the water as the troops noted that the townsfolk drew water from the same wells.

Among the many stories Jenö told Geza as they drank, was a story of a mutual family friend. It was unbelievable, but concerning the possible facts, and because these two knew the man's nature, the story remained with Geza all his life.

Szobodi Sándor (I'm not quite sure this is the correct name, after all these years I may be in error), was home on leave after three years in action, and was on his final days visiting friends in Buda-Pest. Towards evening, as he was walking to the streetcar stop and was singing merrily, happy with the world and oblivious to the fact that he would again be leaving for the front. He accepted it; such is the life of a soldier.

He was challenged by a csendör (gendarme) before he reached the streetcar stop. This foolish csendör drew his sword as he approached Sándor on that quiet and deserted street.

"What do you propose to do with that thing?" questioned Sándor.

"Nothing; It is just to keep you at a distance while I question you."

"About what?"

"You are carrying on in a loud manner; your singing attracted my attention. You may be drunken and disorderly."

"There is no one around. Who am I bothering this late at night other than you?"

"If I choose to say you are drunk and disorderly, then you are drunk and disorderly."

"Look, this is my last day of leave. I'm returning to my barracks, and then to the front line action within a fortnight. Let me alone, look my pass will"... Sándor was interrupted.

"Where are your papers?"

"In my pocket; I was about to... "

"Let me have them."

Sándor did not like that tone of voice. If the csendör had asked to *see* them it was one thing, but he asked to have them. This implied another thing altogether to Sándor. Why he may even keep them or worse still, rip them up. Why the son-of-a-bitch can keep my papers and he can then give me a hard time.

He is trying to give me a hard time!

"Look officer, I intend to get on the next streetcar and be on my way to my barracks tonight. I am not drunk."

"You are singing loudly." The csendör again had an implied threat in his voice. "What does it matter if I sing? I am happy so I sing. If I sing badly is that against the law? There is no one but you in the street to object to my bad singing," chuckled Sándor.

"Shut up, I will ask the questions." He approached Sándor with the sword in his hand. He surely did not know what he was doing!

"Damn you! I have spent three years in hell, commanded to kill...I killed, and avoided being killed, and now you threaten me...?"

Sándor swiftly stepped into the sword arm; turning his back bodily against the man's chest, his back was against the front of the man and with both his hands now on the sword arm extended forward; Sándor then pushed the man backward bodily with his own broad back. The fool did not expect this unarmed soldier to fight of course. He thought that he had the advantage, and so he received the unexpected. Forcing the sword from the man, Sándor swiftly reeled about and now faced the man, holding the sword casually at his side.

Sándor implored. "Now let me be. I don't intend to be held back."

The gendarme reached for his holstered revolver!

"Don't do that!"

But the man did not heed the warning and attempted to draw the gun anyway. Before he could level the gun to shoot, Sándor side stepped swinging the sword and cut off the forearm. The hand, still clutching the gun, fell to the ground.

The csendör was now wild-eyed and, though his right hand was gone, he shakingly reached for his police whistle with his left hand.

"Don't for God's sake man leave well enough alone," begged Sándor.

But the man pulled the whistle forward on its braided cord and, shaking with trauma would have moved it to his mouth except...Sándor again swung the sword and cut off the left hand at the wrist.

The csendör was now screaming! It must have dawned on him what a *very foolish thing he had done to confront this veteran.*

He screamed with pain.

He no longer needed the whistle.

If he kept this up his friends would soon come swiftly to his aid. Certainly they would help him... and detain Sándor... permanently. The csendör, helpless on his knees in front of Sándor continued to scream.

Sándor was angry as hell, and most furious with the man!

A few minutes ago they were both hale and whole; now look at what this ass had done! Why had the fool brought this upon himself? Taken up with his authority, the pompous ass had picked on one soldier too many. Sándor would be the last soldier to be challenged by this fool.

Sándor was the last sight the csendör saw;

Because Sándor could not let him continue screaming, he swung the sword one more time taking the man's head off.

Dropping the sword beside the headless body, Sándor walked on and caught the next streetcar to the train station; the train then took him on to his barracks.

"Jenö why did you tell me this?" exclaimed Geza.

"Because I thought you would appreciate the story of what a determined man will do; he will do what must be done. You have to admit, to get away with something like that a man has to be bold, calm, and have the courage to go through with it. It required lots of guts."

"Well, Sándor certainly has the guts. I hope for his sake that no one finds him out. My gosh! How did you get to know about it?"

"He told me."

"When you were home last?"

"Yes. It was his last furlough before he shipped out again, and Geza, you are right. No one should know about it. It is now just the three of us. Let's keep it at that, okay young friend?"

"Certainly; that is how it should be. Let's not tell anyone else."

And that is why Jenö confided the story to Geza; another act of confidence to cement this new found friendship. How better than to show a complete trust in the young man? Now Geza became Jenö's good friend just like his older brothers.

On the following day Jenö was back with his regiment, and Geza's regiment pushed southward. The fighting was not too furious as the Italians gave ground easily now that they were being forced by a greater number opposing them. The Italian officers were also trying to regroup, and so on some fronts they gave ground more readily because they were moving to form a more solid front, hoping to counter attack.

One of the German Officers of the 83rd led his men into battle by shouting at them from behind.

"Vorwart!" He kept shouting after his men as they crawled on bellies against the Italians. "Vorwart!" Always forward.

A gypsy boy expressed the unanimous feelings of his fellows, and acted upon that feeling.

"Vorwart...vorwart? Always forward, you bastard; while you stay behind? Yes. I know that you will be in the front when we run in retreat. You will show us the way as we see your ass hightailing out of danger ahead of us."

While crawling forward during an enemy engagement, the gypsy boy rolled over onto his back, leveled his rifle along his belly and just above his feet, aimed, and shot the Officer! Since the bullet entered the front of the body, as the Officer was facing the enemy, and the backs of his men, no one was the wiser. They shipped his body home and, as with many officers before him, the report stated that he died in action while leading his men.

When they shipped Sulé Jenö to the Italian front, he got into a difference of opinion with another sergeant. The Captain had made the mistake of assigning both sergeants to the same company.

"Your luck just ran out." Jenö told his adversary. "Before we even get in front of the enemy I'm going to throttle you; you are as good as dead."

They were in the same company but commanded dif-ferent platoons of thirty men each, so the threatened sergeant finally complained about Jenö to the Captain. The Captain saw it the best part of wisdom to place the complaining sergeant into another company to save his life.

He wasn't about to reprimand the 'hero' Sulé Jenö. The Captain needed men like Jenö more than he needed the other sergeant.

There were thirty men in a szakasz (platoon or section). Four szakasz was a squadron, which was made up of 120-125 men and officers. Every szakasz had one machine gun. Machine guns of each platoon were placed 20-30 feet apart. The machine gun positions were placed such that the field of fire of bullets overlapped the next machine gun's field of fire and there were no gaps in the field of cover fire described by the bullets.

The remaining men of the platoon waited, lay in cover on their bellies, or in temporary shallow trenches until the order to advance, or whatever. The corporal or sergeant in charge of an eight-man machine gun crew scanned forward with binoculars. Aerial spotting was done from above while the spotting aircraft signaled down with hand mirrors to the corporal on the ground. The person in the aircraft indicted the distance of the enemy, or effectiveness of the fire through a simple alphabetic code A, B, C, and D, in which each letter signified some command. Was the enemy under cover? Were they still advancing? Are the bullets on target? Etc.

At start of 'fire', the aircraft requested a 'location' or 'range burst', again by mirror codes, and the corporal commanding the machine gun on the ground complied accordingly. The aircraft signaled to 'continue' if effective, and 'hold' until ordered to cease-fire. Continue to fire, or cease-fire was up to the lieutenant or sergeant on the ground. With various instructions from their officer, the machine gunner fired accordingly. Just one burst to locate; he may be attempting to reach a point 100-300 meters distant, or by elevation, to actually arc over a hill.

Eins, zwie, drie...one, two, three bursts; if the gunner could not get the spot, he tried until the burst fell on target. It is amazing to believe that the officer on the ground could see that one burst. But they must have, because they shouted; "thirty meters shorter" or "twenty meters to the left" etc. "Einceg", (once more) to verify the burst. If it was on target; "garbe" (good).

Then they opened with a continuous fire

There were no incendiary bullets for machine guns in 1917. The phosphorescent 'tracer bullets' were developed much later. There were however, bullets that 'ignited' or 'sparked' when they struck. These 'lightning bullets', as they were called, marked the bullet path with bursts of illumination when they hit an object or the target.

Nightly machine gun fire was awesome, and ignited bursts showed the gunner's accuracy with much the same purpose as today's tracer bullets, but as stated, the illuminated ribbon of bullets was not yet developed.

GEZA RUNS
FOR HIS LIFE

Because Geza was a licensed 'steel worker' in civilian life, he was permitted to work in the Military blacksmith's field shops where he sharpened scythes for the neighboring farmers, shod horses too, and whatever metal forging was needed for repairing horse drawn artillery carriages. This welcome relief from battle lasted about four weeks.

The three friends Vyko, Geza and Horvath Jószi wandered into town; on the way they found hundreds of soldiers waiting in line near a house. The young friends joined them and asked what the line was for.

"What's up ahead, food, drink?"

"Two sisters in the house up there," indicated the sex-starved soldiers. "They don't mind consorting with the enemy if the price is right."

"No kidding? All you guys are waiting to use the same girls!"

Just then, one of the girls appeared at a side window and hurled out a dishpan of water. She smiled and cheerily addressed the line of soldiers as she waved at them.

"What the hell was that all about?" asked the young trio.

"You can see that they're clean about their service, huh? See, they are washing after every guy," replied an anxious soldier.

Not if it took ten years could young Geza stomach that. It was disgusting! He and Józsi prepared to leave. "You guys must be sick." They murmured. "What do they do about their lice?"

"Ah come on," replied Vyko, "Don't be squeamish. You guys are just as hard up as we are. You could stand to 'saw off a piece'. It would do you good."

"Not on your life Vyko. Come on, we can do without that. Who knows? There may be some girls in the city who are just as anxious as we are but don't prostitute themselves as blatantly as these two."

The three were being teased by the older men that continued to stand in line as the young friends argued with Vyko. Then suddenly the 'serviced wash water' was once again tossed out the same window by the other girl.

"Oh my gosh! While we stand here and argue with you they have serviced at least four men," said Jószi. "I saw at least that many go in." He replied with a lump in his throat.

"They're using the same water for many men. That's not sanitary," replied the innocents.

To think that this was repeated again and again, as the hundred soldiers waited in line like so many dogs waiting to service the same bitch was too disgusting. Józsi and Geza left; Vyko waited.

During this same time period, as the soldiers received rare twenty-four hour passes, there was an incident concerning another trio, Kenyérés Jancsi (John of the bread). John got this name because he ate his food, bread, as soon as it was allotted to him, and saved none of it. Why save it in your knapsack was his theory, you may die anytime here. He and two of his friends went into the city deliberately looking for 'tail'. They stopped at the edge of town because Jancsi had spotted an attractive 'rump', as the woman bent over working in her vegetable garden. The soldiers exchanged greetings with the woman, and boldly asked if she had any daughters. She stood erect, feet still astride the row, and turned to look at these soldiers who spoke in atrocious Italian.

"Yes," she replied. "But she is in town and won't be home for a while."

"Too bad," said the soldiers.

She shrugged her shoulders, not knowing their intent, turned and bent over again.

"Damn it! That woman has an attractive ass. Look at it fellows; hey why don't you go into town without me, and I'll try my luck with the mother."

"Don't be stupid Jancsi. How could you possibly get that woman interested? She's intent on her work."

"Leave it to me," replied the confident Jancsi.

"Come on. You would only be wasting your time. Can't you see she's busy? No way does she look like she could get passionate, even though that position turns you on, it is probably the furthest thing from her mind."

"How do you know that she isn't thinking right now, bent over as she is, thinking that she wishes she were younger? We did ask about her daughter; she may be thinking how lucky she would be if she were younger. She knows what we want."

"Jancsi you're deluded."

"Go on guys, leave her to me."

The two friends went on without Jancsi, and that damned fool walked into the field where the woman was working. Who knows what he said to her. No one knows exactly what transpired, or how long it took him to make a fool of himself.

A dead fool.

This is the story as it was pieced together following the investigation: Jancsi had attempted to rape the woman once he had coerced her into letting him into her house. How he got her into leaving her garden, we could only surmise; he may have asked for a drink of water, wine perhaps?

But the daughter had returned when he was forcing himself upon the mother. With the mother struggling under him Jancsi fought to keep his dominant position.

While a hysterical daughter clawed at him from above, the mother clawed at his throat and face. Jancsi maintained a hold on the mother's throat. The damned fool may have even strangled her if the fight had continued.

The daughter saw the futility of this fury of hands, and so she ran to the woodshed. Jancsi was not too sure if he had won the struggle and now concentrated on the lone woman under him...the daughter returned too quickly. Jancsi was in total disarray and could not fend off the axe.

One blow was enough to kill him.

Mother and daughter then dragged the body outside where they hid him between the house and some ornamental shrubs. They returned to clean up the blood in the house and waited for the darkness of night to properly dispose of the body.

They were in the process of burying Jancsi undercover of darkness when Jancsi's two friends, returning from town, stopped by to reclaim their comrade. When no one replied to their knocking, they entered the house, and found some broken furniture. They noted that the house was also ominously silent. The friends quickly left through the front door and, in circling the house caught the two women in the act of disposing of Jancsi.

The two friends could not believe what they were seeing, and shouted at the women in alarm. The women, so busily occupied in their ghoulish act, screamed, dropping hoe and shovel. The daughter ran into the night, screaming as she escaped. She knew that the two soldiers could do her harm, and now, would probably harm her mother.

She summoned the neighbors. One of which was sent for the military police; then as a mob, others hurried to the mother's assistance.

"Rape! Murder!" They cried, as they crowded about the two friends who now eagerly released the woman.

In the ensuing days of the trial, such as it was, the regimental major did nothing to the women. He laid no charges on this family.

"They were defending themselves." He told his troops. "And if any of you dare try what that young fool tried you will be shot. I give you my word on it. There are enough whores to satisfy all of you. Don't dare to molest the citizens. They are under our protection while we are here in their country. Not any one of you should dare threaten them or steal from them."

The Major's words became law.

Geza's friend Vyko agreed; there were many prostitutes who were more than eager to relieve the men. Rape was inhuman.

Jozsi and Geza laughed at their friend Vyko's attempt to justify his actions in going to prostitutes.

They were moving out again to a new forward position; then a few days later to another. Without adequate meals during the march, when the troops passed a gristmill near a flowing stream; as tired as they were, hunger prevailed. Some men broke ranks and scooped up a helmet-full of wheat or corn to put into their knapsack. Carried away in their exuberance some of the soldiers wanted to scatter the remainder on the ground by simply casting helmet-fulls away.

One soldier picked up an entire bag of corn and shouldered it. He surely would have tired of it in a short while, and then, forced to leave it somewhere along the route of march it would have been wasted.

"What the hell are you trying to do? That is nonsense. Put it back. Can't you see there is not that much left? Look at the poor miller. What will he have to feed his family? What about the people of the village serviced by this mill?"

The soldier put the bag of corn down.

Geza took a little corn also, and put it in his knapsack. Over all, most soldiers came to their senses, and remembering the Major's threat. They took only what they thought would make a bowl of soup or loaf of bread.

Sure the miller was angry. He must have hated those soldiers, but after realizing they could have destroyed him, or taken all his grist, he must have understood that even in hunger, the troops did show considerable restraint. For that, he may be thankful someday, if he reflected upon it at all. Yes, he would be very grateful...as an after thought...it could have been worse.

The troops were hungry and thirsty, but remembering what they were told...the wells were poisoned. They were also told not to steal food, but still, hunger prevails, four soldiers early one morning ignored orders, and stole a sheep from a nearby farm. They could not lead it away from its barnyard mates, and reluctantly would it be carried without braying loudly.

One soldier immediately slit its throat to quiet it.

They bled it, and then carried it remote from the farm to a place alongside the road. Here they skinned, gutted, and quartered it, so they could stuff the meat into their knapsacks. The quarters proved to be too big to pack into their 'sacks' without displacing or throwing away other equally important meat parts. So, they further reduced the size by slicing large chunks off each quarter, and giving the chunks to their buddies. Geza got a piece also.

During each rest break on the way to the front, these soldiers lit a fire and tried to roast the mutton. But each break was too short; they were ordered to be up and on the march again just as the mutton began to simmer. Marching several miles with the partially cooked meat, they again tried to roast it on an open fire at their next stop. During that day's march they tried to complete roasting the partially cooked flesh at each stop but it was just not enough. They truly felt bad about wasting it because they now felt the guilt of having killed the farmer's sheep. They ended up eating partially raw mutton in order to conserve what they had killed. It wasn't working out as enjoyably as they thought it would and, they tried to appease their conscience by eating it no matter that it was not completely cooked.

They tried to justify their action because they were desperately hungry, but now they had no water to wash the greasy mutton down as they ate it. They entered a village near the mountain stronghold of Monte Grappa and the villagers greeted them with wine. Now the thirsty men over indulged themselves with the wine...the greasy mutton-wine combination got many of them sick.

--- — —---

The majority of Italian General Cadorna's troops were now on the eastern end of the Italian front holding the two plateaus, Bainsizza and Carso, and the valley beyond the Isonzo River.

As the Austro-Hungarian army pursued the Italians from the Udine westward, they entered the Cisalpine Mountains (Present day Venetian Alps). Mules and small ponies carried munitions and supplies because large horses were not good pack horses. They could not endure the load, and negotiate in this rough terrain. The larger horses slipped, and rolled until a boulder or tree stopped their cartwheeling. The infantrymen also slipped, running from tree to tree, and boulder to boulder, down the steep slopes but the little animals were more sure-footed.

The Allied gunners did not shell them as they pursued their course down the precipitous slopes. But when they stopped to rest, no matter how small the spot at any elevation, artillery shelled the trails above. This strategy intended to bring landslides down upon the resting men.

The AustroHungarian forces and their Germans allies were now on Cadorna's left flank, north of his position, headed for the main rail lines at Udine, and threatening to disrupt the main lines of communications upon which the Italians were dependent.

On the northern end of the Isonzo River, German agents had infiltrated, and now corrupted the demoralized and passive Italian Second Army troops. These Italians did not want to fight, and wanted no part of Cadorna's discipline in this "governments' war". With information given them by the German agents, they feared this build up of Austro-Hungarian and combined German forces to their rear, and on their left flank. The agents led them to believe that resistance would be suicidal, and that they were grossly outnumbered. They were encouraged to follow the Russian example to desert the front line fighting and go home to their loved ones.

Survival became their only thought...the hell with patriotism and the glorification of Generals. They threw down their rifles at the slightest threat to life, and preserved life by surrendering.

The Austro-Hungarian troops that had established themselves in the forward positions around Monte Grappa were now under the enemies' positions as the artillery concentrated firepower within the foothills that rise leading up to the mountain. Monte Grappa is between the Piave and Brenta Rivers, and proved to be a very strategic position held by the Italians. It lay directly in the path of the Central Powers' line of approach into the south of their spearhead into Italy. While Central Powers troops were under shear walls and ascent-ways approaching the mountain; the artillery above concentrated on the lines of troops attempting to reinforce the Central Powers troops below.

The military cooks tried with their best efforts to provide food to their assigned companies while under cover of trees if they were in wooded areas or under shelter of over hanging rock. They devised every means at hand to conceal the smoke from campfires; they tried to improvise, planning that aircraft or artillery spotters should not detect the cook fire smoke.

The artillery batteries of the Allies on the other hand, shrewdly awaited the noonday meal by the clock. Having spotted the slightest wisp of smoke they zeroed in and waited, deliberately not shelling the spot, and not giving forewarning to cooks or soldiers. Then at dinnertime they opened up with a heavy barrage that caught camp cooks and hundreds of soldiers gathered closely together for dinner.

The green troops ran in all directions like so many chicks from under a mother hen. The old timers dug in, or ran back to the trenches.

It was actually safer in the trenches at any mealtime.

Invariably, friendly fire intended to knock out the artillery positions on the mountain top, or concentrated on the granite trenches where the Italian troops sought refuge from the shelling, brought pieces of mountain toppling down upon their own troops. Italians, Austrians, Hungarians and Germans were buried alive together as one fell down upon the other from a common shell burst.

In death they minded not in the least their mortal differences. They were now united in immortality...equals once again, as God had intended them to be from the beginning.

As the Central Powers' artillery swept the mountain weakening the Italian return bombardment, the infantry pressed onward and upward upon the Italians dug in the mountain trenches. The incessant Allied shelling was furious and granite slabs burst down upon the troops without discriminating their National loyalty. The Austro-Hungarians charged from one Italian trench line to another, charging the second trench line they also occupied it. The fighting was intense and horribly devastating.

Geza's St. Christopher, locked in that iron box hung around his neck, took a beating as it jostled about inside. At those times when the troops could finally sit down, Geza would take the Saint's likeness out of the locket, to peruse it, and think about his Mother's many prayers.

"How's he doing in that iron box Geza?"

"He seems to be more protected than protecting," replied his friend Jószi.

The young soldiers laughed heartily at the thought. Inside the iron box was certainly a good place to be when charging an enemy position.

"His nose is about worn off, and his shoulders are taking a beating as he bangs against the locket sides," replied Geza.

The young soldiers gathered around Geza to examine St. Christopher. They unanimously agreed that he was becoming more a disfigured ornament than a statuesque saint.

"Yes. But look how he protects Geza." One jeered. "He hasn't done too badly, Geza is still whole."

No one could disagree nor argue that point, be they religious or atheist; Geza was still in one piece. Eventually one of his superstitious comrades did take Saint Christopher out of the iron box while Geza slept, perhaps for his own protection, seeing how well the Saint took care of Geza. Geza did not realize it was gone of course, until a later time, when they had run forward and found shelter, Geza opened the locket as he had so often before, only to notice that St. Christopher was no longer with him. Geza never did find that little figure and no one owned up to having taken it. He then took the iron box and chain from off his neck and pocketed them.

Some of his companions took this missing Saint as an ill omen for Geza; surely the young soldier will meet with some horrible tragedy, now that the blessed saint was gone from him.

An evening in October 1917, around October 23, Feast of St. John is how Geza remembered, as darkness descended first upon the battlefield valley, and then upon the mountaintop, the young soldiers were on edge. There was an ominous silence, the silence that fills a warrior's soul with anticipation.

Many young men were afraid.

The old veterans cursed them in quiet whispers; as some young men crawled out of the trenches to fall back a short distance to relieve their nervous stomachs and bowels in an attempt to stop their shaking, anything to ease their tension. Geza told the old veteran sergeant, Jószi and Vyko that he also had 'to go'.

"Don't unload your nervous shit in here...go to hell...but go quickly and quietly. Get out of the trench to shit or I'll wipe your nose in it." The sergeant cursed.

Geza was no more than twenty meters from the trench and to the left of the sergeant's position when the first shell struck! The shell fell about fifteen meters to Geza's left. Truthfully he was surprised, even though he had been closer than that to exploding shells in the past. This one had penetrated the darkness and silence too sharply...and then another struck too suddenly to his right, about fifteen meters distance.

He would run, pulling his pants up, he tried to run away from that line that the shells had indicated...toward the trench. Because he now felt those *shells were hunting for him.* Someone over there had spotted him and may have been using him as the "line of sight" for a trench line barrage.

And then it hit!

The third explosion was almost upon him as it struck dead center between the previous two shell bursts. It hit the position where he had been when he began his sprint for the trench...it most certainly buried his shit, but...

It had found him!

When the first shell exploded the old sergeant suddenly unwound like a broken watch spring. He turned to see the shell burst behind the trench and near Geza. He commented amusingly to Geza's friends that the allied artillery was out to get Virag. When the second shell struck to the other side of Geza, the sergeant was grim faced and now had no comment. Having experienced many bombardments and seen this pattern before, he knew what was coming next. The three men saw Geza silhouetted beyond the trench in the flash of the second explosion.

It is certain that the Allied spotter also saw that same silhouette.

His friends would have yelled to him, even the old sergeant wished to encourage him to run, to hurry, but remained grimly silent and spellbound. There was nothing they could do but watch him begin his race with death!

When the third shell exploded he was gone!

They could not see Geza.

"They got him. Good Lord they've killed him," exclaimed Vyko.

The sergeant was the first to react, perhaps he felt guilty for cursing the young man out. After all, he was just a seventeen-year-old kid. He had a right to be nervous. Now was he dead?

"Come on you slow witted bastards, don't just stand there let's help him," yelled the sergeant as he rolled out of the trench.

Leaping to his feet he ran to rim of the third shell crater. The young friends and several other soldiers quickly followed, so that this particular section of trench had few men left in it. Earnestly and with eager hands they fell to the somber task, digging about the dirt tossed perimeter, oblivious of the bombardment now concentrating upon the line of what the Allied artillery spotter thought was a trench full of enemy.

They dug with their bare hands, clawing up the dirt, feverishly searching underground for their buried companion. Some dug with bayonets, swiftly scraping rather than prodding, to find the body under the upturned earth and granite shards.

If he was still alive, if he had a heartbeat, there was still hope for him.

He may be buried but alive!

They found him!

Minutes after that dreadful explosion they pulled him forth from the grave into the open air.

He was not an encouraging sight to his companions.

At the threat to personal safety they had risked their lives being exposed to the artillery fire in open terrain. They had hoped to dig him out alive. Now as they saw his shell-shocked body, blood gushing from his nose, his mouth, from his ears and, some say that blood even flowed from his eye sockets.

They wiped the bloodied dirt from his face, tore open the tunic to allow the chest to expand, and freed his legs and arms. Hopefully he would suck in the air to feed the suffocated body, the evacuated lungs. Hurriedly they half carried, half dragged his lifeless body from the dirt. Then they lifted him and carried him back, back behind the line of trenches to the medical post beyond the field of fire.

The medical corpsmen worked on him there. They cleaned him up and found no wounds. There are no wounds on a body suffocated by the earth of artillery bombardment. Concussion is grievous enough, and all the damage is internal. His body waited while the artillery continued to harass those German and Austro-Hungarians who remained in the trenches.

His friends had brought him back into the world; they had given him life! He had been "resurrected".

Those who had brought him from out of that hell, the old sergeant, Vyko, Jozsi, others, now returned to where they would be more useful.

Those three shells that were placed to strike Geza were the first three of a major artillery duel. The Allied artillery concentrated on the enemy trenches below, attempting to break up the massing of Central Powers troops. But the Central Powers' artillery returned reply so furiously and effectively on the artillery above that they prevailed. There were heavy casualties on both sides, more Italian guns were silenced and the Central Powers troops swept forward and upward to the trenches on the slopes. The bombardment lifted and the troops advanced eagerly to route the Italians from the last stronghold facing them. The Central Powers won the battle begun in October, ending in November 1917.

At Caporetto the AustroHungarian forces also succeeded in breaking through that same October 1917, and now pushed the Italians relentlessly back. This was the offensive that succeeded in destroying the Italian armies. It was planned to be executed one year earlier, May 1916, but it was aborted on June 3 of the same year (the reader will recall, because of Russian General Brusilov's timely intervention and invasion from Galicia upon Bukovina and Galicia, German reinforcements were sent to meet that threat. Reinforcing the Italian Campaign was postponed to 1917).

The unrelenting forces of the Central Powers now threatened the main lines of communication and the main lines of retreat.

Those Italian forces to the north and east were in serious threat of being totally trapped and cut off. The battle now developed into a race for the Udine railroad center, with the Central Powers pushing down rapidly from the north. The fleeing Italians were desperate as they approached Udine from the east... and a goodly number won the race... to escape by train. The Italians thus saved a large part of their effective fighting force.

In this race upon Udine, the Central Powers did intercept the escape route of the greater force however, and drove a wedge between the retreating armies cutting off the majority before they could retreat. Many thousands were killed; 250,000 were taken prisoner as immense stores of ammunition and large quantities of guns were captured.

(I have before me a newspaper clipping, circa 1979, titled "Italians Uncover Arms Cache from World War I, *Gorizia, Italy* – U.P.I. – A large cache of World War I ammunition and explosives has been found buried under a field in northeastern Italy, officials said Sunday.

Army demolition teams have unearthed more than 8,818 pounds of large-caliber artillery shells, and explosive nitro gelatin, incendiary bombs and hand grenades remain to be dug up, the officials said.

They said the munitions were apparently abandoned by the retreating 3rd armored Corps of the Italian Army that did not have enough time to destroy them during the World War I Battle of Caporetto.)

As the Central Powers pursued the retreating Italians from Udine, Caporetto and strategic points in the east, Geza's regiment surrounded Monte Grappa and drove the Italians from between the Piave and Brenta Rivers of the

Venetian Plains. He was on his way back to Vienna, Austria, with the many hundreds of wounded.

The Italian army was fleeing with General Cadorna and offered little or no resistance. The fight had been taken out of them and the Central Powers progressed rapidly. General Cadorna continued to fall back until he reached the security of the opposite bank on the west of the Piave River. He and his troops crossed over, and here he was stripped of command to be replaced by General Diaz. Diaz continued to make a stand; the river lay between the tired Italians and their relentless pursuers.

The Central Powers came to a stand on the east bank along the entire length of the Piave, having actually crossed it in a few areas. October and November of 1917 placed the Central Powers in a decisive position for a 1918 spring offensive.

The Allies had no choice but to send help to their beleaguered and desperate ally. American, British, and French troops sorely needed on the Western front in France, were now dispatched to fill the breach. If the Austro-Hungarians succeeded in crossing the Piave River with a new offensive, nothing would deter them from a quick victory in Italy. This would bring a new and very serious threat to the allied armies in France, the Central Powers would be free to attack from the Southeast and into France.

The Italian Army was never again an effective fighting force. It had been crushed, shattered as planned by the German High Command. General Cadorna's incursion onto the Bainsizza and Carso Plateaus appeared as great victories but were, in essence, a climactic tragedy. The unexpectedly well-reinforced Germans had fought back hard, thus overwhelming them.

But Monte Grappa still remained in Italian hands!

The Austro-Hungarians had crossed the Piave and were now on both sides of the river in this salient, leaving the heavily defended mountain surrounded.

Should the Central Powers succeed in crossing the Piave further southeast, and downstream, the war in Italy would soon be over. To prevent this, the Italians flooded the 'Venetian Plain' and thwarted this possibility. They continued to harass the enemy with artillery, mortar and allied aircraft, as the enemy attempted to make a bridgehead by ferrying troops and weaponry across the flooded plains.

This description, by the correspondent mentioned in the writing that follows, is of that November 13 and 15, 1917 offensive: taken from "History of The World War", page 780, Volume 2, 1916-1917; Copyright 1920, by the Grolier Society.

"On November 9, 1917, the retreating Italian armies reached their positions on the west of the Piave River. Within two days the German, Austrian-Hungarians had taken much of the Upper Piave and Val Sugana. In this action the western and eastern sides of the Piave were united and in the enemies control."

"Working eastward down the Brenta Valley from Val Sugana the Austrian mountain troops and some Hungarian divisions drove the defenders toward the last ridges at Monte Tomba and Mount Grappa, and approached the end of Val Frenzia. Meanwhile, the Italians eagerly watched the mountains for the first signs of the expected snows.

The snows came late."

"On the Piave, (Austro-Hungarian Field Marshal) Boroevic's forces crossed to the west side at Zenson, only eighteen miles from the sea, on November 13, and took a bridgehead farther upstream. When at the mouth of the river, Hungarian battalions crossed the canalized stream and started over the marshes to the old riverbed, Piave Vecchia, or Sile. The Italian engineers opened the flood gates which had been built to reclaim land in the delta and control the rise of waters in the lagoons of Venice less than twenty miles away. Of the conditions after the floods were let loose on November 15, we have this account by a correspondent."

"FLOODS DEFEND THE ITALIANS ON THE LOWER PIAVE"

"The water effectively holds the enemy at most exposed points and fifteen miles on the west bank of the Piave. The flooded area is about seventy square miles, and the water is a foot to five feet deep and twelve miles in width at some points, making the district impossible of occupation or movement by the enemy troops. The enemy clings to the west bank at Zenson, but is crowded into a small U-shaped position relying on batteries across the river to keep the Italians back"

"The lower floors of the houses in such villages as Piave Vecchia are under water, and the campanili stick up from the mud-hued level of the flood like strange immense water plants; and here in the silence of the floods the enemy is moving boats and squelshing over mud islands. Peasants, awaiting rescue from the inundation, see him arrive with feelings much like those shipwrecked people who hail a passing sail and find it is a pirate craft."

--- — — ---

That is a huge amount of area in this remarkable description of a river flood plain of seventy square miles! Twelve miles wide in some areas and having been deliberately released by the engineers opening the flood gates that had been built to reclaim land and control the rise of water in the lagoons of Venice less than twenty miles away. Italians did this to assure drowning the thousands of Hungarian and German troops, as well as their own citizens in those villages!

With a raging river now in front of them, the Central Powers would have to find another method of attack

Both sides dug trenches paralleling the river Piave, and waited. The Central Powers for regrouping and preparation for a new offensive to cross the river. The Italians...Just because they had to. They had to stand until their Allies came...and as long as this flooded river separated them from the enemy.

That winter of 1917-1918 also had heavy snowfalls, which again, aided the defending Italians.

The Allies came to their aid in the spring months of March, April and May 1918.

The Battle of the Piave was yet to be fought.

RUSSIAN REVOLUTION

Jószi Virag fell sick that winter, in the New Year of 1917, and with his sickness came depression. No matter how his countrymen encouraged him, no matter how his cousin János Virag reminisced about the good times. János even boasted to the other Hungarians about Jószi-Falcon-Virag's attempt to fly many years before anyone in the village had even seen an aero plane.

"Too bad that you could not have joined the flying forces Jószi, you surely would have been in your element. But no matter, soon the war will be over and we can all go home. Then you can learn to fly a motorized airplane." encouraged János.

"The guards are even talking," replied another inmate. "They feel that they will be going home soon. Something is amiss in Russia."

"Have hope Jószi," begged another Hungarian.

But Jószi lost his will to live; perhaps he felt that life had already passed him by. Others, who had not known anything about flying when he was experimenting, were now flying and fighting aerobatically in the air. The imagination of his dreams was being realized... by others. He didn't give a damn about learning to fly anymore.

With his illness and in the abyss of depression he saw no way out.

Jószi died.

He was put outside with the others who had died that winter. The dead froze quickly and were stacked one upon the other like cordwood because it was impossible to break the frozen ground. Not one of them was to be buried individually, and with the customary respect given Christian burials. The procedure was to wait for the ground to thaw when the weather became moderate. In Siberia that year of 1917, it was July before the ground could be broken. Even then, petrol was poured onto the earth, and set on fire to accelerate a 'spot thaw' in the concentrated area. The prisoners then dug a deep, long pit, into which all the frozen bodies were re-piled, side by side and on top of one another, again, like so much cord wood.

They were then covered over with the dirt removed from the open pit.

But there were so many dead the dirt pile rose into a huge mound above the ground level. The burial parties had to climb the mound with wheel barrows to completely replace all the dirt that had been removed.

When the revolution broke out in 1917, news of its success was slow in getting to these remote Siberian outposts. The Russian captors who had not seen their families now eagerly opened the prison gates when the news was finally verified, allowing their captives the freedom to return home. Some guards had been stationed at this God forsaken icebox for over three years.

"Come with us; share in our new future; you are free, and we are free." Was the happy response the Russians gave their former enemies.

In their haste, the captors left their captives to their own fate. If the former prisoners chose not to share in the 'New Russian Destiny' it did not matter. There was no longer such a term as "enemy" among these who had shared the common Siberian cold.

They were, captors and captives, now wretched kindred spirits.

The enemy lay in Russia.

The new enemies were those who opposed the people's desire for change.

János Virag went to the stables and fed "his" horse. That faithful animal that he had been captured with in 1914, had also survived the mean winters. While the horse ate, he gathered a few pieces of rags that the prisoners called clothing, and a few crusts of dried bread. Then, he too started for home, heading south. The Hungarians would begin their westward travel when they were in a warmer and more comfortable Southern Latitude. He shared the road with fellow prisoners and Russian guards, riding the horse bare back at times. He progressed a good distance, and traveled faster than those on foot. (I marvel that the Russians did not confiscate the horse for their own use, after all, they were armed and the Hungarians were not.)

At times János walked and led the horse, but always with that same 1914 halter on the faithful horse's head, and once again they passed through Uralski Vida.

When he neared the Russian–Roumanian border, for some reason fear got the best of him. He thought that the border guards would give him a difficult time and take his four-footed friend; perhaps imprison him as a horse thief. Reluctantly he removed the halter off his faithful horse, and set it free. The horse had earned its freedom. He left it grazing in a secluded wooded area, and then alone, he walked across the border and on towards home, to Hungary, carrying that halter all the way.

He would remember that horse for a long time.

A cousin, also named János, states that on his returning walk from a concentration camp in the Russia of 1917, they relied on the kindness of the Russian people in all the counties that they passed through. Cousin János did stop to work, helping a kindly landowner. The room and board was so agreeable that he remained for a while. His arrangement with the landowner must have been compatible because his 'short stay' lasted for three years. When finally he returned to Hungary in March of 1920, he admitted that he did not have it too bad for those last three years.

Many soldiers traveled in small groups, these must have appeared as a threat, unshaven, and poorly dressed as they were. Locomotives carrying freight, or passengers, would not allow the returning soldiers passage, not even within the borders of their Hungarian Homeland. Although a single homeward bound soldier could not have been much of a threat, and should have been treated differently, the engineers of freight and passenger trains alike, did not even slow down for them.

But Virag János did make it home: home sweet home, and to a happy reunion in the summer of 1917. How ironic, cousin Jószi may have returned also, as János and many other prisoners had, but he just could not endure the suffering and the energy that was necessary to make it.

János preceded Jószi to that Siberian camp and was destined to be with his cousin for the last days of the boy's life. Perhaps God intended János for that purpose? Jószi needed help and consolation in those last, trying days, and his cousin János was there; he would also be the messenger to carry the story of Józsi's death to the bereaving family. Without the will to live, it is certain that Józsi would have died anyway and the relatives would have always wondered about his fate, as relatives always do when a soldier does not return from war.

It set Jószi' s parents mind at ease...a little, that he died among helpful, consoling countrymen.

(The greatest irony is to presume that Jószi had traveled the very same route that Gergély had, and that Gergély had also preceded him into that same town of Uralski Vida...into that same prisoner detention area near the Old Kulak's farm before Jószi was forwarded on to Siberia. Had Gergély but known. But the Fates are sometimes cruel, and the Fates will that some must die.)

--- — — ---

The Old Kulak had one daughter and two sons, both officers in the Czar's army. The daughter took a liking to Gergély, as did the Old Kulak, much to the consternation of the two sons. Since Gergély had served him well, the Old Kulak made him foreman of all his lands. Now in 1917 the daughter and Gergély were getting serious, and it is certain that the brothers would have stopped the romance because they wanted their sister to marry a Russian; perhaps marry into Russian nobility.

The two brothers did not like this foreigner and stated their objections to their father often, but because of the internal turmoil of revolution imminent in Russia, they were not in a position to prevent it from happening.

With the disturbances in Moscow in the early spring, the two sons were summoned back into service for the Czar. During the 1917-1918 internal struggles with the "transitional government", and the opposition to it, in which Red communist Russians fought White Russians loyal to the Czar, the sons were actively engaged on the Czar's behalf. It is possible that after the Czar's execution they continued to oppose the Revolution with the few remaining Loyalists.

They never returned to the Old Kulak's Homestead. It is presumed they were either killed in these battles or escaped to foreign lands as many Loyalists had, but they were never heard from again.

The Old Kulak now had no heirs but his only daughter, and the father was naturally partial to his daughter's feelings. In the fall of 1917, after his sons had been away for several months, Gergély and his daughter were married. In this manner Gergély became the Land Lord. The revolution and its changes, land confiscation, and collectivization would still take a few years to reach this happy household.

The certainty was that *change would reach them*. Twelve hundred acres of land would not stay a possession of one family, and untouched by the Reds for long, but in the meantime it would still be farmed by the Old Kulak's serfs and many other hired help. It would stay a one family possession because so far, the peasants liked the ancient and customary arrangement where someone took care of them, and provided for their needs. They did not have the responsibility of thinking for themselves, but were told what to do and did it well, for food and lodging, and a pittance of pay.

--- — —---

With victory over the Russians at Pinsk in mid September of 1916, Von Mackensen was now called upon to deal with the upstart Roumania. Using the Central Power's new Ally, Bulgaria, as his base of operations, he attacked, and drove hard into Dobruja between the Black Sea and the Danube River.

General Von Falkenhayn attacked Roumania from Transylvania in the north. Hard pressed to cope with the situation that she had created, Roumania now called out to Russia for help. She had brought the wrath of Germany down upon her, and she was being sorely distressed for it.

But Russia could not help!

Her armies had been shattered at Brest-Litovsk by Hindenburg and at Pinsk by Von Mackensen. Even now, what little order remained within this remnant of the Czarist armies was being usurped and corrupted by Russian traitors and German secret agents. What little help Russia did send Roumania was not enough and Roumania retreated.

October and November of 1916 was disastrous and hopeless for this Russian ally that had procrastinated in getting into the war. She had entered too late with too little to be any good, and now, the Germans were punishing her for it. Russia could have done without that added stress and aggravation... of coming to Roumania's aid. She was experiencing misery enough because of her greater losses. Russian troops could only provide a cover for Roumanian troops as both withdrew from Mackensen's pressure.

December 6, 1916, the Central Powers entered Bucharest. The Roumanian army retreated under the Russian umbrella, to retire with the Russians, beyond Sereth. The war was over for Russia and Roumania. No more active engagements were to be forthcoming from these sectors of the Eastern Front.

The Russian Bureaucracy, like all bureaucracies, had become confident in their many deceits in exploiting the war for personal gain. In their high, untenable positions within the hierarchy, they deliberately began to corrupt normal government, because they cared not for the needs of the people...and were greedy. Their greed in turn promoted mismanagement, and, finally, to cover up their corruption, greed and mismanagement, they kept the truth from the people. Like partners in crime, the officials lied and invented stories to aid one another's deception of office.

With this stratagem, the next step became betrayal; betrayal of the regime that appointed them to positions of trust; betrayal of the Czar, and betrayal of their own people! Blindly they staggered about in circles of self-preservation. But they always stumbled deeper into the pit of lies; never once thinking that their disgusting lack of patriotism, their false front of loyalty, would lead to Russia's ultimate loss, and betrayal of themselves.

Their "apparent" ineptness in allocating supplies to hungry troops ill supplied with arms and clothing was actually for personal enrichment, at the expense of the troops. The much-needed supplies failed to reach their destination because of the treachery within the many layers of bureaucrats.

Rumors, and stories of this graft, corruption, and treachery, began to reach the men of the fighting armies of Russia. They soon learned that these leeches forced the harsh circumstances, and the hardships upon them. They also heard that some army officials, and in some cases generals, had sold information to the enemy. These poor souls enduring the enemy, were also suffering grievously those rumors and reports from home. They were suffering physically during that cold winter of 1916-1917, as the most wretched army, ignored and forgotten by those in more comfortable positions at home.

German secret agents operating in Russia became aware of this increasing disaffection and disenchantment by the Russian enlisted men. They began stirring up even more dissention and trouble, assisting the communist radicals, Socialists, and Bolsheviks. The German agents promoted and encouraged revolt. They joined subversive organizations under the guise of ideological Russians sympathetic to the revolution. Victory in the overthrow of the Czarist government would serve the Central Powers ideals equally well, far better than expending German lives in a direct and general warfare.

When the allies were defeated in the west, there would be time enough to deal with the communist revolutionaries, and then Russia would be added to the Great Middle European State with Germany, Austria and Hungary at its center.

For months the Slavic forces, Roumania and Russia held the Danube-Sereth front. The fighting was only moderate anyway, since Germany pushed no more offensive here. She knew that she could win politically now, so she took the majority of her troops from the Eastern Front to where she was meeting the greatest opposition, in France and in Italy.

Russian desertions ran high that winter, and troops homeward bound were numerous. When they arrived in large cities near their homes, they met with agitators advocating an overthrow of the government. These agitators reinforced the stories of greed and corruption of high officials that the troops had heard. The agitators emphasized the bureaucratic disregard for the soldiers and peasant classes. These rag tag men, the rank and file of the Russian army who had fought, bled, hungered, and suffered the humility of defeat for lack of supplies and true leadership, became blind to reason. Their ferocity at the unjust administration that ignored the needs of their families at home, while they were away fighting the war, was more than the anger they experienced at their own forsakenness. They reinforced the number of workers in dissention, and finally, in Petrograd on March 11, 1917, the revolution started. Enlisted soldiers in uniform joined the workers and deserters in a demonstration.

As news of the demonstrations filtered to those men still in the trenches on the Eastern Front, the Russian army became further reduced in numbers until they remained in a pitifully helpless strength. The new leaders of Mother Russia, Kerensky, Trotsky and Lenin, ordered the standing Czarist Army to demobilize.

The Czar abdicated on March 15, 1917.

Kerensky had favored continuing the war and holding Russia true to its commitment to her allies. He must have also become aware of the subterfuge of the enemy agents operating inside the fledgling Communist Party. His intentions were to form a representative government much like that of the United States. However, extremists, radicals, and Bolsheviks, harassed Kerensky at every turn, stating that Russia had bled enough, and suffered enough for the Czar's 'Imperialist' commitments.

As the attitude of the revolutionary extremists began to surface, Germany sent even more agents into Russia. Russia now became flooded with secret agents and agitators. Combined with the Russian Communist leaders; the agents demanded a government that would ignore the Czar's commitment to the allies. Kerensky knew the intentions of this alliance and what was plotted, but he was helpless to divert it.

The peasants and returning soldiers were easily influenced. The illiterate and ignorant peasantry, so long in servitude to the aristocracy, cared nothing for, nor did they know the differences in the forms of government awaiting them. It was their choice, and understandably so, to stop the 'Russian' war first, and then bring loved ones home from the fighting, to reunite families. In spite of the eloquent pleas from Kerensky, the rabble had their way.

Lenin would be capable of accepting help from Germany in money and men, in order to bring Socialism to the people... and he probably did accept German assistance.

He was once quoted as having said that he would make a covenant with the devil in order to overthrow the Capitalist Systems of the World. He may have thought that after he had succeeded in overthrowing the Czarist regime, he could later outwit, or betray the Central Powers.

Not so: that is for certain, had Germany not lost the war to the allies, she would have annexed Russia in short order. Germany was already helping herself to Russian grain. If Germany could hold out a few years longer; even two years, she would be recruiting from among the Russians.

March 3, 1918, Russia entered the peace conference at Brest-Litovsk; through her Bolshevik agents she made terms with the Central Powers.

March 4, 1918, Roumania also signed a peace agreement with the Central Powers at Bucharest.

The three front wars had drained the Central Powers of much manpower and material. Now, free from the burden of maintaining this, the longest front, the Central Powers were able to allocate the troops from their Eastern Front to where they were sorely needed, in France and in Italy. The situation in 1917 was such, that the Central Powers were already recruiting below the age of twenty-one from within the German States in a desperate effort to reinforce their lost manpower.

The sands of time were being swept away from the footings of the once solid foundation that had been set to construct the "Great Middle European State".

Time was running out.

GEZA
RETURNS HOME

It took many days before Geza regained consciousness. He awoke to find himself naked under clean sheets, in a hospital bed, and not knowing how he got there, or what he was doing there. His last recollection was of the trenches in Italy.

Happy to see him conscious, the doctors informed him of his good fortune. They also enlightened him about the extent of his injuries, concussion and sziv hártya szakadas (literally, 'ruptured heart membrane'; the membranous sac about his heart had actually burst). In this latter analysis he was told how extremely fortunate a young man he was. His friends most assuredly had saved his life by uncovering him as swiftly as they did. He was convinced of his good fortune every day as he sat up in bed and saw that his swollen heart was still beating, but behaved as though it were fighting to get out of his chest. It expanded too far forward, pushing against his rib cage, and threw his entire chest outward against his nightshirt.

He spent one month in the hospital. By that time his heart had calmed down, somewhat. Once he was on his feet he had to learn to walk again because of the trauma and weak equilibrium, his balance was fragile. With the assistance of two canes, one in each hand to steady him, he looked very much like a shaky old man trembling as he placed each foot slowly forward, and leaned heavily upon those canes.

He was most anxious get home again to see his family. Even in his unstable condition the doctors realized that a change from the hospital environment would do him good. If he were among his friends, his family, perhaps he could get a grasp on reality again. So it was that the doctors permitted him to go home. He would spend the month of November 1917, at home.

On the train homeward bound for Porpacz, he thought of the last homecoming just a few short months before. That had been in March just before his seventeenth birthday, when he returned from basic training. How ironic that he had aged, and felt so much older than the short nine months that had passed. Who would be there to greet him?

He did not wish to alarm his mother about his injuries and so had not written home while he was in the hospital. This unexpected visit would be a surprise. Would any of his brothers be there?

He stepped off the station platform and quickly made his way home over those familiar streets. He passed a few old acquaintances of his civilian life, but they did not recognize the wobbly old veteran on canes. He was now a few yards from his home, that white washed exterior so familiar and in his every thought while hunkering down in the trenches. He could not restrain his aching heart any longer; the two canes were now very over worked to steady his palsied young body as he hurried forward. He let out a youthful eager cry, joyful to be alive and at home.

"Mother! Mother! It's me, Geza! I'm home. Mommy I'm home."

Like a boy again, he wobbled hurriedly to cover the last few paces and, just at the door of home his mother stepped out. Incredulous and surprised, she had not expected such a pleasant possibility that day. Her youngest son was home from the war! But when she saw the supporting sticks held in each hand, she was fearful. Both her hands reached up to her mouth and stifled a scream. She looked at his young face and saw that very wide youthful grin and the tears of joy in his eyes.

Instinctively she knew that he would be all right.

She threw open her arms and mother and son met in a shameless, loving embrace. Dropping both canes he squeezed her dearly to his weakened chest. He was not yet eighteen years old, but he was also not that much of a man that he would not shamelessly show his love for her. She held him close, and through tear filled eyes told him that she knew God would bring him safely home again.

"My son what have they done to you? I let them have my youngest son and they send him home to me an old man... with canes for support. Oh how terrible! Then hurriedly she added, but you will agree Geza, that God is kind."

As Geza wondered, and doubted about God's kindness, she continued.

"János is home! Your brother is home from the Russian lands."

And so it was, two of her sons had made it home!

Mother told the entire village; some had seen him outside their homes as he passed them and were curious to enquire about his well-being. Others had heard that an old veteran had been seen on the streets that day, shakily walking with two canes. There was only one soldier in uniform in the village could that have been Geza?

He would explain his injuries in due time, if he wished, otherwise it is best to let things be. When mother asked about the Saint Christopher medallion however, he told her that the Saint too had taken a beating in all the rushing about in the battlefields. He also mentioned that he had not lost St. Christopher, for he had the locket, but somehow the Saint had fallen out...or someone had removed the Saint from the locket when he was sleeping. Perhaps the individual was as superstitious as mother...about the good luck it had provided Geza up until then.

Mother was only temporarily disappointed about the loss of the Saint. (Was it, she thought to herself, the reason

that Geza had been injured, after the Saint was gone?)
Mother went to church, not that very day – but the next
morning while Geza slept late. She got up and went early to
light a candle, and she also told the Old Priest, father Sekés
that Geza was home.

"Do come over to see him Father." Pleaded mother Virag.

His eyes twinkled with recollection of the German
tobacco and wine that he had shared with Geza's father.
"Oh I shall, I shall, I would like to see my altar boy again,"
came the eager reply.

The time was much enjoyed and well spent. Geza had
recovered considerably in just two weeks at home. He had
spent a lot of time with his older brother János as they walked
together to visit friends and relatives, slowly and with János'
help when the canes were weak support for his legs. They
also visited the prison camp to see their friends, Miska, that
Serbian POW, and Tegla Karol. Miska felt genuine sorrow
for the boy, now a soldier and a wounded veteran.

"Geza you have aged a lot." He remarked sadly.

Geza asked jokingly if he had killed any more Hussars.
The friends were light hearted at this visit, so Miska had an
opportunity to expand on the story he was narrating, but
had not finished earlier that year, when Geza stopped him
so abruptly...wielding that sledge hammer.

Miska's commanding officer may have doubted Miska's
accounting of this action and so had asked him to go back
to check on the Hussars they had shot. If they took a head
count or brought back a body, Miska and his men would
receive medals for this action.

That he had the nerve, and cold courage is exemplified
very much so in the fact that he did lead his men back to
the same spot. They saw Hungarian infantry and Hussars
recovering the dead. He left well enough alone. This was an
entirely different situation, his enemy was well armed and
in greater numbers now, moreover they were primed for a
fight. He was not entirely foolhardy.

Miska and his men very cautiously stole away, slinking back across the lines to their friendly forces. Confrontation would lose their lives. They preferred to lose the promised medals.

Now on the retelling of this bold adventure, the friends laughed at the incident. They could picture Miska and his men stealthily sneaking away to safety.

How strange, veterans appear to be forgiving of their enemy after the conflict.

János and Geza had traveled between Porpacz, Szombathely and Vasvar, and to the surrounding villages of their youth, sometimes by train. They talked a lot, and reminisced about the past three years. Geza kidded János about bringing home the halter but not that faithful horse.

"What difference would it have been? You cared for that faithful horse for three years. It was yours, surely you could have smuggled it through the woods and beyond the border. Now all you have to remember it by is that darn halter and some fortunate farmer uses the horse." He laughed.

János was scheduled to return to Vienna; he had been reinstated to active duty and now his four weeks of leave were up.

"Don't go," insisted Geza.

"But they know I am home; they expect me to return."

"Stay another two weeks. Return with me. My furlough is over in two weeks we will go back together. Stay home."

"But they might think I deserted." János balked.

"They can call it what they will. But before they realize it, and send troops to fetch you, you will be back. János I think it stinks. Here we are, just the two of us when there were four brothers; we both served our time and we have to go back for more. It is just not right. Ignore the month leave. They are going to take you to the front anyway. The longer you can stall the better; it makes no difference to them. But it certainly makes a great difference to you, me, and our family. Believe me brother they won't put you in jail, they need recruits too badly for that to happen. We have fretted about you once while you were on the Russian front. We survived that period of worrying, and revived at your homecoming. Now we put our parents through the anxiety of another departure for...who knows what?"

He also told János that he should have stayed in Russia until the war ended. Geza had two more weeks but did not look forward to a return to active duty. He was now much steadier on his two legs and leaned less upon the two canes. He correctly guessed that within the next two weeks he could walk without the aid of the canes. Then he and János could go back to the barracks together since they both had the same Head Quarters; both were assigned to the Közös Ozség (International Troops).

One day while in the house by himself, Geza spent a lot of time in front of that *Holy Wall* of mother's. He pondered the Saints pictures, and those of every brother and sister, cousins and nieces. Did the saints answer mother's prayers? Do they really have awareness? How could those inanimate characters care what goes on in our lives? How could mother have such faith and believe so much?

Is there a God?

Could one so kind permit man to wage war, and permit the whole scale slaughter of innocents? Why was man, who was created in His image, such a murderer of men? Each time he questioned, and each time he doubted, and yet, he was spared. Had he and János not been spared?

"I don't know. I just don't know," puzzled Geza.

His sisters had visited with him a lot but Antal's wife was indisposed, and had not come to see him. Bobbie had returned to Austria, to the home of her parents. She could not get accustomed to being without her much beloved husband. In her mourning for him she neglected the children more and more. She was becoming hopelessly despondent, and needed help with the children. Mother Virag was quite concerned for Bobbie and had been very instrumental in helping her come to that decision, to go home to her parents. Bobbie would be more comfortable at home with her parents; in due time she may, it was hoped, forget her deceased husband.

In the familiar surroundings of her native country, scenes of her childhood might assuage her wounded heart. Perhaps the childhood scenes would help her forget, help heal the broken heart by bringing back memories of another lifetime, another world of her childhood.

But it was not to be; she sank ever more into depression, and rambled on in incoherent conversations with herself. She continued to slowly lose her grasp on reality.

One evening, while János was away from home visiting with old friends, the priest, Father Sekés dropped over for a visit, to see Geza of course before his leave was up. But he brought his long curved-stem pipe with that characteristically big tobacco bowl, just in case, to puff some good tobacco while visiting. He knew that the young soldier always brought the best German tobacco home for his father's pipe, and if he planned it right, the reverend Father might just place himself in a position to take advantage of the old man's tobacco.

Somehow, while he puffed on his pipe and talked the evening through, he expressed his opinion about the way the war was going and that; – "God is on our side. Those soldiers who die go to a glorious death."

That was the wrong thing to say!

Geza jumped to his feet.

He stood shaking above those seated at the table, and now as he stood up shaking as he was, he certainly needed the support of both canes. The room was suddenly silent at his unexpected reaction. The adults were amazed and wondered what set him off so abruptly. They could not believe what came forth from this boy-soldier in the next few minutes.

"To hell with that glorious death you old goat!" Geza cried, "You sit at home and preach the road to salvation leading young fools down the horrible path to enlistment and death. He gets his salvation all right, in an early grave!

Why don't you and your type preach Peace on Earth? Tell those who wage war to stop! Tell them...don't you know that we are all brothers? Preach to discourage wars damn you... and don't bless rifles!"

Geza had seen how God was helping the troops as bloodied bodies clasped hands in prayer before drawing their last breath. He had also seen how the 'religious padre' was serious enough to bless the rifles, and preach salvation for those who die in action, but was himself the first to run for shelter from the enemy aircraft when staring death in the face.

"It is hypocrisy to ask others to do what you dare not do yourself."

"Geza my son, what's come over you?" mother Virag exclaimed, and to the priest; "Forgive him, He is distraught. The war you know...he doesn't mean what he's saying."

"Like hell I don't! Mother, for God's sake – "

"For God's sake. Son stop."

"Mother! It is one thing to preach about a glorious death but certainly another thing for those who experience it.

Pointing to the Saints pictures on the wall with the smaller picture of the Virag children shoved between the wooden frames. "Look at your saints upon that Holy Wall of yours. Do they show any compassion? When you pray do they listen? Do you hear them reply?" He leaned heavily on the two canes now.

"I prayed for you...your safe return...they returned you..."

"They did no such thing! They're still on that damned wall...where they have always been for as long as I can remember. Their pictures are bigger and more important to you than the smaller photographs of us, your children... stuffed randomly in the framed corners. Did they help Antal? I did not see one of them above me in that piece of ground when hell opened up.

They didn't dig me out from where I was buried alive. It was my buddies...with their bare hands. It is to them that

I must be grateful, my comrades are my Savior. Man helps man! There is no other way."

With this last emphasis, Geza swiped at the pictures on the wall with the cane in his right hand intending to wipe them all off the wall and out of his mind. But he was so livid with rage, and he was now trembling so much, that the left hand and one cane were not secure enough to support his excited body. The other cane hit the wall, and it did strike the pictures in their frames. Some of them did swing back and forth dizzily for a moment threatening to fall; but they did not fall. And because mother screamed at such a sacrilegious act; calling out loudly for the saints' forgiveness, Geza left off this threat to the saints, and stormed shakily out of the house.

What was he to do?

Everything seemed so unjust. In these two short years he had thought he was the last survivor of four boys. He thought he was alone. Antal was dead, and he died such an agonizing, ugly death, having suffered so much, having endured so much to be brought home to his loved ones. Then...just fade away none-the-less; how unfair Fate had been to Antal and his wife Bobbie, who even now was on the brink of madness. Did God care about her as she lost grip on reality and abandoned her children?

Assuredly, Geza felt that his oldest brother Gergély was also dead. It had been so long now that he was not heard from, long gone from this life, and who knows where his body lies? How terribly wrong things had turned out.

And yet, as much as he dreaded the thought, he had to go back again. His medical leave was up. He must return to Vienna for a new assignment to active duty. Would he survive? Would he ever again come home?

While he was home, he had been informed of yet another heartache that had befallen his Aunt and Uncle. Uncle had not wanted to tell Geza, and yet, could not restrain himself from telling the painful story.

It is that way.

Sometimes a man must unburden his heavy heart, to remain sane.

While visiting them, Geza had enquired of the Aunt with genuine concern, how her two sons, his cousins were. He had wished them well, and all that was good for them, knowing they were on the Western Front. The fighting on that front was every bit as fierce as on any of the fronts of 1917. The allies were being steadily reinforced with fresh troops from abroad. The Americans had entered the war with fresh troops, more guns, and more supplies to be used against the Central Powers.

The winds of war were becoming very hot; like the heated wind that sears the standing grain in fields already parched and cracked open with drought. This ill wind was no respecter of persons; the best of men were being cut down, just like the grain at harvest. Men with best of intentions were cut down in their prime, along with the "war lovers" and the devils, those generals who drive men to their graves.

Geza's uncle took him into the strictest confidence during this visit. The exact truth should be kept from his aunt.

Cousin Ferenc was an infantryman. His brother István was a medical corpsman and had just recently been assigned to the same division but had not been able to hunt up his brother. The division was in constant battle readiness and fought sporadic engagements too frequently, and regularly on a daily, unscheduled manner to keep the allies from advancing toward their entrenchments.

The story that István's father told Geza went something like this:.....under cover of artillery barrage the infantry attacked allied trenches. When the barrage cover ceased, the allies retaliated, and fierce fighting ensued. There were many wounded lying in the field of battle between the trenches, and Istvan set about with the other medics, and stretcher bearers, to tend to the wounded. As he crawled, and ran bent over, from one soldier to another, he talked to them with words of consolation, but always enquired about his brother Ferenc. He gave a sip of water from his canteen, and saw to their anxieties with knowing compassion. He made sure that the chaplain, also making his rounds among the wounded, would pray for those who were beyond help, so that they died in peace. Finally, after no clues or acknowledgements from those he attended, he came upon his brother lying in that field of hell.

No sooner had he made the heart palpitating discovery, than the battle began to rage about them again in no man's land...that is exactly what it was ...no place for man.

The allies were counter attacking. His brother's leg wounds were bad enough that he could not walk on his own. István administered to the needs of his flesh and blood, in spite of the chaos now unfolding about them, bandages were applied, and the bleeding abated.

Not willing to be out in the open as the murderous fighting ensued, the stretcher bearers had all returned off that no man's land. There were none to carry his brother now as the allies commenced to harass their enemy. István on hands and knees, dragged his brother back a considerable distance to safety behind a clump of battle hazed stumps, aside from the conflict of running men. He comforted with words, and gave Ferenc a last drink from his canteen ...always encouraging.

"I shall return for you Ferenc, after the fighting, I promise you I will be back. But others out there need my help now also, so I must go to them you understand."

And of course Ferenc understood. He felt relieved; his mind was at ease, wounds bandaged, his thirst quenched. He would not deny his comrades the same care. What is more, he knew that he would be safe. After the counter offensive István would return and would care for him and take him back behind the lines. He would see to it that Ferenc was safely returned home. Ferenc crossed his arms about his chest and in spite of the noisy tumult in that salient, closed his eyes to rest and wait.

326 ~ Anthony E. Virag

With a smile to comfort, and one more last farewell, the duty bound Istvan reluctantly left his brother to tend to those who moaned and cried, still lying in the tumbled terrain of mortar holes and the deeper shell craters. Swiftly he moved about the field of blood and death, as though his hurrying would bring the battle to a close sooner. Anxiously he mended wounds with cloth, and assuaged the minds of crippled men who thought that they had been abandoned.

And then the worst of fears!

The allies opened up with an artillery barrage to cover the withdrawal of their infantry from the open areas between the trenches. Hurriedly István crawled among the wounded, dragging some back, one at a time nearer to friendly forces. He could not do more, and he had another commitment, for blood runs deeper than duty.

He dragged one last wounded soul back, back toward that clump of battered stumps to where his brother lay safe. But the additional shell holes now slowed his progress; the earth was torn up and transformed about him. Many who were previously wounded felt pain no more; the shells had ripped them apart. István crawled dragging that fortunate soldier as he went. But he could not find that clump of battle-hazed stumps. István was already there, where he remembered leaving his brother. The terrain had been recently torn up by new shell bursts, so he left the wounded soldier momentarily to search among the torn bodies scattered about.

With palpitating heart, and fearful for Ferenc, he became fearless to the threat upon his own life. He looked about in that hell, still crawling on hands and knees, and again he looked at one corpse lying on its back. Shredded stones and uprooted stumps were around it! He hurried to the cadaver that had arms and legs outstretched in all directions...the head had been blown off! Dreading the worst and still denying the possibility, he examined the body. The recent bandages that he had applied indicated the possibility.

Frantically he searched the pockets and found proof that this had been his brother.

István crawled to that man whom he had brought this far, aside from where the combat had taken place, and dragged the stranger to security. Better to leave that mangled body that was once his brother, to be buried with those who died that day. He did not wish to retrieve it for a return to home, what would be the use? His mother would panic and scream to view the body of her son one more time, and that could not be. It would kill her to see that ungodly sight without a head.

And so it was, no doubt, with many wounded and bandaged soldiers left in the field that may have survived had not that offending barrage blown them apart. His mother should never know. She should never know how Ferenc died. Let her thoughts be what they may, to think that he died in action was good. Never to know how, was best. István would tell her only that he saw his brother that day, and he was well. Then he never saw him again.

István would carry that question with him to the grave. Why had he not taken Ferenc back to the safety of the trenches when he had first found him wounded?

István had told the truth to his father.

Father understood the chaos and confusion of battle, and respect for others wounded that required assistance. He forgave István, and father and son had kept the secret. Now the father had told Geza and urged him to secrecy also.

Only three people knew the true story as István had experienced it.

It would have also been best not to tell him.

His injured heart began to swell again within his chest. How heavy it felt with this additional burden.

A sad heart is a heavy heart.

As he was departing home again, he wished he had not known his cousin's fate. That tragedy certainly did nothing for his morale. Why do his elders burden him so with such terrible truths?

How could he escape death when so many had not?
Would he ever again see his loved ones?

Geza and János were both returning to Vienna for re-assignment to active duty; János two weeks late. They were
both afraid, but kept their fears disguised for the sake of
family and friends.

Tears and sad farewells from loved ones; loving arms
that embraced to hold them, and futily try to restrain them...
to stop time in its motion in that little piece of the world,
while time passed elsewhere and the war ended. Then perhaps their loved ones lives could be spared.

*It has been stated that artillery killed more soldiers in WWI
than did bullets.*

FLIGHT
EXPERIENCE

G eza reported to military headquarters in Vienna expecting to be shipped out immediately, but he was pleasantly surprised to find that he was reassigned to the Machine Gunners of the 83rd. This meant more training, and therefore, a delayed return to active duty.

János was re-assigned to the Hungarian Regular Infantry. He had been in the "Közös Ozség" (International Troops) as had Geza, but now would be allocated to an all Hungarian Regiment, commanded by Hungarian officers. Head Quarters didn't even make an issue of János unlawful extended stay of two weeks; they appeared to be happy to have an experienced war veteran back. Good thing he had listened to his kid brother. A group of soldiers had been mustered out to the front just one week before the two brothers returned to Head Quarters, and János had missed that muster. He would now wait for the next group before shipping out.

As soldiers returned from leave, they were expected to stay within the Head Quarter's compound. These were made up of those like János Virag, returning from Russia, and those who were wounded but now recovered, like Geza. All personnel were on-call for active duty assignments. These men kept returning at random times from their leave, and flowed into the barracks. When a group of 100 or 200 able bodied had returned, they were mustered out together, and sent off to various front line active duties.

329

Geza underwent a brief training period. He could now tear down and rebuild the machine gun blind folded. This was certainly to his credit, but when they took him up in an airplane he puked his guts out!

As the airplane maneuvered, banked and did loops and rollovers, the pilot was forced to level off or get vomit over himself. They landed and once on the ground Virag attempted to crawl out of the rear cockpit but the officer put a halt to that.

"Hold it! How do your feel?"

"Terrible. I puked out everything...even yesterday's supper."

"Good! Then you've got nothing left to bring up." To the pilot, "Take him up again."

And that damned pilot did as he was told.

Twice more they took him up, and he was twice proved a liar; he did have more to vomit out. When they landed the third time and the aircraft had stopped, Virag somersaulted out of the airplane's rear cockpit.

"To hell with them; they could shoot me if they wish but I'm not going up again." He thought to himself.

He struggled to his feet while the pilot climbed out, and ran with the "ground officer" to his side.

"I can't do it." He mumbled before they could ask him anything.

Officer to pilot; "What's wrong with him?"

"I guess he just doesn't have a stomach for flying."

"Damn it. He's such a good shot on the target range; he clusters more bullets than many more experienced gunners. Well, too bad. We'll just have to use him on the ground."

And that was the length of Geza's flying experience. Desperate for skilled rear gunners, they seriously wanted him in a two-man fighter aero plane.

Coincidental to this time, while in the Vienna barracks, Geza received a letter from Sulé Jenö. Among the bits of news and information contained in the letter was this comment: "Geza, what do you think these fools are trying to do with me? You'll never guess. I'm a machine gunner in an airplane! Doesn't that beat anything? These damn fools think I can fly. Oh well, I'll try it for a while. I do like getting up to the fighting and coming back from it quickly to clean quarters and proper meals. It sure beats the dirt and mud ground fighting of the trenches. We'll see you my young friend. I'll probably be back on the ground soon. Take care of yourself."

Obviously, Jenö could do anything; he didn't even get air sick.

Jenö was reported missing in action shortly thereafter.

"Of all the luck," mused Geza, when he heard this through the barrack's news. "I wonder if his aircraft was shot down. I thought that man was indestructible. As often as he was wounded and captured, he always turned up again. I still don't believe he's gone. Captured maybe? But not dead; he's too tough to die."

János agreed. The brother's both had confidence in Jeno's survivability.

On the Italian front in 1917-1918, when the Central Powers aircraft took to the air without specific targets, they would make wide circles over the countryside over the enemy positions, waiting for signals from the ground to indicate a proposed target. If a target and destination had not been assigned, and these same aircraft had been aloft for some time, they became vulnerable to ground fire. With no signal given to drop their bombs, the pilots refused to continue circling above enemy lines; besides, their excuse to flee was that they suddenly saw they were low on fuel.

Those bastards would drop their bomb load on any village in enemy occupied territory; perhaps enemy soldiers were in town? But truly, they couldn't care. Secure in their aircraft, they gave no thought to women and children cowering in that town below.

What was worse, if by some quirk of luck they did strike an enemy munitions cache in their random bombings of those helpless villages, then all hell broke loose as bombs, bullets and gunpowder mixed. Most villages, as small as they were in that era of the early 20th Century, were nothing more than simple cross-road with eight or ten homes and blacksmith's shop. These could be wiped out in any such incident, but the military mind saw it only as a "lucky hit." Who cares what numbers of innocents lost their homes or died in such a well found strike?

That's war!

The aircraft moved back and forth in groups of six when possible, striking columns of reinforcements or supply convoys. It was expedient to get as near to the front as possible with troops or supplies, and if a train was spotted traveling toward the front on the enemy's side, there need be no ground signals for the circling bombers. They attacked to destroy it before it got to its destination.

When ground bound supply reinforcements could not get to them, front line troops needing ammunition were re-supplied by airdrops. It was then that allied aircraft would intercept the supply aircraft, and dog fights erupted. The Americans, British and French always had more aircraft in Italy than the Central Powers. Geza narrated this as fact, and the following paragraphs are his words to the best of my recollection:

"When British or American aircraft went out, there were about twelve in a fighter wing. There were only six at the most in the German flights. Therefore the Germans always tried to get above those greater numbers when possible. Striking quickly into those aircraft on the ends of the squadron wings, getting in their quick licks, they would continue to dive, to get out of there. Invariably, this strategy worked well, when it could be executed. At times, the fewer in number chalked up a better score than the greater number, because these would suddenly mix-it-up. The Allies saw first a German to the left of the squadron, then one on the right diving away. In pursuit of the Germans, they sometimes did not see still other German aircraft diving after them.

"The few planes separated as they flew through the allied formation. Firing into the greater number they were most likely to succeed in downing one. The remnant of the Allied formation broke off into groups. Each group pursued at least one Central Power aircraft and, quite frankly, often got in one another's way. They were not as likely to score on the fleeing Germans in these situations however, as the Allied aircraft randomly following one another in the chase did not shoot wildly for fear of striking an ally.

"A single fighter shooting against many as it dove into them is likely to hit one; he then continued the dive to escape the many shots fired after it hurriedly, and poorly aimed. Those random shots may not be fatal.

Why, if there were three or four Allied planes approaching over the front lines, one German aircraft in the air was bold enough go after them...if he had not been seen by them. He went off in pursuit of the quarry, and did not shoot among them until he was certain of his target. He just kept circling, gaining altitude, in an attempt to get above the group.

"With two machine gun positions, two front guns for the pilot, one for the rear gunner, those pilots were bold!

These air crewmen also carried grenades. If one or the other of the two-man crew did not get satisfaction with machine guns but were now close beside their target, he would toss a grenade at the adversary. The trick was to throw the grenade to the left or right, or even back over their own tail, as the pilot executed an unexpected maneuver.

"Either the rear gunner or pilot, could drop the grenades through an open trap door between his feet on the cockpit floor. A grenade explosion was totally unexpected, and surprised the aircraft maneuvering underneath. With just a little bit of luck, the exploding grenade damaged the wing fabric, or whatever, and could force the enemy plane out of the fight. The grenades were a weapon of "chance" that was more often wasted. But it kept the Allied aircraft maneuvering, and wary to get out of range of shrapnel, as well as bullets.

334 ~ *Anthony E. Virag*

This German was very bold, very daring, and his grenade-toss-bombing caught on with a few other aircrews. The officers were pleased that their pilots dared to challenge when outnumbered.

"Things changed dramatically as the Allies gained air superiority over the Italian front however, and the Central Powers could no longer commit aircraft to the conflict".

It was during his machine gunnery training that Geza met a Company Sergeant Major from Vasvar, named Gaspar Pista. The sergeant major took a liking to the young soldier who knew many people in his home town, and the young soldier intended to take advantage of this camaraderie.

Geza knew a lot of people in Vasvar having served his apprenticeship in that area, and some of those proved to be mutual friends of the sergeant major as well. Pista was a nine-year veteran, having been in the army since 1910, and he had a girlfriend in Vasvar, but he also had a girlfriend in Vienna.

Because he had gifts for his sisters, or had purchased goods for his parents, he was continually asking, "Hey Virag, wouldn't you want to go home? Why don't you sneak out, if your friends can cover for you, spend the time at home, and take a few things for my folks?"

And so it was that Geza went home quite frequently, more to avoid being mustered out to active service, than as a favor to Pista. He looked upon these escapades as a mutual benefit; the sergeant major's wishes were satisfied as was Geza's wish to avoid being shipped to the front.

János had not yet been re-assigned to the next troop compliment that would be shipped out, and Geza stayed close to the sergeant major who assured him that he would not be mustered out with the others...if he were not available. With this assurance, Geza remained in the barracks but told János to go home again with Pista's goods. In this way János could do the sergeant major a favor and, hopefully, he would also miss the next troop muster to ship out.

"If you aren't here when a compliment of troops are to be sent to the front, the better for you, they will get you anyway when you come back. You will go sooner or later, attempt to make it later," advised Geza.

But János was too timid, and did not want to do what was not militarily proper. He was not as bold as his kid brother, and feared military retribution, as odd as this may seem; but Geza continued to coerce him. The younger brother was being a bad influence on his older brother.

Geza went with János to the railroad station to advise him about a device that worked for Geza when he went A.W.O.L while on the sergeant major's "errands".

"When you see an officer approaching pick up your pace smartly and get into step with him. When he shows his boarding pass to the guard, and steps to get aboard, you step lively right after him. Don't even look back at the guard unless you are challenged. The guard will think you are the officer's batman. Otherwise, the guards ask every soldier to show their pass on boarding the platform."

An officer came by, the brothers saluted him; Geza nudged János.

"Step lively now after him, and don't you dare come back to the barracks until they come after you," whispered Geza. "If the guard stops you be bold. Say you are his batman and push yourself past. The guard won't chase after the officer to verify your statement that's for sure. He is too busy attending to those entering the coach."

János took off after the officer. The guard did stop and challenge him but János spoke boldly. Geza couldn't hear what was said, but saw that the guard did step back allowing János to board. János stepped quickly onto the train with his bulging duffle bag, and rushed down the aisle after the officer, as though he were hurrying to catch up. When the officer took a seat, János simply walked past him and into the next coach where he sat down.

Geza had observed all this through the coach windows.

Satisfied with himself, János smiled and in a further attempt at boldness and, to be frugal, Geza found out later, resolved to pay only the fare necessary to get to the next town. From there he would travel free, surely the conductor could not remember everyone's destination. The conductor would be told that this soldier had already given him a ticket for passage. That it was not for the entire trip didn't seem to bother János. He appeared to be bold when pinching to save his own money.

János remained home for two weeks that time, however on his return to the barracks he was immediately shipped out along with one hundred others headed for the Italian front. Well, they finally got him, but there was nothing he could do about it. He had milked his leave and had again cheated an additional two weeks being A.W.O.L., thanks to his kid brother.

A few weeks later Geza again sneaked home to bring some news to Gaspar Pista's girl friend about the sergeant major. He also informed his own family that János was now on the Italian front.

Geza did not go A.W.O.L. alone this time, there were five others, one was a corporal, and the group schemed that he would be "their corporal". They were to be a patrol being transferred to another command. Their ruse would be; they were traveling to their new assignment.

"If you are challenged, show this paper," addressed the corporal.

The paper was something from headquarters and may have had a military letterhead; folded, placed in a tunic pocket it was intended to look like military orders. Because other soldiers would be on the platform, the corporal would call out the enlisted men's names. They in turn would line up for him.

That is just how it worked. The corporal called out the names of his five men, and they lined up for him. Then as they relaxed he ordered them to: "stand to! Damn you— until I order you to get on board."

Maybe he shouldn't have been so officious.

There were officers embarking and disembarking, and of course, one officer getting on board noticed this corporal when he shouted at his men. Noticing their uniforms and their regimental ensign, the officer turned from entering, and disembarked; he approached to question the corporal, because the "83ʳᵈ regular infantry" were expected to be shipped out again soon, and so, he stated, they should not be traveling.

"But aren't you from the 83ʳᵈ? What's your business here?"

Without hesitation the corporal faced the officer. "We are temporarily re-assigned sir. We are a 'Transfer Group'. We'll be back before they ship out the next hundred."

The officer accepted this answer quite naturally, and challenged the corporal no further. They all got onboard, and as soon as they were onboard the six separated into groups of two. Each two sat in different coaches so that each pair would now have to take care of themselves. When the conductor came by to stamp tickets he may also ask for their military passes. If a soldier had a military pass he would not have to purchase a ticket, the military pass was his ticket.

"Tickets! Tickets! Soldiers show military passes," cried the conductor as he came through the coach.

Well, these two soldiers didn't have tickets and they didn't have military passes. None of the six soldiers, now in groups of two, had any right of passage.

"I'm with the Transfer Group that's on board," replied Geza.

"Where is the officer in charge?"

"My corporal? I don't know where he may be seated, all I know is he ordered us all to get on. He threatened that none of us should dare stay behind, so we sat where we could."

It was an unusually very crowded train, and in some coaches passengers were forced to stand in the aisles.

The conductor tapped Geza's companion on the shoulder, since he was nearest to the aisle. "Come with me, point your corporal out to me as we go through the coaches."

"Like hell I will. If I get up another person will take my seat. You go about your rounds; you'll find him. He's in the next coach and he has a boarding pass for all of us."

"How am I supposed to find him? How will I know which corporal it is?"

"You'll find him, just look for a corporal from the 83rd. If he is not in the next coach he will be in the second one, but he's got to be there. He is in charge of us."

The conductor was insistent.

"Stay here," said Geza to his buddy, seeing that the conductor was bound to take one of them. If the friend refused to identify the corporal the conductor would surely have him put off at the next station, and he may be locked up until the Military Police or regimental sergeant came to claim him. He would then be immediately shipped out to active duty.

"I'll go with you," Geza replied to the conductor.

They walked on, Geza and the conductor. The conductor continued to punch tickets and challenge soldiers and passengers as he went through the coach. It was slow going and Geza stopped whenever the conductor stopped.

Because of the crowded coach conditions and having this soldier standing in the aisle beside him as he stopped occasionally to punch tickets and make change, the conductor finally said; "You go ahead. Find your corporal. I'll be there eventually,"

Geza went on ahead. "But I don't know if he is in the next coach."

"Go on until you find him. Go on now." The conductor motioned with his hand for Geza to go, opening the aisle for passenger to pass more freely.

Geza went into the next coach, and the next. "The conductor will be a little while before he gets through this one," he mused. Sure enough, the corporal was seated in the middle of that second coach. Geza was at one end next to a "coach sentry" (örmester, the nearest I can conclude is that the man was responsible for creature comforts of the passengers on the coach, and perhaps handling their carry-on luggage), and beside a window.

"Vigyázon, örmester ur. (Watch out Sentry sir)". Geza stepped between him and the window. "Please step aside for a moment. I want to open the window and go out."

"What...go out...where?" The man was quite alarmed, wide eyed, and incredulous.

"Onto the roof of the coach," replied Geza.

"How in God's name do you intend to get up there...the train is traveling swiftly. Why must you go out?"

"That damned conductor is coming. He's in the coach back there. I'm sure he will put me off at the next station if I don't disappear now."

"Go on out the door between the coaches, there may be a way up to the roof there. But why do you propose to endanger your life attempting to go through the open window of this speeding train?"

The coach was too crowded for Geza to work his way from one end to the other end of the coach, and he wasn't sure he would find another way out and up without causing more attention than he already had with this individual. So he raised the window, crawled through, turned around with his legs inside the coach, and sat on the edge. He lowered his head and shouted back in to the man.

"Close the window when I'm up."

With his body facing the outside glass window, he reached up with both hands and grasped the "drip rail" on the roof of the coach with his fingertips. He pulled himself up so that his feet were now on the edge where he had sat; then he swung himself up onto the roof.

The 'sentry' immediately closed the window after him.

The conductor searched for Geza in vain; while the coach sentry smiled at the audacity of the young private. Without Geza the conductor couldn't find the "Transfer Group" corporal either. The train sped through the first two stations and finally stopped at the third.

Geza let himself down between the coaches, and again boarded the train in a dignified manner. He found his friends, and they continued the trip together as though the conductor hadn't challenged them.

A.W.O.L RISKS

"Hey Virag, do you want to go home?"

It was Gaspar Pista, the sergeant major at it again. He was thinking of his girlfriend in Vasvar. He would send a letter and a gift home to her by way of Geza, while he remained in Vienna to date his Austrian girlfriend.

The regimental cobbler, an artisan skilled in the ages-old leather craftwork, had made a pair of fine boots for each of Pista's two sisters, for a handsome price of course. The boots were made of the finest tanned leather that the military could provide, and were also finished in their tanned-yellow (sárga) color. Other officers had requisitioned the cobbler to make saddles, bridles, and even harnesses for their fathers' farm horses. He was paid well for his efforts and was happy to oblige the many personal requests.

Pista wanted Geza to take these two pair of boots to his sisters before the wetness of spring weather set in. He had already written them about Geza's arrival date, and they would be waiting at the station. Geza was to give the girls their boots and tell them when he planned to return. The sisters would prepare a package for the sergeant major; sometimes it was ten kilos of flour that Geza put into his knapsack and carried back to Pista.

Because milled flour was rationed in Vienna, Pista gave it to his Austrian girlfriend.

It became Geza's "method of operation" to be among the last to board the trains so that he could run and hop onto the train thus lessening his chances of being caught by the guards at the station. If they tried to stop him he continued running and yelled at them over his shoulder; "Hey, I'm already late...I can't stop for you!"

He did not buy a ticket, and the sergeant major had not given him a pass. Soldiers traveled free with a pass. Without a pass, even a ticket was useless because M.P.s and police were on the lookout for soldiers attempting to go A.W.O.L. As luck would have it, there were many times that the station boarding platform was crowded. He would have to push and jostle through the crowds of travelers, their relatives and friends that remained on the platform waiting for the train to pull out.

Now, with two knapsacks, one on each shoulder, he also carried the two boots in a separate small kit-bag in his hand. With the three bags, it was quite an awkward and difficult load. Just as Geza jumped up onto the coach the strap that secured the hand held kit-bag broke. He fumbled to retrieve it before it rolled off the coach platform but to no avail. Then, with those two pair of boots it fell down and landed on the gravel bed of the railroad ties between the coaches just as the train began to move.

Geza quickly un-shouldered the two knapsacks onto the coach floor and jumped down between the moving coaches picking up the defective kit-bag with one swift sweep of his hand. As the train moved forward it could have knocked him down to the gravel also, but he quickly jumped back up to the coach deck. If he hadn't jumped down, he would have certainly lost the boots, as it was, he almost lost his life. He stuffed those damned boots further down into the open mouthed kit-bag.

"You had to be the one to break didn't you? It couldn't be the one with my clothes in it. I could have lost my life just because I couldn't face that damned sergeant major, having lost his sisters' boots."

He made the flaps secure with improvised tying. He was so vehement about the securement that he found he couldn't untie it later, and it remained fastened until he got to Vasvar.

With the parcel for a friend's family in one bag, Pista's gifts, in addition to the clothes, and food Geza packed away for his own family, he actually had three bags full of valuables about his neck and shoulders. When he got to the first station he had to transfer to another train. This was most unusual and not the norm. There were trains going back to Vienna and others that branched out from here but it wasn't often that a passenger had to change trains; they most often would go non-stop into Hungary.

On this occasion, his bad luck continued. Geza in his burdened condition was now required to get off and onto another train.

As he stepped onto the platform to make this train transfer, a military policeman stopped him!

"Leave me be. Damn it, can't you see how loaded down I am? I'm carrying these for two of my friends. We are to receive our marching orders shortly. If you jail me, it will be my good fortune and I won't have to ship out. But damn it; don't embarrass me to my friends by escorting me back to Vienna without having delivered their parcels. It would be most insulting!"

The M.P. looked at Geza, sizing him up.

Surprised as he was, he was also impressed by the brash youthful soldier's answer. But he wasn't about to condone Geza's behavior. For those few minutes between trains Geza managed to bull shit the M.P. with a barrage of half-truths, admitting to the M.P. that he would soon be shipped back to the front, and this is why he took the chance on sneaking home. He was bringing some rare food staples to his folks one last time.

"Only God knows if I will ever see them again."

Not to avoid the truth entirely, Geza explained that he also had what may be the last parcels and gifts of two friends for their families.

"In essence I am the only one of the three that would make time for this trip. That is why I dared to try it. I am the errand boy." Geza repeated what he had said when first challenged. "We received our marching orders, and my friends stayed in the regimental barracks preparing for departure. As soon as I return, we leave. You stop me and I will surely not have to go. It will be my good fortune to be thrown into the stockade."

The M.P. bought it!

He let Geza go. He didn't even look into the bags.

Geza had not lied completely. His regiment was constantly shipping out returnees as they showed up when they numbered a hundred. The sergeant major was simply assisting Geza's delay by allowing him to be absent when the compliment of one hundred was shipped out.

Geza's prime concern was that he would lose face with Gaspar Pista if military police escorted him back to the barracks, and the sergeant major would not get the 10 kilos of flour that Geza was expected to bring back!

As he continued on his homeward journey, now transferred and boarded this second train, he met Forgács Jószi from the 83rd. Jószi had a military pass and also had a knapsack. When the train approached the Austro-Hungarian border it would stop, and customs officials would board the train to check for tickets, passes and baggage.

Everyone was expected to open the luggage for possible inspection.

Truth is, these customs officials did not too often bother soldiers that were burdened with knapsacks and headed home. Understanding this only too well, Geza told his friend, "Since you have a pass and I don't, say that these knapsacks are yours also. Watch over them for me. I'm going to get lost now, but I'll be back when they leave."

As the customs officers approached from one end of the coach, a military policeman accompanied them to help the customs people with soldiers that may give them problems, and to find those who were A.W.O.L. Geza left the coach from the opposite end, and in the space outside, between the coaches, climbed onto the roof of the coach. He waited there until the customs procedure was through, and the train continued speeding on to the next station.

The train stopped at the border station and the military police left the train. From his perch on top of the coach, Geza noticed that they were escorting three privates. Poor guys, they were probably traveling without passes. The Company of privates and military police disembarked onto the station platform. Geza quickly slid down the opposite side returning to the station side, and boldly boarded the coach walking back to Jószi.

"Well. I'm back again. I noticed three fellows under military escort; I guess they didn't have a pass."

In this manner Geza slid through once again.

The train reached their destination after midnight, about 1:30 am. The cabs started their schedules at 6:00 am, but the one these friends had to take on their respective paths, would not be around till 7:00 am. So they slept on a bench in the station.

Geza had traveled often enough in this unpredictable and risky manner, and had learned from other soldiers traveling with knapsacks, that they could be stolen while a weary soldier slept. There were gypsies, and other thieves smart enough who actually listened to a fellow for sounds of slow, deep breathing, which suggested the traveler was fast asleep. The thief was then emboldened to lift the person gently off the duffle bag or knapsack "pillow". Geza therefore kept the duffle bag straps twisted around his arms and wrists as he slept on them. He cat napped in this manner, but awoke suddenly to find someone tugging on his knapsacks. As groggy as he was, Geza almost socked the man in the face but because of his awkward sleeping position, with wrists twisted into the straps of the knapsacks, his punch was useless.

It was Jószi! He was pulling at Geza's knapsacks presuming that one was his. He was looking for his own knapsack.

"How did you get my knapsack entangled around your wrists?"

"Your knapsack, what are you talking about? I'm happy that I could contain these three never mind yours."

They looked the bags over, proving that the three bags were indeed Geza's. Jószi' s was gone. It had been stolen while he slept on it!

He felt ashamed because he too carried gifts for a friend's family; it had been their way, with soldier comrades. First one would go home carrying foodstuffs to both families, and then the other friend would take his leave and do the same. Jószi and his friend, alternated, sometimes sneaking home without a pass, as Geza had often done. It was a compatible arrangement that Geza understood only too well.

"Jószi, I'm taking care of three 'sacks', don't you see, and you couldn't even watch over one? Do you see this? This one has most of my sergeant major's stuff in it, that son-of-a-bitch. But no more, no sir; I am not bringing anything home for him again. I'm not coming home again for his benefit unless he issues me a pass. It's not worth it...the risks I take! Suppose they would have caught me? One M.P. back there did, but thanks to his good heart; he let me go after hearing my bullshit. If he had escorted me back, I would be on bread and water till they shipped me out. But the embarrassment and the shame; that sergeant major's anger!" He shook his head. "They didn't catch me yet. But even now, when you travel with a pass, your gifts and your friend's gifts are stolen. That is quite a price to pay isn't it?"

"Yes," agreed Jószi. "But the worst of it is, my dear old mother bought me a new change of underclothes, and now they are gone to," he commented sadly, "and all that good food."

"That is too bad" agreed Geza. "If we reach home safely, I'll give you a change of underclothes from my things."

And that is how it was, Geza and Jószi got home with no more unfortunate incidents...that time, and Geza did give Jószi a change of underclothes just so that Jószi's old mother would be content to think it was actually her gift of underclothes.

GASPAR PISTA

When Geza got back to Vienna Headquarters after his
latest escapade, he was determined to tell the sergeant
major that he had, had it! He would definitely refuse to go
home again like that, to sneak home stealing a train ride and
all the hazards associated with getting caught. Even with a
week-end pass, it was getting to be a chore, quite a responsibility really. This 'liaison officer' situation that he had gotten
himself into kept him from being shipped to the front lines,
however, he could also get killed "jumping" coaches!

But the sergeant major, Gaspar Pista, did not give him
an opportunity to vent his anger or to say no:

"Virag, you don't have to muster out with the rest of the
troops. Stay here." He meant, of course, that Geza could
stay in Vienna for the duration of the war. Whenever compliments of troops were to be accounted for to be sent to
fighting areas, the sergeant major could always arrange
for Geza to not be among them. He simply was not to be
'available'.

Pista would tell Geza to go out, anywhere, after the
daily roll call was made; only those on medical leave were
allowed to stay in the barracks. Others who were found
hanging around were soon "mustered out" to the front, or
forced to apply for medical discharge. If they actually qualified for a medical discharge they were drummed out of
the army altogether. All "able" men were needed however;
anyone that had combat experience and could fire a gun
was not likely to be let go. Then again, a medical discharge

was difficult to come by, the military doctors were just not handing them out without due cause.

Pista would have to justify the presence of those who lingered in his outfit, which is why he told Geza to get lost. Go anywhere, out-of-sight-out-of-mind. Geza went out from the barracks and into the local parks or just loafed about. Lying within the compound in the sunshine of an early spring day, the sergeant major came out of his office and was surprised to see him.

But Pista chose to sit with him and to bask in the sun for a while himself.

This was Geza's opportunity!

As casual as the situation was, it was the best time to tell Pista the whole story about the risks associated with "sneaking home"...and about those three bags he had carried; about climbing on top of the coach to avoid being caught, and jumping under the coach to retrieve those damned boots that fell from the duffle bag.

"Virag; you young son-of-a-bitch; you're right on that count. It wouldn't be worth living if you lost those two pair of boots. It would have been better to stay under the coach, or to hang yourself. I promised my sisters that Pista Bacsi (the regimental cobbler) would make them the finest boots that could be had. I knew that if anyone could, you would be the one to deliver them intact, defying the devil himself, if need be."

"Yeah...well the devil and the train damn nearly had me!"

As they talked Pista dropped the news to Geza; "Nah, Virag, what do you say?" He had given that 10-kilo bag of flour to his Austrian sweetheart, and it was no doubt that he wanted more scarce, country goods from home.

Is it time for another trip? Geza stopped Pista's amicable thoughts.

"No. Sergeant major, sir, I won't go; Pista. I won't go!"

Pista was very disappointed that Geza would not make this trip home. He did not force the issue however, because he still looked to Geza whenever he needed a private that

350 ~ Anthony E. Virag

could be relied on for unusually personal and clandestine assignments.

The next few days went by uneventfully as the sergeant major was doing the clerical work associated with his duties. Geza, on some occasions visited with him for friendly conversation. At times such as these, Pista would often say "Go get me a cup of coffee. Tell the cook it is for me."

Invariably the cook, who was ready to please Pista, would always give Geza one too, whereas a cook in the Austro-Hungarian army of WWI would never give a private a cup of coffee between meals.

As they talked, Pista dropped the news to Geza, an unusual assignment was coming. Pista's Hungarian sweetheart from Vasvar had come to visit him *unexpectedly!*

"Virag, please pick her up for me will you? She's at the station now, as we speak!"

Geza knew Kuhn Erzsi (Elizabeth Kuhn) very well. He knew her from his civilian life, and in his other non-military 'assignments' for Pista. He had dropped around to see her often enough with a message or a gift. The sergeant major could not leave his scheduled "drill exercise with the troops", but he could excuse Geza from the exercise; if Geza did him a favor, as it was all the time with Pista. He could make excuses for Geza's absence most of the time, even if he would not give him passes.

Because of the many passes that would have been required, the frequency of passes written to one individual private could be questioned, and preferential treatment was not tolerated. Pista knew that Geza took the greater risk, while his risk was minimal. In a pinch, he could deny that he let Geza go. This explains why he allowed Geza home as frequently as Geza chose to risk it.

There was one technicality about a soldier not being present if someone had reported him "present" when he was actually A.W.O.L, and that was the menászi kártya (chow card). Geza and his cohorts always arranged to have a friend pick up this "card" and also to present it for the cafeteria meals. In this manner, an absent soldier was not necessarily found out. If a soldier did not claim his chow card to get the daily meals, the soldier's absence was readily obvious, and questioned. A severe reprimand was the mildest punishment, again, in these trying times of 1918, being activated and shipped out immediately, was the worst reprimand that could be expected.

Geza had gone A.W.O.L. an undue number of times, actually too frequently. There was a buck sergeant (szakasz vezető) who had responsibility for the food supplies, and chow cards. This buck sergeant had a grudge against the young private Virag because he was sure that Geza had covered for his friends when they had gone A.W.O.L. Geza made sure that someone always got the absent soldiers chow card and rations, even if Geza had to get them himself. When this buck sergeant suspected something, he did question Geza, but of course he got no satisfaction from the young private. From that time forward, the buck sergeant was out to "get Geza". He intended this young upstart to "show him respect".

The kitchen help got to know only some of the soldiers by sight, none of the men stationed in the Vienna barracks "Replacement Company" (Pottó Szakasz) remained for more than three months. When soldiers left, they were out of mind. So it was relatively easy for one soldier to cover for another, if he were bold enough.

In like manner Geza had told a friend to pick up Geza's chow cards and meals while Geza was on one of Pista's errands and homeward bound. But the son-of-a-gun lost his nerve, and did not pick up the cards! No one could have known that Geza was gone, until they traced the cards, and they hadn't been picked up for those days of Geza's absence. When Geza returned to the barracks on the following Monday he thought everything was okay. They allotted the chow cards on Mondays and Thursdays, so he went boldly in to pick up his new allotment for the next few days cards and was confronted by the buck sergeant.

"Where were you?" very gruffly spoken. He was short and stocky, and the man tried to make up for his small stature with his big mouth.

Geza knew immediately why the confrontation. His friend must have failed him, and had also failed to warn him!

Now he had better not lie.

"I wasn't in the barracks. I was on the outside," replied private Virag.

"Where did you go? You aren't allowed out without a pass. Who issued you the pass?"

Geza had few choices and fewer excuses not wanting to mention that he was on an 'errand' for Gaspar Pista. There was nothing he could do. He was caught, and he repeated, "I was out of barracks."

The buck sergeant grabbed Geza's nose between his fisted index finger and forefinger. "Jump into it!" He commanded.

Grabbing the sergeant's wrist Geza pulled the hand off his nose before the man could do him harm. "I'll jump into it...," gritting his teeth, "at some other time; time will come for that." Geza did not want to give the man the satisfaction at this time, but the buck sergeant laughed as though he had "won one" over this kid. In the future he now continued to goad Geza for what he had said.

Gaspar Pista was asking Geza to skip the machine gun disassembly drill and go meet Erzsi. "Your proficient enough at this anyway, Geza skip the afternoon drill."

He was a strict officer but a good man; one who knew how to get along with enlisted men. He could be a friend to his men, just as he could be their senior officer. For this, the men respected him. There were sergeants, lieutenants, corporals and regular enlisted men in his instruction classes. They would all take turns telling war stories, the sergeant major no less than the others.

"Boys," he would say, "keep your eyes on the door. I'm supposed to be teaching you about machine guns, let's have it that way if a ranking officer shows up."

One of the trainees would sit on the floor at the machine gun, while they had a good spell of exciting stories from the veterans, or just plainly funny stories of barracks and the soldiers' life. The man at the machine gun would jump to the task of dismantling the gun if a warning came from the trainee on guard at the door, indicating an officer approached. If the men had been too boisterous at the officer's approach, he of course, had heard them, but the men fawned as though they had been heckling the man at the gun. The officers were fooled most of the time, and each man caught at the gun took the joking with a grain of salt.

The sergeant major was a masterful man with his men. They needed a veteran like Pista; it gave the recruits confidence and courage they may have lacked otherwise.

Soldiers did much more for a man like that.

Gaspar Pista gave Geza instructions before he left to conduct the drill. He stated what hotel to check Erzsi into, and to handle her luggage.

"Tell Erzsi I will be over to see her at 4:00 pm, as soon as I can get off duty."

Geza did as he was told. He checked Erzsi into the hotel of Pista's choice, remembering his request, "a worthwhile room mind you, and it better have a sturdy bed!"

Returning to the barracks, Geza reported that his 'mission was accomplished'. "She is expecting you to be there at 4:00 pm sir."

"Virag, I'm giving you a pass for this evening".

This almost bowled the young private over.

"I want you to meet me and Erzsi in the kocsma (tavern) after 5:00 pm."

This surprised Geza even more. He was delighted that the sergeant major was finally giving him a legitimate evening out, let alone to have this eighteen year old meet him for drinks and dinner also. The pass was for a return to barracks at 11:00 pm; this meant he would leave the establishment earlier to make curfew. The sergeant major and Erzsi planned to leave soon after, and spend the night in the hotel room.

Geza again did as he was instructed, and Pista willingly bought his drinks.

Pista and Erzsi were already seated when Geza arrived. Coincidently, the buck sergeant of the "mess hall" was also there, seated at another table with several of his buddies. The buck sergeant watched as Geza crossed the room to sit down. Because protocol demanded it, Geza turned and saluted the table of officers when he walked by them. As his hand left his head in breaking the salute, he muttered and expletive.

Geza sat down. The three friends drank, and cordially visited. They had a genuine good time, as common friendship would dictate. This seemed to bother the buck sergeant, for he was seen to look quite often into their direction. When the sergeant major, Pista, got up to go to the men's room, and Geza was alone with Erzsi, the buck sergeant took the opportunity to beckon Geza to his table. Nodding his head he mouthed the words, "I want to talk to you."

Geza, in turn, lifted his hand and waved him off, and mouthed the words. "le vad szarva." (shit on you). He was not about to leave Erzsi alone at the table, courtesy and common sense was obvious.

This did not please the buck sergeant at all. He got up and approached, planning to deal with Geza, and finish, before Pista returned.

Geza stood up and, taking one step away from the table, he was the first to speak, to throw the buck sergeant off. "This is the sergeant major's sweetheart."

It worked.

The buck sergeant was temporarily set back, and now puzzled. Turning his back to Erzsi, and leaning into Geza, he asked in a subdued voice, and a congenial manner, "what

is the sergeant major to you?" He turned to look back at
Erzsi, smiled and, turning once again to Geza continued
quietly, "relative or friend?"

"Yes. He is...a...relative," just slightly hesitant. Geza lied.

"Why didn't you tell me about this?" queried the buck
sergeant still speaking in a subdued voice.

"What business is it of yours? I have no reason to talk to
you about anything...except to say you are a son-of-a-bitch
and that you are the dirtiest buck sergeant I know," replied
Geza in a low voice.

Erzsi appeared not to detect any hostility from either man.

Geza went on to say, "Do you know, if I told Pista
about you," he used the first name to back up his claim to
be related to the sergeant major. Though he did not like
doing it, he was more than pleased, and rewarded to see
the twinge it created in the buck sergeant's demeanor. He
continued, deliberately to make the buck sergeant squirm
uncomfortably.

"He would not only have grasped your nose between his
fingers, as you did mine, he would have torn it off your face!"

The sergeant just glared unbelievingly at Geza, at this
bold kid, this upstart private.

"You didn't tell him?" now spoken with relief, and in a
controlled calm manner.

"I didn't tell him," declared Geza.

"Then don't tell him, and...let's be good friends, you and I."

"Never!" exclaimed Geza, "Never! Now, if I didn't have
him to look after me, you would continue to shit on me, and
merrily set about making life miserable for me."

They hadn't quite finished when they both saw Pista
returning.

"Don't say anything to him," replied the sergeant and
left before the sergeant major got to the table.

Geza sat down at the table once again.

Pista also pulled up his chair again. "What was that
pumpkin (tök) boy doing here?" He asked.

The description suited the short, stocky sergeant.

Erzsi declared, "He seemed to be trying to intimidate Geza. Surprisingly, I noticed that Geza appeared to have turned the tables on him."

It was then Geza realized she must have heard some of the conversation. Geza did not answer. He was reluctant to divulge his clash with the buck sergeant over his being absent without a pass. He actually did not want to provoke any more trouble for Pista or himself. He was also embarrassed to admit that a friend had failed to cover for him concerning the 'chow card'.

Pista pressed the question a second time, and it was then that Geza told him everything. Maybe the sergeant major, Pista, would now understand why Geza refused to volunteer to sneak home anymore.

No passes, no trips.

"That shit house (szarház) always made life miserable for me when I returned from the A.W.O.L. escapades. And, I suppose he should have. It was his responsibility. But he always argued with me about the unclaimed chow cards, more often than what I actually had gone A.W.O.L. It is a good thing he didn't have me locked up; damn good of him not to inform on me. But his ulterior motive was to make me obliged to him, just like he intimidated the other privates in similar situations."

"Why didn't you tell me of this?"

"And why should I squeal on him? The many times that I did sneak home, it was my good fortune that he did not squeal on me. He made my life uncomfortable but, I did slip by, many times, didn't I? This way no one actually got hurt, or reprimanded."

"I guess there is a lot of truth in that," agreed Pista.

"Don't speak to him about this discussion. It is just as well that he doesn't find out I finally told you," advised the young private.

"In the future Virag, if he acts with too much 'authority', let me know. He'll get it from me."

The buck sergeant did not act with too much 'authority' after that confrontation in the tavern.

Pista did not tell Geza until quite a while after the incident that he had actually talked to the buck sergeant about his handling of "the men", in general. He spoke in a manner that the sergeant could not detect that any one soldier had complained. Pista stated that, "the boys were complaining that you are too strict with them. I don't mind that at all. That is the way it should be, but just don't let it get too personal about paltry infractions." There was an implication in Pista's words, that some of the boys are not treated equal to the rest.

What Pista had actually implied in this confrontation, was that the buck sergeant should not expect Virag to do as some of the others had done. These others made a point of bringing something from home, a gift for the buck sergeant if they were a day or two late. Virag would not "brown nose" for favors. This is what angered the buck sergeant, and why he was trying to get Virag to "bend". The buck sergeant no longer held ill feelings toward Geza after this encounter.

Whenever Geza had to arrange a room for Erzsi, Pista would also send him with a message to Eadie (Edith) the Austrian girlfriend.

"Tell her I'm on maneuvers and I won't be able to see her till tomorrow night and...that tomorrow is not for certain either."

He did not want to loose either girl. He wanted both of them, for now. While Erzsi remained at home in Hungary, and Eadie in Vienna, he had the better of two worlds. But during this particular incident, Erzsi stayed for four nights; five days! Geza had to cover for Pista again the next night.

"The sergeant major has not been relieved of his obligations yet," He told Eadie.

This could only work a limited number of times on a smart girl like Eadie. She showed up at the barracks gate on the fourth night, and waited for Pista to "finish for the day". Since he lived outside the barracks, and had his personal accommodations, she planned to walk to his rooms. She had already checked his residence before appearing at the barracks. She simply did not believe that he was on maneuvers. Not believing that much, she didn't trust him to be sleeping alone these nights. She knew that he did not like to sleep in the barracks. What she did not know, yet, was that he was sleeping with Erzsi.

As luck would have it, Geza saw her among the girls waiting there that evening, and he quickly turned to avoid being seen. Soldiers met their sweethearts at the barracks gate after the day's drill ended, or after maneuvers on the military base and, locked arm in arm, walked away for the night.

Eadie saw Geza before he could escape, and came running through the barracks gates into the compound.

"Where is Pista?"

"I believe he is still on maneuvers Eadie. But if you wait here, I'll check his office."

He left her and, on the double, hurried to warn Pista before the sergeant major came out of the office leaving for the evening rendezvous with Erzsi. Pista surely would not want to run into Edith unexpectedly like that. Geza finally found him.

"Sir, do you know that Eadie is in the compound waiting for you?"

"Here? Damn it, Virag. You go and stall her, before she finds her way into this office."

Geza then stepped out; Eadie saw that he had just left Pista's office. He waved to her immediately, not wanting her to get nearer the office.

"Pista, where is Pista?" spoken in her not too bad Hungarian.

"I'll go into the Captain's Offices and ask them where I could find Pista... they may know where he is," replied Geza.

Pista was sitting at his desk inside, while Geza went into the next office where there was another door access to Pista's office. "Hey! She's getting closer. She's right outside your door. If I'm too long in here, that stubborn lady is going to step in after me."

"Tell her I've been shipped out—as an aid—an officer's replacement within another regiment—for four or five days. Tell her that right now, and you don't know what regiment or where it is. All you've been told is, the regiment is "in the field" somewhere on maneuvers...or at bivouac. Tell her something man! I've got to slide through this last day with Erzsi."

Geza stepped out, and told Eadie that the sergeant major, her Pista, was temporarily re-assigned to another regiment, and that if she liked, he, Geza would go to that regimental Headquarters located in another office to find just where the assignment is.

"I'll go with you!" She replied anxiously.

"No. No. You just go back to the courtyard. The sentry may come in after you and evict you. Be patient, and walk if you must, but stay in the courtyard where I can find you. I'll be right back." This got her away from in front of Pista's office.

Geza ran to the end of the barracks building, but when he got to that office, he did not enter. He continued running and circled the buildings. Be damned if he could enter that office as an unknown private, they would surely challenge him. Who knows what trouble he could get into if he just barged in on them like that? He slowed to a walk now as he got around the building, attempting to kill some time and think of what to say to Eadie. After a reasonable length of time Geza went back to Eadie.

"They have sent Pista on patrol, but they don't know exactly where he may be on patrol in that area at this time. You know of course how much they like Pista.

"Every commanding officer has confidence in him to do a good job. That is why he is constantly asked to help them out. They told me," he added, "in that office," just to sound like he was actually in that office, "that he should be gone for at least two more days. It is possible that he just hasn't finished the task. The patrol has to stay on routine exercise until their drill is complete Edie; he has to stay until he is finished or until they order him to return."

She thought for a while, on the verge of tears. She did not disbelieve this young soldier, he was just barely eighteen and, she no doubt thought that he was too young and innocent to lie. None-the-less, she had puzzling thoughts about such an indefinite assignment for her sergeant major.

Geza escorted her back to the barracks gate, where she thanked him for helping her. She also apologized for any trouble she may have put him through.

"That's alright Eadie, I was happy to be of help. Sorry that things didn't work out better than this."

They said their goodbyes and she left to catch the streetcar.

Geza returned to Pista's office.

"Has she gone?" enquired Pista.

"Yes."

"Are you sure?"

"I left her at the barracks gate. She walked toward the streetcar stop."

"Damn it! Why didn't you walk with her and see her off? You should have waited until she got on the streetcar. That girl is capable of waiting at the barrack gate if she suspects something fishy. Then I'll be a sorry son-of-a-bitch if she spots me. Why didn't you wait her out? Go right now damn it. See to it that she is not still there. Elizabeth is more than frantic by now that I have not showed up yet, hurry, I have to spend this last evening with her. She catches the 12:00 pm train out. I'm late already because of Eadie, and I don't dare step a foot out of this office till I know she has truly gone home. Damn it," cursed the sergeant major. "If Eadie sees me, she'll bawl until I agree to escort her home. And if I don't show up soon, Elizabeth will be bawling in her hotel room, certain that I stood her up on this last night."

"My God," murmured Geza, "now I have to run again."

Forthwith, he was out the gate once more. He arrived at the streetcar stop; no sign of her. He crossed the street to the opposite streetcar stop. She was not there, nor could he see her among the crowds on the street. He looked in a few shops just in case, before running back to the barracks, and into Pista's office once more.

"She's gone! I did not see her anywhere on the street. I walked about, and looked into a few doorways also. Sir, I'm sure she has gone home. Heck, she was twittering like a bird, not wanting to cry because of her disappointment, nonetheless, she was twittering. I'm sure she went home to cry."

With that affirmation, Pista laughed and slapped the private on the back. "Alright Virag," he was pleased, pleased that the young man hadn't entirely fumbled it. "Are you going to be at the tavern tonight?" He asked Geza.

"No sir. I can't go even if I wanted to. I don't have an overnight pass."

They had a good understanding, this "older man" and Geza.

Geza saw Pista with Eadie often after this incident. Erzsi, (Elizabeth) continued sending Pista letters and packages; Geza knows that much. But Pista was reassigned to night duty, or volunteered for it. Geza is not sure; he didn't see the sergeant major much after that. Geza too, was finally shipped out soon thereafter.

This incident with Eadie and Erzsi was early in 1918, during Geza's recovering and medical leave. It was the period when he was waiting in Vienna for troop redistribution and reactivation. These are the weeks where he spent considerable time with his older brother János — being a bad influence on his older brother — always attempting to delay János' re-assignment.

When the war ended, Pista married Eadie. He did not return to his Hungarian sweetheart Erzsi, preferring his Austrian girlfriend.

BATTLE OF THE PIAVE RIVER

G eza was shipped back to Italy with a complement of reinforcements, and was to rejoin those of the 83rd regiment with whom he had served and suffered. The march carried them east of the Piave River, where they remained for a few days before embarkation to the front lines. The nearer the troops got to the action, the more reluctant he became, so he went for a walk in the country mountainside to ease his nerves. As he walked toward the heights, he noticed Austrian and Hungarian uniformed crews digging into debris at the base of some of the high precipices under the sheer mountains. He curiously approached closer to see what on earth they were digging for, and suddenly, he wished he were somewhere else. He should not have given in to his curiosity; he could now detect the smell on the breeze.

He had been near those heights before, last year, when they had advanced onto the Italian lines. He saw plainly now what they were digging to retrieve. Rotten, uniformed bodies, as they were uncovered were brought to a clearing, and lay side by side.

Where they were totally out of site in October of 1917, they now became exposed. The spring rains of 1918 had washed the dirt off corpses covered by landslides and avalanches created by shell bursts. A hand here, a booted foot there, sometimes just fragments of clothing from uniforms, revealed to the burial parties just where they should dig to uncover what was left of a whole body. Enemy uniforms, friendly troops uniforms, bodies contained within any uniform, were treated with one common courtesy for all those who died in that October-November Offensive.

He shuddered; to think that he was once like anyone of them, buried alive in that fierce fighting months ago. When would his body have been found if his friends had not uncovered him as they did? How many will remain where they are? Buried beyond the reach of the diggers, and not exposed by the summer rains, *will they ever be uncovered?*

Many will stay where they are beneath the earth, but those uncovered today would receive a decent burial in the valley flat lands.

He was somewhat relieved to be ordered out finally with the rest of the new troops. The advance took them nearer to the fighting, and they made another stop just behind the second line of trenches. Here fresh troops moved forward, wounded and "old service" troops were moved rearward.

Allied prisoners under guard were also being taken to prison compounds in the North. He met some of his buddies that were among the wounded; they were boarded onto ambulances, any makeshift carriers, and were going home.

Home sounded too good now that he was so far away from home, and near the fighting again. The friends eagerly embraced one another, and fondly hugged the young man. After all, he was also a veteran of combat. These friends in particular, were happy to see one whom they had given up for dead.

They said their goodbyes, wished one another good luck, and parted.

Leaving with the fresh reinforcements, Geza reached the main units of the 83rd that were still on the east side of the Piave River. Many of his old comrades embraced him. Some of the group of men who had dug him out of his internment now anxiously surrounded him to shake his hands and cheer his presence.

"Virag, Saints be praised! We thought you were a goner for sure."

"Hell, you were as good as gone," said one.

"Glad you're back — alive that is. Too damn bad you had to come back," said another.

"Truth is you gave us a terrible scare young buddy. The bleeding, the mess you were. Your body didn't offer much encouragement for our effort."

"You had no sign of life!"

The old sergeant was there, the one who initiated the entrenched men to dig Geza out. "Son, it's good to see you alive and well. It's good to have you back with us again. I do mean it. I'll never chew you out again. I had hoped the best for you, somehow, that you would not have to return."

"How did you get out from under that direct hit? Do you remember us digging you out? All hell broke loose along the trench lines as we dragged you back to safety," cried another.

"Boys, I don't remember anything about that night. The doctors in Vienna know more about my 'accident' that night than I do. They say two shells missed me, the third one got me. They told me how you guys had," he chocked up, "had saved my life."

Stammering awkwardly, but then, like a man proud of his friends and grateful too, he said "Thanks. What more can I say? I'm happy that you risked your lives in that barrage to dig me out." Then, to relieve an awkward situation, he added, "I understand it was one hell of a fight, and I missed it."

He did not actually mind missing it, but he knew it would make them feel better if he appeared envious of their getting a bigger share of the action, and it sounded like "soldier talk".

Elated, the soldiers went into detail, great detail. Each bragged about their individual escapades. Some exaggerated, embellishing their adventure. Others remained completely quiet. But all the men felt better for seeing this eighteen-year old returned from the grave.

His survival was good for their morale.

They enjoyed a slight respite from battle.

The troops were waiting; they would have at least two hours respite at their position, and so three "older" veterans got their heads together.

"Let's take these kids to a whorehouse before we are shipped out. But let's not tell them where we are going. Lead them to think we are just going for a few drinks, and the fun that goes with the drinks."

There were among these kids some boys who had never been away from home. Had it not been for the war, they may never have traveled farther than the next village near their homes. Among those who chose to go with the small group was one named Örövest, a very husky, tall farm boy, fair haired and fair of face, with ruddy cheeks.

When they got to the house, the madam exuberantly let them in, pleased to see a large group of men like this. "Come girls, line up in a row: on the double, now. There is a group of eager soldiers; on the march...March!"

"Show them your best parts," hollered the boisterous older veterans, in the central foyer.

And the girls did come.

They lined up, some deliberately scantily clad for this review. The older men selected from the row. Some girls bolder than the rest, and more curious to teach than to be taken, selected from those kids who appeared to be shy, or backward.

"What's this?" murmured a young naïve soldier.

"Their taking partners; to drink with," laughed the old veteran.

Couples then went off to separate rooms.

One girl had quickly thrown both arms around his neck, and now clung to this tall, good-looking, fair-haired youth.

Örövest was too dumbfounded and unsure of what was happening as he was lead like a lamb, up the stairs.

When the older veterans, and some of the "boys" were through, they gathered once again in that central foyer where they had first selected the girls. Some laughed knowingly and the "boys" grinned shyly. The worldly wise and older men, simply asked the madam for a drink, and gulped down the wine. Others, too young and inexperienced, were embarrassed and behaved sheepishly.

"Well, are we all here?"

Looking about, they realized that one of their numbers was missing.

Then they heard a sudden commotion from one of the rooms upstairs off the foyer.

"You bitches! Let me out or I'll..." The door partially opened momentarily, was slammed shut again.

"Örövest?"

Many voices blurted out the name in unison as all realized who it was that was missing. They stormed up the stairs.

"Open the door!"

But the girl inside would not open to them.

The veterans with prior experience knew that the girls would often "work" together on a man that did not pay. Because the man changed his mind, and did not participate, does not mean to say the girls would let him "go free". These girls would attack a man, and together beat him up.

Because he would not play, doesn't mean to say he should not pay!

The men forced the door open, and quickly pulled the four occupants apart. Three girls in various stages of undress were reluctant to let the disheveled, but still clothed and now angry Örövest, get away. His friends quickly pushed him out of the room, and ushered him down the stairs.

On the way, as they walked back to their salient, the men heard the full story of what transpired.

"That shameless woman undressed completely," stated Örövest slowly, and in a voice of one that sounded completely ignorant, yet attempting to be manly. He blurted out, "then she got some stuff and rubbed it into her pee-hole. She came near to me to undress me but I pushed her greasy hand away. She then lay on the bed and patted her hairy patch. She wanted me to do the same. She reached for my hand when I wouldn't. She then reached into my trousers and tried to grab my prick. I slapped her hand, and swore at her."

The older companions could not contain themselves as they roared with laughter.

Örövest told his story now the more reluctantly, wondering what all the levity was about. But he did continue. "She then jumped up: she tried to come near me. When I backed away, she turned around and opened the door of the adjoining room. She said something to the two girls in there; they all came at me like clawing cats when I tried to get out of the room. They pulled me back in and slammed the door shut; before I knew it they were all over me, trying to take my pants off. I told them that *no one was going to abuse my prick.*"

This was too much! The older men laughed till tears came to their eyes. They had to hold their stomachs from the pain of laughter. The more they pictured in their mind what poor Örövest had experienced, the more they laughed.

When they came to their senses, the men realized the girls had attempted to rape him. Failing that, they were going to rob him.

All the men who had accompanied, and been accomplices to his embarrassment, made a promise of secrecy. They would tell no one of Örövest's experience once they got back to the main group, otherwise the poor farm boy would be the brunt of many jokes and become the regimental clown. His friends would not want that, for they realized it was their fault that misfortune had befallen this virgin.

In June of 1918, the Central Powers began an offensive along a one hundred mile front. Their intention was to drive down the Asiago Plateau, around Monte Grappa, the Montello and also to cross the Piave River. The forces crossing to the west side would outflank the Italians by sweeping down from the north, to meet up with those successfully crossing the river in the southeast. Indeed, they succeeded to such an extent initially, that they captured 30,000 Italian troops.

The Austro-Hungarian officers in this sector exercised a very respectful camaraderie with the enlisted men. With the lull in battle, they allowed the men to move freely among the outlying villages in the valley. The troops were warned however, not to molest the peasants or their possessions. The villagers had small garden plots next to their homes, which they nurtured and cared for. In many instances it would be that little garden plot that sustained the household now that their fate was unsure as the war raged around them.

Because of this curtailment of mingling with the Italians, their women, and possessions, most troops stayed within the perimeter of their own camp, effectively putting temptation at a distance.

Geza's friend Vyko came into camp one day extremely sick. Jószi and Geza concerned about him asked what had happened.

"Damn it boys, God is punishing me."

"What did you do?"

"I took some fresh green onions from a garden."

"You ate them?"

"Yes, damn it."

"Without food or bread? You damned fool."

"But it tasted so good; fresh green onions. I didn't know you could get sick from them."

With that declaration he vomited; his friends saw that he was already bringing up blood!

"My God Vyko, go to the doctor; you're going to die."

As things turned out, the Company doctor stated that Vyko was extremely sick, and he was immediately fed something to neutralize the onion-acid, and lots of bread to cut the onion's action. Because of the blood, the doctor took no chances; this was serious!

"His stomach lining may already be damaged, and he may now have bleeding ulcers," declared the doctor. He wrote an order to the Company Captain, and Vyko was sent back to have the medical experts in Vienna to correct his problem. He went with the many wounded being shipped back that day.

"How about that?" exclaimed the friends. "Boy is he lucky!"

They were inclined to try some of the onions themselves. As the next few months of action unfolded, there were those who would not deny that the onions may very well have saved that fool Vyko's life.

The men played cards in the open, and just passed the time away while waiting for orders of the day, or for their detail of guard duties. At one of these card playing sessions their sergeant approached the group of men, as there were always those loitering few observing while the others played cards. It was not uncommon to see six, or even ten men, in one of these groups.

The sergeant asked for volunteers, promising medals, citations, or even a weekend pass to those who would venture forth to once again "mark the river's edge", and thus determine the measured amount of river recession.

From this data the army engineers would estimate, along with the previous readings of earlier days and past measurements, the maximum recession they would need for the attempted river crossing. Some bold volunteers had even waded into the river measuring its depth, while ignoring the snipers across the river. These bold incursions gave valued information in selecting the most favorable crossing points.

The Central Powers had been doing this since May. They knew that the spring rains, and the thawing snows coming down from the mountains had influenced the river's rise above the normal water mark. The data compiled from these volunteers was to mark the river's recession back to its normal levels, or below them, as chance would have it.

Often, as the need arose, groups of four men would volunteer. Their buddies chided them openly, and called them fools. The lower echelon officers joined the friendly banter, and old veterans frightened the new recruits who had volunteered. The higher-ranking officers finally told them to "ease off", lest the volunteers have a change of heart.

The men were not selected for this dangerous undertaking; it was strictly voluntary. Most of the officers left volunteering as a free will decision of the individual since many had been killed attempting to approach the river in earlier daylight attempts. The sergeant simply stated that, when they were ready after dusk, come to him.

The first few groups of daylight volunteers suffered casualties because of allied sharpshooters from across the river; volunteers would now conduct these probes primarily in darkness. Even then, if they were unduly noisy, or made sudden movements, searchlights suddenly flashed on from the opposite side of the river and menacingly scanned their side of the riverbank. If the searchlight beam found the men, bullets from snipers and sharpshooters behind the searchlights would follow. Even artillery opened up on them making death almost certain.

Meanwhile, their buddies observed it all from cover and at a safe distance, wagering upon the outcome, and betting either for or against their fate. Those in the security of the darkness never returned fire in an attempt to shoot out the searchlight to save their friends, fearing to draw the fire and artillery upon themselves.

The Piave River's slowly receding level was, nonetheless measured and recorded.

It was around June13, 1918; Geza, Horvath Jószi and Vajda Sandor were positioned on the sheer slopes of a mountain precipice. The mountains originate in the Tyrol, forming the Carnic Alps. There are two mountain ranges that run from the Carnic Alps almost at right angles to them. These are the Venetian Alps and the Dolomites. The Piave flows between these. (Geza called the mountain he was on "Tyrol". This could of course mean no more than that they were in the Tyrol mountain range. He was on the east side of the Piave and that may actually have been the Venetian Alps?)

He started his "watch" on that mountain position at 9:00 pm, and it rained: it rained all night. As he stated, not a portion of his body was dry, not even under his belt buckle. All night the cable cars from the mountain top carried troops, Austrian, German, Hungarian, to where? They were certainly an awful lot of troops and supplies lowered, and transferred that night. Geza was so close to the swaying cable cars that he had to stoop, and duck his head when they approached. Every cable car load carried a full cargo of supplies, or a load of silent soldiers. The young troopers on watch were also silent, hearing only the steady sound of falling rain, and the occasional squeaking of the car's trolley wheels as they traversed the cables.

Vajda Sandor was to the left and Jószi to the right. "Hear that?" Geza whispered to Sandor as the trolley wheels squealed past. The cable car was within arms reach and he could have actually touched it had he reached out at arms length.

"What is it?" whispered an equally nervous and giddy from their capture. The anxious Sandor.

"I don't know? For sure; some are carrying troops," replied Geza quietly. The friends remained silent, for silence was their order.

They remained at their post until 8:00 am of the next day, when the rain stopped. The three friends had been relieved and they changed from their wet clothes to go for breakfast. A strong rumor was circling that the expected offensive would start that day. The great activity about, and above the east side of the river, was the deployment actions of many troops.

At midnight of that day, June 14, the Austro-Hungarian forces advanced toward the river, down the dry flood plain, and onward toward the designated shallow crossing points. It was seven kilometers across (4.3 miles approx) from the east bank to the west bank of the dry flood plain. But within the river bed and at the flowing river's narrowest, it was no more than ten, in some places twenty meters (approximately 30 to 60 feet) even at the widest expanse of water.

The men would have no trouble wading through with rifles held over their heads.

Early that morning of June 15, the Central Powers' began a violent artillery bombardment.

A French observer with the Allied forces on the west bank, Henri Kervarec, stated: "it was three in the morning and the general attack launched at four."

The Allied artillery returned fire on the enemy artillery positions.

Their spotters on the west bank saw the riverbed suddenly come alive as it filled with moving masses of humanity; the masses were moving toward them. Allied artillery then opened up on the oncoming masses; all along the river their shells exploded making huge gaps, gaps that again closed, and filled with men.

The infantry forces of the Central Powers continued to move forward, first at a deliberate pace, and then because of the artillery bombardment, began to run on the double. Their own artillery on the east bank of the river now shot over their heads in a duel with the Allied gunners on the west bank.

Geza was with a Company of two hundred men, machine gunners and their crews, riflemen, and munitions carriers when the river crossing infantry waded into the shallow river. His Company was on one of the roads that led to a series of bridges. Each bridge crossed a small, shallow stream far below. These many streams made up the compliment tributaries of the now receded parent river. The two hundred men had not completely crossed the first bridge when it was blown up from under their feet!

Splintered wooden beams remained of what was once a roadway over the water; still they went onward having lost a few men. Those who remained on the eastern side of the abutment moved forward over what remained of the shaky beams. They approached the second bridge on the double. The two hundred, missing a few, now became a strung-out group moving as fast as they could.

Anticipating the worst; it came!

The skilled Allied gunners blew up another bridge as the men were in various stages of having crossed completely; some were crossing it, and some about to cross it.

Again they lost a few men.

Those of the infantry making the crossing in the riverbed ran forward; for death lay behind them within range of the Allied artillery, and they desperately tried to get under the shell trajectories. The Italians and their Allies could see, as far as their eyes would see through the morning light and shell fire, those thousands of men, up and down the riverbed, they were racing across to the west bank...when... it happened!

A *wall of rushing water came down upon them*; a wet whirlwind loudly whistling in the grey dawn as it roared like a torrent whisking up men and horses like leaves in a swiftly flowing stream. It brushed the skirts of both sides of the river bed rising above and onto the wide flood plain!

The roar became a rumble as it picked up the human debris, churned and twisted it, crushing them against boulders, and tumbling the boulders too!

Geza's Company was experiencing their own hell on earth, as each bridge was blasted out from under them. And there were more bridges ahead, more to go, and more men to die at each bridge. But they could also see that fate worse than theirs below them!

374 ~ Anthony E. Virag

The seven kilometer wide flood plain was now completely engulfed with foaming, filthy water that fetched up screaming men and boys.

In vain they flagged their arms about for help; in vain they tried to swim above the flood. As many as ten men, locked arm in arm to support one another, hoping that the strength of ten would perhaps hold them firm against the fury.

But it would not. And the ten were swirled away to continue with the water, as it pursued its course to the sea and, through the valley of the shadow of death.

Men holding together in mortal fear, swirling in circles with the river's roiling eddies, were swept into eternity.

Some men, fortunate to have made it onto little mounds, now islands, stayed where they were, hoping against all odds that the dirt they stood upon would be higher than the water's crest. And some mounds of dirt remained as islands above the swollen river, while too many were also swept clean.

The river was filled with screaming men.

Knapsacks on their backs supported some that bounced like corks upon the terrible flood. Others, whose knapsacks carried weighted materials were like stones, tumbled and sank from view.

The moving mass of humanity that a short time ago rushed forward within a shallow riverbed to reach the west bank, were no longer feared by the Italians as a threatening, oncoming fighting force. They had been affectively swept away by the turbulent, swiftly flowing floodwaters.

"Dear mother..." Screamed a boy in panic. The filthy frothing waters filled his mouth to stifle forever his incompleted cry as he was swept by under the bridge where Geza and his little band of frightened soldiers stood.

Soldiers helped soldiers at the bridge abutments.

They formed human chains to grab and hold onto their "companions in fate", and they saved a few. As strings of men streamed by holding onto one another, they grasped out and succeeded in hanging onto the human chain, and were spared.

Other strings of men at different locations succeeded in holding onto that human chain in vain, for those men, who were once safe themselves and had formed the chain, *were also swept to their death by the grasping hands that tore them loose from* the secure position.

The unrelenting flood was too fierce. The puny power of scores of men could not help their fellow man against the shear weight and swift current of the unnatural volume of water!

Again another bridge was blasted, and the men divided... in their minds as well as physically, for they saw the surging flood below, and the fiery hell ahead. There were those who froze and refused to go forward. What was the use? Death was ahead of them; death was behind them; death was in the flood below them. There were no commissioned officers left among them; a sergeant ordered them to stop.

"My God save me from that fate please." Prayed Geza, as he looked down upon the raging river that was now rising quickly upward against the bridge footings; then to himself he cried, "If they don't kill me now, they never will." He thought he should surely drown, or be blown to bits. He had been spared from a horrible death once before, how fortunate could an unfortunate soldier hope to be?

They were actually nearer the west bank with only two bridges to go, but seven bridges had been blasted from under their feet!

How many of their troops would make it forward to the west bank?

How many of them would die trying to make it back to the east bank? The Allies appeared to be hitting the bridges as the troops massed in crossing them. They were not random shots; they were precise and deliberately accurate.

Geza's group decided to go back!

So they made their way back, fearfully and under constant bombardment, with that constant steam of flotsam below, bodies of packhorses, and men floating face down, others on their backs, their knapsacks were holding the corpse faces up.

The most hardened of them now walked nimbly and gingerly across what remained of the shattered beams and bridge remnants, mindful of their footing, trying to keep their eyes off the carnage floating swiftly beneath them. These remnants of what once were the bridges they had crossed so fearfully, now became their only lifeline back to friendly forces.

They could see that the surging river water had beaten the other railroad trestle bridges apart, just as affectively as the artillery had done to their bridges.

Will their bridge footings hold?

When that once two hundred strong Company of men returned to their friendly side of the river, only fifty remained. Within the fifty were those fortunate few whom they had pulled from the flooded river.

The entire river valley was now flooded.

Only the bridge abutments, portions of elevated road, and some small mounds of earth remained above the wide, swollen flood plain.

Those few sectors of safety were covered with men, too few, considering the thousands that were effectively slaughtered in the swirling soiled water.

The crossing of the Piave River was doomed to fail!

The Allies knew that a crossing would be attempted after the spring thaw and spring rains. And they intended to thwart the crossing as they had in November of 1917. A dam was constructed at the head waters of the Piave River, somewhere between the Dolomite and Venetian Alps. That it was successfully concealed while holding back the water for so long after the snow melt and the spring thaws was, of itself, a brilliant engineering accomplishment.

With the spring rains, the snow melt, and the rains of June 12 and 13, dammed up in some reservoir, there was a huge volume of water to be released upon the invading armies of the Central Powers. The enormous amount is obvious as it came in a great, crested torrent that suddenly enveloped the seven kilometer wide valley (4.2 miles), and covered all that was in it, Italian farmers and peasants as well.

The *seventy square miles of water* was certainly a formidable barrier now and an eternal resting place for those under the water. (reference Chapter 33, pages 303 and 304, that describes the Italian engineers deliberately flooding the Piave to thwart Austro-Hungarian Field Marshal Boroevic's forces from securing a bridgehead on the west side of the Piave in 1917.)

It is possible that there was again seventy square miles of water, or more, on that flood plain and in the valley at the "Battle of The Piave" of 1918.

When the Central Power's forces moved forward onto the river bed, entered the river, and were committed to their advance, Allied artillery spotters saw their lines in the river. Observing this positive commitment to the 'crossing', they radioed to open the dam.

It matters not how this dam was opened; the Italian engineers could have simply opened the gates. What matters is that such an inhuman act as this is possible in war and deemed necessary.

The rain alone could not have been the only contributor to this cataclysmic and sudden rise of the river. The Central Powers would have been aware of a rise in river level since they were monitoring the river's recession with nightly patrols to the river's edge. The so called 'rain swollen' river would have shown an increase in depth when the volunteers checked the water line — but it did not, *and troops waded across.*

In any event, the onrushing flood from one or two nights of rain could not alone fill the entire valley. That the river rose is true, but that man contributed to such a sudden and devastating rise by artifice, has not been disproved, though it has been denied by those who perpetrated it.

It is written and recorded in history that the Italian engineers flooded the Piave River valley in November 1917; they certainly were wise to prepare for the 1918 offensive in the same manner.

It was simply, horrifically brilliant!

The following is a reference taken from a Pictorial History of The Great War, S.J. Duncan-Clark. The J.L. Nichols Co. Ltd. Toronto; page 206:

"In the middle of June the Austrians did attack, but after an opening success of considerable dimensions, *nature opened the flood gates of heaven and severed communications with the far bank of the* Piave River, and the Austrian offensive collapsed."

Page 267: "On June 15, the Teutonic Allies began a great offensive over a front of 100 miles from the Asiago plateau to the sea and along the lines of the Piave River. The first force of the drive carried the enemy across the Piave in places, and the Italians, who had now been reinforced by a considerable force of British and French and some American troops, lost 30,000 prisoners. But any initial success was quickly offset by a counter offensive."...

..."Nature had intervened in behalf of the Italians. The Austrian and German forces had crossed the Piave on pontoons, bringing up with them heavy guns. Torrential rains had fallen after their advance and Allied airmen had bombed and destroyed the bridges behind them. Cut off, they were slaughtered in thousands."

It was not raining during the day of the offensive!

There is a second reference I would like to quote here. It is a very important one that describes the nature of the Piave:

"Its depth and width vary very considerably according to the seasons of the year, a fact which had an important bearing on the operations along its banks. In its lower reaches its bed is a vast extreme of gravel, *only filled in times of heavy rains or at the melting of the snows.*" (Encyclopedia Britannica 1957, Vol. 17, page 204.)

The italicized words are mine, to emphasize particular points that will be discussed here:

Proof of the Allied foreknowledge:

Henri Kervarec, a French observer wrote: "It was very clear, towards the evening of the 15th, that the results hoped for had not been attained. The Italian High Command, as a matter of fact, had foreseen the attack: *it would seem that it had been informed of the time and choice of points specially aimed at.*"

#1. The river was dammed months ahead to hold back the winter snowmelt.

#2. Everywhere the Austrians and Germans concentrated there massed armies and weapons; the Allies were there to meet them with a concentration of troops and weapons.

#3. When the Central Powers reverted to alternate strategies after the river was flooded, they were followed through and met by the Allies.

#4. The Allies met and deployed as though they knew about the incursions in specific areas; just as Henry Kervarec has stated above.

The German Generals in command in Italy knew what had happened in 1917. Italian engineers opened the flood gates onto the lower Piave, and they knew that it could happen again. Planning their river crossing to begin in the dark of night, they may have hoped to have completed crossing it before the Italians were alerted.

They gambled and they lost.

The Austro-Hungarian and German forces were slaughtered by the thousands in that *man made flood,* and the survivors were cut off. Those that made it to the west bank fought like devils of vengeance. They stormed forward to kill this ruthless foe that opened the floodgates upon them.

Forty thousand troops penetrated deep into the Allied occupied side of the Piave, and took Montello Hill. These troops stated that when they set foot upon the west bank, they did not see a single Italian!

They did see that the Italians had thrown down their guns and had run away. Perhaps the Italians thought, rightfully, if the flooded river had not stopped these fearful fighters then neither could they!

This is how it was.

The Central Powers troops succeeded in penetrating Allied territory where troops no longer waited to engage them, and so they pressed forward. Encouraged, they sent signals across the river, "Bring us bullets for our guns and we shall endure."

These troops successfully held their positions, and fought on for several days against counter attacks that were now coming to drive them from the west bank. Engineers on the east side lashed makeshift rafts together and poled reinforcements across as they had in 1917; many rafts carried heavy artillery guns across the now receding river. On their return, these same rafts plucked Italian families from their roof tops where they had clung desperately to escape the sudden flood. But with each crossing the rafts were constantly harassed by Allied aircraft that dominated the air and succeeded in annihilating the many reinforcement attempts.

In this haphazard manner the Central Powers could not provide enough reinforcements and supplies to these troops. The troops, still confident that they could prevail, heroically stood fast, and continued to signal for ammunition and guns.

"We can live off the Italians cast-off food supplies."

Indeed they did; finally resorting to using the cast-off Italian guns and ammunition as well against the Allies.

Somewhere in the German hierarchy there were those who just could not, or would not get the message straight!

The result was that these troops got airdrops, but they were food drops! The frustrated fighting men using Italian weapons, again and again strove to get more signals through. And again and again they received bread and rations. In a futile gesture of insult and resentment, the furious troops threw the loaves upward into the air at their own aircraft.

Why did they not receive ammunition?

The 40,000 became demoralized, and much of that army simply quit trying after June 23. The Hungarian Officers knew of a certainty that the plan of attack was thwarted in every effort. Even those food drops, in place of bullets continued to gnaw at them.

That their date and time of attack was known to the enemy, and positions on the Piave *where they would take place were also known*...was now obvious to many officers.

Those few officers who expressed this horrible deception, and had a close bond with their enlisted men felt a common betrayal. But they were quickly rounded up and silenced. There was to be no dissention among the ranks if the high command could avoid it.

Betrayal of the troops in the field was common knowledge now to those who had been victim of the failed crossing attempt. *The plan of attack was known in advance by the Allies.*

Empress Zita, wife of Emperor Charles 1st of Austria-Hungary, was also of Bourbon and Parma (Parma is in Northern Italy. Bourbons were French royalty; their relatives ruled in France, Spain and Naples. Naples became part of the kingdom of Italy) The Austrians and Hungarians in the field now suspected that she was the likely informant.

She got her information first hand, or overheard the plan of strategy. She also knew that, when Germany demanded a show of power from Austria-Hungary, that Italy would have to be the place and the Piave River was the only place for a show of force. A triumph for the Central Powers in Italy would help relieve the pressure from the German troops on the western front in France. Had Austria-Hungary succeeded, the Allies would have had to rush reinforcements from the western front in France to meet the threat coming to them in the South of France through Italy.

Allegedly, Empress Zita relayed the plans and strategies to the Italian High Command through her emissaries as she was sincerely concerned for her country.

The Emperor however, *apparently disregarded the threat to his countrymen,* or was naively deluded and, maybe totally ignorant of how the crucial plans were divulged; if that is possible.

The critical plans and alternate strategies were too well prepared for them to fail.

They could not have failed!

The Hungarians felt that the Empress corrupted the Emperor.

Perhaps, this late in the war, he may have been concerned more about world politics, hoping to salvage concessions that would benefit his hold upon his empire after cessation of hostilities. He may have, in his stumbling manner, made concessions to plead a separate peace for Austria-Hungary with the Allies.

To this day, survivors of that ill-fated river crossing attempt believe as they did in the aftermath; they were betrayed. Someone had sold them out.

"The Austrian command has accused the Slav troops of having betrayed the cause of the Monarchy in this supreme battle." The quote is from the notes of the same French observer, Henri Kervarec. (Stated above)

A Hungarian newspaper of that era, "Az Est" of June 30, 1918 also states "...Headquarters accuses the Jugo-Slavs of having betrayed, of having revealed to the Italians not only the date of the offensive but even the principal of the offensive. 'The exact moment', says this note, 'must have been revealed by the South Slav deserters'..."

This was a futile attempt, first by the Austrians and then the Hungarian Parliament, to deny and refute strong rumors of the "Royal Betrayal", by directing blame onto the Southern Slavs.

How could South Slav deserters know the High Command's strategy? Jugo-Slavs were unenthusiastic conscripts, it's true; but conscripts do not know their officers plans or strategies, and could not reveal targeted river crossing points. As conscripts they merely obeyed orders, even though they may be the first to drop their rifles and surrender.

In doing so, they were deserters, but they certainly did not know their Army's strategy.

The Azjsag of June 28th relates the speech of the deputy Ladislas Fenyes of the Hungarian Parliament:

> Whatever the Minister of National Defence may say, it has been reported that in the battle of the Piave many Hungarian regiments suffered tremendous losses, or were completely annihilated.

> Even if the reports circulating in the country are untrue, it is nevertheless necessary that the voice of Hungary should come to the ears of the Austrian command, so that Hungarian blood, sacrificed so often in vain may no longer be shed in torrents.

The Az Est of June 30th utters the same complaints and enables us more and more measure the greatness of the Austro-Hungarian disillusionment:

The greater part of the 100,000 men we have lost on the Piave was composed of Hungarians. We no exact information as to the proportions of nationalities, but the description of the battle show us that the Hungarians were in the center melee.

The Hungarian regiments have been sacrificed. It matters little to us that the enemy losses superior to ours. Our grief is sore indeed when we think that we have suffered the loss of hundreds of thousands of men, at the end of the fourth year of the war.

To attenuate the effect produced y the disaster on the Piave, and attempt to disculpate itself, the Austrian Staff threw the responsibility of the check upon the Czechs.

We have unfortunately found that some Czech soldiers have gone over to the enemy, and that a certain number of their comrades are in contact with the Italians, whilst carrying on within our lines a dangerous propaganda.

Another issued by Headquarters accuse the Jugo-Slavs of having betrayed, of having revealed to the Italians not only the date of the offensive but even the principal points of this offensive. "The exact moment," says this note, "must have been revealed by South Slav deserters. The enemy made arrangements to meet the expected bombardment with gas.

The government of King Charles 1 perhaps hoped to reconcile the Austrian and the Hungarians by throwing them on the Jugo-Slavs and the Czechs. These tactics, which were so long those of the Hapsburgs, were not to succeed this time.

The Hungarians were not satisfied; the Jugo-Slavs were not any more so. The building was crumbling away on every side. The victory might have bolstered it up. The defeat suffered on the Piave on June 20, 1918, dealt Austria-Hungary the coup de grace.

Remnants of the first two divisions that succeeded in crossing the river now fought their way back to the east bank. The others, who were in the majority, simply gave up. Not being reinforced, they refused to fight; they were taken prisoner by the Allies on the west bank.

Many Italians, French, British and Americans continued their pursuit of the Hungarians and Austrians to the east bank, confident to gain a foothold there and to also sweep that side clean of the enemy. It was the Allies now that crossed over on pontoons, rafts, and remnants of the bridges.

They thought that the entire enemy camp was routed and in retreat. They erred.

The Austro-Hungarians and the Germans who had not successfully made the crossing, and those remnants that had made it back to the east bank, were there to offer stiff resistance to the approaching Allies. Now the Central Powers got back at the Allies as they crossed in their pursuit of the retreating few Central Power troops and, the Allied troops that did get to the east bank were too few in nu0mber to resist being captured.

The 83rd Mutiny in Vienna

It was around June 29, 1918; the Feast of Peter and Paul; two weeks after that fateful 'river crossing' day. As they waited, they lay in the ditch along the side of a road, out of sight of enemy sharpshooters and artillery spotters. It was a peaceful sunny morning. Looking up from the ditch where they lay, the young laughing soldiers longed for the cherries on the branches of the tree above them. Fearful of exposing their position and getting shot at, they cut a long branch from the bushes that were in the ditch. Using the "hook" of the forked limb, they improvised a means of hooking and bending a bountiful branch down toward them into the ditch, or at least within their grasp. They tugged upon the branch more and more, to bend it downward upon them and as it bent, coming ever closer, it failed and broke. The cherry filled limb fell upon them into the ditch, here the young men eagerly shared the fruit...and then the bugle called, forward to glory, or would it be death?

The Allies had by now cleared much of the opposition from the west bank, and regained most of the important positions in the northern mountainous regions. These incursions became bolder and always with a greater number of Allied troops. There were British, Americans and Canadians who were reinforcing the Italian build up. Soon these men would begin to mount an offensive against the Central Powers and cross the Piave, while others swept down on the east bank from the northern mountains. This would be a re-enactment of the Hungarian and German June offensive but in reverse; it was the Allies now pushing the Germans back! The pincers action from the north would catch the Central Powers between the Allies crossing the Piave in the south.

There had been many incursions onto the east bank by the Allies during these months, and some had been repulsed. Now in October 1918, a strong probe by the Allies placed many men on the east bank. These could not be easily repulsed, and a major struggle ensued in which the Central Powers found themselves taking Allied prisoners. Austrian, Hungarian or German soldiers, sometimes as few as six, found themselves guarding as many as twenty, while twenty Central Powers soldiers may have to watch over as much as a hundred prisoners.

Officers of the Central Powers repeatedly found that the fighting men they needed to stop the Allies were being assigned to guard duty, or were leading the prisoners back behind the lines to prisoner concentration points.

It did not help the Central Powers depleted numbers that within the next few days the prisoners were loaded onto trains and, under guard taken to Austria. The Central Powers soldiers guarding the prisoners were thus reducing the number of fighting men available to contend with the Allied incursions.

Geza, Jószi and Vajda Sándor and three other soldiers, found themselves leading a group of prisoners back behind the lines, they customarily stopped at least once before getting their captives to the prisoner compound. It was not an easy task, and could prove 'trying' if there were belligerents among the prisoners. At the rest area, the six guards encircled the 18-20 prisoners. One in particular kept his hostile eyes on Geza. Perhaps he thought this "kid" was meek and no match for him if he were to attack the boy. Oddly enough, he boldly approached Geza instead of staying put, sitting on the ground as the other prisoners had done.

Geza turned to face the man, their eyes met; and just as suddenly the man lunged at the gun cradled in the left forearm that was across the boy's chest. Before the prisoner could get his hands on the rifle, Geza had, with his right hand swept it forward, his left arm now held the barrel at the bayoneted end. In this manner, the man got the rifle pushed into his midsection with the force from Geza's right hand. The wind knocked out of him, he hesitated temporarily, but grasped the rifle with both hands to pull it toward him and, he thought, take it from the boy.

The boy held strongly. They struggled and Geza's hand slipped *onto the bayonet*. He immediately pulled back that hand suffering his thumb cut. The sharp blade almost sheared off the thumbprint of his left hand. In pain and now furious, Geza kicked the man in the crotch. The man left off his grasping of the rifle and bowed over, both hands at his crotch. Geza brought the rifle butt down onto the back of the man's head. The prisoner plopped forward face down into the dirt. Geza would not have stopped there; perhaps he would have continued to pound the prisoner with the rifle butt, except the other guards were now shooting rounds into the air to warn the noisy mob of prisoners as they rose in defense of their foolish companion.

Those warning shots also stopped Geza.

Vajda Sandor hollered at Geza. "Good God, don't kill the man!"

Left thumb bleeding furiously, Geza replied; "The damn fool would have killed me! Look at what he did. Damn it hurts."

"Wrap your handkerchief around it...tightly. We will get it properly bandaged at the prisoner compound."

The guards now ordered the prisoners to lift, and carry the injured man. His head bleeding, he was unconscious but alive.

The prisoners were interred, and Geza's thumb was bandaged by the medical corpsman at the prisoner staging area. Geza, Jószi, Vajda Sándor, and the other three returned back to their sergeant. The Allies attacked to reinforce their earlier probe and more prisoners were taken.

Geza, Jósi and Sándor found themselves shepherding ten prisoners back behind the lines to the concentration point once again.

The major in charge of the prison compound was not at all pleased.

"Damn it! These are your prisoners; you watch them! I have no more men left to shepherd them!" He bellowed.

"But we have to get back to our regiment."

"You will only go back when all prisoners are shipped out. I need you here."

"But our Captain expects us back shortly."

"Too bad. If you go back; take your prisoners with you. I cannot handle anymore with the few men I have."

It was obvious the major was at his wits end and did not know what else to do except conscript the soldiers who brought in the prisoners. Under the circumstance it was a sound decision; he had no choice. The three friends were reluctant to stay, as they feared to disobey their Captain who expected them to return after delivering the prisoners.

"I will take full responsibility," volunteered the major. "I will answer to him. But I need you now."

The boys stayed that day and night. The following day found them on a troop train as prison guards headed for Austria, and they mused at their good fortune to be heading away from the battlefield. They could hear the guns, another big battle was underway, and they were, thank God, ordered away from it.

They arrived in Vienna with hundreds of prisoners and their compliment of guards. The prisoners were handed over to the regular 'Home Guard', and interred for the duration within the Austrian prison camps.

The Central Powers soldiers, men from many Companies of the 83rd, were ordered to report to the Vienna Headquarters of the International Regiment. Here they met fellow Hungarians that had preceded them in much the same way, as prison guards. They too had been forced to shepherd prisoners back on previous trips. Others, who had been released for medical reasons, also gathered here. From the atmosphere in the barracks, the boys quickly realized that there was a great deal of dissention spreading among the Hungarian soldiers.

Many had openly defied their German Officers demanding to know why the Hungarians could not be at their "home barracks". These men were quickly locked up as an example to others who were thinking the same and grumbling about it. The 83rd, as stated earlier in this writing, was originally headquartered in Hungary, Vasmegye (county) at Szombathely (town). Now half were in Hungary, half in Vienna. To return to Vasmegye would have been most welcome to all the Hungarians, but more so for Geza and his friends that were born, and lived in that county.

Within a few days the Allied successes in France, and at the Piave River was common knowledge to these troops.

"They have broken through our lines!"

"They have moved forward making great gains, daily." So ran the rumor, but it was the truth, not rumor. The Hungarian troops accepted it as the truth and wished to return to Szombathely before some lunatic German General re-assigned them to active duty again, in what they knew was now a futile endeavor.

The Hungarians revolted against their German officer; they "Weren't our boys anyway."

Their General tried to appease them, trying to stop them with words. But the words did not sound sincere to these mad Magyars. They turned their backs on him, and a full-scale rebellion broke out. They stormed the barracks prison, releasing all the Hungarians locked up in there no matter what the infraction was that caused a fellow Hungarian to be locked up. As the native sons cleared the cells of prisoners in one lockup, they were greeted with noisy and confident cheers, complimenting one another on their boldness.

Above the noise they heard a stronger voice boom out:

"I am Magyar too! Let me out."

The crowd stopped momentarily; locked in a cell at the far end of the prison corridor they were surprised to see a lieutenant. A few soldiers ran with keys to release him. "How the heck did we miss you?"

"I don't know? You damn fools must have thought I was German," laughed the happy lieutenant.

The Magyar soldiers laughed in unison at lieutenant Gyula (Julius) Rakosi, he just as suddenly became their leader and instigator; he would get them home.

The Hungarian soldiers packed their kitbags, and knapsacks, but kept their rifles. They had expected to confiscate machine guns too, but the officers had preceded them. Some how the officers had been informed about the Hungarian intentions and they had anticipated the soldiers' actions. Whatever, the officers had removed the "hammer" (I don't know what this is. I can only presume Geza meant the "firing pin") out of them. Without the firing pins the machine guns were useless.

"Damn it. We confiscated the machine guns and cartridges, carts to carry them, and horses, expecting to march home to Szombathely."

The Hungarians had not meant to be unruly, that is, to cause a "civil disturbance"; this was to be Hungarian soldiers against German officers, so they did not plan on commandeering public transportation. Theirs would be an orderly march to Hungary, Vasmegye, and Szombathely, the 'true' regimental home of the 83rd.

The plans suddenly changed. They did not need the horse carts to carry their supplies, machine guns, and related ammunition. So they didn't need the horses either.

"Leave those things. They would only hamper our progress now, useless machine guns, useless ammo," stated Gyula.

The reason that they wanted the machine guns was for self-defense. They knew the Germans would not take too lightly to this revolt.

It was outright mutiny.

If they were to be challenged by an "outside element" on the march home, they could fight. They intended to defy all challengers so they now stocked up with rifle ammo filling their belt pouches. With rifles shouldered, Gyula Rakosi at their head, they marched orderly in rows of four abreast. Some with suitcases, others with duffle bags hung over shouldered rifle barrels; they marched through the side streets to the streetcar depot, avoiding the main thoroughfares of Vienna.

They could have commandeered the public transportation but, as stated by Gyula Rakosi, they did not intend to cause a "civil disturbance", so they allowed the civilian population the use of civilian transportation. Once they got to the "car barns" however, they appropriated a sufficient number of streetcars to make their way to the railroad station. Leaving the streetcars to the civilians once again, they then marched in orderly fashion to the freight yard, intentionally avoiding the passenger terminal.

It was in the freight yard that the locomotives and coaches were made ready before pulling into the station terminal to pick up passengers.

They boarded four of the coaches and seated themselves. Three of the soldiers were ordered forward to the locomotive and there they stayed, with the engineer and fireman for the express purpose of ordering unscheduled stops. These unscheduled stops would be to allow members of the regiment to disembark at the stations nearest to their home, once they were in Hungary.

Their German General whom they had deserted at the barracks, now appeared and came to talk them out off this rash action.

"It is a direct violation of military command! Boys, together we will march to Vasmegye through Austria. I want to lead you, but we all lose this way." In his broken Hungarian, this German general tried to persuade the native Hungarians. He tried to sway them with words of patriotism.

"For what...for Germany?" was the Hungarian reply. "We will have no part of it."

"Come with us, if you want to be part of us. Stay on this train. Come home with us."

"I can't. It is against orders. I can't simply go with you like this. It is not right. I must lead you, we must march... not go by train."

"What's the difference? You want a regiment; we are the regiment... the Magyar part of it. That is why we want to go back where the Magyar 83rd belongs, in Vasmegye, Magyarország [Country of the Magyars)."

"But you can't. Can't you see? We are one. All the International Regiment ...all are the 83rd."

"We'll see you in Szombathely."

"Yeah! Get lost. If you want to be our general, we'll see you in Szombathely."

Then he pulled a threatening 'ace' out of his sleeve: "The 63rd regiment (this was a completely German regiment) is outside the railroad station. They are ordered to attack this train if I return without you. They are prepared to take you by force."

"You better leave while you can general, and tell the 63rd we dare them to try and take us."

"This is desertion! Don't you know what the consequences are for desertion?" ranted the frustrated General.

With these last words the general broke down and wept. With tear filled eyes he beseeched the men to return to the Vienna Headquarters.

He was not successful.

Gyula, the lieutenant and rebel leader replied. "Tell the 63rd regiment; tell the German army, if they fire one hostile shot, we will level the railroad station. We will kill all civilians that get in our way. Let every life lost in this encounter be on their conscience! We shall not die easily. We will die spitefully, or go home as free men." He was not entirely bluffing, they did not intend to give in, but truthfully they did not wish to kill civilians either.

The General left.

Within a few minutes the locomotive and coaches moved forward, but stopped at the railroad terminal. The soldiers on board the coaches could now see the troops of the 63rd in columns of four, waiting.

It would hardly be a fair fight; only four coaches of the 83rd Magyar regiment against a full complement of the 63rd German infantry.

Unexpectedly, and surprisingly, civilians began boarding the train and filled the remaining coaches behind the Magyars. When the coaches were full, the engineer received the signal to pull out.

"All aboard," cried the stationmaster and the train moved slowly forward.

A cheer broke out, "We won. We won!" The Hungarians were on their way home. They never saw that general again; perhaps he lost his rank because he had lost his "command".

Is that what he feared when he shed those tears?

The train made all the regular stops in Austria, then after crossing the border, it continued to make the scheduled stops in addition to those few that the engineer was forced to make by the soldiers in his locomotive. Geza got off at a little Village station just before his hometown, on November 8, 1918. He deliberately remained out of site of his village, and other villagers, until the official announcement of the Armistice, November 11, 1918 (clearly he did not want to be caught as a deserter).

He walked the remaining distance to Porpacz, arranging to arrive after dark. When he got to that railroad station who should be there?

Unlikely, and as unexpected as it may seem, it was Miska the Bulgarian prisoner of war who had served in the Serbian army. He had been released because hostilities with Serbia had ceased, and he was now returning home to Bulgaria.

"Don't forget that gallon of whiskey," reminded Geza.

In the European manner, they embraced in farewell.

"I've got a train to catch my young friend. It is indeed good to see that you made it through that awful hell of war. Take care of yourself."

They saw one another no more.

Geza was free also. He was a civilian once more, at age eighteen years and eight months! He had lived a lot; had seen a lot. He reported to the Regimental headquarters the day after arriving home, and got his honorable discharge. No mention was made about the Hungarian contingent of the 83rd that had mutinied against the German orders to stay in Austria.

A cousin of Geza's was taken prisoner in one of the last battles in Italy. As the prisoners were led back behind the Italian lines, he saw that a revolution was in progress there too. As a result, the Italian captors did not know what to do with their prisoners.

"Let the poor bastards go. They fought in a war they did not want, just as we have," said one Italian private.

"Turn them loose," said another.

"Come, help us put down the unrest at home," suggested another.

With this type of advice, and disregard for herding them any longer, the fortunate Hungarian prisoners turned, and headed home.

Even the Italian Officers thought this a wise order, because the Italians would not have to feed and care for these many prisoners, neither would the Italian soldiers in great number be handicapped with guarding the prisoners. It proved to be a wiser decision for the captors to let their prisoners go when the armistice was announced.

Geza's cousin cut a branch from a tree, and fashioning a hiking staff from it began his the long hike home. When the Hungarians got near the northern border they had been days without food. Italian farmers and kind peasants in the border towns gave the soldiers small portions of their personal rations, corn and other food. It appears that the civilian population was happy to have these soldiers leave peaceably; they were only too pleased to get rid of the foreign invaders.

There were those unfortunate few among the returning troops who did not go directly to their regimental headquarters once at home. These, therefore, did not get the required discharge papers to prove their honorable termination of service. When they were caught at home without discharge papers, they were arrested for desertion and locked up!

Some Hungarian soldiers still in uniform, on their way home and found without discharge papers were arrested. These were locked up also. They were still in jail after the war! And because loved ones assumed them to be missing in action with no one to come to their defense, they were as good as dead!

In 1921, when Geza had become of age for "official conscription", and had to register for another three years of service, those unfortunates that were branded as deserters were still in jail!

Many had gone insane by this time. The injustice of it all! Home at last the soldier thought, after four years of hell, only to be completely lost at home, forever.

PÁL AND PISTA VALKO 1918

S ince the war had ended, the Valko family began to enquire once again through the army and the International Red Cross. The army finally notified them, and in this manner they knew that Pista Valko, missing in action these many months, was actually in a hospital in Miskolc. This is all they knew, and the family was not informed why he had been hospitalized. But no matter, he was home; he had survived the war and that was the most important thing.

Pál was home also. He had been home on leave when the rebellions broke out, so he did not return to his regiment. Now Pál went to visit Pista, taking him a little gift from his sisters.

There actually were deadly, heated engagements between regiments of troops who had been stationed on the Hungarian border, in a buffer just outside of Hungary, and those armed regiments that attempted to return home against, and contrary to the Central Powers wishes. (Much like Geza's regiment had).

Hungarian regiments were set upon Hungarian regiments!

The commanding officers had told the 'Loyalists' that the war had broken out again, and that they would have to stop the enemy who was now marching upon their native soil. The enlisted men did not know the truth and so they stood their ground, and fought their returning countrymen.

The weary infantrymen returning home did not recognize the new uniforms of their attackers. The attackers did not recognize the worn, old uniforms of their returning countrymen. Only when the shooting started did they see. No, they heard the wounded cursing them in their own native tongue. Quickly they realized the subterfuge, the deceit, and the lie.

The 'Loyalists' turned upon their officers and joined their returning countrymen. The officers, those who survived the revengeful madmen, quickly learned not to pit Magyar against Magyar; they are spiteful and an unforgiving lot who hate deception. Rebellious troops had to be challenged by Germans or not at all, even this form of challenge proved costly and foolish.

Pista had contracted malaria, and the military had sent him back to Hungary in a delirium with the wounded. Even though he was now in the Miskolc Hospital in North West Hungary, he was so sick and delirious that he could not write to let his family know of his whereabouts. The family of course was only too happy to learn he was so close to home

When Pál arrived at the hospital looking for his 'kid' brother, there was no one in attendance! Doctors and nurses had all left; even the patients who could walk had left the hospital. There were no more than three or four patients in the entire ward where Pista was, and these were there only because they were the most severely ill, and could not help themselves. It was as though the hospital had been evacuated, except for those few unconscious patients.

Pista was happy to see Pál of course, and even though Pál had brought small gifts from his sisters, the first words Pista spoke after their greeting was:

"Hoztál turos tésztat az édes anjámtol?" (Did you bring cottage-cheese- noodles from my dear mother?) In his delirium this must have been foremost on his mind; the good cooking of his mother, and he must have wondered if he would ever eat "turos tészta" again?

Pál states that when he saw Pista, there was but one solitary, ridiculously long hair on his chin. He was so youthful at nineteen years of age that he had not yet begun to shave.

Pál tended to Pista's needs and got him dressed. With assistance from his strong brother, and leaning heavily upon him, Pista was ready to go home to Szálláshhely. It wasn't far from the train station, but for Pista it was a very long, and slow, tedious walk. When they arrived home, Pál led Pista to a window and then backed away out of view as Pista rapped on the glass to his sisters inside.

They looked up, apprehensively at first, because many soldiers were moving about, stealing their way home unauthorized.

(Almost every regiment in the Austro-Hungarian army had Hungarian soldiers that rebelled from their Austrian and German commanders. The Hungarians were all sneaking home without discharge papers or valid authorization, in much the same manner as Geza's regiment had, except these were alone, or in small groups. Villagers never did know what to expect from these wandering soldiers.)

The girls shrieked in surprise, then screams of joy to see their brother. Mother hurried to the commotion, and she joined her daughters in embracing her son. They were so happy to have him home again.

"Thank God that he has brought you home; and Pál is home too," replied a grateful mother.

Both sons had duffle bag and knapsack, and the girls were eager to relieve the brothers of their burden, but the boys stopped them. With deliberate slowness the brothers took duffle bags off, talking all the while Pál replied, "Mother, we must not unpack his sack yet. He has become lice ridden and I fear the inhabitants of those clothes might take up residence in your bedclothes if we do not take caution."

They would not burn the uniform, so mother came up with an ingenious idea. First the boys would have a hot bath. This would take care of the "stragglers", but tomorrow-- -

"After I have baked bread we will put the uniforms in the kemence (outside oven), with the oven doors closed, the heat will drive the lice out and kill them. Then we will wash the clothes in lye-soap. You and the clothes will be as good as new; praise God."

The clothes were baked for three hours, and then removed with a long handled pitchfork. They were shook out, hung up to air, and then laundered with lye soap. When they dried out, the eager hands of loving sisters ironed them.

Pista put on the pressed uniform, but he was still not his cheerful self. The malaria caused him cold shivers on occasion, and he was just not himself. Local doctors seemed unable to help. Try as they may, they were just not familiar with that type of illness.

Mother put extra dunyha (eider down feather bedding) on him in bed and, what would cause a normal man to perspire still saw him teeth chattering with fever! In a few minutes he would appear well, and then he would drop into a delirium again. Mother nursed him, fed him the best of foods, but he remained seriously ill.

After many weeks, father could not stand to see his young son suffer so, and resolved that something must be done for him in spite of what the local doctors had said.

"Son there is a fine doctor in Kormond. He is an old soldier and has had military experience gleaned from campaigns in many countries. If anyone can help you it would be him."

In the ensuing weeks this old military doctor cured Pista of the malaria, and was extremely happy that with his experience he could still be of help to the young soldier.

Because Pista was not yet discharged, he had to report back to his regiment now that he was cured. There was no longer a 'National Urgency', the war was over, and considering that he had contracted malaria, the army gave him a medical discharge. The young man was not wounded, but he certainly suffered a lot, perhaps much more than if he were physically wounded and quickly recovered. He suffered grievously for a long time, from occasional weakness that the malaria brought on in extreme temperature changes.

In the months that followed, with mother's good cooking and tender care, he began to "fill out" again. He soon looked like his old self, full of face and rosy cheeked. He then began to be discontent with staying home and doing nothing. Anxious to be independent now that he had recuperated he wanted to work.

He applied for and got work as a csendör (policeman), and was quickly on his way with promotions. He became a sergeant, then a higher rank soon after. Whenever his Superiors came to visit Pista at the Homestead, not seeing his father, they would ask the whereabouts of the "old man". If told that Mr. Valko was hunting, they would purposely linger on.

Sure enough, the "old man" would always return with rabbits and Mother Valko cooked all the visitors a fine rabbit stew.

He never shot deer. He was too soft hearted to take the life of a species that seemed so peaceful and innocent. Rabbits? Yes, but only when he knew they were plentiful. He knew this by observation, when you see them too frequently in casual walks through the woods, this means there are too many, so when he saw a lot of them in the countryside, he shot them for food and thereby thinned out their numbers in a crude "balance with nature".

The officers knew that if they lingered, they would be invited to stay for supper. What an understanding indeed, what a happy arrangement, a most commendable family attribute is 'hospitality'.

THE GYPSY
VIOLIN 1919

Varga János, the old siege artilleryman of Pryzml, was forty-six years old when he returned to Porpacz from his Russian captivity. When the villagers could finally speak to him in private about young Lajci, they asked; "János Bacsi, how did Kerekes Lajci die?"

"May his mother's God forgive him? He wouldn't eat horse meat; he wouldn't eat cat meat and wouldn't eat dog meat, that's what killed him. Bélé Istenét. (God curse his guts).

Oh! Lajci; you silly young son-of-a-bitch!" He mused as he shook his head in wonder, "Here I am Lajci; I'm home, and you could have been home too...if only...," and then audibly to those who questioned; "He had a curséd squeamish stomach."

"But how did you find food when others starved?"

"Others starved because they would not eat what was around them! They could have had the same as I had, horsemeat, dog meat, cat meat; if only they could tolerate it. I still had a chunk of raw horsemeat in my food pouch when the Russians took us." [And because of this declaration, he was affectionately nicknamed Nyers János (Raw John) from that day on].

While Varga János was in Russian captivity, his captors often gave him vodka to deliberately get him drunk. The Russians theorized prisoners were easier to handle when they were 'tipsy'. But János would over imbibe, get rowdy too often and start a fight. His captors then had an excuse to beat him. They did this quite often, and poor, foolish János, always took the bait... because he liked his drink. But he never forgave his captors for beating him, and taking advantage of him.

A Russian prisoner of war named Elushin chose to stay in Porpacz rather than return home to Russia after the war. He had become a foreman for a Landlord in the area, married a Hungarian girl and settled down. "I had nothing in Russia. I was poor there. Here I at least have something, and can work to accumulate more."

Like Varga János, he too, liked to drink. When he went into a tavern he didn't order a glass of wine, he ordered a liter, and he too, got rowdy!

The citizens soon found that, Varga János and Elushin just could not be in the same tavern at the same time because after a few drinks János would attack Elushin, taking his frustration and hate for his Russian captors out on this unfortunate "resident Russian". Elushin in turn, soon got wise after a few of these encounters. Even though he could wrestle János to the ground, and "best" the old man in a fight, he kindly chose to avoid further confrontations and learned to cross the street when János staggered along the walk.

If he were in a tavern where János chose to drink, Elushin would leave before János confronted him.

When Geza and his friends, a group of four or five young men were in the same bar, singing and having a good time, János would want to "mix it up" with them. Bound to fight and itching for one, he would declare that they were shit, not soldiers. He contended that they had not spent enough time in the service; compared to him that was true. He went into action in 1914, as a 42-year-old veteran, and was hard pressed from the very first day of fighting. His outfit saw too much action and was always under pressure, which may have affected his mental stability. He had also seen action in 1908-1912, with the revolution in the Slavic States,

Montenegro, Croatia and Bosnia. The eccentric old bachelor had his own opinion as to what constituted a soldier.

Geza's cousin Imre, a strong young man was once approached by János.

"Knock me down, I dare you. Go ahead, if you're a man, just try to knock me down."

"No. No. János bacsi I have no reason to." Said Imre, smiling.

János then gritted his teeth "Just try to knock me down!"

The entire village respected him and so they tolerated him. János died in 1953 at the age of 81. Just think; in his older years he even survived the greatest war, World War II. One can only imagine that the old son-of-a-gun may have even volunteered for that war! He had lived a lot, and he had seen a lot in his lifetime.

Lakatos János, a Hungarian Gypsy, had eight sons. He was shrewd in many ways besides making a large family to care for him in his golden years. He made the trip to Italy with his sons at least four times after the armistice. They even went as far as the Udine to gather up herds of stray horses abandoned by both armies. He had returned successfully unchallenged quite often, but on his last trip, crossing the border at Ledov and circling around the guard stations as they had on previous trips, it was not the border guards that gave these gypsy men trouble on this return trip.

As always, father and sons each rode a horse while they herded a greater number between them. Would-be horse thieves, latecomers, bent upon the same purpose as Lakatos János, but reluctant to walk into Italy from the train station, thought they could rob him of his herd.

János was not about to give the 'rustlers' that satisfaction. Seeing what was intended, he and his sons ran the entire herd of horses purposefully forward menacing to stampede over the horse thieves. Caught off guard, a few rifle shots would not stop the charge, and the 'rustlers' scurried out of the way. They would surely have been overrun, and afraid of the onrushing herd they became equally afraid of the "crazy" Gypsy.

He was no fool.

He had won!

All told he and his sons had acquired more than a hundred horses that were there just for the taking by any ambitious entrepreneur.

The Government Factory in Szombathely had expanded, now encompassing a forging foundry and machine shop. Geza went seeking to get his old job back. The new place was growing and provided many jobs for returning veterans. But Geza's old supervisor remembered the impetuous young man, how abruptly and unceremoniously Geza had "quit" when he was conscripted.

He remembered that the conscription officer in 1917 had allowed one week for young men, such as Geza, to prepare for service. But Geza chose to "throw down his blacksmith's hammer" immediately. The supervisor maliciously conveyed this behavior to the Principle Engineer, adding that Geza also influenced another young man to leave just as abruptly, at a time when experienced help was difficult to replace. With this device he hoped to undermine Geza's chance of returning to his old job.

The Principle Engineer none-the-less interviewed Geza, after all, he thought, a sixteen year old should not have been required to go to war. If he did go, because he was forced into conscription, the action and behavior at work could be explained away as a defiant act of frustration and hate of those circumstances. After talking with Geza, the principal engineer acquired a liking for his honest, free spirit, and Geza got his old job back.

1919 was a very climactic year in Hungary; the soldier's rebellions were no sooner ended than the communists began to express themselves. In the spring of 1919, Geza attended a 'Workers Meeting' in Sárvár, at which two powerful communist leaders, Urban Lajos and Kuhn Béla were the prime speakers. To impress the people in attendance, they glorified Károli Mihail, a rich Hungarian landlord who had distributed all of his wealth, and his possessions to the poor before the 1919 insurrections. Karoli Mihail was a Socialist, and now a strong supporter for the communist cause because he truly believed that "the wealthy should help the poor".

The Communist theory came close to his philosophy: however, he did not realize that they desired to take not only the property but, all wealth that the rich had acquired, and distribute it among the peasants in order for the State to control it all. In his naïve innocence, Mihail was not aware that he was being used as a "tool" to further the Communist cause.

Kuhn Béla was a Hungarian Jew and had fought for Austria-Hungary; captured in 1916 on the Russian front. Together with other prisoners, he joined the Russian Communist Party in 1917. Having spent more than a year, and after receiving training in Communist Russia, he returned to lead a revolution in Hungary. Russia's communists were sent to foment revolution in Rumania, Hungary and Czechoslovakia.

Meetings such as the one that Geza went to in Sárvár, caused dissention between those attempting to establish a sound government in the war's aftermath, and those communists who wanted to overthrow the government completely. Those communists hoped to replace it with their personal brand of a "People's Government."

So it was that, once again rebellions erupted.

In many smaller counties and villages within Hungary, communists evicted the rich merchants from their businesses, and landlords from their estates. The uneducated and unlearned peasant leaders actually sat in judgment of these educated "bourgeoisies", as the communists called the aristocrats.

Lenin had advised Rákosi and Kuhn Béla, reminding them to never forget, "land to the people!" Lenin's philosophy was, "if you give land to the people, they will work it. It becomes their home, and they will defend it."

But in 1919 the Hungarian Communist party was too young, it was growing at such a rate however, that decent, trustworthy, learned administrators were no longer easily found among them. As it spread to other countries outside of Russia, the predicament became worse. It was inevitable; unqualified and unlearned men were put into positions of authority.

In Hungary the revolution was indeed short lived. It was finally overthrown because of the greed of their "new" leaders, and the shrewdness of Landlords who manipulated the unlearned leaders. These Landlords played both sides, for survival and personal advantage.

Rakosi had sneaked out of Hungary and somehow got into Russia where he met Lenin during the Russian peasant uprising of 1917. Lenin suggested that Rákosi return to Hungary in late 1918. Both he and Kuhn Béla hoped to foment an uprising in their Homeland. Rákosi was captured and thrown into jail. He would have been executed for certain but for the 1919 uprising. The would-be revolutionaries freed him. With this 1919 revolution's failure he again escaped, returning to Russia.

After World War II, 1945, Russia occupied Hungary, and Rákosi was appointed Premier of Hungary. Rákosi then repeated Stalin's mistakes, he confiscated the land, including small acreages, leaving only one acre to each Landlord or farmer. Each farmer now had nothing more than a family garden plot. Then Rákosi demanded that all farmers bring their livestock, and motorized farm equipment to Central Collective Farms. He theorized, as Stalin had, all farmers would work "collectively" for the good of the Communist State. With the combined equipment and combined effort, many farmers can farm more land more effectively.

He was wrong!

Individual farmers lost incentive on these "collective farms"; there was no "reason" to work conscientiously. In 1956 when the counter-revolution broke out, the people would have killed him and Gerö Ersö, had they not again successfully escaped; another fifteen minutes, and their lives would have ended at the airport.

One afternoon in the summer of 1919, as Geza was walking home from the railroad station, he crossed paths with a poor farmer on his way from Szombathely. Geza greeted the farmer but the farmer was despondent and on the verge of tears, so that he could not meet Geza's eyes.

"What's the matter Péter Bácsi? Things can't be that bad."

"They are my boy, they are. When the Comrades confiscate livestock from the poor, and befriend the rich, it is a bad thing."

"What is that you say?"

"They took my six cows. I just came from talking with them. I begged them as comrades but I was lucky to come away with my life. Son, they threatened my life."

"Who did? Why did they take your cows?"

"The Bolsheviks, that's who, these communists who profess to help make all citizens equal."

"I don't believe it!"

"Son, they are there now. In that white frame house, they made that their headquarters until the communists establish a regional government. Go, see for yourself. They are inside drinking wine with the földesur (földesur would be a landlord owning large acreage. This fellow's name is lost to me now. He was very rich and had hundreds of cows, sheep and horses). They make merry while others sorrow."

With this last remark the poor man continued walking back to his small farm.

Geza was angered; his anger made him curious. He retraced old Péter Básci's steps to that white frame house, the same frame house that Colonel Carpatti had used as prison camp headquarters during the war. Geza remembered it all too well; this is where the Colonel "chewed" him out in mocking chastisement for breaking Miska's ribs.

Once more with intrepidation, as in the past, up the front walk he went but this time he was alone, no guards to escort him. However, there were two armed guards in front of the entrance and they immediately crossed rifles to bar his path.

"What do you want?"

"I wish to talk to your commander."

"For what purpose?"

"To plea a cause for a fellow comrade."

Momentarily hesitant, one of the sentries turned, opened the door and entered the house. He quickly came back and pronounced that the commander would see him.

Geza walked in alone, leaving the sentries outside as they had been.

Sure enough, the földesur was inside with the commander and a few of the commander's cohorts as Péter Bácsi had stated. The commander sat at a desk facing the door, and so he now faced Geza. A bottle of wine was on the table where the földesur and the other communists sat in front of their glasses. This table was to the right of the commander as he sat at the desk.

It was obvious that the communist commander had been sitting there also, but for show and to display his position of authority, he had quickly seated himself behind the desk before Geza entered.

"What is your request comrade?" The commander cheerfully asked.

"Sir, I came to make a humble request on behalf of an old friend."

"Speak up young man, we are here to help. What is it?"

"Well, I was under the impression that this revolution was intended to help the poor, to make us all equals, and there would be no "class structure.""

"What are you getting at? We intend to help everybody. That is the way it will be when the new government is established."

"Then why do you confiscate the possessions of the poor now?"

With this statement the commander was suddenly red faced, and angered by this young upstart. "We confiscate property, possessions...and whatever...to distribute equally when the revolution is over."

"I do not understand. Why do you take from the poor now, when you intend to give it back to the poor later?" answered Geza.

"Are you for us or against us?" bellowed the commander, showing physical irritation. The cohort at the table now faced the drama unfolding before their eyes.

"I thought that I was for your cause, a cause that was for the people. When I passed my old friend Péter Bácsi only moments ago, I doubted him and so I came here to learn for myself. I could not believe that you took all his cows. Six cows are all he had, and this földesur who sits with you has hundreds of them. He has hundreds of livestock..."

With that statement the commander opened the desk drawer, pulled out a revolver and laid it on top of the desk.

"Do you disagree with our actions?" He asked Geza.

"Sir, I was in the war. I served two years in hell. I did not die, though perhaps I should have, had it not been for my comrades. I shed my blood for my country's cause. I do not intend to lay down my life here."

"Then get on with your purpose for being here."

"Couldn't you at least give back one cow to Péter Bácsi? He has a family that needs the milk. Surely the földesur, here," motioning with his hand in the direction of the land-lord, "could agree with that. He knows the value of one cow and what it means to a family. Seeing he has so many to give to the cause, you surely won't miss one cow that a poor man can use now."

"The földesur has nothing to do with that decision, it is mine to make. I say what will be taken," he bellowed, "and from whom; just as I will decide when and how it will be distributed."

Seeing the fire in the fanatic's eyes Geza did not push his luck. Why, the madman would just as quickly shoot Geza and say it was "for the cause".

"I will leave," replied Geza quietly. "But let me leave you with a parting thought comrade. The revolution is intended to take from those who have too much, and distribute from their excesses to the many poor, just as Károli Mihail has done. I was there in that room in Sárvár when Kuhn Béla talked about the good works of this wise Landlord who gave away his possessions voluntarily, *before the revolution*. He knew he had excess, so he chose to live in only one room of his mansion, sharing his personal home with many less fortunate. That is the example shown us; that is the way we thought it should be. This, what you have perpetrated on Péter Bácsi is not the way comrade. If you persist in this unequal manner, the very people you intended to help will be the ones to turn against you."

While the men in the room pondered the statement, and evaluated what they had just heard from this young man who was at that crucial meeting in Sárvár; the young man turned and walked out, closing the door behind him.

Geza had made it!

He had walked away from that madman without getting shot in the back; but neither did Péter Bácsi get his cow.

Three months later this form of communism was overthrown. The földesur, wisely playing both sides of the political fence, continued to hold onto all his possessions. Indeed, he prospered in a manner that indicated that these three months of adverse administration had not existed; he had certainly not suffered.

Even though Kuhn Béla was purported to be a Jew, the Jews suffered from the communists during that brief revolution. Then after the revolution the new government authorities imposed cruel rules that took time to "straighten out" so that Anti Semitism was exercised even after the revolution. It seems that the Jew suffered no matter who was in power. The new administration authorities captured and beat-up Kuhn Béla before he again escaped in 1920, once again to Russia, where he became a member Komintern, and was 'liquidated' in 1937 on orders from Stalin.

When Pista Valko was stationed in Koség as a policeman, Ilona would take a train to that town which bordered Austria, to visit her brother, bringing the home baked goods mother made for him. If Pista's friends knew she was coming to visit, they would drop over on some pretext to visit him, bringing a bottle of "Raspberry Syrup" and a bottle of carbonated water because they learned that the young lady did not drink wine or whiskey, but really enjoyed the carbonated raspberry mixture.

While in Koség, Ilona would walk to her Jewish friend's house on some evenings. Her friend's father had a dental practice in that town. Her friend in turn, would take a train and visit Ilona at Szalashély, bringing her pet bulldog along. The Szalashély police were not as understanding about Jews as the Koség police were however, and they had the unmitigated gall to enter the Valko home and chase Ilona's friend out of their home!

"How dare you let her and her dog into your home?" demanded the policeman.

Mr. Valko, as kindly and forgiving as he was, often had the police commandant come to his home and formally apologize to Ilona's friend for the policeman responsible for this rude invasion of his home; his demands were met because of Pista's position in the police force.

A poem that circulated after the revolution signifies the narrow-minded viewpoint of many.

Meg bukott a Kuhn kormany!	*The Kuhn government has failed!*
Zsidö nincs hazad man	*Jew you no longer have a home*
Erédj, zsido, keres hazad	*Go, Jew, find a home in*
Palistina, Varan	*Palestine town*
Ej! Zsido, zsido, zsido az a elét	*Ah! Jew, Jew, Jew that is life*
Ha meg unom magom	*If I'm bored with myself*
Ütlek ahogyan érek	*I will hit you however I can reach you.*

Asztalös Károly was twenty-one years old having been drafted into the army in 1917, at seventeen years of age. On his return home the young man needed a job, so Squire Simon, (who had caught him, at age nine grazing cows in the Squire's hayfield) made a job available for the youth. The Squire had observed the boy growing up, stubborn, and still too independent in the same foolish manner of his childhood. The Squire hoped to see the young man change and wanted to help him make that change.

With the revolution of 1919 however, Károly now joined the communist radicals and, *turned the Squire out of his ancestral home.*

"Get out!" demanded the angry boy. "Go live in the servants hut. We are taking over your estate."

"Károly, Károly; this revolution won't last. It can't succeed. You are too few in number; it is ill planned and ill timed. Don't do anything rash; anything that may prove too embarrassing later," advised the kind Landlord. The Squire tried to advise the youth as a friend. But the friend was still spiteful and stubborn...still intent on getting even with Squire Simon for berating him those many years ago when he was a boy.

Indeed, the communists, comrades of Károly did evict the Squire and his entire family, but as a sort of "insurance", Károly did no bodily harm to the Squire, his family or his servants.

He did move into the main house himself however, and lived well and 'high on the hog' for the few weeks that the revolution lasted in that county.

It seemed quite all right for him to now be 'affluent', even though it proved to be temporary, but he did not think it right for the Squire to be affluent!

Isn't that the way with fools?

The Squire moved out of the servants' houses and back into the main house when the communist threat ended, and Asztalos Károly hurriedly moved out. The Squire kindly scolded the young man explaining the error of his ways, and let him go for good.

"But I have to work. I need this job," protested Károly.

"You should have thought of that before you became a communist and evicted me and my household from our family home. Sooner or later you must learn to pay for your actions; your action toward my family was not one of kindness, or thanks that I gave you a job. You chose to ignore a kindness and did not respect or appreciate your position."

Károly knew that his actions were wrong, but after more than twelve years, he still persisted in his grudge toward the kindly Squire.

"But he is a Jew," thought Károly, "why should a Jew have more than I have?"

He could not relate to works, wise business ventures, good management, and conscientious effort. Károly could only see the "haves, and have-nots", as most communist see it. That is why they wish to take from those who "have", take from the landlords, merchants, and those who may have worked hard, and wisely obtained their fortunes. Once people made their fortunes they were to be 'relieved' of it for the benefit of those who have nothing. And so it was that Károly once again left the good Squire with these parting words:

"I won't forget this...I'll get even."

Squire Simon's heart suddenly felt like a lead weight. But why should it? *Because he had heard the nine-year-old boy say exactly those words*, and now as a young man the same "boy" persists in persecuting one who would have been a friend. What will come of it?

The Squire sighed heavily; anti-Semitism was not new to him.

"We shall see." He worried.

The communist rebellion was put down. The would-be revolution was over and all the leaders in fear of retribution had fled the country.

The Austrians and Germans were now "on the fence" in their policy toward Communist Russia after the 1919 insurrections. The Hungarians had acted quickly and decisively, wiping out all signs of communist influence in Hungary within months of its start.

In so doing, those countries remote from Russia, opposing the communists in-country, took the pressure off the revolting communists within Russia. The Russian communists then gained a further hold on the Russian people and their internal, local governments.

Communism became stronger in Russia after 1919, and won this final division of politics in the European States. The German military influence withdrew from Russian soil, as did the United States influence. The internal struggle was now between White Russian, those loyal to the Czar, and Red Russian, those intent on overthrow of the Czar and the Loyalists. This continued for another ten years or more.

Károli Mihail went to France.

This once rich, but kindly man was really of no harm to anyone. He meant well, perhaps dreaming of that Utopia in which all mankind live as brothers, and no one need go hungry or suffer for want. His parting words as he left his homeland were: "I shall return again, to once more distribute land in Hungary,"

In 1945 when Hungary was "apportioned" to Russia, he returned as a communist sympathizer once again. But he proved to be an embarrassment to them with his Socialist views. Because of the high esteem the populace held for the old man, the Hungarian-Russian communists discreetly and cautiously reassigned him to a meaningful position (seemingly meaningful in the eyes of the populace. The hierarchy could not simply 'eliminate' the old man). The Hungarian Government appointed him ambassador to France, in that manner they succeeded in getting him out of their way and out of the country once again.

When he died in France, the leaders were again at a loss what to do with him. Finally deciding to return his body to Hungary; they afforded him a Hero's Honor, burying him in his homeland, thus emulating this *Socialist* in the eyes of his countrymen, as *a Communist hero,* the forerunner of the workers' rights movement.

The veterans were returning home with regularity in 1919, but not all of them had been fortunate to get home quickly after hostilities ended. Some, for reasons of their own, elected to stay in the regions where they were interned, and would arrive later than 1919.

Some men returned many years later.

I talked to a veteran of that war, Simon Kovács, who was taken prisoner on the Russian front in 1916; he didn't return until 1926! As a prisoner he was assigned with many Hungarians to work in the salt mines of Russia. News of the revolution within Russia did not filter to these prisoners, and they did not get the news about the war's end until they were actually released from their duty as prison workers, in 1926.

They had been slave laborers for ten years.

Among those returning to their homes in 1919 was a broken hearted gypsy. Geza first heard about him, and the subsequent story through the gypsy's songs. His entire life was endurable because of his beloved violin. He was never lonely no matter where he was as long as he had his violin. Within it were so many precious, musical memories that he reflected upon in his aging years. With it he traveled to almost every country in prewar Europe. Dark haired, beautiful Italian women sang enticing serenades that he translated into music for his violin.

His songs, and the violin's laughing strings, made lovely music, bringing joy to all nationalities. His sad songs brought tears. But the skilled gypsy knew how to play and when to play, to fulfill the needs of youthful passions of his listeners. And how to bring back to older minds the memories of sweet adventures passed, and with promises for the future of a life well spent.

Yes! He and his violin both belonged to the people.

Now he stands among those in the crowds who hear his violin once again, because he plays it no more! He continues to sing in accompaniment the many melodies, to bring back the memories of another life.

Picture a broken man, who's greatest love is his violin; his best friend plays it now as he sings. This is the haunting song that the gypsy leaves for posterity:

I wandered the Czar's Empire and Italy
And before earls, barons, and dukes, performed musically.
I listened to the beautiful Italian women's enticing songs
A long time ago, a long time ago...perhaps it wasn't even so.
A long time ago, one beautiful night in May.

And when the earthly chaos burst upon us
We would all have to go is how I felt.
A rifle was now in my hands where my violin had dwelt.
A long time ago, a long time ago...perhaps it wasn't even so.
A long time ago, one beautiful night in May.

And from my violin far departed those soul-stirring songs
And now again I am here my beloved violin
But without my right arm because while trying to escape
A grenade took away my right arm.
But it was a long time ago, a long time ago, one night in May.

Jartom a 'Szár birodalmát es Italiát,
És musikaltom gruffök, es bárók, es hercegek elöt.
Hallgatom a szép Olasz nök csabito dalat
Rég volt, rég volt...igaz se volt talán.
Rég volt, egy szép Május éjszakán.

És amikor rank szakat a földi zürzavar
Mindnyájunknak el kel meni ugy éreztem én.
Fegyver volt mán a kezemben a hegedöm heljén.
Rég volt, rég volt...igaz se volt talán.
Rég volt, egy szép Május éjszakán.

És a hegedömbol mese el szált a lelkesítö dal,
És most megén it vagyok drága hegedöm;
De nincs job karom mert szökésközben
Egy granád elvoté a job karom.
De rég volt, rég volt, egy Május éjszakán.

Do we not sometimes wonder about the beautiful memories of a long time ago, and wonder, in amazement, could it have been true...perhaps? Did we actually live that wonderful moment in some distant past? It seems like some one else's life, now. Could it have really been me? Was I that fortunate, to live that which is now a memory, from a long time ago?

This Gypsy lived that life, and the part he sang about.

TROOPS COMING HOME

In 1920, Mr. Virag the elder, received a letter from one of Gergély's army buddies living in Körmond. The friend's letter enquired if Gergély was home yet. The letter also stated that Gergély had married the Old Kulak's daughter in 1917. The friend went on to describe that some Hungarian prisoners of war had worked for Gergély, and they liked him because they fared well under his leadership on the Kulak's fiefdom. This was the first news the Virag family had about Gergély since he was reported missing in action in 1916!

The family was overjoyed, to say the least; is it possible that he is alive?

At least four men, previous prisoners of war and now returned home to various cities in Hungary, were also enquiring by letter about Gergély.

The family immediately wrote a reply letter to the friend in Körmond. Their letter stated that, until receiving his letter they were not certain about Gergély's fate, thinking he was lost in action because the Red Cross had not been able to find news or trace him.

"Could you give us a location in Russia? What was the name of the nearest town?"

Even though the friend had removed some doubts as to Gergély's existence, this friend could not resolve their elated confusion. In his next letter however, he confirmed that it was Gergély whom he had worked with in captivity and Gergély had given him the Porpacz address.

Yes, Gergély was indeed alive!

But why had he not written to let his family know that he was well? For four years the Virags did not know what to think. Many of the soldiers, even the prisoners that were exchanged, were now home in 1920.

The friend had provided an address in Russia. Geza immediately wrote to the address, but apparently Gergély did not get that letter... as was to be learned in later years.

Sülé Jenö returned home in 1921, after nine years of service, counting 1913, the year of his enlistment as one year. He had been captured in 1918 during some of the last offensives in Italy, but had been reported missing in action. He did not make an effort to come home until 1921.

He too, could have stated as the Gypsy Patriot had in his melancholy song; "I have walked the land of the Czars and in Italy."

Jenö, the man who feared no man, wounded and captured on the Russian front, captured another time and imprisoned in Russia. Now he related to the Headquarters questioners how he was captured that third and last time. They demanded this from every returning veteran; the questioners were experienced enough by now to determine who had been captured, from those who had simply deserted to the enemy. Headquarters wanted to know where Jenö was when he had been captured. Who was his commanding Officer? What was the situation like that led to his capture?

"I don't know what the situation was like for those others. I only know what my situation was like. There were eight of us when we started at that damn machine-gun emplacement. The ninth was the 'traktor-ferer' who brought us the ammunition continuously from behind our lines. But not one survived that I know of. I was alone at the gun; the enemy was all around me. I didn't know which way to shoot. I kept firing up to the last moment. When my final round was spent I raised both my arms and stood up to surrender. One of those bastards hit me anyway, rifle butt in the back. It was over for us. There was no other way to do it. We were encircled, with nowhere to go; nothing to continue the fight with. I could not run, I would surely have been shot in the back... a useless death... and a needless loss."

"You took your time getting home after the Italians released you didn't you? Just about three years late."

"Maybe I did. But I did come back, after sight-seeing that beautiful country," replied Jenö.

"Humph! Isn't your country beautiful enough for you?" asked the ignorant questioner.

"I love my home. I love my country, and when the battles are over, what does it matter? What more would you expect of me?"

"Nothing more," replied another Officer.

Headquarters knew Jenö's past record and they knew he was no coward. He was a National hero, decorated twice. Those situations proved Jenö's mettle and his reputation held him in good stead. He went on with his story.

"This time I was lucky and uninjured, but the fight was over all the same. I was alive my comrades were dead. I don't know what became of the others in our perimeter."

"Good boy. You did well," replied this second Officer.

They knew the situation before he had told them!

They had known of that battle and its outcome. They knew the commanding officer, they knew also that more than one machinegun crew had been lost. They were merely adding up the pieces that would complete the story of that battle. Now they knew a little more, one member of a machinegun crew had survived. Jenö had been that one who kept shooting to the final moment. There certainly was no escape in that situation, and there was no way out.

They marveled only that he survived unscarred. His record proved that this was now the third incident, which they knew, and each time he had defied all odds and lived. They could only wonder, now that the war was over, if he was decorated twice (the Silver Star and the Iron Cross), he surely deserved a third decoration. And what about the many other battles he had been in...in the air-gunnery service?

Men like Jenö had gone beyond that which is expected to be their duty.

Much later in the company of his friends, when he heard about the 1919 revolution in Hungary, he exclaimed, "boys, if I had been home then! I would have shot every turncoat rich landlord son-of-a-bitch. It would have only taken me a month."

The uprising didn't last much longer than that. Jenö blamed the war on the 'upper classes'. It was these bourgeoisies that drove the uneducated masses into waging "their war".

In captivity he had learned the language of his captors; he spoke Italian and Russian fluently.

Geza had been apprenticed at eleven years of age, working for three years, up to the age of fourteen when he was certified. He was drafted at age sixteen, one month before his seventeenth birthday, and had worked three years at the Hungarian Government Factory (Magyar Alomi), in "Workshop Sciences", (fabricating shop, wrought iron forming, mechanical models etc.). This factory was in the provincial capital of Szombathely.

Geza now worked at the same factory in 1920, forging locomotive wheels. He had spent some time working with Erszebet Kuhn's brother (the reader will recall Erzsi was Gaspar Pista's girlfriend, the sergeant major in Vienna, Austria).

In 1921, Geza had to reenlist. He could not deduct the two years of his active duty service. By law, every man of age twenty-one must serve three years in the military. What had transpired during a national crisis, for national expediency in wartime had no bearing on the law when a man reached the age of conscription. Geza now had to fulfill that obligation.

Geza had served in the army with a village schoolteacher named Károly (Charles), during 1917-1918. Károly's father was a hired hand for a landowner of 2,000 acres and when Károly came home he did not like the thought of working for the same landlord, so he re-enlisted. He was two years older than Geza, and by 1921 was a "corporal first class".

He remembered Geza very well, because they had argued too often in the barracks, sometimes to the point of getting physical.

Oh, yes! The corporal remembered Geza. He remembered too vividly also those differences of opinion. Now this same corporal was with the military contingent that met the new recruits as they came into the compound before the barracks in Vienna, and escorted these, as yet civilians, to their barracks.

Geza told the man straightforward, "Károly, I am not going in, (to the barracks). My girlfriend came with me on the train and I certainly will not leave her alone. I have made arrangements for her return tonight. I will stay with her till then, and register into the barracks tonight."

"Oh no you won't, you have to go with the rest of the men. We have a head count," was the reply.

"I am not going! I am still a civilian, and you do not give me orders...yet. And you certainly cannot have me bound and hauled in Károly. I'll go in tonight," Geza replied as he turned and left the compound..

Geza stayed out that first day, having left his baggage checked at the station, and spent the rest of the day and early evening with his girlfriend. At night he escorted her back to the station, saw her off on the return train, checked out his baggage, and then, true to his word, went back to the barracks to sign in.

He would report for duty that next day.

The "army" promoted him to corporal because of his two years active service; Károly the corporal, who wished dearly to make Geza's life miserable, now did not outrank him, and could not carry through with his malicious intentions.

Geza soon found himself instructing new recruits of his same age in the art of weaponry, specifically the use and handling of the machine gun.

(In 1946 he met a man in Brantford, Ontario, Canada, who remembered those training sessions well. Mr. Dobranyi even related the route marches, weekend bivouacs and the discipline under Corporal Virag. Geza did not remember the man, the incidents were certainly familiar, but those experiences went with any group of recruits. Drill instructors were not expected to remember every private, but now in 1946, both men were personable, and so a lifetime friendship began).

Geza also met his old friend Gaspar Pista while stationed in Vienna; that friendly sergeant major. Gaspar had re-enlisted and made plans for a career in the army. He was already promoted to Captain, having been stationed to a border frontier with one hundred men in his command. This was something like a peacetime National Guard. He had returned to Vienna but remained for only a short time. Since his active service counted for double time Pista retired while he was relatively young. His father had become a prosperous landowner, and his two brothers helped with the family farm. Pista told Geza that he did not want to be a farmer until he was "well off", and then he would be a "gentleman farmer", his military pension would see to that.

In Vienna, Geza also saw those poor fellows that had returned home without discharge papers. Having been detained for desertion since 1918; they were still in military jails. Some had gone insane, so there was no choice but to keep them locked up now. What eventually became of the others? No one knows. Because of this, and other injustices perpetrated by the military minds, and the political minds that required young boys 16, 17, years of age to be drafted into an active war, then demand they serve an additional three years at age twenty-one, Geza plotted to get out. He wanted out of a system that demanded too much from veterans.

Damned if he will serve three years!

Geza therefore made a habit of visiting the regimental doctor in an attempt to coerce the man. He was constant with his plea for a medical discharge, and he was constantly at the doctor's office.

"Doctor I am a wounded veteran. I almost gave my life for my country...serving two hectic years; search my record," he leaned heavily upon active duty years for retirement. "If career soldiers can get double credit for each year of active duty, why can't a wounded veteran," and on, and on, until finally the doctor decided to "work" with Geza.

PISTA VALKO

A landowner in Andrasfa (Andrew's Tree), a town close to Mák Fa (Poppy Tree), and a friend of Pista Valko, had a beautiful tan-brown (sarga) horse. This rich friend admired how Pista Valko could ride that thing. No man could make that horse run as swiftly as Pista could, and there was many an evening when Pista saddled that horse without the friend's knowledge, riding to Mák Fa to dance all night or, he would ride swiftly to Majyaris, another good-time-town where with good companionship he would sing and dance all night. When it was too crowded in the dance hall, the young couples would move out into the graveled main street in front of the dancehall to dance. It was quite easy to wear out a pair of shoes in an evening, dancing in the gravel street.

Then before morning, Pista would ride back, unsaddle the horse, tie him up in the stable stall and the friend was none the wiser.

There were times however, when the friend bumped into Pista at these "parties". Because he admired Pista's singing voice he would forgive Pista and invite Pista to join his table for drinks. They did have good times together, Pista and this rich friend.

"Toni, where is Pál? Is he drinking again?" Asked mother, as Toni entered the kitchen.

"Where is he, what is he doing?" replied Toni, "Why they have probably beaten him up by now. I could not possibly help him; there were too many Mák Fa and Dögön

426

Helyi (Poppy Tree and Beaten Place), youths just itching for a fight (they were all proud, tough guys). I got out of there, but you know Pál, the more he drinks, the more he wants to drink and he becomes unreasonable. I told him to come home with me but he wouldn't. He just may accommodate those youths."

Upon hearing this Pista immediately went out to look for Pál.

Németh János was among these at the tavern. He never did cause any trouble with Pál because at one time he was on the receiving end of a brawl with the "Beaten Place" youths, and they had injured him so badly, that they likely would have killed him if Pál had not stopped them. Pál waded into the mêlée pulling them off János. He then stood feet astride the unconscious youth, no one challenged him as he said; "Don't lay another hand on him, whoever dares to try will have to cope with me."

Arms cocked, fists clenched, he seemed most formidable.

Pál then put János on his shoulder and carried him out of town to a safe place. János parents were very grateful that he had saved their son's life and they made a special trip to the Homestead, to express their gratitude to Pál, his mother and father. They personally endeared themselves to Pál.

The country side simply buzzed about his bravery, that was before Pál took too excessive drinking.

"Pál saved János' life. He surely would have been killed if Pál had not stepped in," was the common understanding in the community.

But then, in the future, the youths plied Pál with drinks attempting to get him drunk, hoping to take advantage of him in his drunken state. His strength, they thought, is no use when drinks make a man uncoordinated. And so the idea was to make him uncoordinated and then beat him up to get even.

Debtors sometimes become extremely jealous, or spiteful of those to whom they owe, and János was no exception. At this tavern, on this evening, he ignored his indebtedness.

Pál had established a respectful reputation as a fighter because of his strength. On this occasion, János thought Pál had drunk to excess, and therefore he could now take advantage of him. If that were the case, János could show off to those "toughs" that he dared to fight Pál. So it was that he suddenly grappled with Pál.

Pál, surprised as he was at János' behavior, good naturedly pushed him aside and refused to fight, mindful of the boy's parents. These grateful old folks had endeared themselves to him. It would break their heart if, now he would turn-about and severely hurt János.

Rather than provoke more aggression, Pál walked out of the tavern.

Certainly there were some who interpreted Pál's action as a sign of cowardice. It did not matter to Pál, he was more disappointment at János' behavior and it hurt, for Pál knew that this ungrateful youth wished him harm. What would János' parents think; if Pál had turned and whipped their son?

In a sad mood at home, Pál reflected upon János' behavior to Pista.

His young brother was so furious he was gritting his teeth. "Don't brood about him brother. If you choose not to teach him a lesson out of respect for his humble parents, or whatever your reasons, I'll teach him respect."

"Don't you dare harm that boy Pista," said mother. "If you do, and he reports you, you will surely loose your position with the police. He is not worth it Pista."

"Forget it," ended father.

"Don't worry; I have learned how to handle this type of situation."

Pista now planned to get even with János.

"He will have to go home on that path through the densest part of Nagy Erdö (Large Forest) to Buja (Hiding). I will conceal myself near that path and I will confront him there." He thought to himself.

This is what took place on that path in the late hours of that same night.

As János approached, Pista in full csendor uniform, belted scabbard at his side, stepped out in front of him to bar his way.

"Hey Jancsi! Stop for a moment." Jancsi, in place of János, now implied sarcasm.

"What do you want?"

"Don't you recall what you tried to do to my brother earlier this night? He wouldn't fight because he didn't want to hurt you, you fool. But you persisted in goading him, even striking him."

"I did not. It wasn't me."

"Don't deny it. You only add liar to your name, you ingrate."

"I won't fight you," replied János as Pista stepped forward.

"Well I'm going to teach you a lesson anyway, whether you defend yourself or not." With that, he went at János with both fists, beating János to the ground. Then, as János, now on his knees covered his face with upraised arms crossed, Pista used his sword scabbard as a club to beat the protecting arms down. And of course, the metal hurt upraised arms and head.

Finally Pista caught himself! He was now beating János with the flat of his drawn sword!

"My God! I could kill him," he thought, as he looked at the bruised and bleeding man. He now wondered if he had overdone what was meant to be a chastisement. Regretting it, he also felt a pang of guilt.

He stopped.

"You will not dare tell anyone who it was that beat you, or I will disembowel you next time; you won't get off as lightly. So help me. If you dare to taunt my brother or if you go to the authorities to tell them, I'll kill you. Do you hear me?"

"Just don't hit me again," pleaded János. "I will not tell anyone, and I won't do anything foolish, ever. I swear!"

"I won't worry about your word on it. You know the consequences." With that, Pista left the beaten János, still kneeling, on the pathway.

When Pista came home later that night, his sisters quietly let him in so that they would not awaken their parents. Anxiously they asked if he had reconsidered and not met János.

"Nope."

"Did you fight him then?"

"It was no fight. I beat him good."

"You beat János?" The girls were as much frightened for their brother, as they were excited about the incident.

"Yep! I sure did."

"Did anyone see you?"

"No."

"My gosh, if anyone did see you and they report it-- ."

"Not me; I tell you no one saw me do it."

"But suppose János tells-- ?"

"He won't...ever tell anyone, anything."

The way Pista hesitated when he said this, further frightened his sisters. "Did you kill him?" They asked clutching their breast.

"Of course not!"

"Then he could still inform on you."

"He won't"

"But suppose---."

"I tell you he won't dare! Now let it be."

Ilona and Annüs (Annie) let it be. But when news of János' misadventure rippled through the village, and finally reached their girlish ears, they had to find out the truth. Had he told anyone? Had he told higher authorities about his attacker? Would he inform on Pista?

János was laid up in bed for a week.

It took him longer still for a complete recovery. Yet in spite of his parent's pleas, the police enquiring about his attacker, he still did not tell who had beaten him.

Ilona and Annüs paid him a visit while he was laid up in bed. They brought Mother and Father Valko's best wishes for his quick recovery. The girls expressed a genuine concern as they talked to János.

"Oh, János! Who could have been so cruel?"

János flushed and fidgeted, "Why it was their brother damn it. They act as though they don't know," he thought, "and I certainly can't tell them."

"Why would anyone beat you so badly? Why they must have used a stick. How many of them were there?"

The girls did carry on, so much like concerned neighbors. But János would not answer.

They changed the subject to more pleasant things.

And János never did tell.

It is amazing that Pista was so cruel in this instance. Ordinarily he was a compassionate person. Perhaps it was because he loved his older brother Pál and that compounded his hate for János' turncoat action.

From his assignment in Koszég he worked his way up in rank and was now transferred to the town of Rum. He was an extraordinary man! When the police caught gypsies (Cigány) Pista's commandant never sent him along to bring them in. Because he expected the gypsies to be beaten, the commandant sent police whom he knew were hardened and cruel, those who carried animosity toward gypsies. A beating would teach them a lesson, whatever the reason for their arrest.

The commandant knew that Pista would not, or could not bring himself to beat up on the gypsies. Other police relished the opportunity to use nightsticks on the poor souls.

Pista preferred to kindly question and plead with the gypsies in a humane manner. This was only a minor flaw in his character thought his commandant, and so both he and Pista worked around it. He would not send Pista out on these "errands".

"Why should I beat the poor souls? They have to live too. If he steals... he steals. Perhaps, since that is all he knows, he thinks it is his profession to steal; that is why he is a gypsy. I can't bring myself to beat him for it. Damn it! At first, in the early days, when the commandant sent me, I went along with the other police beating the gypsies. But do you know, everyone saw that they were not being bruised or bloodied by my blows. I was hitting them mockingly, not hard at all. Can you imagine the pop-eyed look on those gypsies ha, ha, ha, expecting a painful blow from my upraised nightstick? They actually broke out in a relieved, quizzical smile."

"The other police were as puzzled as the gypsies. That is how the commandant learned about my behavior, and now we both avoid any issue that has to do with reprimanding gypsies." Pista explained to his mother, father and family.

He was a policeman for a great number of years in the town of Rum. Consequently, as with most policemen, even if it is in the line of doing their duty, they acquire some enemies. He married a resident girl of Rum, and that of itself provided some animosity for the young men of the town who seemed to think that they should have the first opportunity with the girls of Rum. Particularly if she had a substantial dowry, and this girl had nine acres of land given as a wedding present, she also shared half of a large home. Pista had courted her for a long time, and she consented to his proposal.

Her brother later married Geza Virag's second cousin.

But Pista had many girlfriends, and during his courtship of this girl whom he married, he got one of his other girlfriends pregnant! She was from Kopron, Zala Megye. After he married the girl from Rum...many years after; his past escapade would catch up to him in a very deadly manner.

PÁL AND ANNÜSKA

One late afternoon, as he walked hurriedly toward home and the dinner that awaited him, Pál Valko was taking a short cut through the cemetery when he noticed a woman in black kneeling at a headstone. The tall trees surrounding the cemetery cast their evening shadow over her so that in her dark mourning clothes she was almost indiscernible, except that she swayed as she sobbed.

The kindhearted Pál approached to offer consolation, and to see if he could be of assistance to one whom he assumed was a widow. It would be getting dark soon and he felt uneasy, thinking perhaps one so sad might tarry too long and then find herself alone in the coming darkness. In a simple humane gesture he wished to ease her out of the cemetery while there was still daylight.

"God cares for those who have gone on. They are in good hands. Take care for yourself. Darkness will soon be upon us. It is best that you leave now".

She had not heard him approaching and, startled, she glanced up at him with tear filled eyes.

Much to his surprise, Pál saw a beautiful, pale face look up into his eyes. The woman was young, no more than twenty years old, he thought. He swiftly glanced at the headstone, and read a woman's name; "she sorrows for a loved one, but not a husband," Thought Pál.

As she knelt at her prayers her pious beauty had smitten him.

"Oh God, how lovely," he thought as he fixed his glance on her fragile face. Her dark hair, her dark eyes were stunning, being set off by her almost translucent, white skin. In all his years he had not seen anyone quite as beautiful. He was immediately lost in those eyes!

He introduced himself while helping her up, and offered to walk her home. She introduced herself and they began to walk toward her village, even though it was the opposite direction that he would be taking to go home.

During their walk he learned it was her mother's grave. Her mother was several months buried, but the young daughter was still very much pained at their parting. She visited the gravesite almost daily if weather permitted.

Pál tried to cheer her as they walked. He told her he had a sister with the same name as hers. He talked of his close-knit family of sisters and brothers, his Christian upbringing and their love of family. And she responded in kind about her family, noting, now that her mother was gone she was the cook and housekeeper for the small family.

Pál left Annüs (Annie) at her cottage door but he asked permission to see her again. She consented and smiled happily at the thought of seeing him again; her smile seemed to lift him off his feet. He was hopelessly lost in his love for her, but dared not tell her. She may think he was too bold, and a false "charmer". Who could believe that a person can fall in love so fast?

I suppose, his generation knew no such thing as "love at first sight".

Her face was before him all the way home, and he thought only of her. He thought nothing of the double distance he now had to walk. When he finally arrived home it was completely dark, and he had also missed supper. His sisters and mother would question him but, he had such a love-struck look on his face that they almost guessed what had befallen him; they seemed to know what had happened.

On the next morning, as he sat up in bed and began to dress, the brothers and sisters could hear him singing. His brother Toni looked in on him as Pál was pulling on his boots, still sitting on the edge of the bed.

"What is that you're singing?"

Pál stepped out of the bedroom and walked to the kitchen where he recited this song;

Temetö be latalak meg elöszor	*I first saw you in the cemetery*
Mikor édes anyádat el temetik	*When they buried your dear mother*
Ugy nészté ki djas fekete ruhába	*In black mourning clothes you looked*
Mint az ibolya a sötit erdö árnyékába	*Just like a violet in the dark overshadowing wood.*

(I am not too sure, after all these years, but I have notes that indicate perhaps it went further than the few simple lines above. I have the following verse in my notes.)

Uj sir van a temetö ben	*There is a new grave in the cemetery*
Rajt a viräg koszoro.	*upon it a flowered wreath.*
Barna kis lány a fej fanal	*Brunet little girl at the head stone*
Ne sir, ne sir	*Don't cry, don't cry*
Barna kis lány	*Brunet little girl*
Ne hulladöz a könnyedet	*Don't spill your tears*
Mert aki meg hal onan	*Because those who die*
Mar nem jön visa töbet	*Will never come back from there*

Then his sisters knew for a fact, what they had thought the night before, Pál was in love. Privately, Pál declared to his mother that he was going to marry that girl.

"But you don't even know her," cautioned the Catholic mother.

"I know all that I have to know," replied a love struck youth to his mother. "I know that I can not go through this life without her."

Before the day was through the field hands were singing his song. And that night even the gypsies had put it to music on their violins and dulcimer (cimbalom). Oh, there were some variations, and a few lines may have been added, but it was Pál's song.

Needless to say, before Pál called upon Annüs of his heart a few evenings later, she had also heard the song for it had traveled throughout the neighboring counties. She commented to Pál about this haunting refrain while sitting opposite him in the tavern that evening, never expecting that she was the object of the song and that he was the author.

With gypsy violin accompaniment, Pál then sang it to her in that tavern.

He melted her heart.

It was no secret; the two were hopelessly in love from that night forward. Annüs became his beloved 'Annüska', and Pál became her 'dear Pali'.

But the girl was sick!

Her mother had died of tuberculosis, and her family had kept the girl's strange illness a secret also. Pál of course eventually found out about her mother's deadly disease, and as a result his family now knew. His sisters were adamant about such 'subterfuge'. They did not want Pál to have anything more to do with Annüs. There was great resentment toward this possible union; because it was probable the girl's illness was tuberculosis also, just like her mother's.

Pál saw to it that Annüs visited with his family often. He knew his sisters would get to like her, he also counted on their love for him, that they should show kindness toward her, and welcome her, and reluctantly they did. They slowly accepted her and began to treat her more like a sister than a prospective sister-in-law.

So it was that Páli and Annüska were married in that year, 1921.

But Annüska's sickness became too severe; she weakened. Doctors verified what Pál's family feared. She indeed had tuberculosis, the same dreaded disease that had befallen her mother. Whether the girl knew she had tuberculosis or not before meeting Pál, was never ascertained. But the sisters felt that she had deliberately deceived Pál, and the poor girl just simply did not want to tell him about it while he courted her. It is quite possible that she did tell him, but he loved her too much to let her illness stand in the way of their happiness. They both believed that this was the only chance for them to both be truly happy. She surely desired some happiness...for the short while she thought she may have had left to her.

Despite her illness she also wanted a family, and within the first year of marriage Annüs got pregnant. Her doctor told Pál and Annüs that she could not survive childbirth. It would kill her! (Yes, abortions could be arranged even in those days, but she would have none of it.) She persisted in carrying the child to term, if possible. Perhaps her love for Pál motivated her. Perhaps she had an *intuition that she would not live,* and she wished to leave Pál a bit of herself... both their flesh and blood. In this manner a part of her would always be with him.

She knew and accepted her fate.

There was a doctor in Szombathely, a specialist who had actually some positive results in treating tubercular patients. Pál took her to this specialist because he would do anything to save her, yet this doctor gave them no encouragement. Pál continued nonetheless to take her repeatedly to this specialist for medicine and follow-up diagnostics.

"She should have told Pál before he married her," declared Ilona.

"It was not fair. It was not a nice thing for her to do at all, to deceive us that way," agreed the sisters.

On the way home from one of the many visits to the Szombathely specialist, Pál and Annüs stayed with the Valko family overnight. In spite of their earlier hard feelings, the sisters did everything they could to comfort their sister-in-law. They even bathed her feet in hot water to help maintain her body heat. They covered her with extra blankets as Annüs sat and chatted with them. The poor girl was very happy at these pleasantries. She seemed in no pain at all, yet her cheeks were constantly flushed with fever. Pál's sisters of course had relented, and they now thought of her as a member of the family. She was their brother's wife, and all the bitterness was gone. They loved her and truly wished her well, desiring to help however they could.

Annüs seemed reconciled to the events unfolding around her; she openly let Pál's sisters shower her with affection. She may have known it was in vain for she was dying. When her child was born, it was not a full term baby and Annüs' younger sister ran all the way from their village to Pál's parent's Homestead to announce that the baby was stillborn, and that Annüska was very ill.

"Come quickly," she cried excitedly.

Pál's sisters had their farm hands hitch up a horse and buggy and with Annüs' sister sitting beside them, they returned as quickly as they could to offer assistance. The sisters did everything they could think of for their ill sister-in-law. They cooked for the entire family, loaves of bread and other food staples. They cooked entire meals for her, hoping she would regain her strength, and at least she would live, though the child had not. If only they could conserve her strength.

Annüs' family consumed those good meals; they eagerly ate the scrumptious food. But it mattered not who ate the good food, for Annüska died three days after the baby.

Heartbroken, Pál reluctantly sent the mother after her child.

He buried both in one week.

Annüska had her "little bit of happiness", but left behind a horribly heartbroken Pál, who never did recover from this wounded heart.

A WEDDING; A WITCH

Ilona Valko was once again a bridesmaid in 1922. The bridegroom was from Porpacz and a very good friend of Geza's, so it happened that Geza was a groomsman, and now matched to Ilona for the wedding.

Ilona's boy friend Gyula Rakosi was also invited to the wedding. The name was familiar but, it was unknown to Geza who the young man was, until he showed up to accompany Ilona to the rehearsal at the church. They shook hands; they hugged one another in a warm manly embrace. There was cheerful exclamation between the two young men, much to the surprise of almost everyone in the wedding party. They behaved as long lost friends.

"Do you know one another?" asked Ilona.

"Do we know one another? We almost started a revolution years ago."

When they were in Vienna after returning from the Italian front, Gyula Rákosi was the lieutenant whom the troops appointed to be their leader in the 1918 mutiny of the 83rd regiment. He and Geza got along well for the next few days. They had a lot in common it seems, including this young bridesmaid Ilona, whom now they both had an eye for. Gyula informed Geza that he had been courting Ilona for several months, he desired to marry her and he planned on taking her to South America as his wife.

"What's in South America that you can't have here? What posses you to go there?" queried Geza. "You are well off in your mother country."

"There is a new frontier in that country Geza. They are cutting down the jungle and selling acreage cheaply to those who have a mind to clear it for farming or ranching. I prefer to raise cattle and I will get me a large ranch. Why don't you consider it?"

"I still have a commitment to the army that I am trying to get out of," answered Geza. "Then I propose to further my education, at the Government's expense. Maybe I can do something better with my life than work in the Government Factory till retirement."

"Good luck to you. But I am going to South America with or without Ilona. Perhaps when I am established, and a prosperous rancher, she can be swayed. She is too close to her family, that's the problem. I must be able to provide for her in the manner she has become accustomed with her father's position on that Homestead. That is my greatest hurdle; the family is just too 'close' and the brothers and sisters want to stay 'near family'.

"That's not quite true. I understand that one sister and two brothers have left years ago. They are in North America for some time now, from before the war. Three of eight children; who knows? You may succeed in getting her to go," said Geza.

They talked about those bold times during the war. How they were fortunate to survive it, and were most fortunate to succeed in getting out of Vienna alive in the 1918 insurrection, as the most minor offense of that escapade could have led to a Court Martial.

They danced. They drank, and then those few days too, ended. The two friends parted with cordialities such as, "see you sometime soon", which never materialized.

They did not see one another again.

Gyula expressed his undying love for Ilona in each of his letters, and pleaded with her to join him in South America.

But Ilona had no intention of leaving home, so a broken hearted Gyula continued to work alone in South America. He corresponded with her often, as lonely lovers are prone to do. In one letter he mentioned that he had her picture enlarged. A photograph of Ilona life size over one meter and a half tall. It would stay in the most central part of his living room "until the real Ilona arrives to take its place".

Each letter expressed his undying love for her, each letter also pleaded with her to join him, but to no avail.

Geza met with a fortunate circumstance on one of those many visits to the doctor's office in Vienna. The doctor within his military Company had talked to the General (Ezredés) about this 'persistent young corporal'. Hungary was not allowed to have more soldiers under arms than had been agreed to by International Convention. The "Anton" (actually: Allied National Treaty of Non-aggression), a Control Officer representing the Allied Military Commission of Control for the International Convention, came frequently now to check on the enlisted numbers of barracked men, the number on leave, or otherwise assigned to a regiment. If the numbers exceeded the International "allowance", some would have to be released from duty!

Those who were discharged in this manner generally came from the ranks of veterans who had served more than three years and, or, had been wounded in the service of their country. The term "veteran" did not imply they had to qualify by age however, many young men who, like Geza, had served in the war before their proper age of conscription were eligible for this "convention requirement". If these men could prove, even in the most cursory manner that it would be "pain of body" to serve an additional three years (that is, no truly valid reason to keep their additional three year commitment as it interfered with their careers in civilian life). These were the first to be honorably discharged, by order of the "Anton".

This would still not exempt them from their service should there be a National emergency (another war), when they would be called up again.

Within a year Geza was out of the service with an honorable discharge, and he was also compensated for his active service! He received one acre of land plus one lot to build a house on. Only soldiers that were wounded in their country's service or those who had earned medals would get the land grants. Those who earned the "silver" (a medal the size of a fifty cent piece) received a house lot plus ten acres. Those who won the bronze received a house lot plus five acres (Thinking of Süle Jenö, I have no idea what both the Iron Cross and 'Silver' rewarded this soldier).

Those who had earned these high honors never had to return to active service!

When awarding these grants the Major stated, "Those who deserved it got it." He also added, knowing the impetuous young man, "Geza, you will never build on your allotment."

(How prophetically true those words would be.)

The Major did not generally give land to veterans who were 'city dwellers', or those soldiers from the large cities. At the time Geza got his land allotment he was working in the city of Szombathely, but Geza got along well with the major, and every one knows that helps. Once the land was allotted, no one questioned the major. So it was that Geza received his allotted acreage and house lot in the land around his home town of Porpacz.

When he was mustered out of the military in 1922, he attended night school, paid for by the Government under a veteran's bill. He returned to the Government Factory and worked during the day.

"Ill be damned if I am going to spend all my life in a factory", he wished to do better and he succeeded. In 1924 he got a Stationary Engineer's Degree.

In that era, such a degree was well received and respected by his employer.

With this degree he became an Engineer within the same Government facility, but he was now in charge of a Steam Engine and Threshing Machine. During the grain harvest he would travel the countryside with a crew of twenty-six men and the Steam Thresher. This afforded him a grand opportunity to save money, except for the small amount spent on clothes, because all his travel expenses were paid for. No matter where it was that he threshed the grain, the farmers always fed him and his crew of men and also provided for their lodging.

But Geza did not save his money! He spent it all; always drinking the best wines and whiskeys in the best taverns, and always with more than enough women to enjoy the evening.

Because most farmers hauled their sheaves of grain into stacks, the threshing season lasted almost until the first frost in late September. These stacks were enormous; some were as high as a barn and, as wide and long. Men pitched the sheaves from these grain stacks into the stationary, belt driven threshing machine. Geza would return to work at the Government Factory only after the threshing season, unless they used his steam engine for plowing.

Plowing was another interesting process, now that we look back at it from this distance in 'their future'. One steam engine was placed at each end of the field to be plowed. By means of a continuous cable between the two engines; one of the engines pulled a four-bottom plow to one end of the field. The plow was pulled back to the opposite end of the field by the second engine. The plow went back and forth between the two engines, and across the length of the field. Each engine indexed along the "head land" ends of the field and was moved along the field once the plow reached the end of the furrows.

The plow had a set of four mould boards above with another set of four bottom mould boards under these. It was not uncoupled from the draw cable to be turned about; rather, the entire apparatus was rotated, turned over, at the end of the field and the plow was pulled back toward the pulling steam engine. Then once again flipped over and the top set, now on the bottom, was pulled back toward the second pulling steam engine; the furrows thus were all rolled over in the same direction onto one another.

As with the summer threshing, custom was that the landlord or the farmer fed Geza and his plow crew. In one incident, that he laughed at as he recalled it to me; an old woman gave him a bowl of kocsonya (jellied soup, some may have chunks of meat within the soup, others had pig hocks in them) which had cooled to jell in her dirt floor basement.

There were no pig hocks in this one; two eyes blinked back at Geza from within the kocsonya. The old lady, far sighted as she was, of course did not see what Geza saw; a frog had fallen into the soup while it cooled. It was now jelled within. Geza respectfully declined this gourmet meal.

Geza worked all day, but in the evenings he danced, drank, and enjoyed life to the fullest. He always dressed in the finest clothes and was seen in the best restaurants and taverns. He went where he wanted, when he wanted. Because of his job, the Government Factory issued him a pass that allowed him to travel anywhere on the railroad system free.

Even if a single locomotive were going to his destination, he would hitch a ride sitting with the engineer and fireman.

He would tell his friend Tibör, "dress well, behave in a dignified manner and all sorts of people, great and small, will treat you with respect."

When they were in Budapest one day, both young men were dressed in fine tan (sarga) suits, and tan shoes. A conductor addressed them as "fiatal tisztes úr" (honorable young sir). When they were seated, Tibör whispered to Geza, "Damn, old friend, you were right! He thinks we are some duke or lord."

One adventure at home in Porpacz that Geza recited is as follows:

He was walking home after an evening of dancing and drinking, but was startled by a hen that suddenly darted out of the darkness and onto the path he was walking! (Any farm boy knows that this isn't so! It is not natural! Chickens do not roam the woods or paths at night. They generally set up high on tree branches, or perch to roost for the night above their ground bound predators, as most warm blooded fowl do. Only ducks and geese fly at night...not chickens.) Geza picked up his pace to walk faster, when suddenly the same hen again scurried to get in front of him!

"Damn you," he replied as he picked up a stick from the side of the road and tossed it at the hen. Amazingly, he struck the bird on the side; it squawked and tumbled into the roadside ditch, then scurried away into the woods in an attempt to get out of his range!

Geza continued homeward, but now at a more brisk pace, muttering under his breath, "Why would that *silly witch bother to follow me*? Has she nothing better to do than frighten me to death in this early morning darkness?"

Two days after this incident he saw "the witch" walking outside her cottage. She was holding her side, and indeed limping with a cane for support.

Geza yelled greeting to her, "Nah! Have you given up your night time prowls for a while?"

"You young fool," she exclaimed, "some day you will know better than to drive away those that would protect you in the dark of night."

"I don't need your help Sweet Grand Mother (Edes Öreg Anyam). Geza replied sarcastically, amazed at why she intended to protect him, of all people.

It is remarkable to me, reflecting upon this era of 1920-1925, where there were "actual incidents" witnessed by many villagers. Of course in that era there were many uninformed and uneducated people, these tend to be the superstitious ones, just as the superstitious of today claim to believe "incidents". Perhaps that is what makes witch-craft "authentic".

But Geza was better informed than most, and he was educated; yet he states this incident to be fact!

PÁL AND ILONA
LEAVE HUNGARY

Ilona's brother Pál became restless, and truly did not know what he wanted; he just could not find peace or contentment after loosing Annüska. His wife's death had left him forlorn and, he was lost without her.

Their sister Theresa had gone to America in 1908, when Ilona was about twelve years old. Ilona remembers that event well; walking Theresa to the railroad station. On the return trip home from the station it began to rain and Ilona was drenched to the skin.

The two older brothers had been in Chicago since 1908-1909. All three had written enticing letters continually; "Come and join us here. It is a land of opportunity. Leave your old lives and come try this new life."

Pál began a communication with his two brothers in Chicago. He was serious about leaving Hungary, and enquired about the experiences the brothers had run into in the "New World". The brothers of course had gotten over their initial trials and tribulations of the different customs and the language learning. They both now had a good grasp of the American English, and stated they would meet Pál in Windsor, Ontario. From there they would assist their brother in getting across to Detroit. (The United States had a quota and Hungarians did not get an opportunity to immigrate as easily as they might to Canada). With the two as interpreters, they could make it easier for Pál at the American Customs offices. He should have no difficulty, as they were both now residents within the United States and would sponsor this new immigrant. A point in time was set.

Pál took the necessary actions to obtain a passport, and made arrangements with an agent to leave Hungary.

In 1924 Pál had been widowed two years; obviously he was running away from the memories that continued to haunt him. But it was not easy to leave the country in 1924. Hungary also had restriction intended to keep citizens from going abroad. (I truly do not know what it was, except that many had left the country immediately after the war to seek a new life abroad, going to South America, as Gyula Rakosi had, others to the United States, and some to England, Australia and Canada). Perhaps the reduction in territorial size of Austria-Hungary after the annexations of territories gone to the Victors of 1918, worried the Authorities about population loss, worker shortages etc. Now, prospective migrants would have to use creative methods to get out of the country. Arrangements were made in secrecy, and it was almost a clandestine action to get out of Hungary without proper representation or authorized permission.

Pál had managed to talk Ilona into going to Canada with him! It is truly amazing how he managed to do this, when Gyula Rakosi had failed to convince her about leaving home. Perhaps she looked at this trip with Pál as an exciting adventure, and thought correctly, that she could return if things did not work out as the two older brothers in America stated it should..

When that day arrived, her son and daughter were packed, and with their luggage in hand; Mother Valko took out her handkerchief and constantly wiped her tears. (Women had pockets in their aprons, and also pockets in the sides of their dresses, these seemed always to have handkerchiefs in them).

"Stay. Don't leave. Stay home, here."

"Poor mother, I could see her even now, after all these years, true as life before me, with her brown eyes;" recalled Ilona. "She was always slim, not so much because it was stylish, but because she had always been troubled with stomach ailments." She had my hand in hers as she pleaded, "Don't go my little girl, don't go."

They left nonetheless.

But the Authorities caught Pál and Ilona at the Border Crossing into Austria, sending them back. (Ilona believed someone informed on them.) People could just not pack up and leave that easily, as they would today. They actually had to apply for permission, and thus, get a permit to leave, or pay an agent to smuggle them out of the country as Pál seems to have done.

Mother Valko was so overjoyed to see them return. She thought that they would surely stay now that they had been caught, and forced to return. Getting out a second time would not be easy; the authorities would be on the lookout for familiar faces that they had deported.

But they were told by their 'agent' to meet again in three days. And so it was that they put their mother, that poor woman, through the agony and heartache of another farewell. How sorrowful it must have been for her; such sadness, to see those brown eyes again welled full of tears, and once again to make Ilona's heart ache to see her mother so moved at their parting.

Pál and Ilona met their agent at the appointed place, and utilizing a pleasure boat (tourist excursion type?) that plied the Danube River, he took them into Austria. Halfway through this journey, the agent met a German sailor on the tourist boat. Their agent struck up a conversation in German, not aware that Pál understood and spoke German. Because of the attempt at secrecy intoned in the conversation between the two men, Pál now spoke out in German.

"What is it you are saying? Why are we, my sister and I in a separate cabin remote from the other passengers?" Pál wondered if they were planning something unscrupulous.

The Hungarian agent was surprised, and the look on his face showed that surprise. The German in turn replied for him most cheerfully, pleased that Pál could understand him without the Hungarian as an intermediary.

"It is alright," he replied. "We will be docking soon, and we don't want you to be seen again as at the last time. You know, they would make it bad for all of us if they caught you a second time. You shall also leave separately from the off-boarding crowd while we try to guide you past the Custom Authorities."

When Pál and Ilona disembarked into Austria, the two agents took them separately, each taking one of them; so they would not be seen together. If they were together the Customs Officials may recognize them as the illegal couple from a few days ago. They took one after another, brother and sister, and led them smartly, around those specific officials.

And they were through!

Now at a safe distance, Pál and Ilona saw the same Austrian Customs Officials that had sent them back three days earlier at a different gate. The officials had not even noticed them. The Hungarian agent then left, and they were to follow the German's instructions. He would get them out of Austria and Germany also. He put them directly on a train that swept them out of the Tourist Docking area. He smiled, pleased with himself. He had gotten brother and sister out from under the officials' noses.

"Well," he said in German, and then in Hungarian, "Isten veled MagyarOrság (God be with you Hungary)

They were on their way!

But as the train wheels on the track sounded their 'clickety clack, clickety clack' in Ilona's mind she kept hearing her mother's words, 'daughter come back, daughter come back', but the engine continued to speed farther, and farther, from home and all the familiar places.

They were off to another country, and then on to a New World, a new life, perhaps? At home in his native land, Pál would surely have gone crazy. All the past would now, hopefully, seem unreal and as though it was another place, another lifetime ago.

And it was! He started a new life in a New World.

Pál did not know then, and he did not realize that he would never forget.

We cannot run away from the ghosts that haunt us in our solitude, they are with us forever.

TOWN CRIERS

While his brother Varga János was away at the war, Ferkó was the only means of support for his mother. He did not allow his handicap of one missing finger and two lacerated palms interfere with his life. He could use a scythe as well as any man, and just as any man he could tie the grain in bundles. He worked hard during harvest and managed to earn just enough for them to live. However, he spent most of the winter and fall getting into trouble, and into jail. His poor mother complained often about Ferkó's bad habits, and of those there were too many.

Why, he even chewed tobacco much to his dear mother's chagrin, and he didn't care where he spit the 'tobacco chaw'.

He had a large tomcat appropriately named Kandúr (Tomcat). This cat even slept with him at night, although one would wonder why the cat would be endeared to him. He was known to spit on the cat if he had to get rid of the tobacco chaw, just so his mother would not be angered that he spit on the floor. The cat caught it instead!

By the light of a full moon, Ferkó often went out to hunt to bring home some wild game, fresh meat for him and his poor mother. This was outright poaching; he knew it, but deliberately violated the law. In planning the possibility of being caught, he had hidden his rifle and shells in the hollow of an old tree. Whenever he wanted rabbit, he would go for a walk into the woods; of course no one saw him carry a gun into the woods, but many did observe that he returned with dead rabbits strung around his neck, swinging to the left and right on his chest as he walked proudly home. If he shot a deer he would sling that over his shoulders, and bodily carry it home. There he would skin his animals, and dress the meat; thus he and his mother would have meat for a few days or, weeks if it were a deer.

But begrudging neighbors must have informed the authorities about Ferkó's moonlighting and the police set a trap for him one evening. Two police observing him from the security of an adjoining corn field watched as Ferkó walked into the woods. They waited anxiously for him to return observing that he walked empty handed into the woods. They were genuinely puzzled to see him return within a short time with a deer over his shoulders. One policeman barred his way, while the other closed in behind him and with rifles poised they barred his path.

"Ha!" exclaimed Ferkó. "You certainly have me. Caught me red handed," he laughed heartily.

"Where's the rifle?" demanded one officer.

"I have hidden it, and there it will stay. It is fortunate that you saw me first, for if I had seen you, both of you may have been like this," he patted the deer draped over his shoulders.

With that threat on their lives, and knowing Ferkó, they thought it best to tie his hands securely, and in this manner escorted him back to the village with the deer still draped over his shoulders. They paraded him through the length of the village, as an example to other would be poachers as Ferkó continued to vehemently curse them, and spit on them all the way.

He spent time in jail. Jail was not new to him as he had been jailed many times before, and many times afterwards. The police had all heard about his reputation, and therefore were always alert when Ferkó was in their area, as much to defend themselves, as well as to stop him before he became unruly.

Geza's father reminisced on one adventure of Ferkó's. It was hard to believe that he would eventually "straighten out" and amount to something. So that when he did, his actions of the past sounded the more unbelievable.

One night Geza's father heard the village dogs barking furiously, so he went to the door to look out to discern the reason for the commotion. He opened the door just as Ferkó reached the street in front of the house.

"Nah! Ferkó are the dogs barking at you?"

"You had better close the door and step back into the house,"

"Hey Ferkó?"

"János bacsi, I'm telling you, you had better get in!"

Mister Virag thought this command over, but only momentarily; wisely closing the door and returning to what he was doing before the barking dogs interrupted.

Village Custom required someone to "watch" the village houses, barns and properties for one half of the night; much like the "Town Criers" of the Colonial United States. When his watch was up, the first watchman returned to the house of the "second watchman". Assured that the second watchman was up and about to do his "watch", the first watchman returned home and went to bed. The second watchman commenced his rounds, and stayed at it till daybreak.

The second watchman was most often awake and waiting for the first watchman to end his rounds by arriving to summon him. In many villages as small as Porpacz of the 1920s, two men were sufficient and adequately circled the village and its few streets.

Nagy bácsi, the village watchman on the "first watch" of that night, was thirty years older than Ferkó. As he did his allotted rounds, walking the row of backyards, he stopped under the long overhanging eaves of a thatched roof. Things were quiet, and the night peaceful, so he lay down to rest. No one would notice if he fell asleep for a while. Besides, if anything out of the ordinary happened, some villager's dog would notice and bark.

"I could wake up then and investigate what the dog was alarmed about," he thought, as he got more comfortable lying down for a nap.

Memories of Magyars Passed ~ 455

No one knows for sure how it happened; did Ferkó trip over the sleeping man? Angered at the man who should be alert and about his rounds, or simply angered that the sleeping body caused him to stumble and fall? Did Nagy bácsi wake up when he heard Ferkó approaching or the dog barking? Maybe Nagy bácsi startled Ferkó attempting something unlawful.

Ferkó struck him and beat up the old man.

What was Ferkó doing under the eaves of that house anyway?

In any event, Nagy bácsi did not show up at the second watchman's house on schedule, therefore, the second watchman called the police. Together they walked the appointed rounds until they came across his body. He had been beaten unconscious, and was still lying under the over-hanging eaves.

Mr. Virag could guess that Ferkó had just come from "beating" the old man when the dog's barking had attracted mister Virag's curiosity.

Nagy bácsi recovered. He told the true story to the police, and once again Ferkó went to jail. Two weeks in jail for that incident.

This is a good place to insert Geza Virag's experience as a night watchman in Porpacz, circa 1922. In his own words:

"I was a night watchman one evening; that is, I took that responsibility for my older brother. It was his turn and I said "Heck, I'll do the rounds for you. Stay home with your family."

I intended to walk the village rounds once, and I did. Then I dropped in to see a girlfriend. But I overstayed my visit. When I left her it was after two a.m. It was too late to awaken the second watchman, I thought he probably was up already and doing the rounds anyway. So I went home to sleep in the barn because I didn't want to awaken my brother's family with my late entry. I lay down in the straw and had a good sleep.

But the second watchman had gone to the police, and had walked the appointed rounds hunting for the first watchman. This would be my brother János. Of course, when they could not find him they went to his house. He was fast asleep when they pounded on his door and woke everyone in the house.

"Aren't you supposed to be the watchman tonight? You didn't wake the second watchman after your rounds."

"My younger brother Geza took the watch tonight in my place. Is there something wrong? What happened?"

"Where is he?"

"If you could not find him he must be sleeping in the barn. He does that when he comes home late. He doesn't want to wake up the household. Let's see if he is there."

They came to the barn, brother, second watchman and police. Making quite a noise they awakened me on the straw, shouting my name for all to hear.

"Did you take the responsibility for the first watch last night? They asked.

"Yes I did." I immediately knew I was in hot water.

"Well then, where were you that you couldn't summon the second watchman for his turn?"

"I was at my girlfriend's house. It was already too late when I left, so I just came home."

"Do you realize the seriousness of your actions?"

"No. I guess I don't. Did something happen on my watch?"

"No. But three of us spent a good amount of time concerned with finding the first watchman."

The next day I was summoned to appear before the lower court judge to answer for my dereliction of duty.

"Young man, did you take it upon yourself to be the first watchman last night?"

"Yes."

"Do you realize how serious the responsibility is? The entire village is counting on the two men who keep watch for them each night. You must not take that responsibility lightly. What were you doing that was more important than your duty to uphold your brother's watchman responsibility and your commitment to the community?"

"Well, sir; since things seemed quiet and peaceful, I decided that, while I was near her house anyway, I might as well stop in to see my girlfriend. You know how that is, and you could imagine that within five minutes I could just not excuse myself. The truth is, after five minutes we were quite taken with one another and, since I never did take a night 'watch' except in this one case, as a favor to my brother, I simply lost track of time. Before I knew it, it was well past the morning hours."

"Young man, you knowingly took a serious responsibility from your brother. You also took with it the responsibility to the community."

"Your honor, I admit my error. I am ashamed that I let my brother down, more ashamed for that than the disappointment of the community. I won't do it again."

"You will take your punishment then?"

"Yes sir. Reluctantly, because I cannot understand what harm was done.

Though it could have, nothing eventful actually happened; except maybe, the search for me by the second watchman and the police. This was the biggest inconvenience. My attentions for the girl overcame my sense of duty. What more can I say?"

And so, as the judge and I talked openly and quite freely about my irresponsibility, he relented.

"I cannot dismiss the negligence. I have to enter something in my case file about this incident because it is already recorded," replied the judge.

"I understand that sir. And I agree to whatever you think is reasonable."

"The fine is all you will have to pay. No lock up; five forints (five dollars)."

So I went home and told my brother János. "I paid the fine. You won't have to. I told the judge I wouldn't do it again, and I won't. That is all there is to it. I'll be damned if I'll take another 'watch' again."

"How did you get away without getting locked up?" János asked.

"I have no idea."

"Normally the judges are very strict about these dalliances from duty," said János. "For a matter as serious as leaving the communities open to vandals, they usually submit the man to a fine and lock him up for a while."

"They may do that if you let them. But don't forget; judges are human too. I was honest with him about the girlfriend, and spoke freely to him. I was wrong and admitted it. He was pleased to hear me admit my error. I made no excuses, and did not humble myself under his questioning. I stated that the situation with the girl was foremost in my mind, not the night watch.

He was young once. Perhaps he decided to be human with me. I thought he was a pretty decent fellow."

Ferkó had a csendör friend whom he knew from childhood; they had grown up together. This man was very upright and honest. He had served his time in the army, and because he was a veteran, he was given the first opportunity to apply for a position with the police department. His physical stature and military record succeeded in getting him the job. He always wished the best for Ferkó, hoping that Ferkó would get a respectable job and amount to something. Finally in 1928, when Ferkó was thirty-five years old, and this friend was now a high ranking officer in the police force at a distant village. He asked Ferkó to apply for a vacant position there. (Perhaps Ferkó's reputation had not have reached that distant place).

The friend had recommended Ferkó to the wealthy citizens as a commendable applicant for the position of police private. This friend even bought Ferkó a new suit of clothes, that he might be more presentable at the job interview.

Everyone in Ferkó's home village admired such a friend-ship "between *that good* and *this bad.*" Still, they took bets that Ferkó would not last long even if he got the job.

"The clothes don't make the man," said the old timers.

Ferkó was sure to loose his temper one day, and then he will beat someone up. Just as surely as he gets into trouble here, he is going to get in trouble there!

But he surprised them all!

He got the job!

He stayed in that village, becoming self disciplined, and he became respectable. Of course he was pleased with the authority and respect that the police uniform brought.

Maybe that is all he needed, a little respect.

They even gave him a rifle! (Now he could shoot all the game he needed, if he had a mind to, and if he did it dis-creetly, no one would know. But he did not.)

Furthermore, he got married to an attractive young lady and had a family! Whenever they visited Porpacz it was Ferkó who lovingly carried their baby and cradled it gently in his strong arms. He had become domesticated, and a good citizen of the community in his new capacity.

COMMUNIST RUSSIA

The "Red" Russians of the young Communist Regime permitted the Old Kulak to maintain 2,500 acres of the original 5,000, as Lenin had decreed. Lenin knew that the wealthy landowners would still be the best providers of food goods. He was not foolish to the extent that, all land should be confiscated from the rich and distributed to the ignorant peasants in one immediate policy change. No! He intended the land to be distributed to those who knew how to work it. Even the previously rich fell into this category; if they were to be left with sufficient acreage from their initial holdings the Communist plan to "divide the land" may work, applied in steps and gradually.

Remember Karoli Mihail? The rich Hungarian Landlord had voluntarily distributed his holdings to the poor before the 1919 Communist uprising in Hungary, and before the so called "successes" of the Union of Soviet Socialist Republics (USSR).

Divide the land? Yes. So that never again would too much be owned by too few at the sacrifice of the serfs who labored on it. But think of what a debacle it would be to kill all the rich, outright, and distribute their land to the poor. Not many peasants knew animal husbandry, and the agronomics that went into farming. They worked hard and well, it's true, but they were only productive under the direction of the wizened landlord. It would be many years before peasants who were permitted to farm individually, or collectively, would actually become productive. Most were inefficient without being told what to do, and what crops to grow.

Under Lenin's distribution plan, the Kulaks could still employ peasants that were willing to work. The Kulaks paid more wages under the communist system, but it became a fairer and more amicable arrangement for the peasant laborers. Lenin was shrewd. He decreed that all large land holdings be halved; and so it was.

But, Lenin died in 1924, and Stalin became the Russian Leader.

It was Stalin who decreed that all lands should be confiscated and distributed indiscriminately to the poor or, when that proved a failure, turned into collective farms. Gergély Virag now managed 2,500 of the original 5,000 acres and so his family had a very comfortable existence and a very good life as yet... up until 1924. Those 2,500 acres that were left were now to be subdivided, parceled out to the area peasants.

Under Stalin's system, all Kulaks and landlords lost everything! Consequently, many of their hired help suffered also because of the sudden unemployment. Stalin erred. History is witness to it, and his example also proved that "Collective" farming just did not work! This "dream" never did succeed in the USSR. Communism formed communes and inefficient "collective farms" in which ambitious and productive people lost their incentive to work.

The Old Kulak did not like the change and he defied it, because he saw what it was doing to the farming community as a whole. The peasants were also suffering, not just the landlords. He would not go along with subdividing the last 2500 acres left to him.

Led by an officer, a troop of "Red" soldiers came to their door. The officer knocked, and the Kulak's daughter answered opening the door. This officer asked for the Kulak by name. When the Old Man approached to enquire about the purpose, he was ordered to go with the soldiers...or else!

The Old Kulak chose not to go!

Four soldiers dragged him from the doorway and out into the front door pathway. Gergély ran after him but was stopped by two armed soldiers and his life threatened. The Old Kulak's daughter ignored the threats and ran past the soldiers restraining Gergély. She was screaming for her father's safety; she wanted very much to hold the Old Man safely, and hug him in her arms. Daughter grasped her father from the soldiers and held him—one last time. Because two soldiers held his arms, he could not return the embrace.

The officer grabbed her long hair and cast her bodily aside. She fell to the ground, whereupon Gergély ran against the crossed rifles of the two soldiers guarding him only to be beaten to the ground. The two small granddaughters cowered in the doorway crying, bewildered and frightened.

The Old Kulak spit into the face of the officer who was already pointing a revolver to the Old Kulak's chest; the Old Kulak cursed the man that killed him. This man, this Red Officer who had torn him from his peaceful home, and from his daughter's embrace, and had rudely parted him from his two little grand daughters, now fired one more shot into the Old Kulak as he lay on the ground before that ancestral home he loved so dearly. The soldiers were now ordered to follow the officer, and they did.

They left the dead man on the ground, on that earth which he loved so much. This ground that had been in his family's possession for generations now would also cover him in his last repose, as it had his father, and his father's father, and many who had gone before them.

His loved ones circled about him. They mourned his brutal execution. Within days, they laid his body to rest in the family plot on the Pusta (Prairie).

In the spring of 1925, Gergély wrote a letter of apology to his parents.

"Please do not be angry at my seeming inconsideration..."

They were elated to finally hear from him after all these years. He let them know that he had a wife and two daughters, and they were all well. A continuing correspondence started with his family in Hungary.

[In 1922, when Gergély's family heard about his life in Russia from the returned Hungarian soldiers, and that he had two little girls, Geza sent him the equivalent of two dollars. Gergély in a return letter told Geza that he had bought two babushkas (kerchiefs), one for each girl. Then he added, "brother do not send me money. I have no need for it. I have all the wealth a man needs." But this reply to Geza's letter took three years to get to Porpacz, arriving in 1925. The letter, which Gergély wrote in the spring of 1925, actually arrived before the one he had written in 1922. Both letters arrived in 1925.]

During the lengthy correspondence that followed, it was learned that Gergély had actually written quite a few letters, the first of which was directly after he had settled on the Old Kulak's ranch in the fall of 1916. He wanted his family to know he was alive and well. He stopped writing when his letters were returned unanswered.

Arguments ensued back and forth, "why didn't you contact the International Red Cross? They would have let us know of your whereabouts." Gergély was also informed now, that Antal had died in 1916, the same year in which Gergély was captured. His parents thought that he had died also, not hearing about him during their Red Cross enquiries.

Gergély did not get Geza's letter of 1920, either.

This period, 1917-1924, must have been one of total chaos and confusion within Russia. Letters from both sides of the border simply "got lost." However, at this era, 1925, and forward, postal delivery within Russia was becoming more "regular"; not as chaotic, and slowly improving.

The 1925 letters from Gergély queried the many aspects of life in Hungary. Could he and his family go "home"? Would he be welcomed? Could he get a job? Most importantly,

"What was the Magyar Government's feeling toward soldiers returning home so late after the war?"

"Why don't you first come out alone? Look things over, and go back for your family," suggested Geza.

"Never! Either we all go together, or we perish together," was Gergély's reply. And those relatives in Hungary could but wonder why he was so emphatic in regard of his Russian family—"or we perish together?"

His parents, his brothers and sisters could not imagine the deadly and precarious situation he was in. He did not write about it in any letter for fear of making them unnecessarily anxious. They would worry again for his safety.

Following a period of correspondence with his Hungarian Family, Gergély and his wife developed a plan. It took some time before they could actually begin to carry it out however. They certainly could not communicate their intentions in writing for fear of the Russian censors finding any intimidating statements about their plans to escape.

Because he was a "foreigner", and had openly defended the Old Kulak's position on land rights, his entire family was being "watched".

Gergély hated the "Reds". The Old Kulak was a good man, a hard working landowner who had been like a father to him. He was not like many of the aristocrats with large acreages that sat back and enjoyed the luxurious living, oblivious of the hardships of the peasant workers who made it all possible. The Old Man worked beside his peasants in the fields and just as hard. It just did not seem sensible, nor was it fair, that the communists could find no compromise but rather, found it expedient to remove this obstacle to reforms.

Gergély spoke out openly against the communist system. Whenever the system bogged down, or proved simply not to work at all, Gergély spoke abusively to the communist leaders. He was unwittingly treading on thin ice!

In 1926, these ineffective communists, uneducated village leaders, threatened this "smart foreigner".

Gergély was in dire straits now to preserve what he had left. What he had left of primary importance was his wife and two daughters. The remaining land mattered not at all! It had, by now, been subdivided again and again, the last remaining one hundred acres was soon to be partitioned out also.

Gergély had to disappear or they would kill him.

He had to drop out of site. Because of his outspokenness to the "cause", and his resentment of land distribution he was being watched even at his daily work in his own fields. The "authorities" wanted any pretext to act out their wishes on him bodily. In the village when he went shopping for the family, in the fields and everywhere he went away from his home, his every action was being observed.

In anticipation of the need for him to "disappear", he and his wife had dug a hole in the barn floor under one of the horse stalls. Actually, he had only the one horse and a single cow left now, out of the many head of cattle and the teams of horses the Old Kulak had before the communists took them. Such was the "fair distribution" of those who had possessions to those who had nothing, (nor could they ever have anything of their own unless it was taken from those who had something).

Isn't this "The distribution of wealth"? Take from the haves and give to the have-nots.

In that area of the barn, they made their secret room, and "planked" the top of the rectangular dug out, so that the planks were the floor of the stall. When it was "strawed" over, no one was aware that it was anything more than what it appeared to be, a stable floor under the horse.

He remained hiding in this underground room until surveillance stopped, coming out only in the dark of night, after evening, to go into the house where he slept with his wife and children. Then in the morning, before light of dawn, in the dark, he once again went back to that underground room in the barn. If strangers were about, Gergély could not be seen. Eventually, even the neighbors missed seeing him. They began to ask his wife where he was.

"Where is your husband? We don't see him around anymore."

To which she would reply that he had left her and the children.

The plan worked.

Even the children, as young as they were, kept the secret from their schoolmates, and from all the others who asked.

"Yes," their daddy had left them.

GEZA'S ACQUAINTANCES

After being out all the previous night, Geza would try to get to bed early the next evening; the new day's work tired him, and he mentally promised to get to bed early that night. On the way home from work however, he would pass a tavern and stop in...for one drink, or for companionship, while he ate his supper. Then he was hooked! One drink led to another; good camaraderie demanded drinking, sociability and, another late evening, and another short night of sleep.

The next day he would promise himself not to drink, not to get to bed late, but, youth is always that way, good intentions overwhelmed by virile ambitions.

The flesh is indeed weak.

With his notoriety and reputation for having a good time, the mothers that had available daughters were chagrined with him.

He had made friends with many a gypsy musician however. Geza had three gypsy acquaintances in particular that spent many a late night entertaining in the bar or tavern where Geza chose to spend the evening. Their names were Kuli Geza, Holdosi Jenö, and Sarkosö Jószi. They called themselves "uri cigany" (rich gypsy).

"I wouldn't ask any gentleman for a drink. I can pay for my own," each of the three was known to say.

But when they played long hours, and had "nipped" a few, and were somewhat inebriated themselves, they would stagger over to Geza.

"How are you doing? How about a drink now, aye? Geza you don't mind do you?"

"I certainly do not mind, but bring your own glass damn you. How's that? You are 'uri cigany' huh?"

They had a hearty laugh at this inference.

"You are not 'uri' (rich) if you can't afford your own glass. I don't mind you having a drink on me, but I won't tolerate you picking up another man's glass to get a drink," declared Geza.

Unabashed with their friend and his remarks, they did bring their own individual glasses and shared his bottle. They played their music all the more willingly for him.

He reminisced about Kuli Geza.

"How much I drank with that gypsy! When I drank, he drank, and still when the evening was through I gave him five forints (five dollars), sometimes ten. He also got quite a few tips from other guests that night.

Whenever I was to be a groomsman, Kuli Geza or his friends would willingly volunteer to play at the wedding.

"Geza brother, let me go."

"How much do you ask?"

"Nothing, just buy the train ticket."

Most major towns could be reached by train. (No automobiles for each man in those days). Train service was timely and quite reliable.

If arrangements were agreed upon, and the village was not to be reached by train, Kuli Geza and his friends would set out by mule cart very early in the morning on the day of the wedding. The three gypsies with their violins, musical instruments and their cimbalom (dulcimer), loaded on that cart made quite a scene as it ambled down the country roads pulled by a solitary mule. They generally played all Friday night, perhaps all day Saturday as well, and Sunday, at a "three day" wedding reception. In those three days they earned enough for the coming week, and the gypsies then provided more than adequately for their respective families.

There was another gypsy flute player (sipös), who had lost his leg just below the knee to shrapnel in the war of 1914-1918. He would limp about on a peg leg with the three other gypsies when he could.

Geza felt particularly kindly toward this Sipös.

The gypsies wandered into town to where the young people gathered in the evening, hoping to play for the young crowds' enjoyment and earn a few pennies. Invariably, not all of them met with success, some were luckier than others and managed to "latch" onto a particular "tavern group".

"Nah, what do you wait for?" addressing the limping Sipös. "Trying your luck this evening?"

"Oh, Geza I would like to earn a few forints, but I don't know which vendeglö (diner) would provide the best luck for me, and it does get tedious to hobble from one to another. It would be best for me to go to one and stay there...if fortune were kind."

(I'm sure he played on Geza's sympathy).

"Go into the 'Sabaria'. There is a good crowd there." Or, if Geza were on his way to a particular nightspot, he would invite Sipös to join him. Once there, the poor man would sit down on a chair by himself, apart from the customers, happy to get the weight off his stump.

Geza sat down at another table, and when the waiter came by, he ordered his own drink and one for Sipös; "a glass of wine and a cigarette for my gypsy friend."

Sipös would sip the wine, drag a few puffs on the cigarette, and then finger a tune out of the flute. There were those customers who were "well oiled", and they would pay the flute player to play their requests also. Geza would give him a little money for that night; in this manner the poor fellow would have a worthwhile evening. That's how it was in those days, if a person had work, life was not too bad. With wise management of the meagerest of wages, a person could still live well, well enough to even support a family.

There were of course too many poor. Many without a job, and these unfortunates couldn't afford a glass of wine for weeks. There were not too many men that earned as much as Geza, but those that did, supported a family very comfortably.

Geza, being single, lived remarkably well!

Let there be just enough to provide a living. That is all that anyone should want. Now, in Geza's case, if he got sick, he received sick pay. And so Geza vowed to live as he pleased, and in the manner he pleased, until he would marry. This was quite disconcerting to the women who had available daughters, and they often openly chastised Geza admonishing him to save.

"Gosh, young man, how fortunate you are to have such a position! Such a good paying job! Why are you so dissolute? You're just like your father."

That is how they would sum it up because Geza's father had exercised the "errant ways". Geza's father would still sell an ox on occasion though he did not deprive his family of their needs now that they were grown up and independent. It was his dear wife that suffered.

Geza would tell these nosey gossips, "I cannot lose all I have, because I am all that I have. I am alone and I am all I posses. I have nothing but myself. That which I drink away today, will be earned again tomorrow! I awaken every morning having added value, like a little colt. Every day it increases in value. I am like that colt."

Among the farmers there is a saying, one farmer to another, as he looked at the young colt and noticed its growth from day to day; 'it increases in value each day'.

There was an Evangelist who traveled that part of the countryside, and occasionally preached to the peasants, sometime to the old men and women, sometimes to the young ladies and young men. The truth is, he would preach to anyone that would listen! He often said: "For those of you, who would chastise the dissolute youth, let me caution you. If a young man strays, better he should stray when he is single. There is hope for him, and he can become a better man for it. Just like good wine that improves with age, so can a youth! Remember, *the grape is also* squeezed *to make the juice.* This juice 'boils' and must 'work itself out' ...by fermentation, once it has 'worked itself enough', if it is in a good barrel it will give forth good wine. If the young man 'works out' his waywardness and revelry, he could be a better man for it."

Words of wisdom are timeless, and appropriate for all generations.

To those women chastising him, Geza would say, "now, I too am working myself out. When I 'boil' out, and finally marry, it is because I have worked myself enough."

Geza met many colorful characters during his tenure at the Government factory, and in the Factory Field service. The following are "vignettes" of but two of those characters:

Rudy Schleicher:

He stunk! He had a very heavy body odor, but why shouldn't he? He never bathed! And he slept in his clothes. He slept wherever he passed out, under a porch, in the open fields, or in an alley. In the winter he generally took up residence at the railroad station. He would sleep on a bench inside the station where it was warm... while they let him. Then, when they helped him out, and locked up for the night, he retired to an empty boxcar on the railroad siding.

Whenever the "Company" needed him in the winter, they knew where to find him, down by the railroad station. Whenever the Company engineers wanted to learn, or if something new they designed needed improvement, they would call "Rudy".

Rudy would come; now that he was needed it had to be important! Whenever he was summoned, he would come spitting profusely. His walk was now determined, and the spitting seemed more determined also, determined to clear the head and system of alcohol, as if that were possible.

He generally spent all of his money on drinking, but if he knew that the next morning required him to be alert, he showed up in time for breakfast. Even if he had no money he showed up for breakfast in the Company Cafeteria. Rudy did have an odd sense of responsibility for his employers, "they would not be calling me if it wasn't important."

Oh yes, the Company paid the few pennies for the ham and eggs, toast and coffee. It was ultimately deducted from his "fee". His position in this capacity was that of an "advisor" (consultant), since he could not be imposed upon to work daily, nor could the Company expect him to work eight hour days, he worked as he "wanted", and only if the requirements of the Company made his advisory position seem necessary.

No one actually dined with him, or drank with him. He did not eat too frequently anyway. It is true that other men shunned his company because he was so unkempt and foul smelling, they simply did not sit at the table to join him. In the taverns it was the same; Rudy did not care. He lived his solitary life, and that was about all he seemed to want.

If he wanted money he earned it, and with the money he could buy anything. Yes, he could even afford the price of a "girl" when his body desired. Rudy was quite a man.

His employers, those who would hire him, would long ago have discarded him, if they did not need his brain. Indeed, the community even put up with him, where normally a bum would not be tolerated, he was. They were reconciled to the fact that, no matter how drunk he got, and how often, he was after all, harmless. As long as there were manufacturers and engineers that needed his knowledge, the community put up with him.

He was, as one might put it, a "utility". One might ignore it, walk around it, and just simply behave as though it was not there, until it was needed. Then one simply "turned" it on.

Rudy had already forgotten more about engineering than many engineers could learn in a lifetime. Invention and innovation came as natural to him as breath. It was just his drinking that was unnatural; but then, one might say that here too, Rudy excelled most men.

Rudy invented a particular type of scaffolding, a very peculiar, but unique device which was most advanced for its time. All it required was level ground for its base to set on. When it was in place, if it was within distance of an electrical supply, it was simply plugged in and switched on. If it was to be used remote from an electrical supply a "benzene motor" (generator) provided the power. When activated it could telescope to reach the highest belfry in town or to engage delivery of men and materials to a high rise building and elevated construction services.

It was a most fascinating accomplishment for a staggering drunkard to build a solid footing which elevated tradesmen.

Yes, they needed him, to help others who knew not how to help themselves to do repairs on industrial chimneys more conveniently, church steeples, and who knows what else. This scaffolding was capable of extending to a ten-story height of one hundred feet!

The telescoping platform was built to his specifications, just as Rudy drew up the sketches for it, and with his instruction. Do not forget that he also provided his own brawn in the building of it. It was then redrawn by the Company draftsmen, and also patented by the Company. Rudy got his drinking money, while they reaped total credits.

Rudy got all sorts of "leads", letters of recommendation, and tokens for food and drink. But Rudy remained Rudy. He was what he wanted to be. He could not be anything other. I guess he just did not care to change his life style for that of anyone.

Who was he? What was he? Did anyone know? They lived and let live, as all good people should. He was not yet 55 years old in 1926.

Rudy Schleiker was quite an extraordinary man.

Béla:

Béla was dark, almost brown, with a swarthy and seemingly dull face. When he sat down to eat with his coworkers, he would immediately begin to draw spectacular wrought iron gates and ornamental fences in remarkable detail on scrap pieces of paper. He was an individual that was also satisfied with what was enough. His wife was always getting after him to be more ambitious, and if he were inclined, he could have made a fortune. But she couldn't change him after all their years together.

They were married, and she wouldn't leave him.

Who would want her? She was uglier than he was.

They had no children but that just made it easier for him, lacking initiative. She would cook only once a week now that she was so disgusted with him. In that case he would simply cook a meal for himself.

Béla could never go to bed early nor could he go to bed sober. But there was no counterpart to Béla; he was the best wrought iron craftsman in the Company, if not in the country. Geza does not know if Béla changed his ways.

He lived the life he wanted.

Ah! What would ambition and success have done to him?

It would have pleased his wife, but it may have ruined the man.

PÁL AND ILONA IN CANADA

I lona talked about a railroad tavern (vasuti kocsma), where she was asked by their German travel agent if she wanted to "have a glass of wine" (frücs, actually a wine and soda water).

"I don't want a drink. I don't need a drink." She was so forlorn. "You know Pál...let's go back. Let's go home," she cried.

"I am not going home! What do you think? Why did I decide to leave?" replied her stubborn brother.

"Well, I would much rather we went back home. I'm confused, there is all this strangeness, and...I don't know."

At this time all sorts of probable consequences crossed Ilona's mind, the uncertainty of a future in a foreign land, things that she had not imagined before. She now began to realize what it would be like in a country where they could not understand the language, nor could they be understood. She realized this as they experienced an example in each country they passed through.

"Well, now we have set ourselves to this course, let's see it through. We shall continue, if we don't like it, we can just as easily return," said Pál (quite possibly not sincerely meaning it at all!).

This is just about the way it actually happened.

Canada had an immigration agreement with many European nations; The agreement was primarily established to supply Canada with able-bodied workers, specifically, young men and women laborers for farms. These young people were shipped immediately to the Western Provinces where help was sorely needed to open up, and develop the Prairie Provinces. Europeans over forty-two years of age were not even considered; Canada needed young Homesteaders.

Once they were in Canada, and had a mailing address, Ilona's father again asked Ilona to return. He would send her the return fare, if she needed the money. The concerned father wrote this letter not so much for his stubborn son Pál, but for Ilona's sake. He knew that his son was the most determined one. It was Pál's idea in the first place, and with reason, he was trying to escape the memories and heartaches of the past. Now that their two children were in Canada, Mr. and Mrs. Valko worried more for their daughter than for their son. They were sorry for Ilona whom they knew was taken up with the thought of an adventure in joining Pál in this migration. They also knew she would experience hardships, and for the first time in her life she may have to work for a living!

Canada's immigration agreement with the European Nations allowed those people who changed their mind and decided against settling in Canada, to be returned by the same boat that brought them.

That's right!

Their transportation back to Europe would be paid for by Canada, if the immigrants changed their mind within their first year. This fact was not made public knowledge too often. So it was not common information to the immigrants. Only those working in the immigration offices of both countries knew of this law.

The Canadian Government certainly did not advertise about the free return trip home. Indeed, the poor and penniless foreigners were under the impression that they were marooned. It was up to them, with their own efforts, to make money somehow, and earn enough to pay for their return. Consequently many years passed before the New Canadians had acquired a reasonable amount of money, and by then, having survived "the slings and arrows of outrageous fortune", many decided to remain.

Yes, they left their wives, and in some cases children in their Homeland; others decided rightfully to send their loved ones the money to make the trip and join them in the New World.

Pál and Ilona did not get shipped out west to the farm provinces. They had money enough of their own to get to a predetermined destination. Those who arrived in Canada with little or no money, poor souls, had to consent to the free rail transportation, and that was a one-way trip to the central farm provinces of Manitoba, Alberta, and Saskatchewan. Pál and Ilona travelled as far west as Windsor, Ontario, to meet their two brothers as planned. Julius (Gyula) and Joe (Jószi) were to come on the prescribed date from Chicago.

The two new immigrants waited and waited for their wayward brothers to show up. A week went by, and then another. It was now obvious that Julius and Joe were not going to show up. In Windsor there was yet another travel "agent" working in the Hungarian community. He informed Pál and Ilona that they could get work for a few weeks, and that they should entrust their passports to him. He would attempt to get them Canadian passports. It would take a while and cost more money but, the agent assured them, it can be done. With the Canadian passports they could enter the USA. They were to trust him.

"There certainly is no need for you to go out West. Those people all have to work hard and for little pay. They won't get a fair wage. Every employer calls them 'foreigner' and takes advantage of them."

So brother and sister settled in Windsor for a while waiting for their Canadian passports. Ilona could easily get a job and was never out of work. She worked in a laundry;

she worked as a housekeeper; she even worked as a cook, baking Hungarian pastries for a restaurant. Ilona had never seen a Negro, except at a carnival back home in Hungary. There, people paid to see the black man with bushy hair and flat nose. He was a sideshow entertainment and billed as an African savage.

In Windsor she now worked with a Negro woman in the laundry. Ilona could iron "professionally" (skill picked up at home ironing for a large household), and was paid well for it. The Negro woman ironed on the "board" ahead of hers. The ironing boards were arranged in a row. Each woman was instructed as to what part of the garments were to be their responsibility, and so the Negress ironed at the first board, Ilona at the second, someone at the third, to be followed by still a fourth and fifth "ironing woman" as necessary. In this way the work was done swiftly and skillfully, just as an assembly line. Those who were more skilled with men's clothing and shirts, ironed men's shirts; some women were more skilled in ironing skirts, dresses, blouses and so forth. The best work possible was done quickly, effectively, and proved to be customer pleasing. This laundry was quite popular in Windsor, and many of the clothes came from Detroit, across the river.

Ilona and Pál were quite financially capable to provide for their own needs because of their earnings and traveling money set-aside from Hungary. It was somewhat reassuring for them to know they could provide for themselves, as they now gave up on their travel agent.

They did not get Canadian passports and their Hungarian passports were gone also. The travel agent had also left this Hungarian community.

They were now stranded in Canada...technically illegal immigrants! They could not return to Hungary without proof of their nationality, and that was only to be found in their passports. They were in a precarious position.

[At this remote place in time we have concluded, 1) Julius and Joe did not intend to meet with them. As much as they had promised assistance to their brother and sister in the encouraging letters from Chicago, they were actually being deceptive. We shall find out 17 years later just what deceivers they were. But for the present, we shall continue the story. 2) The unscrupulous agent took advantage of the new immigrants, taking their money and selling their passports on the black market.]

The Negress would turn to Ilona and grasp her hand when she saw the homesick girl crying at her work. And Ilona cried all the harder then, because she could not talk to anyone; she could not speak the language.

Well, she cried! That's all she could do; she was homesick. Then at lunchtime, everyone quickly left the laundry to go to the Chinese restaurant (American and Chinese food) beside the laundry.

There the Chinese waiter asked each person for their menu choice, and took their orders. Ilona was with her co-workers and she wanted so much to be like them; she was part of them and longed to be understood. But when it came her turn to order they could only speculate as to what she would like to eat. The Chinaman was kind, and quite patient. He would bring her French fried potato chips and some fried meat (whatever it was). He would then show Ilona the catsup (ketchup).

"That good man," reflected Ilona after all these years, "was trying hard to communicate with me in the only way that he knew."

He brought Ilona something similar to what a co-worker in the group may have ordered at lunchtime. Ilona did acquire a taste for French fries and catsup, such a taste that she ate large portions of catsup. Too much catsup! She got sick, so sick that she couldn't work for a week. The catsup had produced acute diarrhea.

A Hungarian woman boarding at the same house as Ilona exclaimed, "Ilös el fogs pustölni! (Helen, you are going to die!)

"Well, it doesn't matter now whatever happens to me."

Ilona no sooner finished in the toilet, and would have to run back in again. How sick she was! And nowhere was there a familiar helping hand. Ilona cried, and got still more depressed as she dwelt upon her loneliness.

"If only I could hear my mother's voice: to hold her hand once more, like she held mine that day, and squeezed it so imploringly. I would now hold hers and be so content."

She remembered.

"Stay. Don't leave. Stay home. Don't go! My little girl don't go," her dear mother's words echoed softly in her mind.

This fine Hungarian woman, boarding in the same house, made Ilona a good meat broth, (or thick soup), and finally, slowly, her stomach accepted solid food again.

Ilona recovered. She resolved not to eat catsup anymore no matter how that Chinaman beckoned her to eat it. She did not dare put it on anything.

At those times, in her melancholy reverie, Ilona would think back upon that letter. Her father would gladly send money to get her back home. But Pál and she had money enough; money was not the issue.

Without their passports they were stranded and could not return.

Ilona would implore Pál, "let us investigate how we can get back to Hungary".

He was firm in his answer. "I won't go. I have nothing to return to."

Ilona knew that Pál was as homesick as she was. She also understood that he had greater heartaches than she had, reflecting on his lost wife and child. How could he return home where every day things, scenes and memories would only bring him daily sorrow? To be home again with constant reminders of his one love, his sweet Annüska, would be more than he could bear.

"If we go home you can get married again. Any girl back home would be only too pleased to make a match with you." Ilona pleaded, because she feared to make the return trip alone even if it were possible.

He was handsome. He was tall and muscular. What girl wouldn't want him?

They did not return to Hungary.

Ilona continued a cheerful correspondence with Geza, and soon realized that she had convinced him to come to Canada. Had she written the truth, Geza would most certainly have not considered such a rash action.

This is very much in the same manner that Theresa Valko had done in writing to her family in Hungary after she immigrated in 1908. She continued to write: "Come out, things are great etc.," just as Julius and Joe of Chicago had done for the past twenty years. Never did they say how bad it was for immigrants. Their letters always suggested that the brothers and sisters should "come", but never "why". Until Pál suggested to the Valko family he "may go". It was then that he took Ilona aside and asked, "Would you like to go with me?"

If only the brothers in Chicago had been honest in their letters. Perhaps they had been too proud to admit they also wanted to return home in the early years. They too, stuck it out and stayed.

Perhaps, now that they were a little more established in 1926, and somewhat independent, life in America was good. Never-the-less, they had not mentioned that life in the New World initially was extremely difficult. Jobs were actually hard to get for many immigrants in the years from 1908 leading up to 1914. If one could not speak the language, they would have to settle for anything just to feed one's self, and that is a bitter pill to take when you had everything you ever needed back home.

If Ilona knew what it would be like she never would have left! Even in her dreams she now walked at home, and talked with her dear mother. The landlady had often told

Ilona the next morning that she and her husband were awakened by Ilona's shouts as she cried out for "Momma", but there was no momma. The poor girl almost died of homesickness, yet she did not go home. She had to get used to the fact that Momma would not be with her anymore.

Pál traveled to Hamilton, Ontario, where he found that he could get a job that paid extremely well in one of the Iron Foundries around Hamilton Bay. He also found that a strong Hungarian community existed there. This was much more to his liking, and so Ilona and Pál made the move to Hamilton.

"Pál and I are both working," Ilona wrote Geza. "There are jobs in Canada for all who want to work. Your Stationary Engineer's degree should get you a good job here."

In 1926, when Geza decided to immigrate, he first had to get released from the military. Even though he was discharged, his military obligation was not ended. He could be called up anytime a National crisis threatened, until age forty-six. In Vienna where he enquired for the military release, the Major told Geza, "Oh, my boy, that won't be easy. We will have use for you veterans. Just go back, go home until we summon you." (Could the major have known something about the direction that Europe was heading in 1926? He must have observed signs of the coming conflict in the politics of Europe.)

Geza went back home without his military release and thought about what the Major had said. Then he determined, "I'll leave the country without it." Geza had begun to earn a pension at age twenty-four, and now at age twenty-six he would loose the two years of earned pension if he left his employment.

He plotted his departure none-the-less. He feigned sickness with the help of his family doctor who verified his sick time off from work. By means of his sister Erzsi, Geza would send the doctor a dozen eggs occasionally as a gift. The doctor in turn would ask Erzsi about Geza's health. She always stated that he was making progress, but at times seemed to suffer a set back. Through her, the doctor carried on the façade, encouraged Geza about his 'recovery', but stated that he should not be too anxious, and that nature would in due course correct the illness and ultimately Geza would get well.

At times, Erzsi had to remind Geza to buy the eggs, or butter, whatever was to be the "gift" for the weekly visit to the doctor. For three months this doctor allowed Geza to continue to "get well". But the Company insisted on giving Geza a medical check-up with their Company doctor. They wondered why Geza was not making progress.

Geza had feigned medical leave, saying it was his war wounds, and he received 85% of his wages during his sick leave. He probably made out better than what two years of pension would have given him. He recouped his would-be losses in leaving the job prematurely, forfeiting his pension for sick leave pay those many weeks.

He was young, and he partied it away every night.

During this time, Geza was also getting everything ready, documents, passport etc., to leave the country. Two Jewish sisters who were good friends of Geza, had a father that took to Geza's free spirit. Even though the man was a Jew, he did not mind this gentile boy accompanying his daughters in town, or of an evening. When the girls knew Geza had made up his mind to leave they sewed a linen pouch, with tie-straps on it, that he could put his money, passport, and valuables in.

"We have been told that you must secure it around your neck. In this manner, who robs your pockets will not get your most important valuables nor the major part of your money."

The ticklish matter of his military release he handled by going to the Town Reeve. He knew the man personally, they had often partied together, and maybe, just maybe, this man could arrange a substitute document in place of a military discharge. But the Reeve too, was reluctant to let his friend go.

"I don't want you to leave. The country needs people like you Geza. What the hell is wrong with you? You have a good job and you certainly do as you please. Damn it. You have freedom and liberty; it is just like 'America' right here! Why would you want to leave?"

(In retrospect, many years later, Geza said the Reeve was right. "Perhaps we could have drank and sung together, even if one considers 1939 and what followed. You know, my buddies in the shop were not conscripted; they were not taken because they were needed in the shop. Perhaps I too could have avoided conscription. Hell yes! When the country is at war all skilled craftsmen are needed in the factories to keep the war machine going. They needed the workers. Even the prisoners of war who were skilled tradesmen were utilized in war plants.")

(In Buda there was a factory built into a hill. When the Russians came in and encircled the city in 1944, those workers didn't know for days that the Russians had been there. The workers slept, ate, and spent the entire week in the underground plant. Only when the occupation commenced, there were those who suddenly realized, "Hey! There isn't a German left in town." Then the workers came out into the light of day and into a different Hungary)

Geza wrote to Gergély, still in Russia in 1926. "I may go to Canada."

"What do you think is there young brother? Do you think the streets are made of kolbász? (sausage?)," was the older brother's reply.

Many thoughts passed through his mind, no doubt the thought lingered, as it had for many of those before him; "if things are not what they should be, I'll return home."

But for now, another Hungarian saying also crossed his mind:

Magyarorság az en hazam	*Hungary is my home*
Magyar nevelt apam, anjam	*Hungarian raised by father, mother*
Magyar az en nemzetisegem	*Hungarian is my Nationality*
Ön fent alö a buskesegem	*My pride is mighty high.*
Egaz Magyar scak ugy vagyok	*I am a true Hungarian only if*
Hazamra bovaradok	*I do not loose expectations of my home.*

Many had said to him then, at the railroad station bar, where the group of friends and well wishers had accompanied him.

"Why in the dog's god name do you want to leave? (Mi a kutya Istenét neki akars el meni?")

In the village, the father of those two Jewish girls who had sewed that money pouch had the same parting words.

"Why in the name of that dog god do you want to leave? You have America here."

By that he implied that Geza had everything that any immigrant to America would hope to find in America.

And that Old Jew was right!

Geza had everything that a well-to-do man would envy. He had an excellent job that provided him a railroad pass to travel anywhere in Hungary.

In that railroad station tavern in Szombathely, where his friends gathered around to see him off, and with each one assuring him of the error of this planned migration, Geza momentarily thought to himself, "I'm going to stay home. I'm not going to go!"

But he did go!

Geza traveled through Western Europe and crossed the Atlantic Ocean on the Ocean Liner Pacific, arriving in Halifax, Nova Scotia in 1926.

He made his way to Hamilton, Ontario, to Ilona and Pál Valko's accommodations. On his arrival he vowed, like the Magyar Hymnists had vowed, "Here you must live and here you must die." (Itt elnéd es meg halnöd kel.) That is how it was. Within two weeks he had gotten a job for twelve dollars a week, temporary he thought, till he can get an engineering job.

The Canadian doctor noticed a scar on one of his lungs during an x-ray examination for this job. Geza related to the Company doctor, as best he could in broken English, about being buried alive in 1917, in Italy, by an artillery shell explosion.

"My heart beat was so pronounced that I was afraid to look at it. What a desperate, rapid pounding it put out! I thought it would jump out of my rib cage. I didn't think I would recover. Surely I would never be the same!" Geza told the doctor, "But I have lived a lot in these nine years since, and did not know, nor did any doctor tell me that I had a scar on my lung."

"Obviously it hasn't slowed you down. You are in excellent physical shape otherwise."

Ilona was making twenty-five dollars per week, combined with Geza's wages this was thirty-seven dollars per week income. When the relatives in Hungary were informed of the good wages, and of his and Ilona's good fortune, Geza's cousin's husband wanted to immigrate. If Geza could get him a job, he too would come out to Canada.

With Geza's assurance and assistance, the cousin-in-law arrived that same year. The trouble is he wanted one hundred dollars a week as soon as he saw the "potential" in Hamilton. He was a good carpenter, it's true, but truer still is that he didn't want to work, he just wanted the money. Carpentry was his trade in Hungary; he didn't like to work too hard there either, but again, he did have a good life in Hungary. And like Geza, he also did not have to come to America. It is just that he, unlike Geza, did not want to work. He just wanted the good life if he had it 'given' to him, then he would stay in America.

Greed for a greater wage drove him. He soon found out that here, as "over there", no one is going to 'give' you anything if you don't have the gumption to work for it!

The cousin-in-law very soon returned to Hungary.

PÁL MEETS EMMA

Ilona and Geza were married in 1926. Things went well for them; thirty-seven dollars a week for one household was excellent income in that era.

A daughter was born to them in March of 1927. They named her Ilona after her mother but, as usual when surrounded by an English speaking community, the neighbors gave her the equivalent English name of Helen. Indeed, mother Ilona also became Helen to her English-speaking friends.

In November of 1929, twins, a boy and a girl were born to Ilona and Geza. They named the boy John (Anglicized from János, his grandfather's name). They named the girl Annie (Anglicized from Annüs, her grandmother's name). The family was beginning to multiply and Geza was still working, as was Pál. Pál was now living with Geza and Ilona and paying for room and board; so the Virag couple's income was more than sufficient. The young couple could easily pay the house rent, having saved money from when they were both working. Now with Pál adding to Geza's income they were quite comfortable.

Three years following their marriage, when the stock market collapsed in October of 1929, there was much concern in the Hungarian community because of what newspapers were printing about the catastrophe in the United States.

"What is a Stock Market, and what is this Stock Market crash?" questioned the puzzled immigrants. Those in the community who could read English kept the concerned people informed the best they could.

"The Stock Market is a place where people invest their money, if they are so inclined, and if they are lucky they profit from their investment."

"What? Don't people in that country put their savings in a bank? Let the stock market suffer," replied the many frugal savers, "it will not affect us".

"It is possible the bank may experience a problem if those people who lost their investments turn to the bank, drawing out their savings to make up for their losses to sustain a living," warned some of the wiser ones.

"The Stock Market is in the United States, it cannot affect us here in Canada," again, wishful thinking on the part of those frugal savers.

"If many Companies lose their investment money, those Companies may have to lay off workers! There could be a period of joblessness."

Those able to read the daily newspapers grew more concerned than the unread community members. Many in Canada, who were still working, felt that what was happening in the United States would not affect them.

In the Hungarian community of Hamilton, Ontario, Pál met a Hungarian girl. She must have been a pleasant person because Pál began to spend a lot of time with her. Her name was Emma, and she lived only a few blocks away from Geza and Ilona's home. Pál would visit her frequently. He still was not certain that he would marry again, and sincerely felt that he could not. Memories of his dearest 'Annúska' still haunted him.

He did need companionship other than relatives however, and Emma provided that. They went 'steady' for quite a while. Pál would get off work, go home, wash up and change his clothes, then catch a streetcar. The streetcar would take him to the James Street car stop at Barton Street where he transferred to the Barton Street 'beltline' car and went to Emma's place of work. He would wait there, at that stop, for her to finish working, and together they would take the return streetcar. He just could not catch the same streetcar every day, because sometimes he got home later from work. By the time he cleaned up, he was off the normal schedule. At these times, Emma waited the few minutes for Pál because she knew that he would be there.

The couple abided by this arrangement ritually.

They were two, lonely immigrants, homesick, and confused about the foreign world around them. They found pleasure in such simple things as holding hands and talking in their native language as they rode home together each evening on the streetcar.

In late December Pál received a huge turkey from the Company and brought it home. Ilona proceeded to cook it immediately; they would have turkey that same evening!

Pál got cleaned up and went to catch the streetcar as he did every weekday evening. When he 'transferred off' the James Street streetcar, two Hungarian friends hailed him down before he could cross James Street to the car stop and catch the Barton Street streetcar to Emma's place of work.

"Boldog Karácsony Pál" (Merry Christmas Paul)

"Merry Christmas to you both," he replied.

"Come have a Christmas drink with us."

"Gosh, as much as I would like to fellows, I've got to meet my girl," he feigned disappointment.

"Oh come on now Pál," said one.

"You know she'll wait. What girl wouldn't wait for a stout fellow like you?"

"Thanks fellows, but no thanks, I've got to go."

"Just one Pál; come now, have a beer with us for the festive season."

Pál wanted to have a beer, but he was not sure his friends would let him leave after just one drink. "Just one then and I really have to go."

The friends crossed Barton Street and went into the Hotel. The conversation was lively, and exciting, with talk of the Holiday and reminiscents about the Christmas festivals in the Old Country. Tomorrow they would have the day off.

His two drinking partners kept him longer than he intended.

Pál realized that he was going to be later than usual for his meeting with Emma and he didn't want her to worry over his tardiness. He always caught that streetcar, or the very next one. He now ran to catch it as his friends followed in feigned pursuit, with words of insincere apologies.

The Hotel is situated so that in crossing the road Pál now ran diagonally across the intersection, thus he was in front of the streetcar as it began its turn onto Barton Street going east. For a moment, Pál and the streetcar Operator actually faced one another. The Operator could be seen through the front windshield at the controls and he saw Pál, but *refused to stop!*

Witnesses admitted later, that the streetcar Operator saw Pál and could have stopped. He certainly had time but deliberately proceeded forward.

Pál was hit!

Pedestrians and passengers alike, yelled at the fool Operator to stop! With the passengers screaming at him, only then did he make an effort to stop.

The drinking buddies standing on the curb outside the hotel looked on in horror as Pál's body was rolled aside by the 'cow-sweeper' front end. They ran to his assistance as all road traffic came to a halt. They saw that he was unconscious and bleeding. Both of them felt a painful twinge of guilt, had they been the cause of his death? They stayed with him, and accompanied him in the ambulance to the hospital. Then they stayed with him until evening, and together they reluctantly took the James Street streetcar south to Geza's place.

Ilona and Geza were beginning to wonder what had happened to Pál when the two guilt ridden friends knocked on the door. Geza answered the door; Ilona was attendant at her kitchen, and the turkey. Geza recognized Pál's friends and let them in, allowing Ilona to continue her work in the kitchen. They whispered hurriedly to Geza that Pál had been injured. He called the men upstairs for privacy as he did not wish Ilona to hear about her brother's accident. She was still breast feeding the twins born in November, and no telling what the fear or shock would do to her ability to continue breast feeding. Ilona, in the kitchen tending to the cooking, with the turkey still in the oven, saw the three men go upstairs.

The three were not upstairs very long. When they came down Geza let the two men out. He went to the kitchen and told Ilona that he had to attend to something urgent; it would take a little while. As he put his hat and coat on he said, "Keep the turkey in the oven. Don't set the table for supper, until I come back." He did not want her to ask 'what' or 'why', for fear of having to tell her a lie, so he left quickly.

But Ilona suspected something serious was happening. It was not like Geza to leave abruptly without explanation... at suppertime, and where was Pál? He should have been home long ago. Because she did not know, her woman's intuition now suspected the worst. She ran upstairs to her twins; her little girl Helen ran upstairs after her.

"What is the matter mommy?"

Arriving at the hospital, Geza learned that Pál was still alive! The doctors were amazed at Pál's tenacity, but were still not certain of the outcome. He had sustained repeated hits to the head on the pavement while tumbling forward of the streetcar. The doctors surmised that he suffered skull fractures and the consequent brain concussions.

Pál had gone through hell in the Great War, and miraculously had come out of it without a scratch, never suffering a wound during his entire military service. Now, after all those years of being shot at, the artillery, machine gun and rifle fire; had he come to this country to get killed? What a terrible tragedy if he were to die because of this freak accident thought Geza. Seeing he could not help Pál, he left the hospital.

It was now dark of course; Ilona and Helen would need consoling. How could he begin? What words of encouragement could he tell them and at the same time indicate a positive hope for Pál's recovery?

By the time he got home the turkey was more than well done, for Ilona could not concentrate on dinner. She could not get off that one path of her thoughts; those men were Pál's friends. Pál was not home, and Geza had left quickly without explanation. This was enough to worry Ilona, and so the turkey burned!

Geza found his family upstairs in the bedroom with the infant twins, Ilona with tear stained face still wet. Helen was also crying, though she knew not why. It was because mommy cried, and that was enough reason for the child to cry. The twins were also fussing as though they felt the tension.

Geza explained it all to Ilona. Pál was seriously injured, it is true, but the doctors admired his strength and, (here he lied), they were certain Pál would pull through. This did not set her mind at ease! She now had more reason to worry about poor Pál. Ilona could not rest comfortably until she saw him. Geza suggested waiting a few days.

He was also concerned about the intensive swollen face and head; these must subside before he would allow Ilona to see her brother. It was Christmas. She should wait until next week.

Geza visited Pál every evening however, checking for encouragement from the attending doctors and nurses.

During his recovery Pál was often in and out of consciousness. In his delirium he talked Hungarian of course, and too often he talked to his beloved Annüska. She was with him, there in his comatose mind, and he would cry out to her, "Annüska", groping and reaching for the phantom. But it was Emma that held his hands in hers. Emma visited the unconscious man every day in those critical first weeks. She saw his body writhing and twisting, fighting the nightmares as much as his pain. She heard him cry out with tear filled eyes his first love's name "Annüska–Annüska", and all the while it was Emma that stroked his feverish head with soothing hands and comforted him.

As he began his amazing recovery, the doctors did not know what to think when he talked, they thought he was incoherent. It was the foreign language of course, but to them it seemed non-sense. And so they feared he had suffered brain damage and was becoming "feeble minded". He acted normal enough when his friends visited because they all talked Hungarian!

The doctors finally realized their foolish misjudgment.

Pál was not "feeble minded".

When Ilona visited she brought little Helen with her. If Pál were up and about, as he was during the long recovery, for he would walk the corridors and visit the other patients. It was on these occasions that the doctors were reassured of Pál's sanity, for he would call softly to Helen:

"Helen, come here to your Uncle Pál," but again, in Hungarian.

And she would run happily down the corridor toward his waiting open arms, as he knelt down onto the floor to greet her. She loved her Uncle Pál.

The doctors saw that this giant of a man also loved, and remembered the child. They had been confused for months, because not only had this man insisted on speaking his native language instead of English, but also the concussion had caused a slight speech impediment. The speech impediment was more noticeable when he attempted to talk to them in English. It was only slightly noticeable when he spoke his native language to his fellow countrymen.

This speech impairment too, improved with time, and finally it was not noticeable at all! When he drank, it became noticeable! But then, again, even otherwise well people slur their words because of drink.

After his release from the hospital, Emma visited him often at home. She helped Ilona nurse him, and that made her happy. Pál often talked to Emma about home, the Old

Country, and how things were in the past, but never did he talk to her about his beloved Annüska.

He did not realize that in his unconscious state, he had said more than enough; Emma already knew! The bits and pieces that she heard as he cried out in his nightmares were substantiated with what Ilona would tell her. Neither woman let on that Emma finally knew Pál's greater pain was his broken heart.

Emma consoled him and nursed him until he was strong enough for extended walks. They went for long walks together on the streets of Hamilton during his recovery. She was a soothing balm for his fractured and tortured mind.

They married.

In later years, when they bought their own home, and had children of their own, Emma would tell Ilona that Pál still cried out for Annüska in his dreams. During his waking hours Emma was his wife, but in his dreams he walked the familiar homeland paths that he had walked with his first love.

He was in that cemetery again where they first met, but he saw only the mother's headstone, not Annüska's. He may have even sung that song, their song, in which a brown-eyed girl mourned her mother and he consoled her, married her, and they lived happily ever after.

This wonderful woman was content to settle for that. She was wise enough to realize that she could not compete with a phantom; Pál would have to continue to cope with the phantom alone, while struggling with the real world in his waking hours.

Pál had an earthly burden that Atlas could find heavy on his shoulders.

GERGÉLY RETURNS HOME

Gergély's wife and daughters kept their secret so well and hidden him so successfully in that underground room in the barn from 1926 to 1931 that the villagers finally forgot about him. Even the gossip, that he had secretly packed up one night and fled the country was accepted eventually as true.

With neighbors and nosey villagers now smugly content that the 'upstart Magyar had done the right thing', suspicious observation, and spying on the wife and children also ceased. It became easier for Gergély to spend nights in the house, but forever cautious, he returned to the barn very early before daybreak so he could quickly hide under the horse stall should neighbors venture near. The family never-the-less concluded they could not continue to live in this manner for long. The five years had proven too stressful; it was impossible to continue, and they knew they were pressing their luck.

Finally they made preparations to leave. His wife and daughters made arrangements that were to be done in the open without his presence, so that it would appear that they were indeed without a father. They packed whatever they could cram into one wagon. Gergély made certain that he had all the letters from his parents in Hungary etc. Then one dark evening, Gergély hitched up that one horse, that horse that had shared so many days near his secret room in the stable.

With wife and children on the wagon, they went to the Old Kulak's gravesite. Stopping momentarily to say words of farewell, and give explanation to the spirits that lay side by side in the family plot, as to why these remaining survivors must now leave their native home forever. Tombstones showed date of death leading back to many generations of ancestors. The Old Kulak had worked the 5,000 acres and it was to be a home for his descendents for many generations into the future. But that was now a figment of a lost dream.

Finally, the living left the dead, and that much loved home, the home that had been so good and had promised so much when they were younger. It seemed years ago.

Communism put a stop to all such dreams. Communism would no longer allow this radical Magyar to live, or leave, as a free man. Communists had piece-mealed the 5,000 acres into 2.500, then 1.250, then 625 and finally, only a few acres remained around the house and barns. The land distribution provided for many neighbors whether they knew how to farm it or not, and many neighbors would now happily report against, and accuse Gergély in any fabricated way possible.

Before sunrise of the next day they were many kilometers and well away, but still not an extremely great distance from their old home. They kept plodding on, stopping only occasionally to rest that faithful horse. When they were a few days of travel distance from home they stopped to seek shelter in a village. Continually frightened with their adventure, they remained cautious. To be captured while still in the interior of Russia would mean certain death for Gergély. God knows what would happen to his wife and daughters.

If people questioned this family as to where they were moving, since everyone could see their possessions cramped neatly in the wagon, they had a story that was plausible, and therefore acceptable. In those years of turmoil during the revolution, too many Russians were moving back and forth from one village to another in much the same manner.

"We are returning to my wife's family home," then they would name a Russian border town. Gergély would say that, "My wife's father and mother are getting old and require someone to take care of their needs in these troubling times."

They had a few stories that they had rehearsed, so even the children would be answering the curious peasants with the same fabrications that their parents had. These stories were compatible with their appearance, a family traveling with all their belongings packed on a horse drawn wagon. If asked to name the place of residence they were moving from, the family had made a rule to mention the village where they had stayed at two days before.

This seemed to work well enough.

When they were close to the Russian border they were stopped by a roving band of ragtag, renegade soldiers. The soldiers did more than question the family; they searched among their belongings, completely unloading the wagon searching for valuables which they could confiscate.

Content that this family had nothing more than an excess amount of cash in rubles and silver certificates, the searchers relieved them of it!

These roving renegades were very much surprised at the amount of money this seemingly "poor" family carried. Setting themselves apart from the worried little group and whispering, they had a heated discussion about what best to do now that they had robbed the family of their cash. They seemed to come to a unanimous agreement that the family provided handsomely for the soldiers and posed no threat of reporting the robbery.

Then why kill them?

After all, this is quite likely their total life savings of many years of hard work, and the woman's old parents may need all the help this little family could provide. The soldiers seemed decent enough...for thieves. They left the family some money, only enough that the soldiers deemed necessary to live on until reaching that fictitious destination, that town near the border.

The family was most fortunate!

In those trying times of the young Socialist Republic, who knows what accusations could be made about any person, especially ones who carry large amounts of readily negotiable currency.

To kill them would have been easy; no one would know who did it even if someone found the bodies. Who cared?

There were too many bodies found that way during the chaos and restless turmoil for the country's stability.

Crossing through the Carpathian Mountain passes they departed Russia, and entered Hungary where they were stopped once again; this time by Hungarian border guards. The Officials would not believe that Gergély was a Hungarian citizen even though he produced those letters from his Hungarian family. Gergély spoke such a broken Hungarian now, that the officials were certain he was a Russian!

What could they expect of him? He had spent over fourteen years in Russia; married a Russian girl, and had talked only Russian for the last ten years. The dubious authorities took the family to an Immigrant Processing Center in Budapest.

Having lived in Russia these many years, he had difficulty getting himself understood by his countrymen. He remained under house arrest for thirty days in Budapest, while the police and immigration officials cross-examined him. He was considered a political prisoner, and as such he did not have the amenities that common prisoners had; he slept on a bed of straw.

His wife and children however were allowed to stay at Gergély's sister's home in Budapest. The Officials would not give him the consideration of a native son because he took so long returning home after the war. The Hungarian Government did not show too much kindness either, because Gergély chose to return this late after the war. Why he may very well be a Soviet spy sent back to foment unrest, to agitate for Communism. It mattered not that father, mother, sisters and brothers were respected citizens. Officials presumed that he had been indoctrinated into communism, as many had been in those months of 1919. The Authorities treated him with suspicion; a radical departure from a Hungarian patriot.

In 1922, Hungary had advertised in Russian newspapers, and in other nations in which they knew Hungarian soldiers had been prisoners. It was a communication to all native sons:

"Let your parents know where you are, if your letters are not answered by relatives, write home to your Regimental Headquarters. If you do not express a desire to maintain your birthright, all who do not reply will loose their citizenship."

It is no doubt that, this is why the authorities gave Gergély a hard time. He had not written anyone in his country. Heck, things were still going good for him and the Old Kulak in 1922. Neither of the Kulak's two sons was around, having joined the White Russian resistance of loyalists fighting the Red Russian revolutionaries. He was in line for a good inheritance! What more could a young man want?

When adversity struck the slate clean however, and his life was threatened in 1926, circumstances became entirely different. He could see sound reason for returning home.

For thirty nights he slept on that straw bed, during the day he picked up, and improved upon his mother tongue from his questioners. His interrogators asked him the same questions repeatedly, but always in a different format, hoping to trip him up. They had him under observation all the while, and even listened in by hidden microphone on his private conversations with members of his family, or whoever else visited him.

He continually told them that he had left Russia because it was no longer home to him, or his wife. The communists had murdered his father-in-law in cold blood, right before his family members' eyes.

"Wouldn't this act alone be cause enough to hate those murders?" He asked.

"You took your time to decide on leaving after that murder, five years wasn't it?"

"I could not leave outright; immediately! I had to plan the escape or they would have killed me. My family would have been trapped in Russia, if they killed me to." He argued.

"If I killed your father-in-law," stammered Gergély in broken Hungarian, "you would surely dislike me too." Reminiscing in thought, he would tell them "This Old Kulak took to me as if I were his own son. He allowed me to farm 5,000 acres with him when his sons did not return from the revolutionary wars. His sons must have been killed. Who knows? But there you have it. My life was threatened, my family was in jeopardy, and I was hiding for almost six years! How could you suppose that I am partial to such a government? How could you imagine I am an agent of theirs when I could not stand them?"

"They dragged the Old Kulak from his family, from out of his house. He resisted. He said it was all the same to him, knowing that if he went they would kill him. If he stayed they would kill him. What's the difference when it comes your time to die? So the Old Man chose to die on his own land.

They shot him.

We buried him."

"My fate would have been the same. I opposed them. I hated them. Had I not gone into hiding I would have been killed for sure? That is why I brought my family; we have nothing but the clothes on our backs. You saw what we carried, all our possessions in one wagon."

Finally the Authorities allowed mother Virag to underwrite responsibility for this immigrant family. With that cleared, no more obstacles barred Gergély's road home.

The Hungarian Government none-the-less regarded him with suspicion. From the day of his release they never did trust him.

In 1935 he still had that photograph of the horse stable and stall, showing the horse in the stall.

"That is the horse with whom I shared a stall to hide under for all those years," he would say to his relatives and friends.

LIFE GOES ON

E ven though the stock market crash of Wall Street had occurred in October of 1929, there were those businesses in Canada that had not yet felt the effect, and continued to prosper. Many men continued to work and had well-paid jobs, as did Geza, and so, remained oblivious to the imminent catastrophe that was to circle the globe; families grew.

Pál and Emma rented a house quite distant from Geza and Ilona, not because they wanted to be far from the relatives, but because the monthly rent in this new location was more economical. The families did not visit too often as a result of the distance. A first child was born to Pál and Emma in 1931; they named her Helen. Another son was born to Geza and Ilona the same year in June. Things were still going well for the Virags because from March to November of that same year, they managed to send home to Hungary, 1,000 Canadian dollars.

As the children grew older the Virag family did visit the Valko family more often, even at their distant place. I remember once, when we visited, Helen Valko was eight years old and her brother Paul was three or four. The two children were like "shy rabbits" and ran from us as we entered their home. Their mother was so protective of them she would not let them play outside with the neighborhood children too often, so they were not accustomed to playing with other children. Emma could not speak English too well, and perhaps she thought, if she does not know what's going on with the children at play, they may be up to no good, and may even harm these "foreign kids", her children. Their parents thus had to fetch and coax them from their bedroom at our visit. This all changed however when Pál and Emma again moved, as did Geza and Ilona; the two families where now just about five city blocks from one another.

We moved from 299 Bay Street to 18 Picton Street, and walked to Bennetto School. The Valkos lived on Farie Street and the children walked to McIlwraith School.

The children would get together more often and played indoor games, Snakes and Ladders (now called Chutes and Ladders). Our favorite of course was Monopoly. The Monopoly games we played took two or three evenings to complete and were generally at Aunt Emma's home. So we would go back each evening until we finally finished the game. We really did quite well at it, enjoying the buying and selling of property with all the play money. Aunt Emma would have a hearty laugh at all our play money riches. She liked to see us play this game because it kept us indoors all evening, and thus she knew where her children were. As stated earlier, she was very protective of her Helen and little Paul.

Now that he was returned home, Gergély bought some land next to Geza's veteran's allotment with the money he received from Canada, so that the complete parcel of land totaled about eight acres.

He proceeded to build a house on it.

But when he went to a Notary Public (Közyegzö) to sign the 'transfer title' and get the required notarization, he ran into a very 'uncivil' civil servant. He initially had difficulty getting through the rude person and transferring the land grant title. The Notary Public then in Porpacz, had a reputation for being rude to veterans from the Russian front in particular. When such men went to him for any service that related to veteran's benefits, he would call them traitors, accusing them of cowardice or whatever came to his simple rude mind.

504 ~ *Anthony E. Virag*

"You are just like the rest of them...all those who gave up, and spent the duration of the war in Russia. That is why we lost the war; you wouldn't fight. You had the remainder of the war easy in Russia."

Gergély was the recipient of similar remarks when he went to this man, but he did not take it lightly as some veterans may have. The Közyegzö expected these veterans to be humbled, and to take the humiliation. They should, after all, if they expected his help! They certainly could not retaliate, could they?

"Notary Public sir (Közyegzö ur), don't dare say those things to me. I happen to know that you were never in action, nor even near the front. You never were in the situation that many of us experienced. You were like most of the fat-headed freeloaders and officers shaking their fists from a safe distance on the home front!"

Another man from the neighboring region, also a veteran, entered while the two were arguing. The Közyegzö would have willingly dropped off this unexpected confrontation that was now getting heated, since a third party was listening to Gergély fearlessly getting the best of him in this tongue lashing. But Gergély continued to press him, telling the 'uncivil' fool how the Virag family had suffered personally.

"All four brothers served, one gave his life, and you imply that I lacked loyalty? You weren't even in action; I recommend that you shut up!"

The newcomer now had his turn at the Notary Public. "I have heard that you dish out that shit to others; all the veterans who come to you for help have to hear your nonsense. You had better listen to this man's advice and shut your mouth. Don't bring such crap up again, not to any veteran that fought the war you didn't fight. One may retaliate on you physically some day."

The Notary Public got a verbal kick in the ass from this newcomer also. He was now fit to be tied. These two veterans had boldly defied him, and put him in his place.

"He wasn't even home." Sputtered the Notary to the newcomer, and pointing at Gergély, "Now he is taking advantage of the army's veteran land grant."

The Notary could not comprehend it, even though it was obvious that the land was given to Geza for "services rendered by a wounded soldier". This foolish man could not understand that prisoners of war, having served, also suffered grievously. Not having had experience in active fighting during the war, or having not been deprived in the manner the fighting men had been, he blamed them all. He was discomforted that Hungary was now suffering the results of a defeated nation. She was once a great nation and was now reduced greatly in area having been partitioned off and divided among the conquering countries. This is why the uncivil man vented his hostility on many of the returned soldiers.

If they had not given up; but he could not understand, he wasn't there! The animosity continued in this man, but not in open verbal exchanges anymore.

The village teacher was one year younger than Gergély, and he was also a very good friend of Geza's. He had been appointed village schoolmaster upon the previous school-master's retirement in 1926. He was not one to flaunt, nor make a show of his medals. On occasion when Gergély and he would take a drink together, he might tell Gergély where it was, and how it was that he got such and such medal.

The teacher had been a lieutenant in the Great War, and he did not hold with the argument that any soldier that was captured or taken prisoner was a coward or had shirked his military duty. But the Notary Public more likely had a clerical job behind a desk somewhere, had he executed his military obligation at all.

It seems ironic to me, wars are fought between soldiers of the opposing Nations, and yet, the soldiers of these different Nations are friendly towards one another after the conflict wherever they meet during peacetime. Yet people within the same Nation are bitter and angry towards their own soldiers who had fought in the war.

When will there be Peace?

Only when we dip equally from the same bowl; only when we realize that we are equals, the richest in the land and the poorest of them all, we will either stand together or die individually.

In 1921 when that Major told Geza, "You will never build on your veteran's land allotment." He was now proven right; it was Gergély who benefited from Geza's land grant.

Jobs begun to get scarce in 1933, and Geza too, finely found himself out of work at the end of that year. The Depression had finally circled the globe. To provide for his family he now bought a bicycle with some of their savings; a car was out of the question. Few people had cars in those days since public transportation was reasonable and efficient. He and his friend Simon Kovacs would ride through Hamilton and out into the surrounding countryside hunting for work on the outlying farms. They enquired of all the 'garden farmers', from Stoney Creek to Grimsby, for work, any work at all, as farm hands. If they were lucky, they worked all day and slept in the farmer's barn at night. When the farmer no longer needed them, they rode home to their families. Many times, these willing workers were away from home all week, coming home only on the weekends with the few dollars desperately needed to feed their families and pay the rent.

They did work, even on weekends when needed, coming home only after the farmer's needs were completed.

In July-August, they picked cherries. In the fall they would pick apples or pears, these poor men worked at whatever was available, until the farmers too, began to feel the pinch of the depression. No one could afford to buy the cherries, apples or pears, therefore pickers were not needed. Geza and Simon were turned away from many fruit farms.

"No Help needed," signs were posted at most every place of business as well, in the factories and on every farm.

"Mister, please, let us take some pears" (or apples, or whatever was rotting on the trees), begged the two men, "for our children. If you cannot pay us to work, if the fruit will rot anyway, let us make use of a few." They spoke in very broken English, as neither man had yet conquered the English language.

Kindly farmers having no money themselves worked the men in the fields for a while and then allowed the men to take a basket or two of fruit as payment for their labour. They bicycled home with their prize!

There were other farmers however who hated their own predicament, perhaps hated the immigrants too, blaming them for the World Crisis, whatever the reason. There was the odd farmer who actually chased these hungry men off their land! Then, later on those nights, if they were still in the immediate area, Geza and Simon would ride back to the surly farmer's orchard and shake all the fruit off as many trees as they could. The farmer was needlessly unkind; the two men needlessly spiteful. At another farm, cabbages would rot in the fields but the farmer denied them one or two heads to take to hungry children. Again, at night, the two men helped themselves and uprooted, cut or destroyed what cabbages they could not carry.

Survival was all-important, and life was becoming vicious.

There was a Brick Kiln on the East side of Hamilton, at the base of the mountain. Geza found himself out there one day, twenty-six miles from home and family. He enquired for a job.

"Anything!" he pleaded.

He was hired on the spot.

Hungry and tired from the long bicycle ride, yet famished as he was, he worked the remainder of the day! The sun was setting when he asked humbly for the day's pay. He pointed to his stomach. The owner understood; he had seen that Geza had not eaten that day. The man paid Geza and asked, "Where do you live?"

"Far away, in Hamilton."

"My gosh man, you will no sooner get home and it will be time to come back. Stay here. There is plenty of straw to sleep on."

Geza did not have to think too much on that, but he was desperately hungry. Two Native American Indians who had also been working for the Brick Kiln realized the immigrant's plight.

"Come with us."

They motioned to Geza that they would be getting some food, and would also be returning to spend the night, and like him would be sleeping in the straw as they had been doing all that week. Geza got into the Indian's old model T Ford, and went with them to a grocery store. He bought a lot of baloney and a loaf of bread. They returned and bedded down in the straw for the night. (The baloney and bread lasted him the remaining two days of that week.)

In the morning Geza awoke with a scream, jumping up onto a pallet load of bricks. The startled Indians immediately ran to his assistance, not knowing what made the grown man scream and turn pale, taking refuge above the ground. Geza motioned to the straw bed he had just evacuated, and the Indians saw what it was. They laughed hilariously as they coaxed the frightened white man down from the pallet of bricks.

"It's nothing Gayzus," they said, not capable of pronouncing Geza. "Those snakes won't harm you, they're garter snakes. They want the warmth of your body, that's all. They crawl all over a man at night. They don't mean any harm."

"Like hell," thought Geza. He had heard weird stories about snakes back home in Hungary; that they were capable of crawling into a human's stomach when the person lay sleeping with mouth wide open. They could only be lured out again, so the old wives tale went, if you placed a saucer of milk on the ground next to the sleeping person the following night.

That night, on top a pallet of bricks, Geza constructed a crude manger of boards. He filled the manger with straw, and slept elevated above the ground from then on.

He maintained that job at the Brick Kiln until the winter forced its closing. He bicycled out Monday mornings, and bicycled home Friday or Saturday night, depending on the Kiln's orders for bricks. The pay was good and the family was fed. The Virags considered themselves fortunate.

Geza invited the Indians home a couple of times. In this manner he got a ride home after a hard week's work, as they drove their model T, and he left his bicycle at the brickyard. These two Indians thoroughly enjoyed a home cooked meal, and particularly, Ilona's Hungarian pastries.

There were some men in the Hungarian community that had managed to get employment in the winter months through the Unemployment Office. They suggested that Geza should also go to the 'work site' and ask the supervisor on the work site for a job. When he got there, he asked some of the Hungarian men who were more fluent in the English language, just how to best phrase his desperate request for work. Not knowing the more fluent man had set him up; he proceeded to address the supervisor.

"Me lazy, you crazy, give me a job".

The startled man could only guess how this unfortunate foreigner had been set up to say such a ridiculous thing. "Who told you to say that?" He asked.

Not exactly knowing what the supervisor had meant by this query, Geza looked toward the man who had told him what to say. The man of course was now sorry he had played this rude joke, as the focus of the supervisor's attention immediately went to him. The supervisor asked the English fluent Hungarian if indeed it was he who had put Geza up to saying that ridiculous statement. Sheepishly the man admitted he had.

The supervisor just as quickly hired Geza and fired the joker! Geza now replaced the Hungarian and had work throughout the winter.

In the following spring, the Unemployment office began recruiting laborers for the Department of Public Works (DPW). The DPW had created a 'Jobs' program as a sort of 'Relief' to the unemployed. Instead of getting a subsistence payment for nothing, the men had to work for the Relief! This is when Hamilton had the entire mountainside and the area about the Incline reinforced with huge boulders and brick retaining walls.

The Incline was a vehicle for passenger and freight conveyance, a sort of 'box car' that ran on rails, broadside up the side of the mountain at the head of James Street. There was a fee to be paid of course. A person bought a street car ticket if they wanted to take the Incline up instead of walking up all the stairs or on the road to get to Upper Hamilton where the Orchards and Farms were.

The laborers received a 'script' note from the supervisors at the work sites; the script indicated how many hours the man had worked that day and the man in turn then went to the unemployment office to receive the payment in cash. He did not get paid on site.

Things seemed to be working out well for Ilona's family in Hungary, as it was with Geza's family in Hungary. Because of the hard times Geza and Ilona were having during the years of the Depression, correspondence now came to an unnatural standstill. These two Canadian immigrants had written often, indeed, even sent large amounts of money home to help their respective families. (But no one helped these two in their time of need.)

Worried, now that she had not received any more money, or heard from him, Geza's sister requested the Red Cross to put out a 'search' for him. And the Red Cross did find him easily enough. He wrote her immediately to set her mind at ease. Their family with four children is well; Pál and Emma's family were also well. He also stated that their fortunes had changed, and that they were all out of a job. They now took in boarders (people we now call roomers). He did not tell them everything they had to do to survive the depression; then again, the relatives in Hungary could not understand the changed situation, as they apparently were not suffering similar hardship during this time.

This correspondence back and forth from the North American relatives, both those now in Canada and those in the United States, to those back in Hungary must have generated a communication to those in the United States, from the relatives in Hungary. The Hungarian relatives informed those in the United States about the plight, and hardships experienced by Geza, Ilona, Pál and Emma in Canada.

In this manner Julius and Joseph Valko of Chicago Illinois, became aware of their Canadian relatives joblessness. Their plight suddenly opened an opportunity to these wayward brothers! Julius and Joseph were serious gamblers and were indebted to many of the illicit 'blind pigs' in Chicago for their gambling losses. They immediately fell upon a scheme to help themselves get out of this temporary mess, using Geza and Ilona as their excuse for getting the money to pay off the gambling houses.

Theresa Valko, Ilona's older sister, had married a Hungarian farmer named Molnar, and they lived in Omaha, Nebraska. Theresa and her husband were informed by Julius that they were collecting money from the Hungarian community in Chicago, and from friends at their places of work, to "help out Ilona and the kids". It is stated that Theresa and her husband also contributed to Julius' benevolent "fund".

We found out in later years that Julius and Joseph collected money often, and in large amounts, *but not one penny was ever sent to Ilona and Geza!* Finally, Uncle Julius and his family visited Ilona and Geza in Hamilton, Ontario. Uncle Julius had married a widow named Theresa, and she had bore him two sons, named Julius and Paul. Paul, the youngest, was about seventeen years old in 1937. Uncle

Julius had not seen his sister Ilona since 1908; that is when he and Joe left Hungary. Now he could hardly speak the Hungarian language, so it was an odd experience to hear him talking the Chicago-American slang, and Ilona replying in her native Hungarian. He could understand what she was saying but could not reply in kind.

These American relatives were doing very well and were all employed. Perhaps the depression was now 'easing' out for them in the late thirties. They had a car and could afford to make the trip from Chicago to Hamilton. The American dollar exchange rate in 1937 was very good in terms of the Canadian dollar.

The Chicago Hungarian community was probably putting pressure on Julius with constant enquiries about "Ilona and the kids". This trip was therefore made on fifty percent cordiality to see the relatives, and fifty percent on the sham pretext that Geza was now in a position to pay back some of the loaned money that Uncle Julius and Uncle Joseph had collected throughout the last few years from the Chicago Hungarian community. But, again, no money changed hands between Julius and Geza since Geza had no knowledge of the subterfuge perpetrated by his brother-in-law. And, Julius did not let on to anyone in his family, or the Chicago Hungarian Community; but continued the charade even long after that visit!

It was during this visit that Julius' brother Pál and sister Ilona gave him hell for his heartless cruelty of not making the promised appearance at Windsor in 1924. He had encouraged them to come to America, promising to meet them at the Windsor border crossing. When the time came he was NOT there. They waited in vain, and lost their passports as a result of their desperate effort to get to the USA. Brother Julius took their abuse, offering a lame excuse that he was not at that time an American citizen, and he too was afraid of getting trapped in Canada should he make the trip from Chicago.

"Why didn't you think of that when you wrote us those many letters of encouragement? You were not entirely honest with us. We suffered so horribly and unnecessarily. If only you would have been honest with us. Things would have been easier for us. As it was we were exploited by English speaking people in that Hungarian community. We even lost our passports to a crooked agent"

After all those years some sense of family prevailed.

Blood does run thicker than water, and though Julius may have been forgiven, Ilona and Pál did not forget. The American relatives did visit their Canadian relatives often thereafter.

Meanwhile, Joseph Valko had begun to drink excessively. He gambled most of his wages away, that which he did not spend on drink. He totally ignored the needs of his own wife and family and finally lost his job because of excessive drinking! He lingered around his old Chicago haunts for a while and then moved.

Up North, the rumor had it.

Rumor also indicated that he tried to straighten out his life.

Nobody really cared.

His two daughters were grown up; both were working and living together in a flat. I truly do not know about his wife's fate. Some say that she had support from her daughters for a while and she may have remarried in her later years.

The last news about Joe was that he was found...dead. Someone may have killed him to rob him. This would indicate that once again he had money. Who knows for sure? The strongest report, and probably most nearest to the truth was that the gamblers caught up with him and wiped the slate clean of his debts!

No relative claimed the body.

When a grown man becomes an alcoholic; when he gambles his savings away, and what he doesn't squander on booze he drops to the flip of a card; he becomes a derelict.

514 ~ *Anthony E. Virag*

He had asked Julius to go with him, up North. Julius was not quite that foolish. He was not an alcoholic, and he did stop his gambling habit, perhaps after he saw what it did to his brother Joe. And perhaps, so that he could stop this deceitful charade of "aiding Ilona and the kids". Julius did stay with his family. Julius was Joe's last contact with the real world. Once Joe left Chicago no one heard from him, and, as was stated before, no one cared.

1936–1945
EPISODES

To supplement the household income Ilona began to work also, and care of the children fell to the oldest, her daughter Helen who was about nine years old. Ilona worked at the Hamilton Cotton Mill. She worked hard, long hours, and did not get ample pay for the effort, nor did most of the foreign women who worked there. As with most non-union shops, the owners, managers and supervisors could do as they wished, and the foremen did play favorites among the women who worked for them. Within a year, I believe it was 1936, the women walked out en masse. They went on strike and picketed the mill.

Ilona was on this picket line, along with many mothers, but she was the only one that brought her child. I was about five years old then, but I still remember how confused I was; happy to be walking hand in hand with Mom, but confused by the large number of women. And I remember these Mill buildings, of which there were three, each one occupied a complete city block, with an alleyway running through them. I remember one young male mill worker, who evidently was the spokesman for the strikers, appeared at a side entrance in one of these alleyways to one of the three Mill buildings. With him were two well dressed rather rotund, Company spokesmen.

The crowd of women fell silent, as the two Company men helped the young man up onto a barrel. He addressed the women; he must have been negotiating inside the mill.

I found out later, on the way home with Mom, that they got a nickel an hour pay raise, along with grievance representation. I do not recall if they formed a union at that time but I doubt it.

During King George VI and Queen Mary's visit to Hamilton in 1938, I was sitting on Dad's shoulders to see over the heads of the crowd. The Royal Train pulled into the Canadian National Railroad (CNR) station on James Street, just a few blocks from our home on Bay Street.

There were all sorts of souvenir hawkers selling their wares.

The one I remember most well, because I could not have one, was a periscope. Dad did not spend his money freely on novelty toys. The periscope was excellent for short people, and children, to look over the heads of the crowd in front of them. It was simply a rectangular tube of cardboard with a mirror angled at 45 degrees at the bottom-viewing end, looking up into a mirror angled at 45 degrees in the opposite direction at the top, to sight forward. It provided an acceptable field of view.

After the Royal visit, adults in the Hungarian community, and adults in the population at large, talked about the "imminent war". The visit by the King and Queen they said was simply a morale builder, so Canadians would now relate to this common tie with their English cousins who were nearer to the threat of war.

Times were still very bad for many families. But as the World moved nearer to another war, the economy picked up, and not too many people were without a job. Geza finally got a steady job at one of the many foundries around Hamilton Bay; he worked at the Iron Foundry, located between the railroad tracks and the Bay Shore. My brother John and I would go down to visit Geza, Dad, at work when he worked Saturdays. Business for this Foundry was picking up and six days a week was not uncommon

As stated above, we lived on Bay Street then, the Iron Foundry was a few blocks down from there and past the 'Hamilton Bridge Works'. We crossed several sets of railroad tracks as a short cut to get to the Iron Foundry. It was a novelty for the foundry supervisor, and the foundry security to have the worker's kids come down to see their Dad work. Security did let us in, and Dad gave each of us a shovel too. We worked the best we could for a ten and eight year old, and tried to help. We shifted the once-used 'green sand' from cooled molds, by shoveling it through primitive, half-inch, and then quarter-inch screens. This sand would be reclaimed, to be used by our Dad in the new mould he was preparing.

He was a good moulder, and he would sometimes work on large pit molds about ten feet deep.

The first Saturday we called at the Foundry, the supervisor was so tickled with the boldness of these "foreign" kids that he gave us a tour of the plant. I also remember that Dad got a raise that year, 1939, he would now be making eighty-nine cents (0.89¢) an hour.

It was also in 1939, when he got a letter from the Hungarian Government recalling him to his Homeland with an offer of military rank. It seemed exciting then, to an eight year old, with all the talk of the coming war. The letter stated that Hungary was in need of its veterans and experienced soldiers, particularly those that had an 'upper education'.

Geza's degree acquired in Hungary had done him absolutely no good in Canada. Prospective employers would not accept his diploma's validation! Now here it was, Hungary was offering him an opportunity for the good life once again if he would return. After all that hard work and sacrifice he and Ilona went through getting established comfortably in Canada, they chose not to return to Hungary.

They thought of their four children and the safety of being remote from Europe where the war would erupt.

They made a good choice.

Gergély and his family struggled to overcome the stigma of 'Russian Displaced" persons, they were called 'Muscovites' by some rude and envious neighbors. With hard work they built a house with a large room, and another nice room adjoining the main house, on the land of Geza's 1921 military allotment.

They made the land return them a good living, planting a lot of nut trees, and grapevines. As he began to prosper, he bought another adjoining parcel of land. The home began to take on a look of the Old Virag homestead in which Gergély and Geza were born; as it looked before their father squandered almost everything.

In the summer one could sit out in the cool shade of the grape arbor. Gergély made that in the shape of a house, built of lathes that provided the support for the climbing grapevines. When the vines were fully matured, they enclosed the entire structure to give it the appearance of a green-leaved-house. Yes! He had made everything himself, just like he and Geza remembered their boyhood home.

He and his family worked hard on the land that Geza gave him, and also those additional acres acquired with the financial assistance coming from Geza in the early 1930s. Like a true brother, he halved the revenue of his earnings with his sister Erzsi.

In late 1939, when others his age (45 years old), were conscripted, the authorities did not want Gergély. They did not trust this 'Muscovite'.

"He will only desert and return to Russia anyway," they thought.

In this manner Gergély was, fortunately, ignored. It is amazing! How he disliked the Russian Communists, he actually hated communism, yet, the Hungarian Government was not concerned with what he showed 'on the surface'. His sister's husband was three years older at 48, and they took him.

At the Szombathély railroad station, during the war, not one bomb struck the network of tracks! The planes were coming in too fast (these must have been fighter bombers), the bombs hit the nearby cemetery, and blasted the graves open with tombstones flying in all directions. The aircraft always came 'in' from over the city, rather than over the open country approaches to the city, which would have been more favorable for dropping their bombs on the targeted tracks. Perhaps, one can surmise, that approaching the tracks from open country, made them easily spotted, and easier targets for anti-aircraft guns. Approaching from over the city, they could not be seen by the gunners, until they cleared the city buildings to bomb the station, and then they were anxious to pull up and get out.

There were over a dozen sets of tracks and the bombs didn't come within ten yards of anyone of them! The train station wasn't even damaged!

The Russians had a better opportunity to destroy these tracks when their infantry entered Hungary in 1945, but they did not choose to do so. They were moving forward at such a fast pace they thought it necessary to keep the tracks intact. They used the railroad to move troops and supplies forward.

Yes! They could have easily destroyed the tracks with their artillery but the Russians did not try to bomb this valuable railhead.

As it turned out, the retreating Germans destroyed more tracks when they pulled back out of Hungary than the allies had in their poorly directed bombing. Explosives were set off on many of the main lines leading towards Germany. But the retreating troops did not have time to destroy every track.

With the American forces involved, their aircraft neared Hungary as the war was drawing to a close. Geza's sister and brother tell the story of German anti-aircraft fire shooting down a black fighter pilot. His buddy, perhaps the wingman, flew extremely low, following the downed pilots aircraft 'in'. Then he made several passes over the downed plane, which had careened and crashed to later burn, having skidded through farm fields into the side of a woodlot. After several passes, with no response from the downed pilot, and the aircraft beginning to burn, the buddy flew away.

The townsfolk however, quickly ran and retrieved the body from the airplane before it was totally engulfed in the flames. They gave the black pilot a respectable burial and retold that story for many years after.

"Yes! The buddy did all but set his plane down, and he may have done that too...if the soft farms fields had permitted landing."

The townsfolk came out eagerly after every bombing run to see if the aircraft had succeeded in destroying the tracks. It became a curiosity, more like a game. They also watched the dueling aircraft with fascination, and the anti-aircraft trying to down the incoming allied planes.

The railroad skirted beside and through those woods. It is possible that the town and the woods were formidable obstacles for low flying fighters to unload their bombs accurately on target. Many farmers continued to work their fields, until they realized that a battle was about to unfold. Some of the pilots, eager to unload their bombs and get the hell out of there, dropped their bombs on the open fields where peasants worked...he was sworn at and considered a son-of-a-bitch.

Though the citizens couldn't truly blame them, these pilots were no better than their WWI counterpart who unloaded their bombs on helpless towns and villages. They didn't want to return with bombs still attached to their airframes. It is possible that, in their righteous frustrations, the pilots deliberately wanted to strike something; even if it was an enemy civilian.

One hundred WWI aircraft did not do the damage that two WWII aircraft could do to the ground troops and civilian population. In WWI, infantry rifle fire could bring down an airplane. A machine gun firing from the ground could damage the fabric of many aircraft, one at a time, and cause them to head home. WWII aircraft were faster and thus more difficult to hit. If they were "shot up", cockpit armament protected the pilot, and he could still affectively continue the fight or make it back to his home base.

When the Russians "liberated" Hungary in 1945, Gergély, and many World War I veterans that had learned Russian during their internment as prisoners in that war, became interpreters for the Russian Occupation troops. Many of his Hungarian neighbors flocked to Gergély then for help, and whatever assistance they could get to survive. They reasoned that he could perhaps plead their cause during this period of frustration and bewilderment.

Poor Gergély!

He was too understanding and sympathetic, most eager to do what he could to help his countrymen, and establish a sympathetic and compromising environment within the ranks of the occupiers. Not many Hungarians were as fluent in Russian as he and his Russian Family. The Russian Officers and soldiers soon learned that he had married a Russian girl, and therefore began to rely with more confidence upon him. As a result, his two daughters also became interpreters, and, if required from a pressing Russian occupation agenda, his wife was available to assist also in Hungarian/Russian language requirements.

He had no animosities toward his Hungarian neighbors having wizened considerably since 1931, and, in spite of his tenure in that horse stall on the Old Kulak's land in Russia, he had no animosity toward the Russian "Liberators" either. Gergély reflected that all men are the same. Suspicious of what they could not or would not understand, human nature makes them what they are.

"Damn it! One cannot escape fate," he exclaimed. "I escaped from the sons-of-bitches because they persecuted my family, and because they threatened my life. Now, here they are; didn't they follow me home? After all these years they have caught up with me. If they carried a record of my activities in Russia during 1922-1931, with them, I'm sure they would not be so trusting of my family, if only because we escaped them. But that was long ago, and they are too intent on pursuing this war to concern themselves with revenge on a single upstart during the formative years of Communism. That is surely forgotten."

Truth is; if they had known the story of his family's escape from communist Russia, they would not have trusted him as an interpreter.

During the Russian advance through Vasvar, Porpacz and the neighboring villages, the advancing soldiers respected the rights of the civilian populace. However, they did need food and lodging, and they preferred to sleep within the Hungarian homes, or their barns. They had spent too many restless nights without a roof over their heads, and now, as time permitted, they expected the civilians to extend a kindness to the "liberators".

Most households co-operated, no matter how reluctantly, but there were three households in Porpacz, that had out-wardly refused the soldiers food and lodging. The advance infantry 'marked' those homes by writing, "these people are against us" in creosote on the yard fence, or the side of the house itself. The occupation troops that followed would "administer" justice to these households. The soldiers did not execute civilians at will, again, because of orders not to aggravate the populace. But angry soldiers could be hateful, just as hateful as the hostile citizens; the troops wanted revenge upon those who refused their comrades the simple courtesy of food and lodging. These troops then, deliberately took the vegetables from the family gardens, eggs from under the hens, and many times the hens as well!

This food was the livelihood for women and children of the household. It is easy to conclude that, many Hungarians simply disbelieved that any request from these soldiers was meant to be an act of friendliness; indeed, they feared every action of these liberators.

When the village came under Russian martial law, the three households and their families were brought to account for their actions and refusal to co-operate with the liberation army. Gergély was the Russian/Hungarian interpreter appointed by the court for the hearings. In truth, he pleaded sincerely and understandingly for these families.

"If they refused food to the soldiers it is probably because they did not have food enough for themselves, or they refused lodging to enemy troops because they could not trust them. The troops had, after all, stolen, looted and misbehaved in many villages as they came across Hungary, even when they were afforded the lodging hospitality of the farmers. Under similar circumstances could any sensible judge find such a family guilty?"

With this type of rationale, the lives of these families were spared. After all these years, his Hungarian neighbors finally accepted him, and no longer would they think of him or his family as 'communist Muscovites'. They began to think of this family as very useful and humanitarian neighbors. He had finally earned their respect!

As the Russian occupation continued, because of his integrity he earned the respect of the Russian military and occupation officials as well.

There were Hungarian army officers, now prisoners, who professed to fluency in speaking Russian to get a more favorable treatment from the occupiers. Some may have been able to understand the language, but were weak in translating it properly into the Hungarian equivalent, or, knowing the Hungarian, they failed to translate a proper Russian equivalent. The Hungarian (Magyar) language is a very difficult language to learn fluently, and then consider trying to turn these words into the equally difficult *Cyrillic* of the Russian words.

As it turned out, there were some Hungarian officers who were deliberately causing mischief and misunderstanding hoping to foment hostility among the civilian population toward the Russian occupiers. They were indifferent to what the consequences of their misinterpretation may cause, and hoped to embarrass the occupation forces, or cause them to exercise injustice that would create a strain on Russian/ Hungarian relations.

Gergély's daughter was present when one of these officers was translating Russian into Hungarian for a particular Russian administrator. Appalled at what she heard spoken in Russian, and how the Hungarian had transcribed it into Hungarian, she felt compelled to interrupt and declare to the Russian administrator that the document was not conveying what he intended. The administrators asked the girl, "What does the translation state? Read it to me in the Hungarian now, and put that into the new Russian equivalent."

Upon hearing a totally different and contradicting intent, the Russian was so angered that he ordered the officer to be shot! The consequences of the misinterpretation were grave enough to be treated with such severity. Indeed, if Gergély's daughter had not immediately ran for her father's help, the officer would have been shot. The administrator accused the officer of willful and malicious attempt to cause the Russian occupation forces grief. He was creating a situation that would falsely have angered the Hungarian populace into revolt at the Russian declaration. The Russian administrator reacted violently against the premeditated action of this officer.

Gergély painstakingly, and in a most diplomatic manner explained to this angered Russian that the Hungarian officer did not knowingly translate the communication incorrectly. It was his ineptness with the Russian Cyrillic alphabet that caused the blunder, and of course, Gergély easily proved the Hungarian's ineptness.

The Russian Administrator immediately discharged the man. With his life threatened, the Hungarian Officer was most willing to return to the prison compound.

So, Gergély again saved a countryman's life. The Hungarian officer was thankful, to say the least, and did not challenge the proof of his ineptness, rightly or wrongly. He had certainly put his life in a precarious position, but he later admitted to Gergély in confidence that he felt, as an officer, it was his duty to undermine the enemy.

The Russians now had more respect for Gergély and his family because his daughter had turned what would have been a most unfortunate "public spectacle" into an acceptable clarity for the citizens. The daughters were often chauffeured about from one assignment to another, and were seen in many counties under Russian escort. The Russian's demonstrated their confidence in this family, and showed their gratitude with clothes for the girls, dresses for mother, and suits for Gergély and son. The grateful Russians showered them sinfully with all sorts of gifts, and money—too much money.

The excesses were distributed to the many Virag relatives.

The Hungarian soldiers now captive disliked their captors. There was not quite the same humane, underlying factor that is pleasantly recalled by World War I veterans. In World War II, most German soldiers and their allies in Western Europe hated the Russian military and considered Russians a "sub human" race. They were taught to make their enemy miserable, and they were taught to be efficient killers of Russians.

In WWI, there was not so much hate (a paradox of war), during lulls in fighting, both sides came out of the trenches and fraternized. Wars had not been fought on such a grand scale before and for such protracted periods of stalemate as the trench warfare illustrated. At Christmas a truce was declared on some fronts. It seems that soldiers understood one another's misfortune, no one really wanted to be there, no one really wanted to kill.

Yes!

It seems that man had learned to create misery on a grander scale in WWII.

TERROR IN EUROPE: PEACE IN CANADA

I n 1944 while the Nazis continued to round up the Jewish people for the 'Final Solution', some Hungarians cheered at what was going on. Many others stood quietly aside, afraid of what they saw happening about them, to their neighbors and old friends. Still others boldly and directly assisted their Jewish friends by concealing them, or helped spirit them out of the country. But too many Hungarians and Jews also, just simply did not believe what was happening. The Nazis or S.S went systematically through the large cities, block by block. Even with this unfolding as evidence before them, the Jews who were several city blocks from those being rounded up, went about the business of their lives as usual; thinking that what they saw happening there, could never happen here, while it continued to happen, block by block in the thorough and efficient German manner. They could have acted; they could have fled for their lives, but many did not.

Geza's sister Barbara had married a man who was of Jewish heritage from many generations back, and now the Hungarian Arrow Cross (same as German SS) pounded on their door. She would not open to them, so they broke down the door and dragged her husband out onto the street.

There, in the center of the road, she tore into the uniformed men, pleading for her husband's life while he cowered on his knees behind her skirt, not believing this women's defiance.

The uniformed men did not believe her defiance either!

"Good woman, we do not have orders to take you. We have been told to take him."

"You will not! If you dare to take him...you take me also, but I will fight you to my death!"

These police looked incredulously at the determined woman and left her in the center of the road with her man still clinging to her skirt. She had, at peril of her life saved his. But all such people were not as fortunate. The Arrow Cross was NOT merciful.

A villager's twenty-six year old son, Swartz Jenö, a Rislinger Jew (Rislinger Zsido) was caught and rounded up with the Jewish family whom he had been visiting in one of the small towns. They in turn, along with several other Jews, were lined up on the edge of a long pit and shot. While the other victims fell into the mass burial pit, Jenö fell where he had been shot, on top, and at the edge of the pit.

The officer in charge of the firing squad walked to him and saw that Jenö was now bleeding profusely. He kicked Jenö in the side, but the boy did not move; he hardly had a breath. The officer must have considered him as good as dead and, amazingly continued to walk the length of the burial pit. He then shouted an order, and the troops in the firing squad marched away.

Just as suddenly as the troops left, a bulldozer began to push dirt into the open pit along with bodies that had, like Jenö, fallen where they were. It worked its way back and forth, dumping dirt over the bodies.

As it neared Jenö, the engine noise and trembling ground aroused him. He crawled desperately a considerable distance out of the way of the bulldozer's path, and amazingly, into thick underbrush. There under the refuge of the sheltering shrubbery, he slipped back into unconsciousness.

That night, Hungarians combing the area for survivors found him and spirited him to a sympathetic doctor. Jenö lived to talk about it, thanks to those friends, and was still alive in 1963.

In another instance, during a Russian bombardment of the twin cities Buda-Pest, the civilians crowded into a cellar for protection from the barrage. There were many old couples and many young couples with children seeking sanctuary in this rubble of a home. They were about twenty-three frightened souls, with them an old WW1 Major of the Hungarian Army and his wife. Among them was a Jewish youth whom they knew, his family was...who knows where. They closed the heavy oak door behind them and sat cowering in the darkness against the walls, hoping no shell would find them.

Amidst the sound of shells bursting, there was suddenly a loud pounding on the door. Wide eyed and frightened they wondered, could it be some other unfortunate seeking protection in this cellar? Three of the younger men hurriedly opened the heavy door and seven youthful boys in the dreadful Arrow Cross Police uniforms burst in. The oldest uniformed youth could not have been more than seventeen years old. Those with him were of equivalent ages or younger. They had pounded the door with rifle butts to be heard above the shelling outside.

"Who is in charge of this group?" demanded the older youth.

"I am." Exclaimed the old Major, and he introduced himself as a veteran of WWI, whereupon the uniformed youths appeared to relax their tension.

"Do you wish to spend the time with us in this crude shelter until the barrage lifts?" asked the Major.

"No sir. We have a job to do!"

"And what is it, that you risk your life in this hellish bombardment?"

"We are searching for Jews, are there any here among these people?"

"There are not. I know all these people. They are my neighbors, and all of them are good Christians, I assure you."

The seventeen-year old leader accepted this answer, saluted the Major, and astoundingly, ordered his 'men' out, to continue to 'do their rounds'.

When the barrage lifted, the small group left the refuge of the cellar, at which time the Jewish youth thanked the Major, sincerely shaking his hand.

"It is insanely remarkable that such a foolish regime is so blinded by this purpose, it sends children soldiers out under an artillery barrage to continue rounding up Jews. Don't they know the war is ending? Can't they leave well enough alone?" remarked the major.

The Jewish youth replied, "They fear the end. They are, as you say blind to the purpose, and blame the Jewish race now for their defeat and failure, as well as for starting the war. And now my old friend, I must leave this city immediately."

"But why, the Russians will soon be here."

"Do you think these Secret Services will let up? You saw how determined they are. I must leave, and go into the countryside where they seem not to be as efficient. I can still find places to hide there. God bless you."

And the young man left.

Asztalös Károly was now about forty-three years old; the Good Squire Simon was about seventy. Károly was now only too happy to report 'Simon the Jew', to the secret police. The Arrow Cross wasted no time; the Good Squire was ordered to pack what he could onto a single horse drawn cart, and get out of his home, and off his land.

With his elderly wife, and two middle aged daughters sitting on the cart, he was escorted out of his ancestral home, and away.

"Will no one help me...my family? Will no one protest? Have I not been a good neighbor, have I not been fair to you?" With tear filled eyes and seated on the tailgate of the cart, he pleaded with both arms outstretched as the cart passed between the people standing on both sides of the road.

The neighbors were as much in fear and disbelief as the squire was. Many had tears in their eyes also, but not one dared to stand in the way of the Arrow Cross or attempt to intervene on the Good Squire's behalf.

They feared for their lives.

Only Károly reacted.

He stood in the middle of the road, looking after the receding cart. The Squire sitting in back, with feet hanging down, arms still outstretched in a pleading gesture, his voice slowly ranging out of hearing.

Asztalös Károly smiled.

He had finally succeeded to satisfy his lifelong grudge against the Squire. Thinking back upon that time in 1908, when the Squire had mockingly whipped his behind for grazing the family cows in the Squire's hay field, then reflecting to the 1919, Communist revolution, brief as it was, and his altercation with the Squire again at that time; to Károly's embarrassment and final dismissal from the Squire's service.

Károly had his revenge.

As unright and as cruel as it was, Károly felt justified in this last, deadly humiliation of the one who had always been tolerant, and even-handed with his neighbors.

"Yes! I showed him," gloated Karoly.

In 1944-45, when the Russians came into Hungary, Sule Jenö was then 52 years of age and he thought seriously about fighting them, as he had in 1914-1917, but thought this way for only for a short interval. He now owned a little hotel and was afraid that his family would lose everything if it were taken from him. It is true, values change with time, but wisdom *is* the better part of valor.

Gergély told Geza that Jenö often reflected on how he had seen Geza in 1914 as a fourteen year old, when Jenö was twenty-one on his way to the Russian front. And how surprised Jenö had been on his return to active duty in Italy in 1917, to see Geza on the Italian front; he remembered that the 'boy' grew up too fast, having to go to war at age seventeen.

"Boy, how he swore when we drank together in the post war years," admitted Gergély.

"God bless the sons-of-bitches," he would say. "I suffered enough for my homeland during the war years."

When Geza visited "home" in 1962, after the 1956 uprising, he told Gergély, "If you had wanted, I could have sent you money so that you and your family would join me and my family in Canada. Together brother, we could have made it easier."

But of course that was not meant to be.

Just after the war, in 1945, Geza decided to move to a farm. From the European experience in the aftermath of 1918, Geza feared a recession or something as serious as unemployment in which the family would again suffer hard times. He could not subject his family to that again; once through a Depression is enough! He felt correctly that, on the farm we could at least provide for ourselves. (We did more than provide for ourselves, we prospered beyond his expectations!) We moved to a 96 acre farm in Waterford, Ontario.

Simon Kovacs (Geza's friend re: bicycling for jobs in Hamilton) had already relocated his family on a farm in a little village called Bealton. It was, we found out, indeed a small village, being nothing more than a cross-road intersection with a General Store on one corner, a Church on another corner across from the General Store, and the Country School House on a third corner; a ten acre field complimented the fourth corner where the school kids played baseball.

Bealton was approximately 9-10 miles from the 96 acre farm my father chose to settle on. Simon and his family had preceded us by one year and as a result made acquaintances of his neighbors, one of which was a Hungarian farmer named Paul Evan. Paul had been in WWI on the Russian front, captured and imprisoned he learned the language before returning to Hungary in 1919. I do not recall when he migrated to Canada.

Paul was a very capable man and had gained fluency in at least six languages, speaking English fluently. I can imagine that he did as well speaking the others; one of them which fascinated me was Indian Iroquois. (The other five were Ukrainian, Hungarian, German, Russian and English) He had picked up the Iroquois while going to the Six Nations Indian Reserve where he went many times when he needed hired help on the farm.

He was held in great respect by the Chief because of his benevolence in paying a fair wage to those Indians that were hired.

He was also a very wealthy manager, running a 'garden crop' farm and Dairy Farm with his two sons Steve and Andy. In the fall his sons drove a large two-ton stake truck throughout the outlying counties to buy up the cucumber crops off farmers, making two trips per week, or whenever the cucumber picking required; this proved to be a very prosperous business as well. Paul Evan made a good profit in reselling the cucumbers to the pickle factories, one of which was in Waterford.

Simon introduced Geza to Paul and the three men got along extremely well, visiting back and forth among their homes reminiscing about the Old Country and current events in general. We children also helped with picking Paul's tomato crop that fall. So it was that when Geza wanted to fill his barn with milking cows to gain a milk contract from the Villa Nova Dairy, he approached the wealthy farmer for a loan of a few hundred dollars with which he would buy livestock for the almost empty barn. He had already bought a few cows, but there was to be a farmer's auction that week and Geza wanted to buy a few more cows before the winter settled upon us.

In a blunt and surprising manner Paul refused to give Geza a loan, with an emphatic "no". He also articulated with his right arm embracing and striking his chest, "Virag, first and foremost what is mine will be mine, and secondly, what I acquire is mine"...embracing and striking his chest again..."and third, what I profit from re-selling is mine", again embracing and striking his chest, "and what is left is for my family alone", embracing and striking his chest one last time.

"I respect your frankness Paul, and apologize for embarrassing you with my request. You have money; I have not. I thought as countrymen we can be approached to help one another."

"Well, you were obviously wrong."

"Let this embarrassment not interfere with our friendship."

"Certainly not; we can still be good neighbors and friends."

Following this unexpected rebuttal, it was a surprise to see Paul Evan drive his car into our barnyard as we were doing chores in the horse stable early that morning. He got out of his car and approached Geza as Geza stepped out of the barn to greet him.

"Virag, come with me. Get into the car."

"Where are we going?"

"We're going for a ride; I want your advice on something." (This was all the more surprising, that Paul Evans would ask my father's advice even after he had turned my father down for a small loan.)

The story related to us later on that Saturday from Geza: Paul drove him to the Farmer's Auction. As the cows were led into the corral individually to be bid on for the sale, Paul would ask, "Virag what do you think of that one?" As things continued throughout the day, Paul bid on seven excellent cows, and when the auction ended my Dad complimented him on the prime cows he had purchased.

Paul stated, "they are not mine Virag; they are yours."

"What? How? Thank you Paul...I am confused, but you know I am grateful. Now, how am I going to get them home?"

"Don't worry yourself. Andy will be here with the truck as soon as he unloads it at the pickle factory."

And that is how Geza began his milking herd. The milk money from the dairy provided for paying Paul back the price of the cows. Needless to say Geza and Paul's friendship was cemented for life.

HAPPINESS; THEN HEARTACHE

In the spring of 1947 we were invited to a wedding in Hamilton in which our cousin Helen Valko was to be a bridesmaid. Helen was very excited about the wedding, very mature for her fifteen years, a tall five feet eight inch young lady she would be sixteen in a few weeks. She looked beautiful in the pink, strapless gown. The odd thing about this gown (I thought it was odd), was the ridiculously large black bow from just below the breasts to end at the belt line with trailing tails reaching to the knees. All the bridesmaids had this 'black bow' regardless of the color of their gowns. The various colors really were something however; there was a pale blue gown, a light green (aqua), and another peach colored. There were about six bridesmaids all with different colored gowns, and one maid of honor.

The bride therefore had a rainbow of colors around her to amplify her white gown.

But our family, and Helen's family looked only on Helen. We were happy for her because it was her first 'formal outing'. She relished in it, and was so full of life. I could see her now, smiling and just bubbling over with a lively spirit, whispering and giggling with the other bridesmaids.

My father and mother, brother John and I had to leave later that evening before the wedding festivities and dancing actually ended. The cows had to be milked early next morning; farming cannot be put off!

536 ~ *Anthony E. Virag*

A few months after this wedding we got word that Helen was sick, very sick. She had contracted tuberculosis! This was devastating news to all of us, particularly devastating to her father, for he had lost his beloved first wife to the same dreaded disease. But medical science had come a long way since 1921-22; surely Helen could be cured.

In those days we had many friends who had contracted tuberculosis and had been confined to the "Hamilton Sanatorium" until they got well. Some had their weakened lung collapsed and removed, or the infected portion of a lung removed. They survived and continued to live a productive life.

Recovery in the "late forties" was quite common.

Doctors assured the family that Helen would be well and back in school that September of 1947. The same doctors *confined her to bed at home,* under her mother's care, coming occasionally throughout the week to administer drugs and "tap" spinal fluid from her. We didn't know what was happening, or why she was not sent to the Sanatorium as we knew others had recovered there. Not having the success he had expected with the home confinement, the doctor finally transferred her to a hospital for a more intense regimen of treatment!

I remember Aunt Emma telling me that Helen would like to see me, so the next time I was in town I did go with Aunt Emma to see Helen in the hospital. She looked terrible, and was completely "out of it". A nurse came into the room and demanded to know what we were doing there. I told her we were related and that Aunt Emma was the patient's mother. The nurse would have none-of-it and brusquely ushered us out of the comatose girl's room. I am certain Helen was not aware of our visit. I truly regret not visiting her when she was still cognizant of visitors; but I also regret seeing her as she was.

A few weeks later she died.

She was just sixteen years old!

Again we visited the relatives in Hamilton for this final farewell of a much loved young lady. Helen apparently had sensed her fate and had discussed it with her mother for she wanted to be buried in her bridesmaid's gown. She looked so peaceful, so beautiful in that gown, lying there in the coffin as though asleep; a sleeping beauty waiting for some prince to awaken her.

Aunt Emma was terribly distraught, as religious as she may have been; nonetheless she said many things totally beyond religious understanding.

"Why did God take my only daughter? There are other families of four children; could He not have taken one of them?"

This reference to a family of four children was not a figment of my imagination. She actually meant my parents' four children! God forgive her, she would rather it had been one of my sisters, or one of us boys.

Uncle Pál was suffering silently through it all, just as he had one generation ago because of this dreaded disease; no doubt reflecting with a broken heart. And surely he was going through all the same soul-searching questions *of that time and now again*, with the all too familiar remorse. He had 'run away' from it then, to erase the memory, and here it was back again to open the old wounds, renewing the old pain. It was the same cursed disease that now took Helen. Why, he thought, could it not have taken him instead of Helen? He had escaped the memories and heartaches once by leaving his native birthplace.

Where could he escape to now that death had taken Helen?

Several weeks later I visited them in that big home, now empty of a precious soul. I had taken the trolley from Waterford to Brantford; the usual routine... a bus from Brantford to Hamilton. Taking a streetcar from the bus station on King Street, it turned down James Street going south, and I walked the three short familiar blocks to their home from the James Street car stop.

Uncle Pál was glad to see me. Aunt Emma was courteous, and hospitable. I do remember the next morning being awakened by Uncle Pál; as I groggily opened my eyes I was surprised. He was standing with a bottle of whiskey in his left hand, a shot glass full in his right hand.

"Sit up! Drink this. It will get your blood moving."

He handed the shot glass to me as I sat upright in bed.

"Come now, bottoms up."

I slammed the shot down. Boy! It immediately popped the 'sleepers' out of my eyes and I handed the shot glass back to him.

"Good. Now get cleaned up, dress, and come down for breakfast."

I did as I was told. When I got downstairs to the kitchen, Uncle Pál was sitting at the opposite end of the table. Aunt Emma had a smile on her face.

"Sit down there," she indicated, opposite Uncle Pál where another shot of whiskey waited. "I'll get your eggs and bacon. Do you want coffee?"

"Yes!" I blurted. "But what's with this whiskey?"

"Drink it. It will aid your digestion," replied my uncle.

Again I did as I was told, and it made me more eager to eat my breakfast. Finally my uncle got up, put his jacket on, and offered me another shot.

"No thanks uncle Pál. I've had enough;" whereupon he slammed the shot down; his third that I knew. He kissed Aunt Emma as she handed him the lunch bucket, and he went out the door.

I have, often since then, thought about this 'drinking' before leaving for work. I have met other men in my lifetime that did the same, and I think I have figured it out. My Uncle *hated his job!* He was doing the work of three men in the foundry, but when he asked for a raise they turned him down. He knew they were taking advantage of him, a 'foreigner' and one with his great strength. But what options did he have? He could not get a better job now at his age.

He had to bear up to the mental abuse and the thankless hard work, so he reinforced himself before going to work.

I am sure that there are many men like him today who are good to their families, suffer alone and endure a hateful job to provide for their children. Who knows what mental anguish such men carry? Let us not put guilt upon them for their behavior. They have their 'cross to carry' and are doing it in a manner that has worked for them without destroying the family.

Uncle Pál suffered many demons, losing his first love, now his only daughter to the same curse of tuberculosis. Perhaps the head trauma from his accident caused headaches from his laborious and torturous thinking. Yet he continued to work everyday at a most hateful and thankless job. We could not imagine what a troubled mind and aching heart he lived with.

As it is with many families having lost a loved one that has left many endearing memories in a home, they now wanted to move. The familiar surroundings only continued to be a reminder of the life that once shared those familiar rooms. Uncle Pál, Aunt Emma and their young son Paul moved to a spacious, one story "ranch style house" on McNab Street, not far from the street car stop that I had often used on James Street. It was now also more convenient for Uncle Pál to catch the street car to go to work.

In early 1948, I again took the trolley from Waterford to Brantford. My brother John had driven me to the Waterford Trolley station. From Brantford I took a bus to Hamilton, and in Hamilton I took that familiar James Street car to the stop close to McNab Street, from which I walked to my uncle's home. They were giving my father a $3,000 loan to buy a tractor and I was to carry the cash back the next day. I did have a chance to visit with my friends however, since I arrived at mid-day and that night would be sleeping at my uncle's home.

When I came in later that evening I was to sleep in a bedroom next to Aunt Emma and Uncle Pál's bedroom which had adjoining French double door, closed now for mutual privacy. The streetlight shone through my front window giving sufficient light to undress, so I did not turn on the room lights as I did not want the lights to awaken them.

What suddenly startled me was a picture of my cousin Helen. In the darkened room *that picture was bright* while all the other pictures on the dresser were indistinguishable! I puzzled only momentarily as I undressed, then I really got a fright!

Standing in a dark corner was an apparition; it was Helen in her bridesmaid gown!

The hair on the back of my neck bristled upright.

I looked about the room, was it my imagination? The light from the street lamp radiated light to the left of that corner of the room. The apparition was in the darkened corner to the right of the window.

I was seeing a ghost!

I could not be mistaken; though the face was not clearly detailed. (I dared not look too intently). She stood there in her pink gown with that ridiculous *black bow* in front.

I was frightened, and jumped into bed, pulling the covers over my head I wondered, what did she want? What did this vision foretell?

I was to find out in the morning.

When I awoke the next morning, it was because I heard voices in the kitchen. It was Aunt Emma talking unusually loud to Uncle Pál; this seemed strange to me because they were not arguing. I thought it might be her subtle way of awakening me. So I dressed quickly, washed up, and joined them in the kitchen.

She continued her conversation with my uncle. Still in a voice which I thought was louder than her normal conversational voice, as she put eggs, bacon and toast in front of me. I sat down, and she poured me a cup of coffee. Sitting across from my uncle, I proceeded to eat the hearty breakfast, thinking that Uncle Pál may be having a hard of hearing problem this morning. As I ate the food in front of me, I noticed *he was having trouble with his knife and fork.* He could not grasp the knife.

He looked at me and mumbled something that sounded like, "son of a gun", as he tried to push the knife, which was now on the table, with his right hand.

He could not pick it up!

I looked at his pathetic effort, and looked into his eyes as he looked confusedly into mine. He could not finish breakfast! He sagged, his back against the chair, and began to mumble incoherently in an attempt to talk.

I dropped my fork, got up, and ran after my aunt who had gone into their bedroom.

"Come quick. Uncle Pál is having trouble!"

We both ran back into the kitchen just as my uncle was attempting to stand up. Once he had pushed the chair aside he had trouble standing on his own, and he had to grasp the table to keep from falling. None-the-less he staggered to the kitchen counter where his lunch bucket was.

He was attempting to go to work!

Aunt Emma and I went immediately to support him. He tried to push us away, to fight us off, but now he knew he needed our support, because he was sagging to the floor.

One arm over my shoulder and one arm over my aunt's shoulder, together we got him into the bedroom .We then helped him onto the bed.

My aunt was distraught and very much at her wits end. She must have realized she had talked excessively loud to him in the morning because he appeared not to respond, and this current behavior indicated why.

What was he going through?

She told me to go to the neighbor to phone for a doctor. I immediately ran next door, told the lady what was happening, and ran back to see if I could help my aunt with my uncle. He was still making an effort to get up out of bed, desperate not to miss work.

Within the hour, the doctor arrived and set about examining my uncle. Attempting to get voluntary movement from his arms, then his legs; the doctor then tried vision tests, holding a finger up to my uncle and moving it from right to left. I remained in the bedroom during the doctor's examination in order to communicate the English spoken by the doctor, into the Hungarian that my aunt and uncle could better understand.

When my aunt went out to the kitchen I asked the doctor what he thought was wrong with my uncle.

"Do you know what President Roosevelt had before he died?" He enquired.

"Yes". I said worriedly.

He then told me to tell my aunt to keep Uncle Pál comfortable. "Don't let him strain himself in an effort to get out of bed." He went next door to use the neighbor's phone and summoned an ambulance.

The ambulance took my aunt and uncle to Hamilton General Hospital. I took the streetcar and walked from the car stop to the hospital hoping to catch up with them in the emergency area of the hospital. Of course I was somewhat later than their arrival time, but I found my aunt sitting alone and crying. I enquired about Uncle Pál.

"I don't know where they took him," she replied in Hungarian.

I told her to stay where she was, and went about the hospital halls to find my uncle. Pushing through a larger door I ran into a young man in white. Surprisingly I knew him, and he recognized me. He had gone to high school with my older sister Helen.

"What are you doing here?" He asked, surprised to see me.

"I'm looking for my uncle", I replied. "They brought him in...in an ambulance about half an hour ago, and my aunt does not know what they did with him."

"Where is your aunt?"

I showed him through the door, and down the corridor. When he saw my aunt, he made the patient-kin-association.

He had seen her with my uncle and the ambulance medics as they brought Uncle Pál into the emergency ward. He turned to me. "Come with me."

He led me into a room beyond where I had first bumped into him. Opening the door I saw my uncle struggling with the linen covers on a hospital gurney. The young man stated: "They are going to remove his street clothes. He is being admitted. You better go now; the staff should not see you here as they remove his clothes."

And that was it!

I told him to keep my aunt apprised of the situation, and let her know of my uncle's room once he was admitted. I returned quickly to tell my aunt that Uncle Pál was being admitted, and he was being cared for. She stopped crying, and appeared temporarily relieved that I had found him.

In turn she said I had better go home now as it was getting into the afternoon hours and I had $3,000 cash in my pocket!

I left her where she sat, in the hospital, and caught a streetcar going to the bus terminal. Then I got onto a bus to Brantford, from Brantford I took that familiar trolley to Waterford.

But my brother John was *not there to pick me up.*

I walked the five miles home to the farm. As I entered the barnyard my sister Annie ran out to greet me with these words... "Uncle Pál is dead! Mom, Dad and John have gone to Hamilton to stay with Aunt Emma."

They had been summoned by a telegram, perhaps an hour before my trolley stop, and had no way of notifying me.

This is why I had to walk home; the family car was in use. My sister and I stayed home to milk the cows and do the chores that evening.

I puzzled over the events that transpired during the past twenty-four hours. I had a nice evening with my teenage friends in Hamilton the night before, only to be confronted with Helen's ghost when I retired to my bedroom. She obviously was trying to communicate with me or anyone in the household, but I was too afraid. No doubt she remained throughout the next day until Uncle Pál died.

They were together again.

She was to be his "spirit guide" and would surely take him for a reunion with his beloved Annüska. He was once more reunited with the two people whom he loved the most 'in this life'.

He must have suffered a 'troubled mind', attempting to figure out life's injustices. Tuberculosis took his one and only first love Annüska. Why? Why had tuberculosis taken his beloved daughter also? Was he cursed to suffer a continuous heartache, another such injustice in this life among strangers in a strange land?

He had escaped the memories and heartaches once, by leaving his native birthplace, where would he escape to now that death had taken Helen?

His death mercifully provided the answer.

His head injuries from the streetcar accident must have contributed to his early demise leading to the stroke.

A troubled mind, an injured brain and an aching heart; one cannot continue to exist for too long with these impediments.

We buried him in 1948, he had not lived in that new house for six months, and it was not quite ten months from the time we buried Helen. They now lay side by side in Holy Sepulcher Cemetery across the Bay from Hamilton.

He was fifty-four years old.

PISTA VALKO'S DEMISE

As we mentioned in an earlier chapter, Pista Valko's wife had nine acres of land and the use of half an old house as a dowry. When Geza visited Hungary in 1962, Pista and his wife were constructing a smaller, two room house because the Communist Collective Farm Supervisor confiscated their old house for his personal use.

It was cold that February, so Pista's wife heated a round fieldstone in the oven. When it was warmed, she put it between the sheets to pre-warm the bed for Geza. The bed became warm, sure enough, but the cold air still 'licked' at his head. Geza told us these humorous stories on his return from Hungary.

Having left the police force, Pista was now part of the collective farm community. People envied him because he had his own horse, and there was always some hostility toward him. Others in the community saw his good fortune as 'spite' to their misfortune. It was also common knowledge that Pista had been a Csendör Officer (ranked policeman), assigned at one time to the border town of Rum, again a cause for envy.

Now, in his later years, he rode his bicycle to work. There was one spot along the road to work where he had to travel past a deep roadside ditch that was more like a ravine. This ravine had a bridge crossing it; the bridge was at right angles to the road, and he turned to cross the bridge continuing down the opposite road side to work.

One spring day in 1965, in the dark of early morning, he rode his bicycle on that familiar road, past that ravine as was his custom...and died there.

They found his body at the bottom of the deep ditch, in that ravine; his neck was broken!

There are conflicting stories associated with this "mishap". Some say that his wife had a boyfriend and together they plotted to get rid of him. Others say that it was an enemy harboring a grudge from the distant past, as some people suppose there is likely to be against a policeman. In his youthful days on the Police force, Pista had acquired some enemies, and there were those local youths who had not taken too kindly to his marriage to a "local" girl, particularly since she had a good dowry.

They resented him for years.

The facts?

One can only wonder. The police report states that his bicycle was found on the roadside, above the spot where his body was found in the ravine. The police conclude that he may have struck something with the front wheel, and was thrown off over the handle bars into the ditch, where he suffered the broken neck. Not likely, as there were no stones or obstructions found near the bicycle wheels.

Some people stated that, as Pista rode that morning, a man suddenly rose out of the ditch where he had been waiting, and barred Pista's way. Pista may have stopped suddenly, and, or, was pushed bodily from astride his bicycle, into the ravine. Being pushed or thrown headlong from off the bicycle into the ravine broke his neck.

Maybe his attacker broke his neck?

The story these people tell explains how it was that the bicycle remained on the road just above where the body went into the ravine.

His wife wrote a letter to Ilona in which she feigned words of bereavement, stating that Pista pedaled his bicycle off the road in the morning darkness, and both rider and bicycle went down into that deep ditch, where he suffered the broken neck.

This letter is puzzling in that it is the only version of the accident which states, in its simplicity, what would be most logical and acceptable. In the darkness Pista inadvertently rode off the road...except for one glaring fact...the bicycle remained on the road; the body lay at the bottom of the ravine.

He had pedaled his bicycle to work along that very familiar route for several years. Could he have been careless? Did he suffer a stroke or a dizzy spell; after all, he was getting on in years. Why was the widow's story the only one that implied that bicycle and rider ended up in the ravine?

The widow ended her letter stating, "Please do not write further asking details about poor Pista. I have told you all I know about this unfortunate accident, and it would bereave me to be reminded again in the future by letters from you."

Pista's sisters, Annüs and Ilona, insist that the bicycle did not go into the ditch, as did the police report. Annüs is more accusative in saying someone pushed him off his moving bicycle into the ditch.

"Because Ilona, that is an evil woman. She had a black soul, a soul as black as the devil's."

The widow had also talked to Annüs after Pista's funeral, and stated that she intended to write Ilona asking for money, on the pretext that the money would be for a beautiful, "carved wooden cross" as a grave marker.

Annüs wrote Ilona immediately, hence the accusatory letter. "Do not send her any money sister, she mocks us. She says that we are all so loving, such kindly relatives, that you will be duped into giving her the money–which she will use for herself and not for Pista's grave marker."

The widow wrote no more. Ilona did not enquire further through the widow about the brother she loved so much.

So we end it.

THE CONCLUSION

In 1949 my brother John and his good friend Leo Drosdowski heard that Clayton Barber of RR#5 Waterford had Orange Groves in St. Petersburg Florida, and was known to hire help for tending the groves before the orange harvesting. John and Leo went to Mr. Barber and enquired if he would give them a job during the Canadian winter since that is when the orange harvest began in St. Petersburg.

As a result, John and Leo worked the next two winters for Clayton Barber in that Orange Grove. And a good acquaintanceship developed between these three; the old man and the two young men. We also learned that Clayton had made more money "marketing" the Waterford area garden crops than he did with dairy farming in Waterford. He would buy strawberries, plums, peaches, apples or whatever, from his neighbors and ship the produce to Brantford from the Waterford trolley station.

Clayton Barber's father had 'wintered' in Florida as many wealthy Canadians in the '30s and '40s had. While in Florida the father bought a few acres of orange trees in a small orange grove, and 'willed' it to his two sons, George and Clayton. When the father died, George did not want any part of the remote few acres of orange trees. So Clayton "bought out" George's interest and now owned the orange grove outright. Clayton added more acreage to it, and more fruit trees He even added a fruit processing shed where a roadside table sold the squeezed fruit juices to tourist and vacationers. As time went on the City of St.

Petersburg also grew and developed to surround the orange grove increasing the property value. Clayton would spend the spring and summer on the 210 acre farm in Waterford, returning to manage the Florida orange grove in late fall and throughout the winter. His hired man had died; the widow, the oldest son, and her family continued to manage the Waterford Dairy farm during Clayton's stay in Florida.

Some altercation reared its ugly head between the young hired man and Clayton during the second winter that John and Leo worked in the orange grove. Clayton was angry enough to evict the widow, her son and the family; but who would run the dairy farm? He was too old to attempt it himself; along with the Florida property it was just too much. In his anger he would not consider another unpredictable hired man.

He determined to sell the farm.

This must have been a painful decision for Clayton because the farm had been in his family for generations. His grandfather received it as Crown Grant land for his years of military service to Queen Victoria.

Had he not been so angered at the hired-man situation, Clayton would surely have reconsidered his decision.

John picked up on this opportunity and asked my dad if he would buy this bigger farm. We all thought Dairy farming would be better than garden crop farming and so dad approached Clayton Barber, struck a deal and the Virags bought one of the best farms in Norfolk County.

Clayton Barber wanted dad to buy the farm on 'land contract' which meant that Clayton would hold the remaining mortgaged amount after the initial down payment, deriving the interest on the yearly installment payments. (That is how things were done in Land Contracts of those days). Clayton's shrewd business acumen preceded him however; dad chose to mortgage through the bank in Waterford where he had already established a great business relationship with the Manager.

This proved to be a wise decision on the part of dad.

Within a year Clayton regretted selling the farm and would have dearly done anything to get it back; of course his hands were tied. Had we bought the farm on Land Contract, Clayton would have hired a good lawyer to breach the contract. But as time went on and the Virags prospered on that farm, Clayton conceded he was getting too old, having no sons of his own to farm it and carry on. This 'foreigner' and his sons were doing the farm justice in the old tradition which he respected.

We bought up a lot of Clayton's farm equipment when we purchased the farm, and now were quite self sufficient, independent farmers, having a threshing machine of our own and corn cutting machinery and hay harvesting machinery; all the things a dairy farmer requires.

Clayton had "Broad Lea Farms – Clayton Barber" painted in white on the large red barn, in representation of the broad meadows. We now changed this to "White Way Farms – G. Virag and Sons" representing the white of the milk our dairy farm was to produce. My dad was extremely proud of this farm and, that as it was me, his son who painted this sign on the barn.

Within a few years we also bought the neighboring fifty acre farm with house and barn on it from "Little John". John was a bachelor and getting too old to farm it on his own. Our farm was now a reasonably larger, 260 acre Dairy Farm.

Doc Drennan came to help us with a heifer that needed veterinarian assistance. Doc's practice was in Simcoe, Delhi and the outlying areas, so he was reluctant to come to Waterford where his friend and fellow veterinarian Doc Frew had the area practice. Doc Frew was on vacation and we needed a vet badly, this is how we got Doc Drennan to help us. He seemed to be a hard nosed cantankerous son-of-a-gun with a quick temper and, I admit, I was somewhat concerned about his attitude. I may have presumed he resented "foreigners"; would my Dad also pick up on that?

Doc was very precise, and very strict in the course of his work, to the point of commanding us what we had to do to help him, and to hold the animal still as we tried to assist him. I did notice though, that he was all the while 'sizing up' my Dad. He must have been musing to himself, how old is this man? His accent is European, I wonder? Finally he said,

"You look old enough to have been in the war," accenting "the war".

"Not this one," replied Geza, meaning not the second war. "It vas the first vun."

"Oh! Yeah. That's the one I meant. I was in that one too. How old are you?"

"Yes? I am fifty-one, vas I sixteen. I drafted."

"Sixteen years old, my gosh." mused Doc. "Where did you serve?"

"I vas in Italy."

"Huh? I was in Italy too. Where in Italy?"

"On the Piave, in Italy, vas my last campaign."

"Well I'll be darned! So was I at the Piave. I was there! We were reinforcing the Italians and Americans there, in the hills above the valley."

"Aha! Vas you up there, on the other side...shooting at us down there in the valley. You know, vas I vit the Magyar and Austrians; it vas we who fought you there."

I was now holding the struggling heifer alone and became acutely aware of the sudden silence, there on that farm in Waterford, thousands of miles from Italy and the Piave River.

Dad, Geza was making himself understood remarkably well, in spite of his Hungarian accent. In that time of listening, Doc suddenly smiled from ear to ear. Geza was somberly shaking his head side to side, indicating emotional feelings of those olden times and, also his disbelief.

After all these years, these "old enemies" must have reflected upon this paradox; the flashes of fear, excitement of pursuit and fire. The death and carnage of the past clashed so dramatically with this peaceful barnyard, the farm and with its humble animals, far from any strife or conflict.

It was Doc who finally broke the silence with that ingratiating smile.

"Here we are now, today friendly, both good Canadian citizens, and I am helping you, as you help me, to treat this heifer. Isn't it a bugger? I would not for the world want to harm you; I know that at the time I was a threat to your life and you a threat to my life."

Now it was Doc who shook his head side to side in disbelief, reflecting on that Hell at the Piave River.

Geza smiled slightly.

"Yeah; Ve just 'bout kill vun another there. Now how foolish it seems." Geza smiled, for he acknowledged that feeling for which words were inadequate. "Yes my friend, we were taught to fight and told to kill, for what? For this?" and he lifted his hand in a motion encompassing an arc, indicating the barn building, chickens, cows and surroundings... as though he were surveying this peaceful barnyard scene, and comparing it with that bursting conflagration which was the hell of thirty-four years ago.

Here he was in his adopted homeland, wondering if it was indeed he, who had lived through that torment, for a land he no longer called "home".

As we worked together now for the heifer's benefit, they talked engagingly, we found that Doc had served in a Canadian Cavalry regiment. Dad also told him about being buried alive on one of the engagements in the advance on Monte Grappa. How he had spent three months in a Hospital in Austria, with a short leave to visit home, only to be returned to that hell which became know as the Central Powers tragic "Crossing of the Piave".

These old veterans now, amazingly respected one another, and Doc Drennan never hesitated to come to our help whenever Doc Frew was indisposed. He truly did not mind helping the foreigner.

STORY OUTLINE

1. 1900; conveys an image of a passive country life, with many picturesque and peaceful villages inhabited by happy, religious peasants, simple people of child-like innocence, raising happy, healthy contented children in a "Country of Contentment"

2. 1908-1912, the coming cloud, and approaching storm; the Balkan wars, a confused country with confused peasantry.

3. The above wars; then 1914, peasants experience fear, doubt, and apprehension.

4. 1914-1917 heartache, hate, defiance, determination; the loss of innocence, perseverance; a disregard for all things military and of the government. Having suffered, the peasants doubt the future.

5. 1918-19 ongoing internal turmoil, revolutions, enlightenment, education, a better life. The once innocent peasants are no longer innocent but justifiably distrustful of Government.

6. 1925-27 immigration; a new country, a new life, homesickness, new experiences, a new found security.

7. 1933 joblessness, doubt, insecurity, endurance, perseverance again, move from city to country; begin farming in 1945.

8. Struggles, 1947 heartache, resolve, hard work. Change of farming method.

9. New life, new experiences, newfound friends; 1951 prosperity.

☼ Only after finishing this Historical Biography did I realize just how the real life characters prevailed during their life and death experiences. For those interested in the old Siege Artilleryman Varga Janos' experiences within Przemyl, I would suggest looking up the "Siege of Przemyl" on the internet.

♣ I would also suggest searching the historical references to the TWO Battles of The Piave River, 1917 and 1918. I have found that there is a deliberate avoidance when describing this historical event. For it does not admit the Italian Engineers opened the "flood gates" of the Piave in 1918, drowning close to 100,000 Hungarian troops!